A Century of Collecting

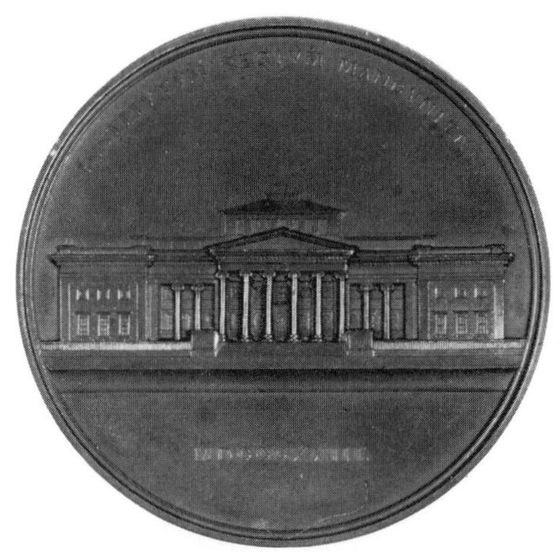

1882–1982

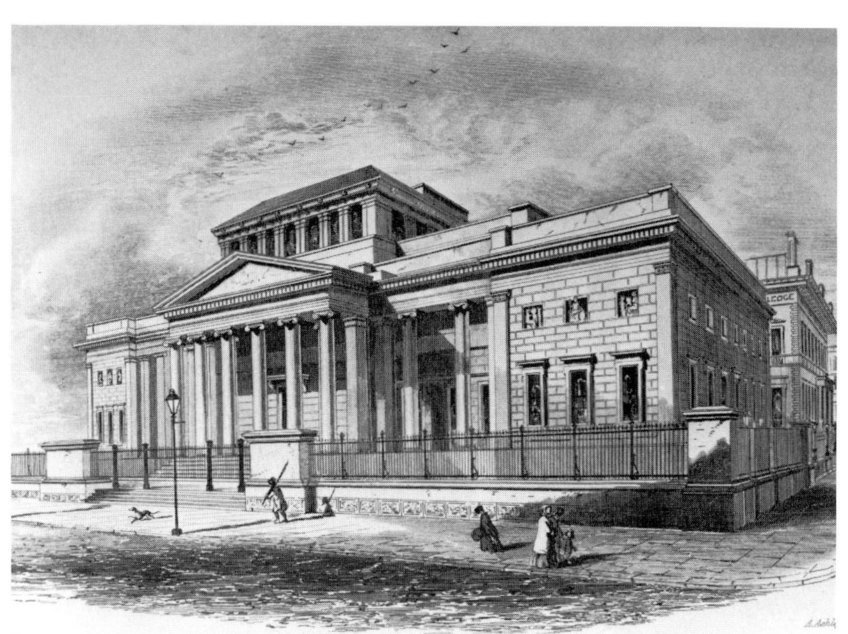

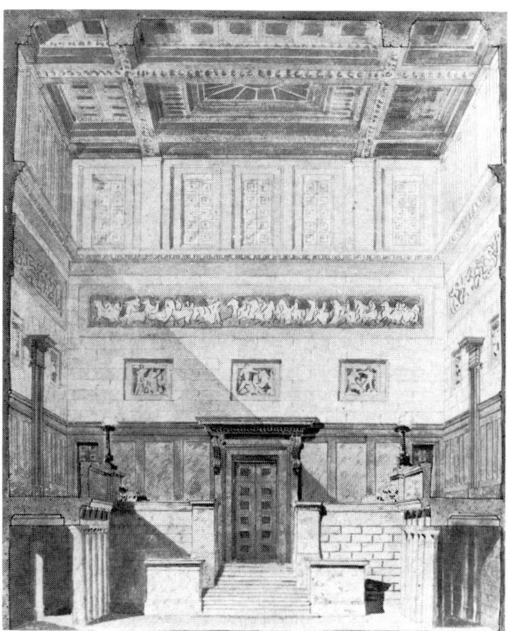

Fig. 2 Barry's Manchester Institution building
Fig. 3 Part of the frieze in the hall
Fig. 4 Barry's second drawing of the elevation

A Century of Collecting 1882–1982

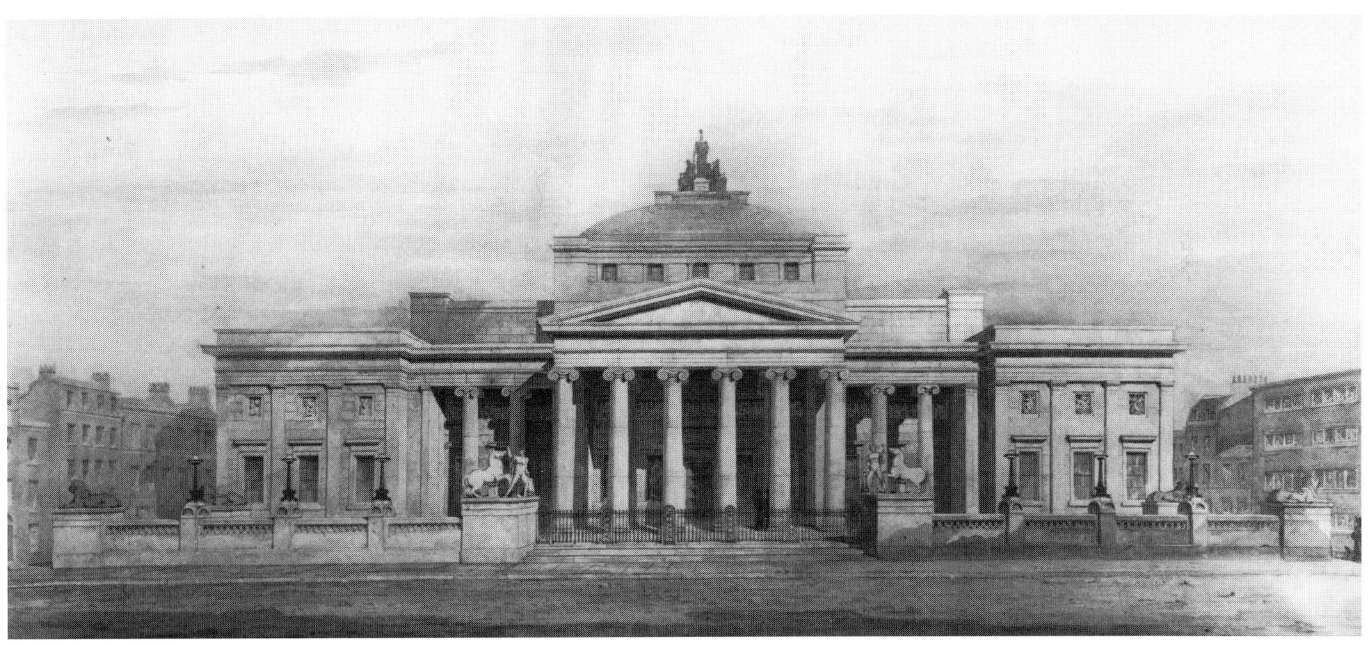

A Guide to Manchester City Art Galleries

Manchester City Art Gallery

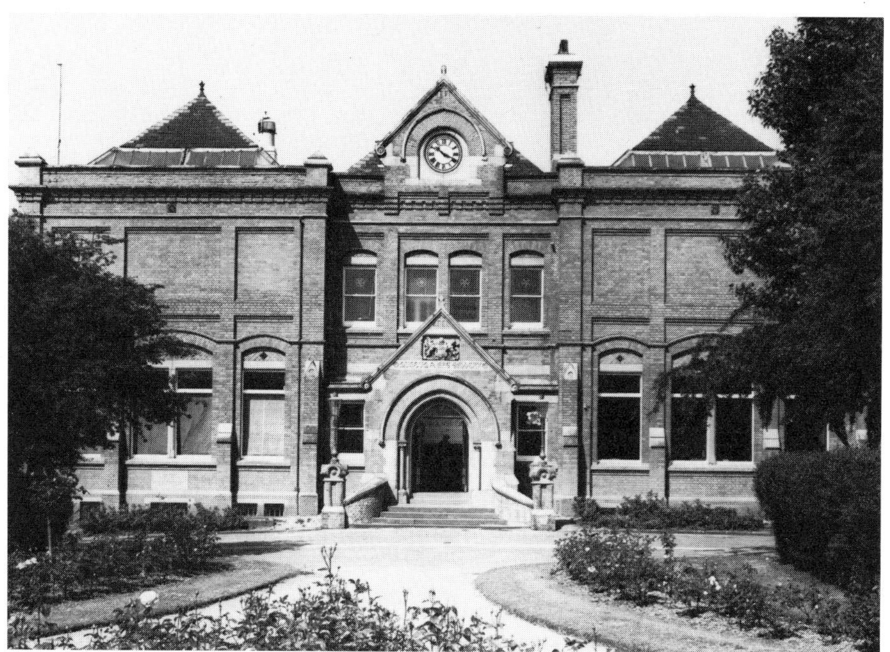

Fig. 5 Queen's Park Art Gallery, Harpurhey

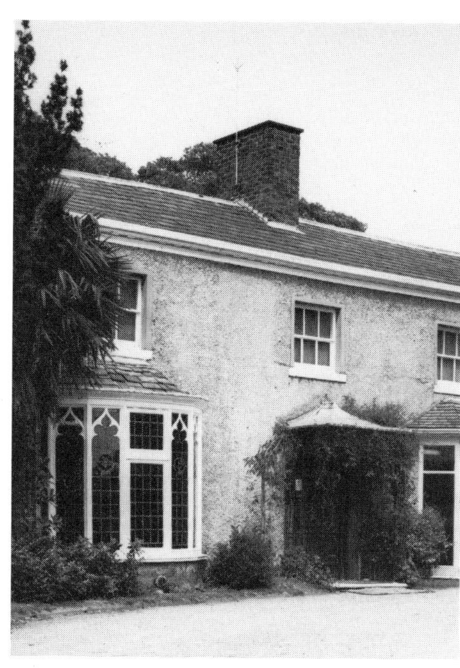

Fig. 8 Fletcher Moss Museum, Didsbury

First published in Great Britain in 1983

ISBN 0 901673 20 X
Produced by the South Leigh Press Ltd
Chilcroft Road, Kingsley Green,
Haslemere, Surrey

Distributed by A. Zwemmer Ltd,
26 Litchfield Street,
London WC2H 9NJ
Printed in England
BAS Printers Ltd
Over Wallop, Stockbridge,
Hampshire

Contents

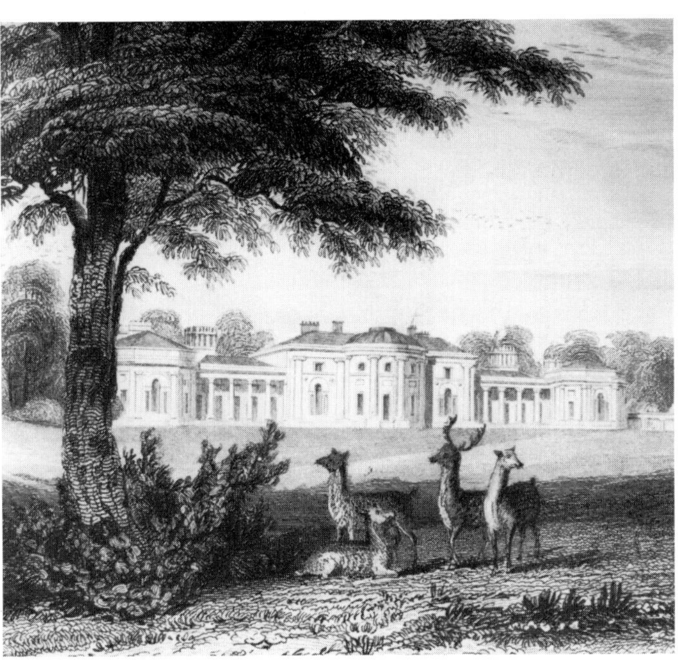

Fig. 6 Heaton Hall, Prestwich

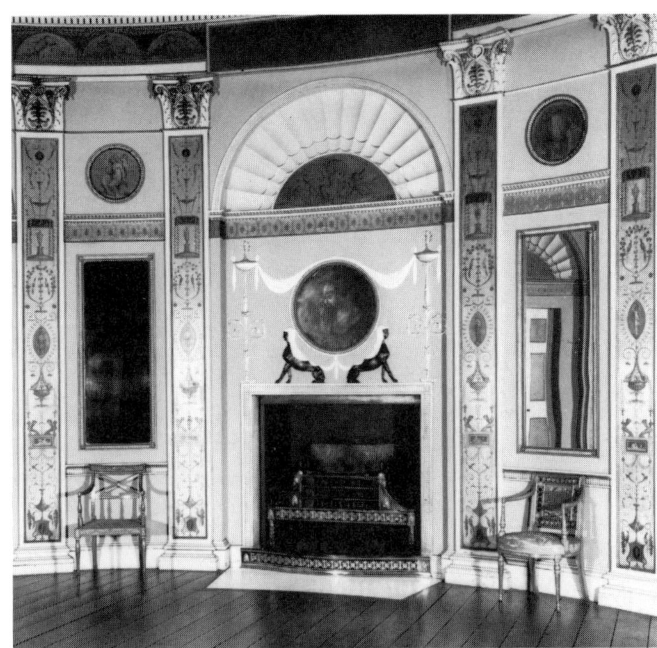

Fig. 7 The Cupola Room, Heaton Hall

Acknowledgements

MANCHESTER CITY COUNCIL
CULTURAL COMMITTEE 1982–83

The Right Worshipful The Lord Mayor,
Councillor Clifford Tomlinson

Chairman
Councillor S. V. Shaw

Deputy Chairman
Councillor M. Harrison

Councillor F. R. Butler
Councillor M. I. Crawford, JP
Councillor T. Egan
Councillor G. W. G. Fitzsimons
Councillor H. T. Lee
Councillor C. McLaren
Councillor P. M. Morrison
Councillor H. P. D. Paget
Councillor A. J. Spencer
Councillor G. Stringer
Councillor M. J. Taylor
Councillor Miss M. A. Vince, JP
Professor C. R. Dodwell, MA, PhD
Mr H. M. Fairhurst, MA, FRIBA
Professor I. M. Kemp, MA
Mr G. North, MA
Dr M. A. Pegg, BA, PhD
Professor K. R. Richards, MA
Mr C. G. H. Simon, MA, JP

Director of Cultural Services
L. G. Lovell, FLA

Director of Art Galleries
T. P. P. Clifford, BA, AMA, FRSA

MANCHESTER CITY ART GALLERIES
DEPARTMENTAL STAFF
Director
T. P. P. Clifford, BA, AMA, FRSA

DEPARTMENTS

FINE ART
Senior Keeper
Julian Treuherz, MA, AMA
Assistant Keepers
Miss Sandra Martin, BA, AMA
Mrs Jane Farrington, BA, AMA
Martin Royalton-Kisch, MA
DECORATIVE ART
Senior Keeper
Richard Gray, BA, AMA
Assistant Keepers
Mrs Deborah Clarke, BA, AMA
James Lomax, MA
Thomas Richardson, BA
COSTUME
Keeper
Miss Jane Tozer, BA, AMA
Assistant Keeper
Miss Sarah Levitt, MA
MILITARY HISTORY
Keeper
P. R. Russell-Jones
CONSERVATION
Senior Conservator
Brian Cardy, BSC, DIP CONS.
Assistant Conservators (Fine Art)
Peter J. Hartley, BA, DIP CONS.
Miss J. Melissa Hughes, DIP CONS.
Assistant Conservator (Applied Art)
Mrs L. M. Matthews, CONS. CERT.
Assistant Conservator (Costume)
Miss I. Bobkiewicz, DIP AD, DIP CONS.
Technicians
W. Bird
G. Lomas
Furbishers
R. O'Neill (foreman)
A. Rawcliffe
A. Boardman
M. Hampson

CLERICAL AND ADMINISTRATION
Administration Officer
Graham Jones
Director's Secretary
Miss K. P. Cope
Senior Clerical Assistant
Mrs S. Taylor
Clerk Typist
Miss Z. Collier
Miss K. T. Walker
Clerical Assistant
Miss H. Knott
Photography
A. Seabright
M. R. Cobley
Security
K. H. Blundell
Superintendant of Galleries
C. Palmer
Foremen (Attendant Staff)
J. Hull
J. Dowding
D. Campbell
P. Baxter
D. Fidler

List of Entries

110 R. P. Bonington: The Doge's Palace from the Piazzetta, Venice
111 S. Palmer: The Bright Cloud
112 D. Cox: Rhyl Sands
113 Sir Francis Chantrey: John Dalton
114 W. Etty: The Sirens and Ulysses
115 Sir Edwin Landseer: Paganini playing the violin
116 W. Mulready: The Artist's Studio
117 J. F. Lewis: The Coffee Bearer
118 Daguerreotype of family group, *c.* 1850
119 Noah's Ark
120 G. F. Watts: The Good Samaritan
121 W. Holman Hunt: The Hireling Shepherd
122 Ford Madox Brown: Work
123 Sir John Everett Millais: Autumn Leaves
124 D. G. Rossetti: Boatmen and Siren
125 W. Holman Hunt: D. G. Rossetti
126 D. G. Rossetti: Astarte Syriaca
127 A. Stevens: Seated Youth
128 Bartolozzi table
129 Pugin plate and Butterfield flagon
130 Lamb sideboard
131 Burges escritoire
132 De Morgan tile panel
133 Whitefriars glass decanters
134 Ary Scheffer: The Holy Women at the Sepulchre
135 A. Yvon: Marshall Ney supporting the Rear Guard during the Retreat from Moscow
136 H. Fantin-Latour: Self Portrait
137 C. Pissarro: A Village Street, Louveciennes
138 P. Gauguin: Le Port de Dieppe
139 A. Rodin: The Age of Bronze
140 J. Dalou: The Reader
141 A. von Wagner: The Chariot Race
142 Minton Prometheus vase
143 J. Tissot: The Concert
144 Frederic, Lord Leighton: Captive Andromache
145 J. W. Waterhouse: Hylas and the Nymphs
146 Sir Lawrence Alma-Tadema: Silver Favourites
147 C. Ricketts: Christ Crucified
148 Dresser egg coddler
149 Bird jar by Martin Brothers
150 Ruskin and Della Robbia vases
151 Pilkington lustre vases
152 Tiffany peacock vase
153 Fabergé bowl and stand
154 Lalique 'L'Oiseau de Feu' lamp
155 Sir William Orpen: Homage to Manet
156 A. Valette: Albert Square, Manchester
157 W. R. Sickert: Victor Lecour
158 A. John: Dorelia in a Hat
159 A. Modigliani: Anna
160 Wyndham Lewis: Portrait of the Artist as the Painter Raphael
161 H. Moore: Mother and Child
162 F. Léger: Painting
163 Boch Frères Keramis vase
164 Sir Jacob Epstein: Bust of C. P. Scott
165 L. S. Lowry: An Accident
166 B. Hepworth: Doves
167 B. Nicholson: Au Chat Botté
168 Leach stoneware vase
169 Thirties wine service
170 Jacqmar summer suit, 1942
171 M. Ernst: La Ville Petrifiée
172 A. Giacometti: The Artist's Mother
173 L. Freud: Girl with Beret
174 F. Bacon: Portrait of Henrietta Moraes on a Blue Couch
175 D. Hockney: Celia
176 D. Petherbridge: The Concrete Armada

ABBREVIATIONS

t.l.c. = top left corner
b.l.c. = bottom left corner
b.r.c. = bottom right corner
mon = monogram

The watercolour by Sir Charles Barry of the exterior elevation of The Royal Manchester Institution is loaned by The Victoria University of Manchester, Tabley Collection. (Fig. 4)

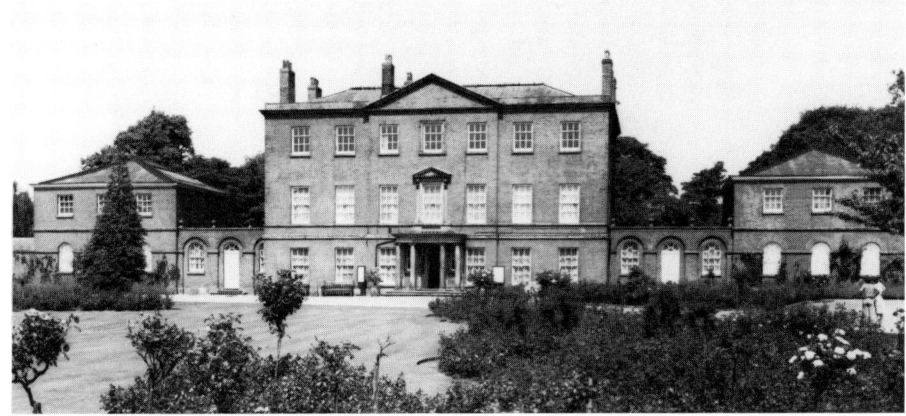

Fig. 9 Platt Hall, Rusholme

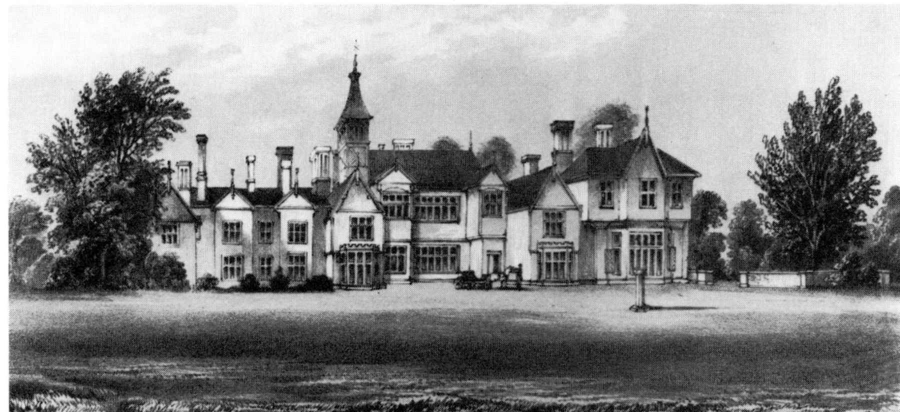

Fig. 10 Wythenshawe Hall, Wythenshawe Park

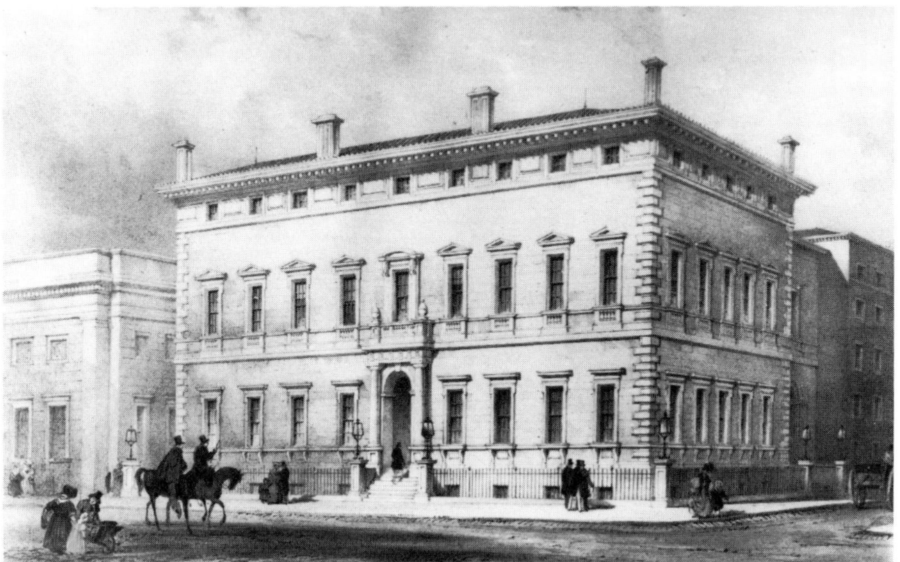

Fig. 11 The Athenaeum, Princess Street

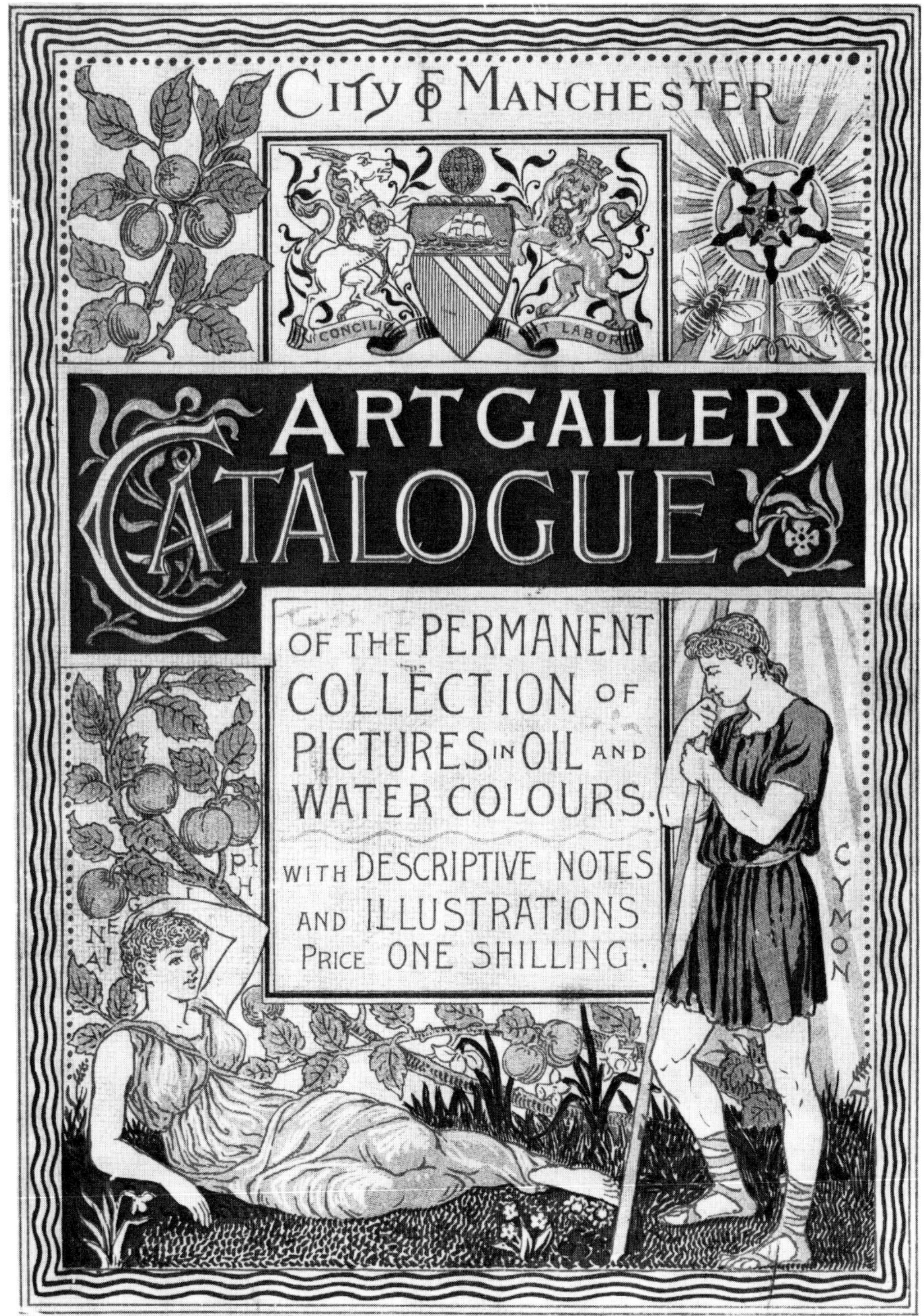

Fig. 1 The Stanfield Catalogue, 1895

Introduction

On 10 August 1882 the Manchester Corporation Act received Royal Assent: the old Royal Manchester Institution in Mosley Street became the City Art Gallery of Manchester, and the Corporation took possession of the building and its collections in January 1883.

It is to mark this historic event that we have chosen to publish a guide to the collections, the first since that compiled in 1956 by the then director, S. D. Cleveland. Previously, the Gallery had published only catalogues of the specialist collections, starting with the *Catalogue of the Permanent Collection of Pictures in Oil and Watercolours* by William Stanfield, Curator, in 1888. Walter Crane designed the cover for the 1895 edition (fig. 1). This comprised 175 entries including nine loans from the National Gallery.

In the intervening century the City Art Gallery has burgeoned from one building to seven and now contains, apart from furniture, costume, ceramics, metalwork and other artifacts, about 2000 oil paintings and over 8000 works on paper. The purpose of this guide is to chart this astonishing expansion, this century of collecting, and to reproduce a small selection of the most beautiful and interesting objects in the Galleries.

The history of Manchester's art collections goes back much further than 1882, as their nucleus can be traced to the Royal Manchester Institution in the 1820s. However, the peculiar history of Manchester itself must be first recounted.

Early 18th-century Manchester grew from a small country town in Lancashire with a native wool and cotton industry to become, with the construction of the Bridgewater canal (1759–61) and the introduction of various labour-saving textile machines, the largest and most important textile city in the world. Between 1758 and 1801 the population of the town had risen from 17,000 to 70,409; exports in cotton rose from £46,000 in 1751 to £5½ million by 1800. Manchester, which was already a centre for the manufacture of precision instruments, now boomed with the production and marketing of textile machinery, the impact of which on the social structure was immense, for it led to the development of the factory instead of the house as the place of work.

The town expanded rapidly in the 19th century, its enormous wealth derived from 'King Cotton'; old buildings came down and were replaced with new ones. By the accession of Queen Victoria, the town boasted many distinguished Greek Revival buildings and could lay claim to rival Edinburgh and Newcastle as an 'Athens of the North'. However, within a few decades many of these buildings were demolished and replaced by new ones, many in the Venetian Gothic style so favoured by Ruskin. The town was created a city by Royal Charter on 29 March 1853, and became the commercial centre for all the cotton towns that grew up in the North West, principally Bolton, Bury, Rochdale and Oldham.

On 1 October 1823 the inhabitants of Manchester held a General Meeting at the Exchange, during which the first resolution of the newly-formed Manchester Institution for the Promotion of Literature, Science and the Arts was promulgated and passed unanimously.

A public subscription was launched to provide a suitable building. Hereditary and Life Governorships were instituted on one payment of 40 or 25 guineas respectively, while Annual Governorship carried a subscription of two guineas. In January, (Sir) Benjamin Heywood gave £500, the income of which was to be applied yearly by the award of a medal or other prize for the most meritorious product of Science or Art which might be offered for inspection at each Annual General Meeting of the Institution. By 5 April 1824 the Institution had already raised £23,000. A month earlier, on 11 March, the Governors had heard from Mr Secretary Peel (himself a cotton magnate) that King George IV had granted Royal Consent for Patronage of the Institution. An architectural competition was launched for the new building. By 4 October 1824 designs had been submitted by Thomas Harrison (of Chester), Charles Barry, John Foster (of Liverpool), Lewis Wyatt, Francis Goodwin and J. B. Papworth.

The architects submitted their plans, with their identity concealed under a motto. The Committee unanimously decided to recommend one with the inscription NIHIL PULCHRUM NISI UTILE (nothing beautiful unless useful), which, when the Governors had approved the recommendation, was found to have been used by (Sir) Charles Barry (1795–1860), who later designed with Pugin the rebuilding of the Houses of Parliament.

Barry, the son of a prosperous London stationer, was then aged only 29. On coming of age, he had spent the money inherited from his father travelling widely, examining architecture on the Continent and in Greece, Turkey, Egypt and Syria (1817–20). The Institution building (fig. 2) is his finest essay in the Grecian taste, down to the casts of the Parthenon frieze in the hall, presented by King George IV (fig. 3). The building, despite ill-use, unsympathetic alterations and, during the last war, the destruction of the original iron railings, remains one of the chief glories of the Gallery itself. Much time and trouble is now being spent on restoring it to something of its former splendour.

Mancunians were evidently proud of the building from the outset. Sir John Leicester (later Lord de Tabley), patron of Turner, founder member of the British Institution and Governor of the Manchester Institution, commissioned Barry to provide him with a second elevation, which he then hung in his gallery at 24 Hill Street, London, for public exhibition (fig. 4).

Despite the fact that the Institution building had been designed in 1824, major construction work did not start until 1827, and the building was finally completed in March 1834. Realising that this delay was bound to have a depressing effect on the subscribers, in 1827 the Committee obtained the assent of the Governors to arrange an art exhibition in temporary premises in Market Street; this show was repeated annually until the galleries in Mosley Street were ready. At the first Market Street exhibition in May 1827 the

Committee bought *Othello, the Moor of Venice*, by James Northcote; in 1832 *The Storm* by William Etty, for which the Gallery now has a brilliant preparatory drawing; and in 1847 *The Chase* by Richard Ansdell, which received the Heywood Gold Medal. In 1856 the Institution bought pictures by two deceased artists, *Phaeton* by De Wint's brother-in-law, William Hilton, and the vast canvas of *The Birth of Pandora* by James Barry (no. 98).

The Institution also received gifts and bequests including casts and marbles after the Antique and after Antonio Canova given by Jonathan Hatfield in 1826 (his own bust by Lorenzo Bartolini was bequeathed in 1957); a cast of *Psyche borne by Zephyrs* by John Gibson RA, a gift of the artist in 1830; a marble statue of *John Dalton* (no. 113) by Sir Francis Chantrey RA, a gift from a group of subscribers; *A Farrier's Shop* (1793) by George Morland, given by John Greaves in 1834; *The Sirens and Ulysses* (1837) by William Etty, given by William Grant in 1839 (no. 114) and *The Good Samaritan* by G. F. Watts, given by the artist to the Citizens of Manchester in 1852 'as an expression of his admiration for Thomas Wright, the prison philanthropist' (no. 120); and a handsome canvas of *St. Sebastian* from Vandyck's studio presented by Richard Holt in 1845.

The first Loan Exhibition of 'Pictures by Italian, Spanish, Flemish, Dutch and English Masters' was held in 1831.

One foreign painting that was bought by the Institution in 1858 and still remains very popular is *Marshall Ney supporting the Rear Guard during the Retreat from Moscow* (no. 135). This grim picture of an historic Napoleonic event was painted in 1856 by Adolphe Yvon, who was the only French artist sent out officially to the Crimea.

The Institution was catholic in its collecting tastes, somewhat reflecting Renaissance cabinets of curiosities. By 1840 there were twelve silver Burmese images, an Ostrich egg, a mammoth tooth, a Peruvian mummy, a Malay *kris* (or dagger) and a portrait medal of Matthew Boulton 'presented by R. Boulton Esq'. In 1842 the Duchy of Lancaster presented over 100 coins from the celebrated Saxon Cuerdale hoard (no. 8). This was an important addition to the growing numismatic holdings.

By 1846, the permanent collection had swollen to such a size that the Institution published its first complete catalogue and opened its doors to the public on a regular basis for three days a week with an entrance charge of sixpence. Under the Monarch's patronage, the regular temporary exhibitions of 'Modern Artists' and 'Ancient and Deceased Masters' were well attended. One of the most distinguished early shows comprised 100 drawings by Lodovico, Agostino and Annibale Carracci, lent in 1836 by Lord Francis Egerton MP.

But the Mosley Street building served other purposes as well. Immediately behind the great Doric entrance hall, Barry had built a magnificent semicircular lecture theatre along strictly classical lines. This was the finest such room in Manchester, and many distinguished persons delivered addresses and lectures there, including Benjamin Robert Haydon in 1837, 1840 and 1844, John Ruskin in 1858 and Ford Madox Brown in 1879. The room was also used for many other activities: on 19 September 1879 Alphonse Legros painted there, before students of the Manchester School of Art, a portrait of Napier Hemy, the artist. The oil painting on canvas was presented afterwards to the Institution.

The mid-19th century had witnessed great activity in the Manchester art world. In 1853 the south wing of the Institution had been allotted to the School of Design, which later became the Manchester School of Art and now forms part of the Polytechnic. In 1857, one of the greatest art exhibitions so far seen in Europe was held in Manchester under the title *Art Treasures of the United Kingdom*; it was housed in a huge temporary glass structure rivalling the Crystal Palace, and was opened by Prince Albert with great pomp and pageantry. Over 1,300,000 people were to visit it, including Queen Victoria herself. In 1859 the Manchester Academy of Art was founded formally and the first of its annual exhibitions held at the Institution ten years later. This Academy still flourishes and from its annual exhibitions Manchester City Art Gallery have bought and continue to buy representative pictures by local artists.

As the century drew on, it became increasingly apparent that the Institution, which fulfilled a very important function for the city, was now seriously under-financed. In 1882 an agreement was entered into with the Manchester Corporation to the effect that the Institution with its land, building, collections and fittings was to be transferred to the City, the Governors retaining their privileges of admission to all exhibitions and lectures. Another provision was that the City should devote £2,000 annually to the purchase of pictures. Representation on the new managing committee was determined as fourteen members of the municipality and seven members of the Institution. This was then drafted into the Manchester Corporation Act of 1882.

At the Institution's own expense, Barry's great lecture theatre was destroyed and replaced by a further picture gallery (now housing the Pre-Raphaelites); the entrance hall was lavishly redecorated with elaborate stencilling and gilding in the Classical Revival taste then so fashionable. This ambitious and complex scheme, apparently the faithful repetition of one of 1846, has now been restored to its former glory by the Manchester Direct Works Department on the basis of old photographs and with the use of paint scrapes and sections (undertaken by the Fine Art Conservation Department in 1980; detail reproduced on the cover.)

The Royal Manchester Institution continued to be represented on the Art Gallery Committee until 1973 when, with local government re-organisation, their right to representation on the Committee was transferred to the University of Manchester, the Art Gallery Committee then becoming the Cultural Committee. As a farewell gift, the Institution presented a handsome *Portrait of a Gentleman in Red Velvet*, attributed to Jonathan Richardson and a bronze bust of *L'Espiegle* by Carpeaux.

When the City took over the Royal Manchester Institution building, it was clearly understood that this was to be a temporary arrangement and that soon a new city gallery would have to be built. Space was noticeably lacking, especially when the Gallery tried to cater both for the rapidly expanding permanent collection and the annual exhibitions. Two more of Barry's fine rooms were destroyed in 1892, amidst protests, to provide further display space. In 1898 the City Art Gallery Committee bought the block of buildings behind the Gallery, excluding the Athenaeum Club, to allow for expansion. But such expansion was suspended and now, a century later, Manchester remains the only major city in Britain without a proper custom-built city-centre art gallery. This would not seem so serious were it not that the collections are very large and that many of the items are of great rarity and beauty. Besides, had Manchester built its own new art gallery speedily it might well have been possible to accommodate a superb collection of oils, drawings and prints, numbering 1,156 items and including oils by Botticelli, Rembrandt, Le Nain, Delacroix, Millet and Degas. As it is, these were given to the Victoria and Albert Museum in 1900 by Constantine Alexander Ionides, a Greek textile merchant who was born in Cheetham Hill, Manchester. Other private collections were also promised but lost through no building being provided for them.

However, new moves to attract tourism to the city centre and the possibility of future government financial assistance to certain key museum and art gallery building projects may mean an end to this impasse. In the meantime, to help store and display its collections, the City Art Gallery has to use various branches, which will now be described briefly.

Queen's Park Art Gallery, Harpurhey (fig. 5) Queen's Park, Harpurhey, is situated some four miles north east of the City Art Gallery. The Queen's Park Gallery was designed by T. Allison, the City Surveyor, in 1883–84 for the old Parks Committee. When first opened it functioned like a miniature version of the South Kensington Museums, with natural history, ethnography, scientific and engineering displays, as well as contemporary exhibitions of paintings and applied art. The building was transferred to the Art Gallery Committee in 1906, and most of the collections dispersed.

On the ground floor is a continuous suite of galleries which are side-lit and now used for picture storage. On the first floor is a corresponding set of three top-lit galleries, one of which is used for displays of militaria (the Manchester Regiment and the 14th/20th King's Hussars); the remaining space houses Victorian and Edwardian oil paintings and other later works acquired through the War Artists Advisory Scheme. The brick-vaulted cellars provide storage.

Heaton Hall, Prestwich (fig. 6) Heaton Hall, seven miles north of the City Art Gallery, is generally acknowledged to be the finest late 18th-century country house in the north west. It was rebuilt from 1772 by James Wyatt for Sir Thomas Egerton, Bart., later 1st Earl of Wilton. A music room was added in 1790 by Samuel Wyatt, James's elder brother, who was also responsible for the stable block. Finally, their nephew Lewis Wyatt added, between 1806 and 1824, a suite of bedrooms, a library, monumental chimney stacks and an orangery. The house contains some spectacular interiors, none more distinguished than the Cupola Room in the Etruscan taste decorated by Biagio Rebecca (fig. 7).

Heaton and its park were purchased by the Corporation in 1901 to provide space for recreation and to allow for a railway cutting in the corner of the park. Early this century the Hall was regarded, according to T. Swindells' *Handbook to Heaton Park* (1906, p. 6), as 'not of interest either to the architect or historian', and the original contents were sold off at auction in 1902 and 1906. In 1906 the Art Gallery Committee was given control of the centre section of the house (except for the dining room and library). The whole building was finally transferred to the Cultural (formerly Art Gallery) Committee in 1981.

The state rooms are now in the course of being redecorated with reference to contemporary documents, using paint scrapes and sections, and are being refurnished closely following early account books. It is intended to furnish the south wing with its kitchens and servants' quarters and, one day, to replace the glass hipped roof of the orangery, returning it to its delightful former appearance and function.

Fletcher Moss Museum, Didsbury (fig. 8) This Museum is tucked in behind the Old Cock Inn off Wilmslow Road, in a small garden immediately opposite the parish church of St. James, Stenner Lane. The Museum was called the Old Parsonage and the living belonged to the Mosley family. It was at first, presumably, a simple two-storied cottage of four bays until it was extended around 1834 in the Gothick cottage-ornée taste. The house was bought by Alderman Fletcher Moss, well known author and campaigner for the conservation of old Manchester. Having 'improved' it to his own antiquarian taste, he left it and its contents to Manchester Corporation. It was opened as a branch gallery in 1923.

The Fletcher Moss Museum has now been returned to something of its early 19th-century appearance and is used for displaying the local history of Manchester and its environs. One room is being fitted with fine panelling by G. F. Bodley and C. E. Kempe (taken from a house in Salford).

Platt Hall, Rusholme (The Gallery of English Costume) (fig. 9) Platt Hall, in Platt Lane, is a red brick Palladian house, built from 1764 by Timothy Lightoler for John Carill-Worsley. It is plain on the outside but with an elegant rococo staircase, starting in one flight and curving back in two, with a good plaster ceiling ornamented with fruiting vines. The dining room in the centre of the upper floor is a riot of rococo decoration: fitted into the plasterwork over the chimney piece and integral with the room, is a very fine painting by Richard Wilson, *A Summer Evening* (no. 67) signed and dated 1764. The entrance hall and staircase have been redecorated to their original colour scheme, and the dining room is now being scraped back to its former combination of textured grey-blue walls with plasterwork in buff flecked with gold. The house also retains much of the costume of its first owner, given by his descendant Mrs Clementia Tindal-Carill-Worsley in 1954.

Platt Fields and Platt Hall, when first acquired by the Corporation, were placed under the control of the Parks Committee. The Hall was transferred to the Art Gallery as a branch in 1927, and used at first for the display of pictures, furniture, silver and glass. Even at this time, English costume and costume accessories were a feature. In 1947 it was opened as the Gallery of English Costume, and contains the largest and most comprehensive collection of its type outside the Victoria and Albert Museum.

Wythenshawe Hall, Wythenshawe Park (fig. 10) This is a large half-timbered house, with the central section dating from at least the early 16th century. It was the seat of the Tatton family since the Middle Ages. The low-storied range of buildings to the south was pulled down around 1955 while the matching group to the north was retained and dates partly from the 18th century. It was partly remodelled, probably by Lewis Wyatt, around 1811, when the house was extended and given additional antiquarian features by Edmund Blore, *c.* 1847. The tenants' hall and half-timbered lodge (dated 1878) are the work of a later architect.

The house and park were brought from the Tatton family by Sir Ernest (later Lord) and Lady Simon and presented to the Corporation in 1926. In 1930 five rooms in the centre portion of the house were opened as a branch gallery. More rooms were subsequently allotted to the Art Galleries, but much is still under the control of the Recreation Committee and used by the Catering Section (including the tenants' hall). The house is furnished in the antiquarian taste of the 1840s, including a certain amount of 16th- and 17th-century English and Continental furniture, portraits, trophies and weapons, treen and a Flemish tapestry.

The Athenaeum, Princess Street (The Gallery of Modern Art) (fig.11) The Athenaeum is situated immediately behind the City Art Gallery, Mosley Street. It was designed by (Sir) Charles Barry in 1836 after the Italian palazzo style of the 16th century. Opened on 28 October 1839 as the Manchester Athenaeum Club it provided lectures, debates, language classes, a newsroom, a library circulating 100,000 volumes annually, a music society and a graphic society.

The Club was sold to the Corporation in 1938 to enable the City Art Gallery, Mosley Street, to be extended. The Art Gallery Committee now possessed the complete block behind the City Art Gallery, bounded by Nicholas Street, George Street and Princess Street. The property is still in their successors' possession.

The ground floor of the 'Athenaeum Annexe', as it came to be called, was opened for a few months in 1939 and again in 1954 with displays of ceramics and local history. Now three ground floor rooms house a very small representative selection from the Galleries' rich 20th-century collections. Cellars are used for technicians' workshops, ceramic and glass storage. On the first floor are the Conservation and Education Departments, but the magnificent theatre, on the top floor, is still an unoccupied empty shell.

To these branches one should be added which no longer exists, although most of its collections became City Art Galleries' property.

Horsfall Museum (formerly Manchester Art Museum), Ancoats This museum was begun as an educational venture in 1877 by T. C. Horsfall, the wealthy son of a card manufacturer. His idea, inspired by Ruskin, was to provide a museum in the slums of Manchester for poor children, whose eyes could thus be opened to natural and man-made beauty. His collections were moved to Ancoats Hall, Great Ancoats Street, in 1886. In Ancoats Hall, formerly a seat of the Mosley family, Horsfall gathered paintings and drawings of birds and flowers, an aviary, model rooms, a history of the life of Christ, a room of art processes, a gallery for the Industrial Arts, a gallery dedicated to J. M. W. Turner, and another to local history. Artists and other distinguished men helped Horsfall in his philanthropic endeavours; the museum was largely financed by himself. Horsfall began lending pictures and reproductions to elementary schools in the Manchester area. However, he found that his enterprising scheme received disappointingly little general support in Manchester. The museum was finally taken over by the Corporation in 1918 and re-opened the following year as the Horsfall Museum. In 1954 the collections were re-distributed amongst the other branches, or disposed of, and the Hall demolished.

Although Horsfall's museum no longer survives, his ideology has formed the basis of much City Art Gallery thinking over the last century. His museum was the first of its type in the world and anticipated by over twenty years the similar museum founded for poor children in Brooklyn, New York.

The name 'Art Galleries' given to the Manchester buildings is misleading for they contain, as this Guide demonstrates, apart from the Fine Art Department (oils, sculptures, miniatures, commemorative medals, prints, drawings, watercolours and photographs), a very large Applied Art Department, ranging from ancient Egyptian artefacts, Greek gold jewellery and a full-scale Japanese *norimono* (or litter), to an early 18th-century Netherlandish pulpit, a variety of ethnographica, and a narwhal's tusk. The military collections, belonging to the 14th/20th King's Hussars and the Manchester Regiment, boast two Victoria Crosses, the silver chamber pot of Joseph Bonaparte captured at Vittoria, a Ferret armoured car and a scout car. All in all, the City Art Galleries perform, although on a much more modest scale, many of the functions of the National Gallery, Tate Gallery and Victoria and Albert Museum combined.

The Collections The Fine Art collection is very rich in the field of British Art, particularly for the 19th and early 20th centuries. For the 17th century and earlier, there are only a handful of works of real quality, like the portrait of *Mary Cornwallis* by George Gower (no. 43) which includes delightful details of costume and jewellery, the curious stilted allegory of *Sir Thomas Aston at the Deathbed of his Wife* by John Souch of Chester (no. 48), *Sir John Cotton and his Family* by Sir Peter Lely (no. 49) and the portrait of *Murrough O'Brien, Earl of Inchiquin* by John Michael Wright: the latter two portraits still retain their contemporary Sunderland frames.

The 18th century fares better, with a small group of great masterpieces such as *The Cheetah and Stag with Two Indians* by George Stubbs (no. 68), *A Peasant Girl gathering Faggots in a Wood* by Thomas Gainsborough (no. 96) the pair of portraits of *Lord Cathcart* (no. 65) and *Lady Cathcart with her Daughter* by Sir Joshua Reynolds, *A Summer Evening* by Richard Wilson (no. 67), painted in 1764 expressly for the rococo dining room at Platt Hall, and the vast canvas *The Birth of Pandora* by James Barry (no. 98), which has been in the collection since 1856. These pictures are by no means the only ones by these artists housed in the galleries, for there are six oils by Gainsborough, four by Reynolds, five by Wilson: while a host of other fine works includes paintings by such artists as Dandridge, Devis, Highmore, Hodges, Hogarth (2), Hone, Ibbetson (4), Kauffman, Lambert, Lawrence (2), Marlow (2), Morland, Romney, Thornhill (3), Vanderbank (2), Wheatley, Wootton, Wright of Derby (4) and Zoffany. These are complemented by a good holding of prints, including what is probably the finest collection of 18th-century colour prints in the country, all in delightful carved frames (the Frederick Behrens Collection); a very important holding of mezzotints, chiefly portraits (Lloyd Roberts Bequest) and a group of drawings and watercolours, boasting works by J. R. Cozens, Dighton, Gainsborough, Hearne, Rowlandson (3), Paul Sandby (3), John 'Warwick' Smith (58), Thomas Stothard (62) and Samuel Wale.

Spanning the 18th and early 19th centuries is a group of miniature portraits (77), including examples by Bone, Bradley, Cosway, Cotes, Engleheart, Hazlehurst, Hone, Richmond and Shelley.

The holding of 19th-century oils is remarkably comprehensive and includes the cycle of eighteen grisaille *Heads of the Poets* by William Blake commissioned to decorate William Hayley's house at Felpham, Sussex; J. M. W. Turner's two grand oils, *Thomson's Aeolian Harp* (1809; no. 105) and *Now for the Painter* (1827); and *The Pays de Caux – Twilight* by R. P. Bonington, a consummate performance, only rivalled by the broken cool blues and yellows of *Rhyl Sands* by David Cox (no. 112), one of eight oils by the artist in the collection. As for Etty's work, it would be difficult to find a better selection anywhere: of his twelve oils, *The Sirens and Ulysses* (no. 114) is the largest and most ambitious, but the Byronic *Self-portrait*, *The Storm* and *A Peacock* all represent the artist in his most dashing and virtuoso manner. As a contrast, Samuel Palmer's little *Bright Cloud* (no. 111) sparkles like a precious jewel, a sonnet to the lush and blessed English countryside. James Northcote, Reynolds' student and *alter ego*, excelled himself in his *Othello, the Moor of Venice*, a profoundly sensitive image. This section of the collection also contains oils by Ansdell (2), Callcott, Collins, Constable (2), Crome (3), Landseer (3), Müller (5), Mulready (2), Pickersgill (3), Archer Shee, Stark (3), Uwins, Vincent (2) and Wilkie. The holding of watercolour drawings of this period is much stronger, including a well balanced group of works by Turner (36), and others by Barrett, Blake, Bonington, Callow, Constable, Cotman, Cox, Copley Fielding, Harding, Holland, W. H. Hunt, Samuel Palmer, Ruskin and David Roberts.

Manchester's most celebrated treasure is undoubtedly the Pre-Raphaelite collection, which is usually claimed to be the finest holding in public ownership. The Galleries have oils by the following members of the Brotherhood and their immediate circle: Archer (2), Brett (2), Madox Brown (29), Burne-Jones (1; he was a Birmingham artist), Collins (1), Collinson (1), Holman Hunt (7), Martineau (2), Millais (11), Prinsep (3), Sandys (1), Shields (9), Smallfield (1), Simeon Solomon (2), Spencer Stanhope (2), Webb (1) and Windus (2). Among the masterpieces are Madox Brown's *Work* (no. 122) and *Stages of Cruelty*, Burne-Jones' *Sybilla Delphica*, Hunt's *Hireling Shepherd* (no. 121), *Light of the World, Shadow of Death* and *Scapegoat*, Millais' *Autumn Leaves* (no. 123) and Rossetti's *Astarte Syriaca* (no. 124), *The Bower Meadow* and *Joli Coeur*. The group of Pre-Raphaelite drawings is richly representative and Manchester's Pre-Raphaelites material is rounded off with a fascinating group of letters, personalia and memorabilia.

High Victorian art is as strongly represented as the Pre-Raphaelites, for this was the period of Manchester's greatest prosperity. The collection largely reflects this wealth, the taste of its businessmen-collectors and the aspirations of the City when it took over the Gallery from the Royal Manchester Institution. The bulk and range of the collection is daunting, for it seems very unlikely that the Galleries will ever have available the space to show anything like its riches. There are, for example, ten oils by G. F. Watts, eleven by B. W. Leader, six by Lord Leighton, six by Briton Rivière and, a little later, eight by Mark Fisher. The collection overflows with famous pictures: Alma-Tadema's *Roman Flower Market*, Lady Butler's *Balaclava*, Frith's *Derby Day* (a version) and *Claude Duval*, Greaves' *Chelsea Regatta*, Herkomer's *Hard Times*, Hook's *From under the Sea*, Leighton's *Last Watch of Hero* and *Captive Andromache* (no. 144), Maclise's *A Winter Night's Tale*, Albert Moore's *A Reader* and *Birds of the Air*, Rivière's *The Last of the Garrison* and *His Only Friend*, and Yeames' *Arthur and Hubert*.

The Edwardian period is equally richly endowed, both in quality and quantity. One of the great treasures is the group of fourteen Valettes. In 1925 the Gallery was given Charles Rutherston's collection of 800 works in all media, encompassing all that was best in advanced British art between *c.* 1890 and 1925. The Rutherston gift, on top of the Gallery's own collection, accounts for the oils by Conder (7), Augustus John (8), Henry Lamb (10), C. R. W. Nevinson (6), Lucien Pissarro (14), Sir William Rothenstein (19), Sickert (13) and Wilson Steer (13). Besides these oils, this is one of the major holdings of drawings, watercolours and prints by these artists, and others like Gaudier-Brzeska, Eric Gill, Paul Nash. The Rutherston Collection laid the foundation of a collecting policy characteristic of the period up to the Second World War, when notable works by such artists as Ben Nicholson, John Piper, Graham Sutherland, Barbara Hepworth and Stanley Spencer were acquired. Post-war collecting, until recently hampered by a minimal purchase grant, has been less far-ranging, but important works by Francis Bacon, Bridget Riley, Howard Hodgkin and Patrick Caulfield have been added.

The collection of Foreign Schools paintings is now growing fast, and contains works of fine quality by artists of excellence – like the *Adoration* attributed to Ridolfo Ghirlandaio (no. 30), an exquisite *Madonna* by the Master of the Magdalen Legend (no. 28), Stanzioni's *Salome with the head of St. John the Baptist*, Reni's *St. Catherine* (no. 39), Batoni's *Portrait of Sir Gregory Page-Turner*, and Bernardo Bellotto's pair of *Views of the Castle of Königstein* (no. 83). Several of these paintings were acquired recently by my predecessor, Loraine Conran, who was also responsible for creating the Art Fund, which merits the Galleries' undying gratitude. His deputy, Dr F. G. Grossmann, had earlier purchased a group of oil sketches, some of special significance, like the Charles de la Fosse, originally for the staircase ceiling of Montagu House, London, and Anton Raphael Mengs' *Apotheosis of S. Eusebio*, for the church of that name in Rome.

The existing holding was transformed in 1979 by the most generous bequest, by the late Mr and Mrs Edgar Assheton-Bennett, of 100 oil paintings principally of the Dutch School. These 17th-century cabinet pieces, once added to the existing Netherlandish collection, put the City Art Galleries in a class quite by itself outside London. It now has small masterpieces by Ter Borch, van de Cappelle, van Goyen, van der Heyden, Koninck, van der Neer and Paulus Potter, not forgetting the superb flowerpieces and still-lifes by Kalf, van Huysum and van Os (nos. 54, 56, 57, 58, 59).

Later foreign paintings consist mainly of works by Salon painters like Bouguereau, Ary Scheffer, Wagner and Adolphe Yvon, and by the Barbizon and Impressionist Schools, the former represented by Boudin, Corot, Courbet, Harpignies, Troyon, plus a large group by Fantin-Latour; and the latter by Blanche, Cazin, Derain, Forain, Gauguin, Léger, Marcoussis, Camille Pissarro, Renoir, Sisley and Vlaminck. Other European countries are represented by the Dutchmen Jacob and Willem Maris, the Franco-Italian Monticelli, and the Surrealist Max Ernst (no. 171).

The Foreign Schools sculpture collection is dominated by the fine marble *Bust of Monsignor Antonio Cerri* by Alessandro Algardi (no. 40), bought with the aid of a national appeal in 1981. The seven busts of celebrated Florentines by Foggini, which were allocated by the Government to Manchester in 1974 through provisions in the National Land Fund, add considerable distinction to the Galleries. *The Shepherd Boy* (no. 104) by Bertel Thorvaldsen, formerly, like the Algardi bust, in the Hope Collection, Deepdene, is a masterpiece of this Danish sculptor and constitutes one of the key works of Continental neo-classicism in England. Although the Galleries house other delightful but less distinguished sculptures from the second half of the 19th century, there is nothing to compare for sheer quality with the four bronzes by Auguste Rodin: *The Age of Bronze* (no. 139), *Eve*, *Bust of Victor Hugo* and *Bust of Alphonse Legros*. These purchases were negotiated between the sculptor and the City by Alderman Walter Butterworth, as Chairman of the Art Galleries Committee, between 21 October and 17 December 1911, and are documented by copies of correspondence with the sculptor in the Gallery files. The Galleries also house sculptures by Bartolini, Barye, Bourdelle, Carpeaux, Dalou, Despiau, Legros (25), Levasseur, Maillol (2), and Zadkine. English sculpture of the 18th century is virtually non-existent, with only a marble chimneypiece of 1790–91 by John Bacon RA at Heaton Hall, and a little Rysbrack terracotta bust, usually displayed in the City Art Gallery, Mosley Street.

The early 19th century is richer, with works by Gibson, Chantrey (3), Henning, Lawrence Macdonald (2), E. H. Baily, Papworth and Theed, while works from later in the century are represented by Bates, Cardwell, Drury, Alfred Gilbert (4), Onslow Ford (2), Ricketts, J. M. Swan (3), Stevens (9), and lesser local luminaries like John Cassidy (10) and J. W. Swynnerton (3). These are further supplemented by a fine array of public statues within the City which come under City Art Galleries' supervision. To complement them in miniature, the Galleries possess an extensive group of 19th-century commemorative medals.

The 20th-century collections lack balance, with a magnificent series by Epstein (12) and works by Atkinson, Butler, Dobson (6), Gill (4), Gaudier-Brzeska (2), Lambert (2), Meadows, Moore (4), Hepworth, Bryan Kneale (2), Havard Thomas (6), and Derwent Wood (2), but, although the Moores are of exceptional distinction, others are perhaps not quite as numerous and distinguished as the Gallery's paintings and graphics of the period.

The Applied Art collection is particularly rich in its English holdings, especially from the later 17th century, creeping conservatively through to about 1820, always avoiding what local collectors must have regarded as stylistic aberrations like the rococo, gothick, Greek and Egyptian revivals. Except for 1884, when a number of showy pieces of Minton porcelain were purchased from an exhibition held at Queen's Park, the Gallery policy was to avoid acquiring examples of modern manufactures, for this area was considered the domain of the College of Art, then run by the City. The Horsfall Museum, however, indulged in collecting to a limited extent contemporary applied art and some of this, including a superb series of De Morgan tiles, was transferred to the Galleries in 1917–18. What early continental pieces there were, found their way into the Art Galleries and were generally of a type considered in the last century suitable for antiquarian furnishings, like Dutch iron coffers, Delft vases, pieces of German stoneware and Italian maiolica. A curiosity is the handsome Dutch 18th-century marquetry bookcase that belonged to Elizabeth Gaskell, authoress of *Cranford*.

In 1933 the Galleries, which were then under the direction of Lawrence Haward, started the pioneering Industrial Art Collection. It consisted of examples of glass, pottery, wallpaper, dress and furnishing material and printing, designed by artists and craftsmen, which were mass produced by commercial firms for large-scale public consumption. The term 'industrial' distinguished these items from the other contemporary works which were mainly produced in small quantities by individual craftsmen for a limited clientele.

English furniture, ranging in date from the 16th to the 20th centuries, is mostly distributed between the branch galleries according to period, although parade furniture is shown alongside the pictures and works of art in Mosley

Street, with more modern furniture fulfilling a similar function next door in the Athenaeum, and the branches still retaining some of their original furnishings. Many of the items were bought in the 1950s and '60s, with the advice of the late Ralph Edwards, then of the Victoria and Albert Museum.

Wythenshawe Hall retains a fine 16th-century oak interior porch, carved in low relief with a scallop shell, strapwork and inlaid with arabesques. The magnificent 17th-century refectory table came from Hever Castle, and the elegant original mahogany library bookcases were supplied by Gillows of Lancaster in 1813. Platt Hall retains Lightoler's rococo dining room with carved chimneypiece and rococo frame surmounting it, incorporating Richard Wilson's *A Summer Evening* (no. 67). At Heaton Hall there are still three splendid curved serving tables in the dining room niche, designed by James Wyatt about 1773–74. Standing on tapered fluted legs, they have mahogany tops, the painted pine frames carved with bacchic masks, oak leaf festoons and paterae. The music room at Heaton was designed in 1790 by Samuel Wyatt with, as the principal feature, a splendid neo-classical organ made by Samuel Green (1790–92), with its case elaborately painted by Biagio Rebecca. The library ante-room retains three of its curved mahogany bookcases, supplied by Gillows of Lancaster in 1824 to the 2nd Earl of Wilton.

The furniture and woodwork section of the collection numbers over 500 pieces. The earliest examples are the Italian Renaissance *cassone* (no. 35) and three 'Elizabethan' beds. There are many 17th-century objects, including chairs, stools, chests, chests of drawers, hall cupboards, tables, and a long case clock by Peter Garon in a superb case with 'sea weed' veneers. The 18th century is represented by a magnificent gilt and white frame designed by William Kent around 1734–35 for Devonshire House, sets of chairs in the manner of Chippendale, Sheraton and Hepplewhite, bequeathed by Sir William Boyd Dawkins, a looking glass designed by Robert Adam in 1774 for Derby House (no. 89), a spinning wheel by John Planta of Fulbeck, near Leeds, a grand pianoforte by Robert Stodart of 1784 (no. 94), a square piano by Longman and Broderip, hall chairs, sideboards, knife urns, secretaires, long case clocks, sofas, fire screens, tripods and consoles.

The Regency furniture collection is of similar quality and scope to the earlier holding, and of especial note are the pair of painted and gilded armchairs in the manner of George Smith, with arms in the form of winged griffons. The Galleries now prefer to buy fine furniture from houses in the region: acquisitions include a pair of sabre-legged black and gold armchairs from Tabley Hall and a painted 'spoon back' chair from Toft Hall. They also collect furniture made in Manchester, and now own stamped pieces by Zanetti and Agnew, Doveston, Bird and Hull, Ogden and James Lamb. Items of 19th-century furniture, especially made to designs by architects and celebrated designers, are becoming a feature of the collection, with examples after designs by Bevan, Blore, Burges, Godwin, Mackmurdo, Morris, Pugin and Waterhouse. The 20th-century collection is thin, although it contains some fine pieces by J. Henry Sellers.

The metalwork collections are rich principally in English 18th-century silver, although Irish and Scottish silversmiths are represented, and there exist excellent examples from earlier and later centuries. As with the furniture, collecting after 1810 seems always to have been subordinated to limiting factors like condition, weight and legible makers marks. The permanent collection was founded on two bequests, that of Dr David Lloyd Roberts (d. 1920), and that of George Beatson Blair (d. 1940), a local businessman who, with his brother James, also gave his superb collection of Turner water-colours. The collections were totally transformed by the munificent bequest, in 1979, of the late Mr and Mrs Edgar Assheton-Bennett, who favoured Queen Anne, George I and George II pieces, principally by Huguenot silver-smiths working in London like Archambo, Feline, Harache, de Lamerie, Nelme, Pantin, Platel and Willaume. As a result partly of their bequest, the Galleries now possess delightful early silver-gilt pieces, like the covered cup from the church of Waterbeach, Cambridgeshire (London 1557–58); the 'Magdalen' cup (London 1573–74; no. 44), probably made for Sir John Byrom, sometime High Sheriff of Lancashire; the Mostyn flagon (London 1601; no. 45), finely engraved with grotesques by Nicaise Roussel and an elegant 'steeple' cup (London 1623–24). Such masterpieces are seen in the context of well over 900 examples, consisting of extensive groups of different pieces invaluable to students, like 225 spoons (including one of *c.* 1350 and another dated London 1480), 90 forks, 43 tobacco/snuff boxes, 39 tapersticks (the finest existing collection), 37 candlesticks, 36 salvers, 35 fish slices (largely Bedford gift, 1977), 22 teapots including the gold teapot (no. 63) by James Ker (Edinburgh 1736), and the gold neoclassical vase and cover made by Parker and Wakelin (London 1772) for John Smith-Barry of Belmont, Cheshire (no. 88). The Galleries have been fortunate recently, to buy a pair of two branched silver candlesticks by Thomas Pitts (London 1769) made for Sir Thomas Egerton at Heaton Hall and an unmarked silver-gilt rococo vase engraved with the arms and crest of the Tattons of Wythenshawe (no. 64). Rococo silver, Regency plate and later 19th-century silver are hardly represented, although a Gothic revival silver flagon and silver-gilt jug after designs by Butterfield (no. 129), a monstrance possibly by Pugin, an Aesthetic chinoiserie teapot after a design by Dresser and a Dresser egg coddler (no. 148) have now been acquired. Art Nouveau silver includes pieces designed by Archibald Knox for Liberty & Co. More London silver was added to the collection with works by H. G. Murphy, Edmund Spencer, Leslie Durbin, F. Newland Smith and James Birchall.

The Art Galleries also house a superb collection of Dutch 18th-century brass tobacco boxes (47; Greg Bequest), largely engraved with exploits in the campaigns of Frederick, King of Prussia, and a group of keys of all ages and all parts of the world (113). The collection also contains watches, fobs and seals (Francis Buckley and Lloyd Gifts), spectacles (193; Llewelyn Andrews Gift), metal fire- and light-making appliances (Greg Bequest) and various items of ormolu, including an elegant 18th-century tripod by Matthew Boulton.

Continental metalwork of the 19th and 20th centuries consists of a silver salt by Odiot (no. 102), a very grand pair of bronze and gilt bronze candelabra by Thomire, and a small collection of Austro-Hungarian pieces in the revived Renaissance style (bequeathed in 1934 by J. E. Yates). There are also examples of Turkish, Swiss and Russian art, including the Fabergé mounted jade bowl and stand (no. 153) and examples of later metalwork by Tiffany and Jensen.

The jewellery collection at Platt Hall contains some 18th-century English paste, memorial jewellery, a group of Berlin iron, cut steel, jet, coral, and hair jewellery. Star items include a superb necklace by C. R. Ashbee (on long loan from the Manchester Polytechnic), and a charming necklace of beads made by May Morris.

Somewhere midway between metalwork and ceramics stands the Gallery's collection of English 18th-century enamels. These number 481 and were almost all bequeathed by Harold Raby of Withington, who died in 1958. The collection, consisting of printed and painted enamels, encompasses all aspects of the subject.

Manchester Art Gallery is undoubtedly best known to ceramic enthusiasts for its magnificent holding of English earthenware, dating from the Roman period up to the early 19th century. Most of it was presented in 1923 by Thomas Tylston Greg. The principal attraction is the rich collection of slipware, with signed chargers by Thomas Toft, William Taylor and William Bird, posset pots, fuddling cups, candlesticks, dishes and mugs. The delftware is rich in London, Bristol, Brislington, Liverpool and some Dublin wares, including 'blue dash' chargers, 'ship' bowls, pill slabs, vases, a set of 'Merry Man' plates, bottles, baskets and tiles. The Nottingham and Staffordshire salt glaze is equally comprehensive, with figures, bears, wall vases, teapots and tea caddies, cream jugs, mugs and toys. Many are richly decorated in peacock-bright enamel colours. Elers-type red wares, Astbury and Whieldon tortoiseshell wares, Jackfield black wares, are profusely represented, as well as Staffordshire and Yorkshire creamwares. In 1906 Miss Anna Maria Phillips of the Park, Prestwich, gave Manchester her fine collection of Wedgwood agates, basaltes and jasperware.

With the notable exception of the selection of Minton purchased in 1884 and referred to previously, the mid- and later 19th- century ceramics holdings of the Galleries until very recently were negligible. This is now being rectified with characteristic examples of the manufactories of Copeland, Doulton, Burmantofts, Brannam, Watcombe, Ruskin, Moorcroft, Della Robbia and the Martin Brothers. Manchester's Royal Lancastrian Pottery, from nearby Clifton Junction, which was founded in 1891, is well represented. It is a very comprehensive collection (237 pieces), especially strong in the characteristic lustre wares, with some patterns especially designed by Walter Crane and possibly Lewis F. Day. Much of it was given by Edward Eason in 1920, and this was supplemented by generous gifts from the Pilkington Tile and Pottery Company (in 1910 and 1937), Mrs Ormerod (in 1964) and Mrs Bessie Coates (in 1977).

Studio pottery was collected especially under the directorship of Lawrence Haward from Annual Exhibitions of the Red Rose Guild, with fine pieces purchased from Bernard Leach, Michael Cardew, Katherine Pleydell-Bouverie and Lucie Rie. Recently items have been added by potters like Elizabeth Fritsch, Colin Pearson, Jaqueline Poncelet, Malcolm Pepper and Siddig El'Nigoumi, and a handsome selection given by the widow of Harold Thornton.

The English porcelain section is very uneven, but includes a magnificent collection of transfer-printed wares, principally Worcester, which had belonged to an early member of the English Ceramic Circle, F. C. Dykes, and was given to the Galleries by his widow in 1948. Other English porcelain was bought by the City or bequeathed, including pieces of Chelsea, Bow, Derby, Longton Hall, Worcester, the Liverpool factories, Bristol, Swansea and Nant-garw.

Continental ceramics come largely from two sources, the Leicester Collier Bequest of 1917 and the Lacks Bequest of 1981. Leicester Collier, of Skiddaw Lodge, Keswick, gave a fine small group of Italian maiolica, including a circular plaque of *St Bonaventura, St Francis and St Louis*, after Catena, made in Venice and dated 1550 (no. 34), and good examples of Castel Durante, Urbino, Faenza, Gubbio, Deruta, Savona and Castelli. He also donated a delightful group of Italian porcelain figures and groups from the factories of Capodimonte, Cozzi, Doccia, Naples and Le Nove. The German porcelain comes mostly from the bequest of Doctors Frederick and Erna Lacks, who had built up an enviable collection of continental pieces, especially early Meissen. To this the Galleries have added further pieces of Meissen, Ludwigsburg, Fürstenberg, Vincennes, Sèvres, Paris and Este; they also possess small groups of German stoneware, French, German and Spanish tin-glaze and Dutch Delft, including a remarkable 18th-century dish, elaborately decorated and inscribed with the Lord's Prayer.

Compared with the post-mediaeval pottery and porcelain, Manchester's glass collection is less comprehensive. There are over 3,300 pieces of pottery, as compared to 857 of glass, but some are quite exceptional. Leicester Collier bequeathed some splendid continental glass in 1918, including a late 16th-century South Netherlandish bell decorated with horizontal milled trails and lion mask prunts, a 17th-century German goblet engraved in diamond point with St Francis, and a neo-classical ewer, wheel-engraved by Quirin with Napoleon receiving the surrender at Austerlitz (no. 101). In 1922 Mrs T. T. Greg gave a delightful little translucent white mug, decorated with a huntsman, almost certainly after J. E. Ridinger (1698–1767), and made in Germany or Bohemia around 1755–60. Dr David Lloyd Roberts, the watercolour collector previously mentioned, gave 221 items in 1920, while Francis Buckley, four years later, presented a group of Lancashire and other provincial English items. However, the largest single gift came from the late Professor F. E. Tylecote, Alderman of the City, and sometime Chairman of the City Art Galleries Committee. His collection of over 250 pieces includes English and Irish wine glasses, jelly and sweetmeat glasses, decanters, tumblers, jugs and rummers. There are some particularly delightful items, like the sweetmeat bowl and cover of *c.* 1700–25, decorated with scalloped and pinched bands, the cover surmounted by a swan finial, the cream pail and ladle of *c.* 1700–50, with handle surmounted by the figure of a bird, three wine glasses enamelled by the Beilby family, and a grand rummer boldly engraved on the wheel with a representation of Nelson's funeral car, dated 'Jany 9 1806'. The Galleries also have typical examples of later English, Continental and American glass, a carafe enamelled with water plants after a design by Richard Redgrave RA, decanters and wine glasses by James Powell and Sons, an iridescent Favrile vase with peacock eyes by L. C. Tiffany (no. 152), and the 'Oiseau de feu' lamp by René Lalique (no. 154).

The oriental collections at Manchester are little known, but include some fine things. They came into the Galleries from four principal sources. The Chinese porcelain (580 pieces), principally of the Kangxi (1662–1722), Yongzheng (1722–35) and Qianlong (1736–95) periods, was largely bequeathed by Leicester Collier and Harold Raby. Collier's friend, Sir John Scurrah Randles, bequeathed his superb collection of Qing porcelain and some Ming wares in 1953. Leicester Collier also bequeathed some fine earlier pieces, and this period has been added to by the Galleries with purchases like a Wei duck, the Han wine jar and the Tang tomb figure (no. 13).

The collection of 69 Chinese cloisonné enamels of the Ming dynasty and later were largely bequeathed by Sir William Boyd Dawkins in 1920. In 1934 John Yates presented 118 jades and hardstones, mostly 19th-century in date, but of splendid quality. A magnificent Song dynasty Guanyin (Goddess of Mercy) of carved wood, covered with gesso and delicately pigmented, was given to the collection by G. F. Williams in 1935 (no. 14). The Earl Egerton of Tatton bequeathed most of his fine collection of oriental arms and armour, including 89 swords, 76 daggers, 14 muskets, 10 shields and 9 axes. Additionally, 124 Japanese sword guards came through the Horsfall Museum. The Tatton Collection is particularly strong in Near Eastern material, much of which was well described and well provenanced, for the Earl wrote the standard work on the subject. Dr Craven Moore of Manchester University put together a fine collection of over a hundred Japanese woodcuts which were bequeathed to the Galleries in 1978.

Manchester's collection of English costume consists of around 18,000 items and a substantial library, containing about 7,000 books and periodicals, some 8,000 photographs and 2,500 loose fashion plates. The collection was started by Mrs Mary Greg, wife of Thomas Tylston Greg, who gave a group of dresses in 1922. The nucleus was soon extended by many gifts, mostly from families in the Manchester district. Lawrence Haward wrote on 21 January 1933 to Mrs W. Heelis (Beatrix Potter) at her cottage near Ambleside, clearly trying to coax out of the authoress items of costume. Beatrix Potter proved to be very generous, giving fashion plates and watercolour drawings by Caldecott, Cox, Bonington, Prout, W. H. Hunt, and an oil by Lord Leighton.

The actual 'Gallery of English Costume' was only established in 1947 when the collection of Dr Willet Cunnington was bought for the City, mainly by public subscription. Dr Cunnington was one of the first students of the history of dress, and collected specimens for their sociological importance as much as for their decorative qualities. Thus, the coarse woollen shawls and wooden clogs once worn by Lancashire mill workers are as highly prized as the costliest ballgown, since everyday dress is rarely preserved.

There is also an extensive collection of lace, embroideries and textiles, many of which were collected by the designer Lewis F. Day and presented to the Gallery after his death by his widow. Large quantities of dress and furniture fabrics were added by Haward when he built up the Industrial Art collection after 1933. It was, above all, the Gallery's first Keeper, Miss Anne Buck, who transformed Platt Hall into a museum of international importance.

The Platt collection includes magnificent examples of brocaded and embroidered dress from the 17th and 18th centuries. A special feature are the wardrobes of Thomas Carill-Worsley, Sir John Stanley of Alderley and his son John, 1st Baron Stanley. Platt Hall also contains the clothes of Victorian men and women and the collection is brought right up to date with dresses by designers such as Zandra Rhodes, Caroline Charles and Laura Ashley, and even a 'punk rocker' outfit.

Some especially fascinating items include the court dress of Frederic, Lord Leighton, PRA, and a frock designed by Edward McKnight Kauffer for his wife, Marion Dorn. The City Art Galleries have posters and cotton bale labels designed by McKnight Kauffer, and a carpet designed by Dorn. Among the various accessories are handbags, fans and umbrellas as well as the less obvious ones like toothpicks, curling tongs, wigs and chest expanders.

Allied to the costume and textile collections now at Platt Hall are the extensive holdings of wallpapers, including a magnificent group by Owen Jones, mostly bound in volumes and stored alongside the Galleries' graphic material. There is also a large collection (over 900 items) of dolls and dolls' houses, toys, furniture and china, presented in 1923 by Mrs T. T. Greg.

The objects in the Antiquities collections were not collected for anthropological or archaelogical reasons, but principally as distinguished works of art in their own right, as the source of much Renaissance, Neo-Classical and Egyptian Revival art, and as elements documenting the history of enlightened taste and connoisseurship. The Egyptian collections (only 107 items) consist of a group of bronzes, a large quantity of vases, phials and jars from Pre-Dynastic times until the Roman period, made of alabaster, granite, porphyr, schist and earthenware. Then there are blue and green faience *ushabti*, beads and scarabs. The collection ranges from large canopic jars surmounted by animal heads for preserving human viscera, to a tiny carving of a frog in basalt with gold eyes and a Ptolemaic gold comb head. The majority of these pieces were given by John Yates. Other items were excavated by Professor Flinders Petrie, like the mummy masks from Fayoum given by his financial backer Jesse Haworth, the Manchester newspaper proprietor, and the fragments of wall decoration found by Petrie at the Ramasseum and given to the Horsfall Museum.

The cream of the Greek and Hellenistic antiquities (about 170 items) are the red and black figure vases that belonged to F. T. Palgrave. Many of the items came in turn from the Pourtalès and Magnoncourt collections. The entire group was purchased through the assistance of C. P. Scott, proprietor of the Manchester Guardian, with a grant-in-aid from the Science and Art Department in 1885 on the British Museum's advice. It consists of a magnificent series of Corinthian vases, including a superb alabastron painted with a confronted lion and lioness and an olpe. Then there are some delightful Attic kylikes, a cup by the Tleson painter (no. 5), one by the Brygos painter showing a revelling youth returning from a drinking party and another by the Elpinikos painter showing a reclining youth playing *kottabos* (an after-dinner game; no. 7). As a contrast in size and gravity there is an amphora painted with Homeric subjects by the Towry-White painter, a satyrhead kantharos and a ram's-head rhyton. Various vases were added to these, including a handsome hydria by the Nausicaa painter, which came from the Horsfall Museum in 1918, and a boldly painted Apulian column crater given in 1981 by the Wellcome Institute of Historical Medicine. The Galleries also own Tanagra statuettes, a few bronze items and marble sculptures, including a head of Jupiter Serapis and a relief of fighting Greeks and Amazons, which is a fragment of a 2nd-century marble sarcophagus found in Asia Minor and given by the National Art-Collections Fund in 1931.

The Roman collections consist of some 569 accessioned items and nearly all come from the 19th-century excavations of the Roman fort and *vicus* of Manchester. They include fragments of stone, pottery and bronze – the finest items being a bronze statuette of Jupiter Stator, from the Ellesmere Bequest, and a handsome stone altar.

The Roman material is the foundation of the Galleries' Old Manchester collection, which consists of local archaeological finds (including Saxon coins from the Hexham and Cuerdale hoards and a Viking brooch; no. 8 and 9), pictures by local artists and of local sitters and topography, prints, models, photographs (including groups by James Mudd and Samuel Coulthurst). There are groups of exhibits dealing with the political and economic agitations associated with Manchester, such as the Peterloo meeting of 1819, which culminated in the Reform Bill of 1832; the Chartist and Anti-Corn Law movements of the early years of Queen Victoria's reign; and the Suffragette Movement. These collections, which are at present housed at the Fletcher Moss Museum, also contain local commemorative medals, trade tokens, locally manufactured furniture, clocks, watches, barometers, pottery (Royal Lancastrian) and glass.

As an extension of local history, the City Art Galleries at present house on loan, at Queen's Park, the collections of the Manchester Regiment and the 14th/20th King's Hussars. These comprise colours, guidons, uniforms, medals, vehicles, weapons, drum sets, models, paintings and photographs.

In spite of the breadth and depth of the collections, Manchester City Art Galleries are still actively buying and improving the quality of their holdings, and even though potential donors suffer heavy burdens of taxation, the City continues to attract remarkably generous gifts and bequests. To this end they are admirably assisted by the Friends of Manchester City Art Galleries and the Patrons and Associates of Manchester City Art Galleries, bodies established respectively in 1978 and 1979. The Patrons, a Charitable Trust, are unique in Great Britain as, through their agency, groups of pictures and sculptures from the reserve collections are lent out to businesses which, in turn, make donations of £500 or more annually to the Galleries. These monies are then put by the Trustees at the disposal of the City Art Galleries for making acquisitions.

From this introduction it is clear that the quality and quantity of supporting material in the Galleries is impressive, but what the City needs above all are a few more paintings and works of art of superlative quality that are worthy not just of a detour, but of a special air ticket to Manchester. What pre-20th century pictures and works of art are in Manchester, are displayed in such a sumptuous and intentionally reactionary 17th–19th-century manner that they appear abrasively progressive. Ceilings are stencilled, painted, and gilded; floors are strewn with Persian rugs; sculpture, ceramics and glass are shown in carefully conceived juxtaposition; and labels are intended to be thorough, informative, but unostentatious.

Most of Manchester's collections are in store because of the acute lack of display space. One day the Galleries will have an extension, something they have been waiting for since 1897. When that happens the stored collections, like a wrinkled brown chrysalis, will undergo a metamorphosis into that magnificent and brilliantly coloured butterfly which at present lies dormant.

We hope that the following illustrations of pictures and works of art, which have been carefully chosen from the collections and described by members of the curatorial staff, will remind visitors of some of the items that they have enjoyed in Manchester, and will tempt others to come and delight in our collections.

TIMOTHY CLIFFORD
February 1983

Catalogue

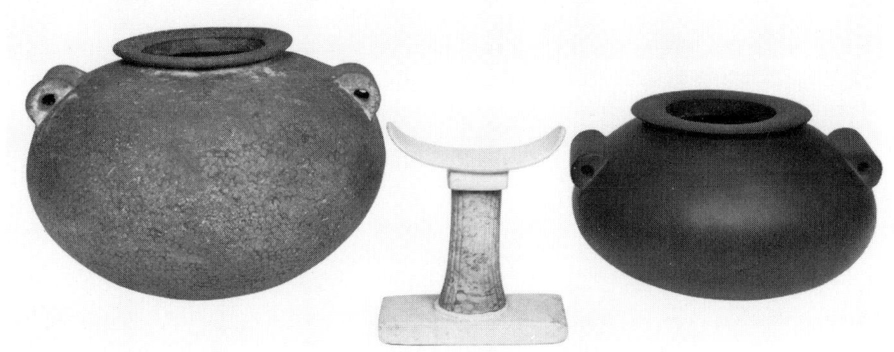

1

1 *Egyptian Jars and Headrest*

STONE JAR

Globular jar made from solid green schist, with tubular lug handles.
Egyptian, Predynastic period (*c.* 3000 BC)
Height: 15.2 cm (6 in)
John Yates Bequest (1934.295)

The production of stone storage jars began during the Badarian culture (fl. *c.* 4000–3700 BC) when isolated basalt vessels are found; many more were produced during the Nagada I culture (named after a site in Upper Egypt, fl. *c.* 3700–3300 BC), usually of cylindrical or beaker forms. The very finest were produced under the Nagada II culture (*c.* 3300–3100 BC) and Early Dynastic period (Dynasties I–II, 3100–2686 BC) in a variety of hardstones, and in forms paralleled by contemporary pottery. By the beginning of the Old Kingdom (Dynasties III–VI, 2686–2181 BC) they were superseded by simple clay vessels.

EARTHENWARE JAR

Globular round-bottomed jar with tubular lug handles, everted rim and short neck, decorated with red iron oxide slip in a fine scale pattern over the body, and with a net pattern on the rim.
Egyptian, Predynastic period (*c.* 3000 BC)
Height: 21.6 cm ($8\frac{1}{2}$ in)
John Yates Bequest (1934.294)

The end of the neolithic period in Egypt was marked by a considerable increase in artistic production. Under the Nagada II or Gerzean culture there was a predilection for unglazed but finely decorated pottery jars of various shapes, mainly globular or cylindrical, with lug handles for suspension. They were made from the calcareous clays of certain valleys of Upper and Middle Egypt. The decoration took the form of figures, or geometric motifs, as in this example. An almost identical example, excavated at Hu (Diospolis Parva) is in the British Museum, and another, found at Aulad Jahia, is in the Cairo Museum.

HEADREST

In three parts, the base plinth and top rest of plain speckled alabaster, the central column of ochre and black veined marble.
Egyptian, Old Kingdom (2686–2181 BC)
Height: 16.9 cm ($6\frac{11}{16}$ in)
John Yates Bequest (1934.284)

Headrests in this style form a usual part of Old Kingdom tomb furniture. The first intact tomb chamber of this period, discovered in 1925, that of Queen Hetephras, wife of Snofru (*c.* 2613–2578 BC), first pharoah of the 4th Dynasty, contained a headrest stylistically identical, made of gilt wood (*c.* 2580 BC), while an alabaster piece in the Kofler Truniger collection (Lucerne) is inscribed on column and plinth with the name of its owner, Nefermaat (6th Dynasty, *c.* 2200 BC). In addition to its usual domestic function, the headrest was used to support the head of the mummified body. Chapter 166 of the *Book of the Dead* was composed to effect this purpose by magical means.

Such simple but monumental forms were to be much admired and of great influence on pioneering artists of the 1920s and 1930s like Henry Moore, Arp and Brancusi.

2 *Egyptian Jar and Bronzes*

FUNEREAL JAR

Alabaster, the lid carved in the shape of the head of the dog-headed guardian of the lungs, Hapy.
Egyptian, New Kingdom (1567–1085 BC), probably 20th Dynasty (1198–1085 BC)
Height: 43.1 cm (17 in)
John Yates Bequest (1934.271)

These jars, in which the viscera were placed in burial, are usually called Canopic jars; this misnomer is derived from an early observation at Canopus, on the Nile Delta, of human headed vessels, which were in fact a form in which Osiris was worshipped there. In funerals, they represent the four sons of Horus, jackal-headed Duamutef, falcon-headed Qebehsenef, human-headed Imset, and dog-headed Hapy, and were used as containers for the main organs of the body. This practice was continued through the New Kingdom period, but

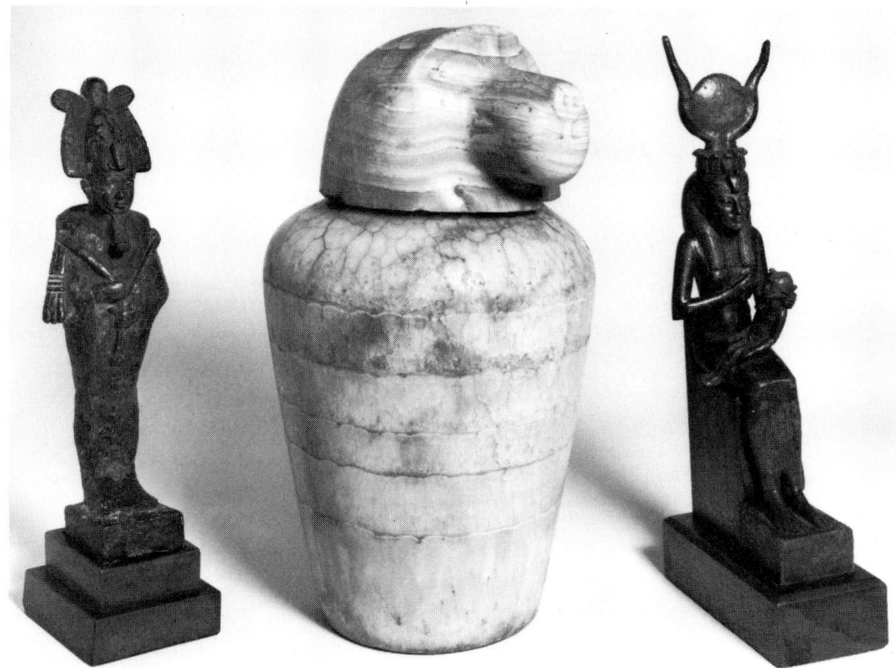

2

declined under the 21st Dynasty (1085–945 BC) when the embalmed viscera were returned to the mummified body.

OSIRIS

Cast bronze, the god represented as a mummy with arms crossed over the breast, holding a crook and a flail; he has a narrow plaited beard and wears on his head an *atef* crown, the white crown of Upper Egypt with two red feathers.
Egyptian, 26th (Saite) Dynasty (664–525 BC)
Height: 36.9 cm ($14\frac{1}{2}$ in)
John Yates Bequest (1934.258)

One of the most important gods of the Egyptian pantheon, Osiris was the god of fertility, having the power of granting life from the underworld in the form of vegetation and the annual flood of the Nile, and the judge and ruler of the Underworld, as the personification of the dead king. The story was that the pharoah Osiris was drowned or otherwise murdered by his brother-in-law Seth, who scattered his body, cut into fourteen pieces, over the world. These were recovered by Osiris' wife Isis and her sister Nephthys, who buried them, giving a new life to Osiris in the hereafter.

ISIS AND HORUS

Cast bronze, the goddess represented as a woman seated on a throne, the hieroglyphic symbol of a throne on her head, holding the infant Horus, her son, on her lap.
Egyptian, 26th (Saite) Dynasty (664–525 BC)
Height: 39.7 cm (16.6 in)
John Yates Bequest (1934.259)

Isis had three major functions as a goddess, that of the mourner of the death of Osiris, hence the principal deity in the rites of the dead; as an enchantress, she could cure the sick, revivify the dead, or inflict disease; and as the mother of the new pharoah, Horus, she was also a giver of life, and protector of Horus until he could exact revenge on Seth for the death of his father Osiris. From the reign of King Psaemtik I (*c.* 664–610 BC), Isis was the best known Egyptian goddess.

3 *Portrait of a Woman*

Wax encaustic on panel
Egyptian (Fayoum), 2nd or 3rd century AD
30.5 × 22.5 cm (12 × $8\frac{13}{16}$ in) irregular
Unsigned
J. Haworth Bequest (1937.128)

This realistic portrait of a woman wearing earrings is one of about six hundred recorded portraits from Fayoum, a province of Egypt south west of Cairo. Another example is also in the Galleries' collection. They date from the mid-1st to the mid-4th century AD and were painted on wood or linen, in wax encaustic or sometimes in egg tempera. The portraits were originally painted from life and hung at home, but were later re-used to cover the faces of mummies, according to the Egyptian custom of burying the mummified body with a likeness of the deceased, thus preserving its identity in the after-life. These flat painted portraits succeeded the three-dimensional mummy masks. Remarkably lifelike, their relaxed attitudes, with slightly turned heads and arresting, natural expressions, are quite

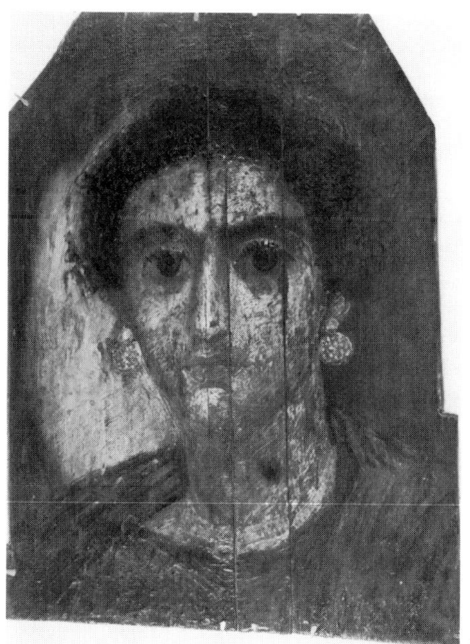

3

unlike the frontal hieratic stylisation of ancient Egyptian art.

Many of the sitters were of Greek origin. Though Egypt by now was a province of Imperial Rome, it had been settled by Greeks, whose prosperous way of life preserved many Greek customs. Portrait painting in the ancient classical world is recorded in literary sources, but these portraits, from a later epoch, provide almost the only surviving evidence of it.

A large find of Fayoum portraits was made by Sir W. M. Flinders Petrie, the great English archaeologist, during his excavations at Hawara in 1888 and 1911. The Mancunian Dr Jesse Haworth, who bequeathed this example, was a friend and sponsor of Petrie and a benefactor of the City Art Galleries and the Museum.

4 *Greek Pottery*

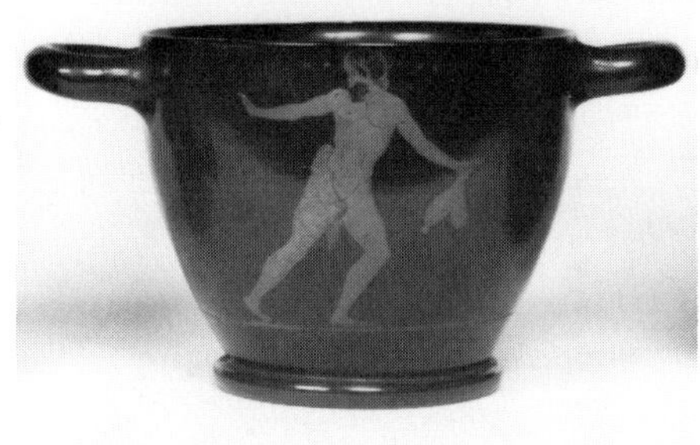

4

SKYPHOS (DEEP WINE CUP)

Red earthenware painted with black slip in classical Attic red figure style.
Greek (Athens), *c.* 460 BC
Height: 12.6 cm (5 in)
Purchased from the Palgrave Collection with the aid of a grant from the Science and Art Department (1885.21.Aa.29)

The cup is decorated with two satyrs carrying bloated wineskins, each superscribed *kalos* (beautiful). It was painted by an early classical vase painter, known only for his *skyphoi*, which are called the Mount Holyoke group; his work is related to that of the better known Lewis painter. The piece comes from the important French collection, the Pourtalès cabinet.

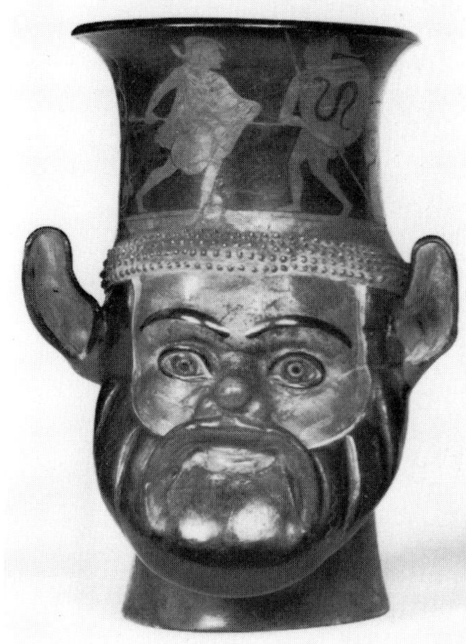

4

KANTHAROS (CUP)

Red earthenware moulded with the face of a *satyr*, with single handle, decorated with black and white slip in classical Attic red figure style.
Greek (Athens), *c.* 430 BC
Height: 22.3 cm ($8\frac{7}{8}$ in)
Purchased from the Palgrave Collection with the aid of a grant from the Science and Art Department (1885.21.Aa.31)

Painted on the neck of the cup is a scene of a hoplite, or heavily armed soldier, in combat with a peltast, or lightly armed man, between palmettes. The piece belongs to a group of 'head vases' called the Manchester group after this vase, which was previously in the important Magnoncourt Collection.

OLPE (WINE JUG)

Buff earthenware painted in black slip with crimson details in Early Corinthian style.
Greek (Corinth), 620–600 BC
Height: 26.4 cm ($10\frac{3}{8}$ in)
Purchased from the Palgrave Collection with the aid of a grant from the Science and Art Department (1885.21.Aa.2)

The jug is decorated with four animal friezes, between broad bands of tricolour scales, comprising lions, goats and a swan between two sphinxes, more lions, and running greyhounds. It is typical of high quality early Corinthian export ware.

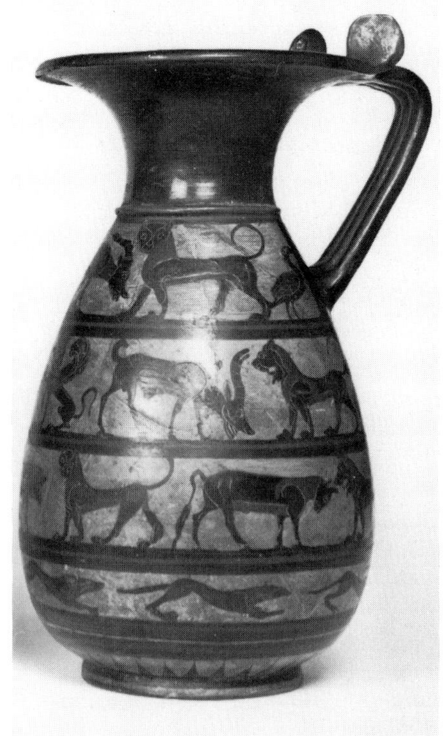

4

5 *Kylix (wine cup)* *pl. 1*

Red earthenware painted in black slip with crimson and white details in mature Attic black figure style with a single band of rams and swans.
Athenian, 550–530 BC
Diameter: 20.9 cm ($8\frac{1}{4}$ in)
Purchased from the Palgrave Collection with the aid of a grant from the Science and Art Department (1885.21.Aa.17)

Some of the finest 6th-century Athenian vase painting was executed on 'Little Master' cups of this sort. The decoration is confined to a single exterior band around the outside, and hence the type is called the Band Cup. Although unsigned, this cup is probably by one of the finest cup painters of the period, Tleson, son of Nearchos (also an important painter). Although his signatures only record him as a potter, it is now generally considered that he also painted his pieces. His figures are usually of animals, and complement his characteristic miniaturist detail and lavish use of additional colour.

This piece was found in 1802 at Kamiros on Rhodes, the market for considerable Athenian exports in the 6th century, and passed into the great Pourtalès Collection. From there it moved to the Palgrave Collection, from which it was purchased by the Art Gallery.

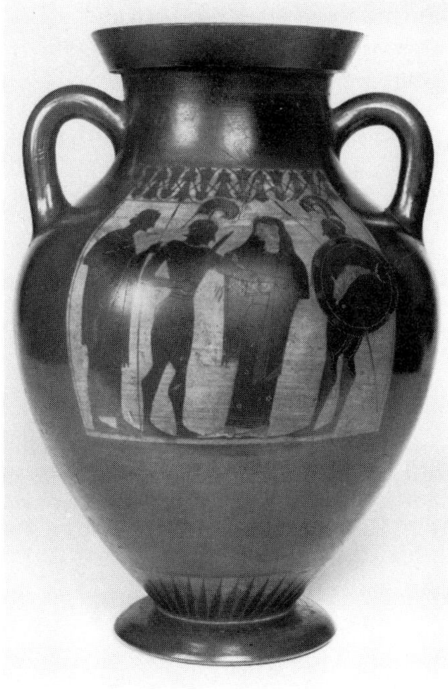
6

6 *Amphora (wine jar)*

Red earthenware painted in black slip with white and crimson details in Attic black figure style.
Greek (Athens), *c.* 550 BC
Height: 40 cm (15⅞ in)
Purchased from the Palgrave Collection with the aid of a grant from the Science and Art Department (1885.21.Aa.45)

The principal use of the *amphora* was the storage of wine, although it could also be used for olive oil, honey or water. Two main shapes were common, the continuous curve, as in this example, and the neck *amphora*, in which the body of the vessel has a distinct shoulder from which the neck rises. The whole vessel was thrown on the wheel in one piece, apart from the base, which was attached later. The lid, with which most *amphorae* were equipped, is usually lost.

This piece belongs to the archaic period of 6th-century Athens, during which some of the finest vessels were made. It is painted by the Towry-White painter, so-called after another *amphora* in the Fitzwilliam Museum, Cambridge, from the Towry-White Collection. He belonged to the generation preceding Exekias, commonly acknowledged as the finest painter of Attic black figure vases.

The vessel is decorated with mythological scenes on shoulder panels. These are taken from the epic cycle describing the Trojan War, of which the *Iliad* and *Odyssey* of Homer form a part. On one panel is a confused battle scene, in which one hero on a chariot fights another, while the obverse, shown here, depicts the recovery of Helen from Troy by Menelaos. This is one of the scenes in the story of Helen which is most popular for vase decoration.

7 *Two Greek Kylikes*

KYLIX (WINE CUP)

Red earthenware painted in black slip in Attic red figure style with, on the inside, a drunken reveller within a central medallion.
Athenian, *c.* 470 BC
Diameter: 21.8 cm (8⅞ in)
Purchased from the Palgrave Collection with the aid of a grant from the Science and Art Department (1885.21.Aa.37)

The central scene shows a reveller reeling home from a drinking party clad only in a cloak (*chlamys*), his hair bound with a fillet, the composition completed by his dropped walking stick. Although unsigned, this cup is by one of the most important early classical Athenian cup painters, the Brygos Painter, so called after the potter Brygos with whom he usually collaborated. Wine cups of this period are frequently decorated with subjects associated with wine drinking.

KYLIX (WINE CUP)

Red earthenware painted in black slip in Attic red figure style with, on the inside, a *symposium* scene.
Athenian, *c.* 500 BC
Diameter: 19.9 cm (7⅞ in)
Purchased from the Palgrave Collection with the aid of a grant from the Science and Art Department (1885.21.Aa.24)

By the Elpinikos Painter, after the inscription *Elpinikos kalos* (handsome

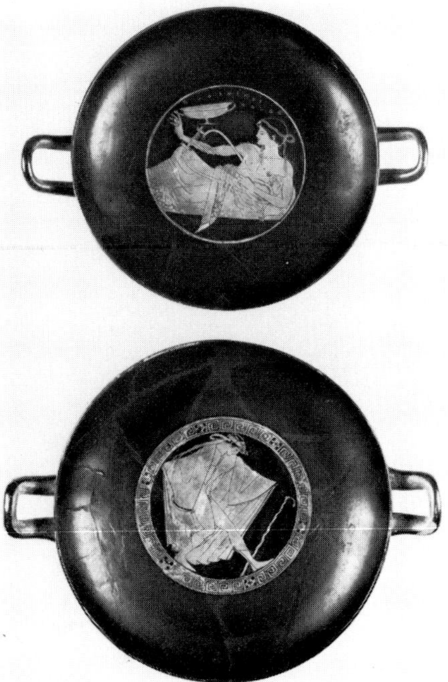
7

Elpinikos) which appears on all his cups. The subject is shown here reclining at a drinking party, holding a lyre with his left hand, and with his right playing the game *kottabos*, in which wine-lees are flicked from a cup across the room into a bucket. Originally from Vulci in Italy, north-west of Rome, subsequently in the Camino Collection.

8 *Three Saxon Coins*

SILVER 'SCEAT'

Obverse: dotted square containing
Reverse: plumed bird motif
English, Kingdom of Mercia, 700–40, or Frisian
Weight: 1.23 gm
Gift of Nathan Heywood (1909.472.5)

BRONZE 'STYCA'

Obverse: Eanred
Reverse: Fordred
English, Northumbria, King Eanred (825–54)
Weight: 1.24 gm
Royal Manchester Institution: Hexham 17

SILVER PENNY

Obverse: +CVN.·.NFTI·:·
Reverse: CNVT R E X .·. around patriarchal cross
Vikings of Northumbria, King Cnut (*c.* 877–903)
Weight: 1.40 gm
Royal Manchester Institution: Cuerdale 1

The Manchester hoard of *sceattas* is the most significant find from the city in the Anglo-Saxon period. Nine *sceattas* were found while digging the foundations of St Matthew's church, Campfield, in 1821, while eight 'copies' were given to the Queen's Park Museum in 1909 with a different provenance. Silver *sceattas* formed the earliest currency in Mercia, and their design may derive from late Roman silver coins. The Hexham hoard was found in 1833 at the west side of the transept of Hexham church in a bronze vessel. The date of the deposit of the hoard is *c.* 850–60, and it contained *stycas* of the Anglo-Saxon kings of Northumbria, mostly Eanred and Ethelred II, and Archbishops of York, mostly Vigemund.

The Cuerdale hoard, discovered near Cuerdale Hall, Lancaster, on 15 May 1840 by a group of workmen, was one of the most important hoards of early English coins. The hoard comprised over 7,000 silver coins, over half of which were Northumbrian, the remainder English, French and Islamic, together with silver ingots, neck chains and rings, all in a lead case within a wooden box. It is dated *c.* 903, and may have been hidden during a skirmish between Anglo-Saxons and Viking settlers. Silver pennies replaced *sceattas* as currency in the late 8th century; they were copied from Merovingian French *deniers*.

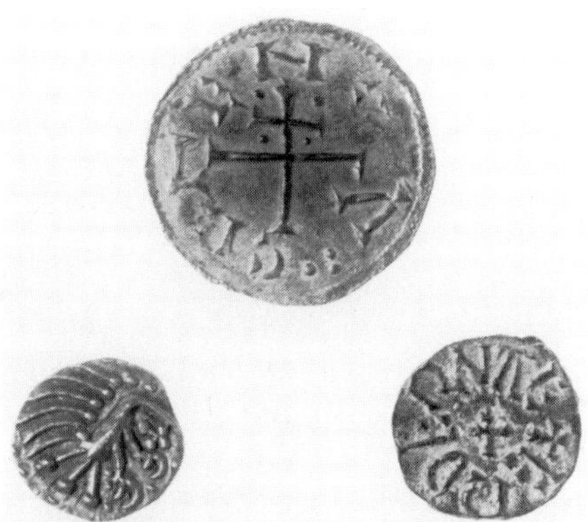

8

9 *Two Brooches*

RING BROOCH

Gold, set with alternate garnets and sapphires in collets, between each of which is a raised boss with punched decoration, and surmounted by an open fruit pod. A sapphire is set on the pin.
English, *c.* 1300
Diameter: 4.5 cm ($1\frac{7}{8}$ in); weight 20.67 gm
Purchased with the aid of a Government grant (through the Victoria and Albert Museum) (1977.168)

The brooch was discovered in 1971, on a mound of earth excavated from a trench in Victoria Street, near the

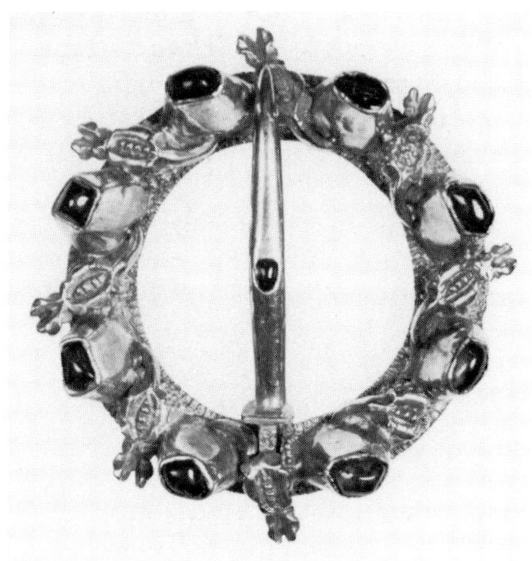

9

cathedral, the centre of medieval Manchester. The use of the medieval ring brooch as a fastener at the throat for the ends of a cloak can be seen in contemporary sculpture, for example on the west front of Wells Cathedral (1240–50). The form was introduced in the 12th century and was popular during the 13th and 14th. The only other complete brooch of this type in England is in the Victoria and Albert Museum, and is one of a group of four. They are all made up from collets and naturalistic foliage motifs and believed to be French in origin. The Manchester brooch may be unique in having stamped bosses between the collets, and is assigned an English origin by comparison with a silver brooch found with English coins at Dumfries in 1878. It may be dated, by the decoration of circular punching, to the period of the Coventry coin hoard brooches, *c.* 1300.

DISC BROOCH

Alloy of silver, tin and copper with a quatrefoil interlace pattern, surrounding nielloed roundels containing pellets.
Viking, *c.* 900
Diameter: 2.6 cm (1 in)
Earl of Ellesmere Collection (1909.408)

This brooch was discovered in Manchester between 1828 and 1832, during the construction of the

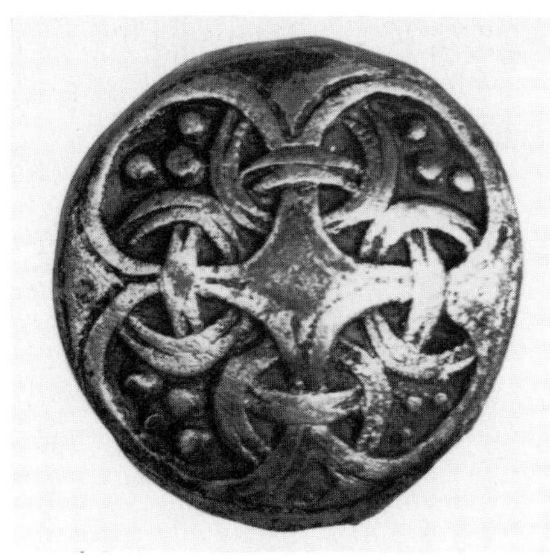
9

Bridgewater Canal, in the Castlefield area of the city. Castlefield was the site of the Roman auxiliary fort of Mamucium, which gave its name to the early medieval village which grew up nearby. The brooch is one of the few finds from early medieval Manchester, and is particularly interesting as an indication of Viking influence. Comparable brooches have been excavated from Saffron Waldon in Essex, and in Sweden from Hedeby and Birka.

10 *Follower of Daddi*

c. 1290–1348

VIRGIN AND CHILD WITH THE GOLDFINCH

Italian; tempera on panel
62 × 32.2 cm (24⅜ × 12$\frac{11}{16}$ in), arched top
Unsigned
Inscr(b.): AVE.MARIA.GRAÇIA.PL
Purchased with the aid of a Government grant (through the Victoria and Albert Museum) (1959.29)

Bernardo Daddi was a leading and influential Florentine artist of the generation immediately after Giotto. In his work, the monumental qualities of both Giotto and the sculptor Giovanni Pisano were combined with the decorative stylisation of Sienese art. This panel is probably by one of Daddi's close followers. It is one of three replicas of a painting in the Berenson collection at 'I Tatti' near Florence. The others were formerly in collections in Parma and Florence. Doubt had been cast on the authenticity of the Manchester panel, but scientific analysis has revealed nothing inconsistent with a 14th-century date.

It was possibly the central panel of a polyptich (or altarpiece with many panels), showing saints and scenes from the Gospels. Each panel would have had a carved and gilded Gothic frame, and have been decorated like this one, with haloes and subsidiary motifs punched into the gilded background. The inscription, 'Ave Maria Graçia Pl[ena]' (Hail Mary, full of Grace), is the greeting spoken to the Virgin Mary by the Angel Gabriel at the Annunciation (St. Luke, ch. 1, v. 28), a scene which may have been represented elsewhere on the altarpiece. The goldfinch, or *cardellino*, is often seen in images of the Virgin and Child. According to legend, the goldfinch received its red markings on the road to Calvary: when flying over Christ's head, it drew a thorn from His brow and was stained by a drop of His blood.

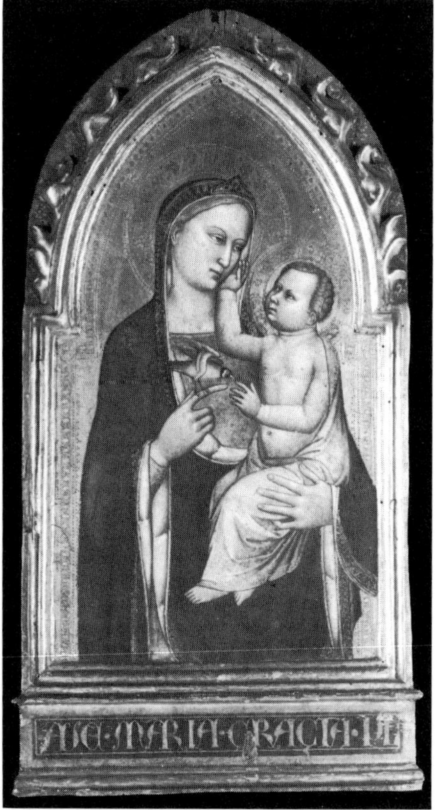
10

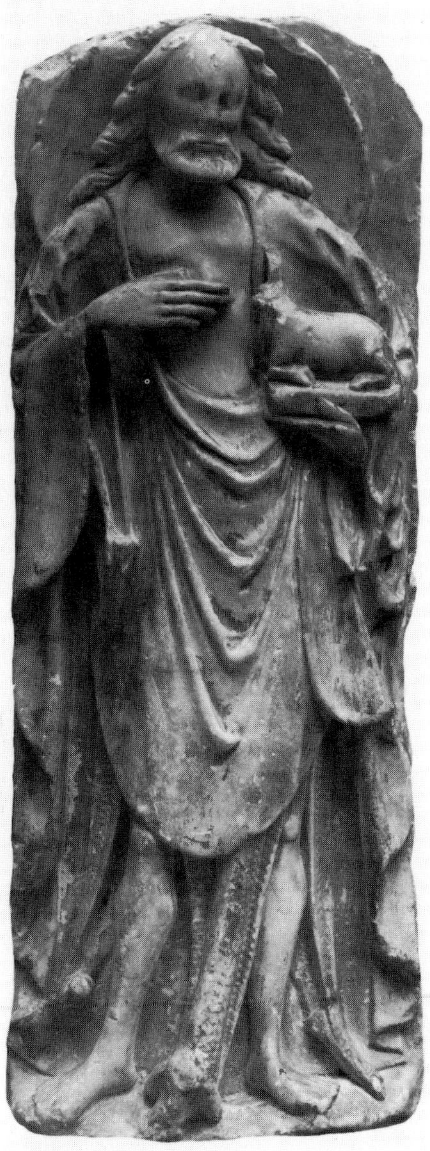
11

11 *Nottingham Alabaster*

ST. JOHN THE BAPTIST

Alabaster
English (Nottingham), *c.* 1400
34.3 × 12.7 cm ($13\frac{1}{2}$ × 5 in)
Purchased (1951.124)

Alabaster reliefs were made in large numbers in England from the mid-14th to the late 15th century, mainly in the Midlands, near the alabaster quarries at Nottingham and at Chellaton and Tutbury in Derbyshire, though there were also workshops in York and London. Alabaster, a sulphate of lime or gypsum, was plentiful, cheap and easy to carve; such panels were exported across Europe and have been found as far apart as Iceland and Italy. In this country, many were destroyed by the iconoclasts of the Reformation. It is rarely possible to assign to these panels a precise date or place of origin.

The alabasters were richly painted and gilded, and often grouped in wooden frames to form altarpieces of five or seven broad panels with scenes from the Life of Christ or the Virgin, flanked on either side by single saints on narrower panels like this one. A trace of yellow colour remains on the saint's right sleeve.

St. John the Baptist is holding his attribute, the lamb (see Gaulli's *St. John the Baptist*, no. 42), and under his mantle he wears the 'raiment of camel's hair' described by St. Matthew (ch.3, v.4). This has been shown by the carver as a complete camel skin, the head at the bottom centre and two feet dangling on either side with bone and hoof attached. This iconographical peculiarity is seen in other alabasters of the period, including a slightly later altarpiece in the Victoria and Albert Museum. It demonstrates how the workshops mass-produced these images to standard patterns. A second relief, *The Betrayal*, is also in the Gallery's collections (1951.123).

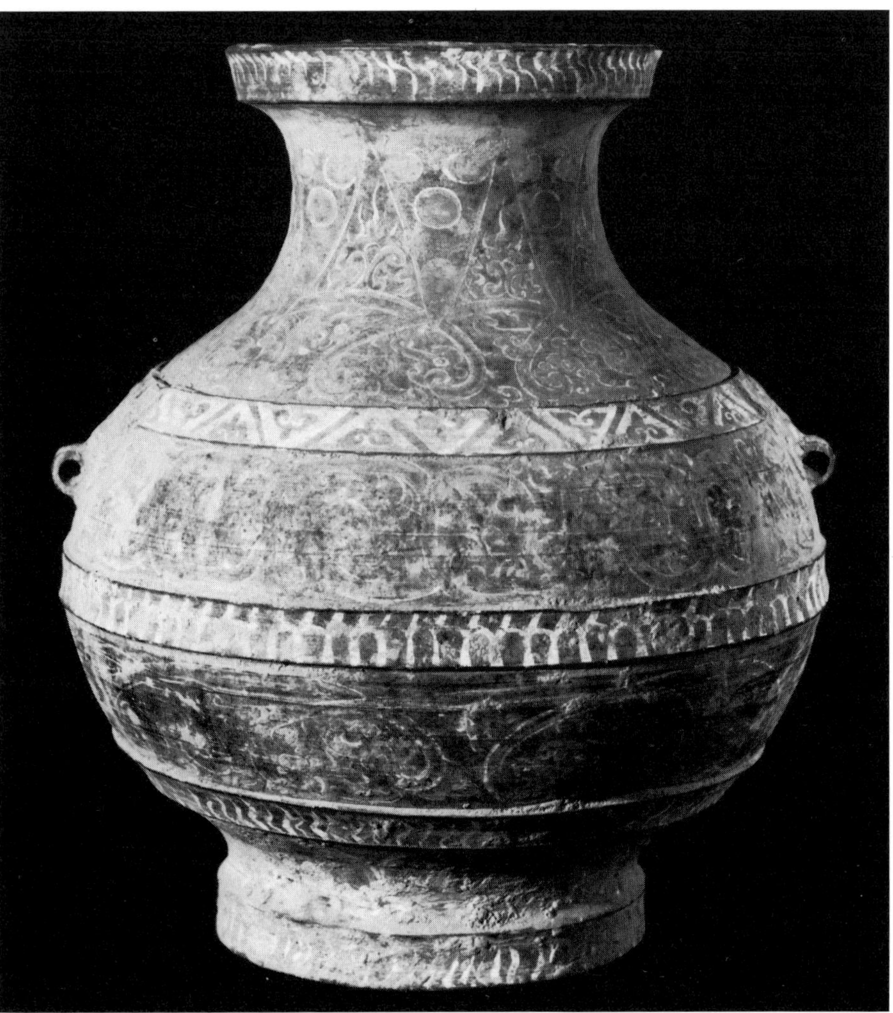

12

12 *Wine Jar (Hu)*

Earthenware, unglazed, painted in unfired red, blue, green and white pigments.
Chinese (Henan province) Han dynasty (206 BC–AD 220)
Height: 41.8 cm ($16\frac{1}{2}$ in); diameter: 36.1 cm (14.2 in)
Purchased (1935.155)

The tombs of the Han dynasty were abundantly furnished with all the requisites the dead might need in the afterlife, including food and wine. This wine jar belongs to a type produced exclusively for funereal use, being flamboyantly decorated in polychrome colours, but relatively cheap to produce. The form and decoration of this *hu* derives from contemporary but much more costly bronze pieces, which were typically adorned with functional ring handles suspended from animal masks (*shouhuan*). This style was developed with the *hu* in the Eastern Zhou period (770–256 BC), as was the decoration of interlocking triangular panels on the neck. On the ceramic versions such ring handles are purely decorative.

Similar vessels, also for funereal use,

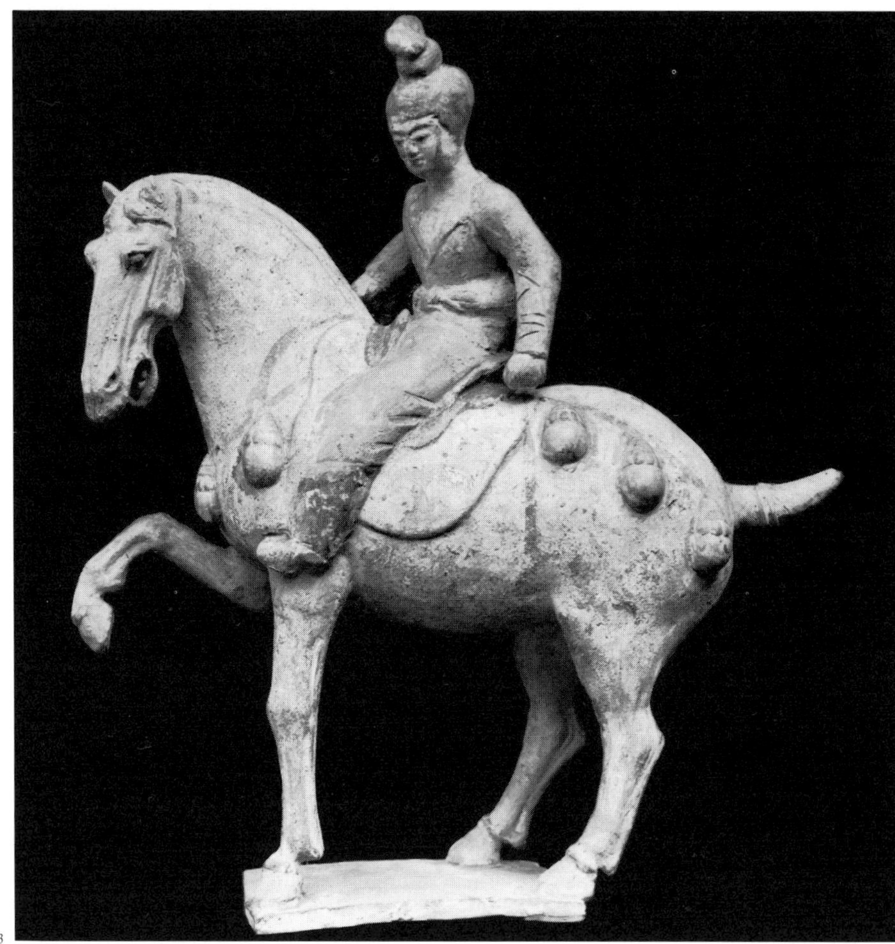

13

were produced in central China, in Zhejiang and Jiangsi provinces, but these were made in high-fired stonewares with grey-green felspathic glazes, and led directly to the development of the fine *Yue* wares and subsequently to the celadons of the Song dynasty. Excavations of brick-lined chamber tombs in the region of the Han capital Luoyang, in Henan province, show the quantity of such vessels used. In a single tomb as many as twenty-five may be counted. Thus the replacement of bronze with pottery represented a considerable saving of resources, and apparently provided the dead with the same facilities.

13 Tomb Figure

Horse and female rider, earthenware painted in unfired white, ochre, red and black pigments.
Chinese, Tang dynasty (618–907), *c.* 706
Height: 38 cm (15 in)
Purchased (1935.139)

Tomb figures, representing the retinue of the deceased, appeared in the Qin dynasty (221–207 BC) and reached their peak of sculptural achievement in the Tang dynasty. They, along with food and other tomb furnishings, provided the dead for their needs in the afterlife. The finest Tang figures were produced in the first half of the 7th century.

The year 706 saw a series of remarkably affluent burials, notably those of Princess Yongtai and Prince Ide, and this tomb figure is of the same style as those excavated from their tombs. It was very popular in this period for women to wear male dress for riding, especially in and around the capitals of Luoyang and Changan.

The fashion is described in the *Treatise on carriages and dress* in the *Old Tang history (Jiu Tang Shu*, by Liuxu, written *c.* 945): 'At the start of the Kaiyuan period [713–42] the palace ladies who rode behind the imperial carriage all wore central Asian hats, exposing their painted faces, without a veil. The families of the multitude of officials followed the fashion, and the style of the veiled hat [*weimao*] was absolutely out. After a while they also exposed their hair whilst riding; some were wearing men's dress and boots. Highborn and lowborn, men and women, could not be distinguished from one another; all looked alike.'

14 Buddhist Boddhisattva

Wood sculpture, painted in red, blue, white and yellow
Chinese, Song dynasty (960–1279), 1150–1250
Height: 117 cm ($46\frac{1}{8}$ in)
Gift of G. F. Williams (1935.175)

The Boddhisattva is depicted seated on an advancing lion led by an attendant, and represents either Guanyin (the God or Goddess of Mercy) or Wenshu (the Lord of Wisdom). Since none of the formal attributes of either are present (for Guanyin the *kalasa*, ambrosia bottle, or a lotus flower and miniature Buddha in a niche; for Wenshu the sword, book or blue lotus) and since both are usually depicted riding on a lion, identification is not yet possible.

The carving is typical of the fine, flowing, naturalistic style of the Song dynasty, quite different from the stiffer,

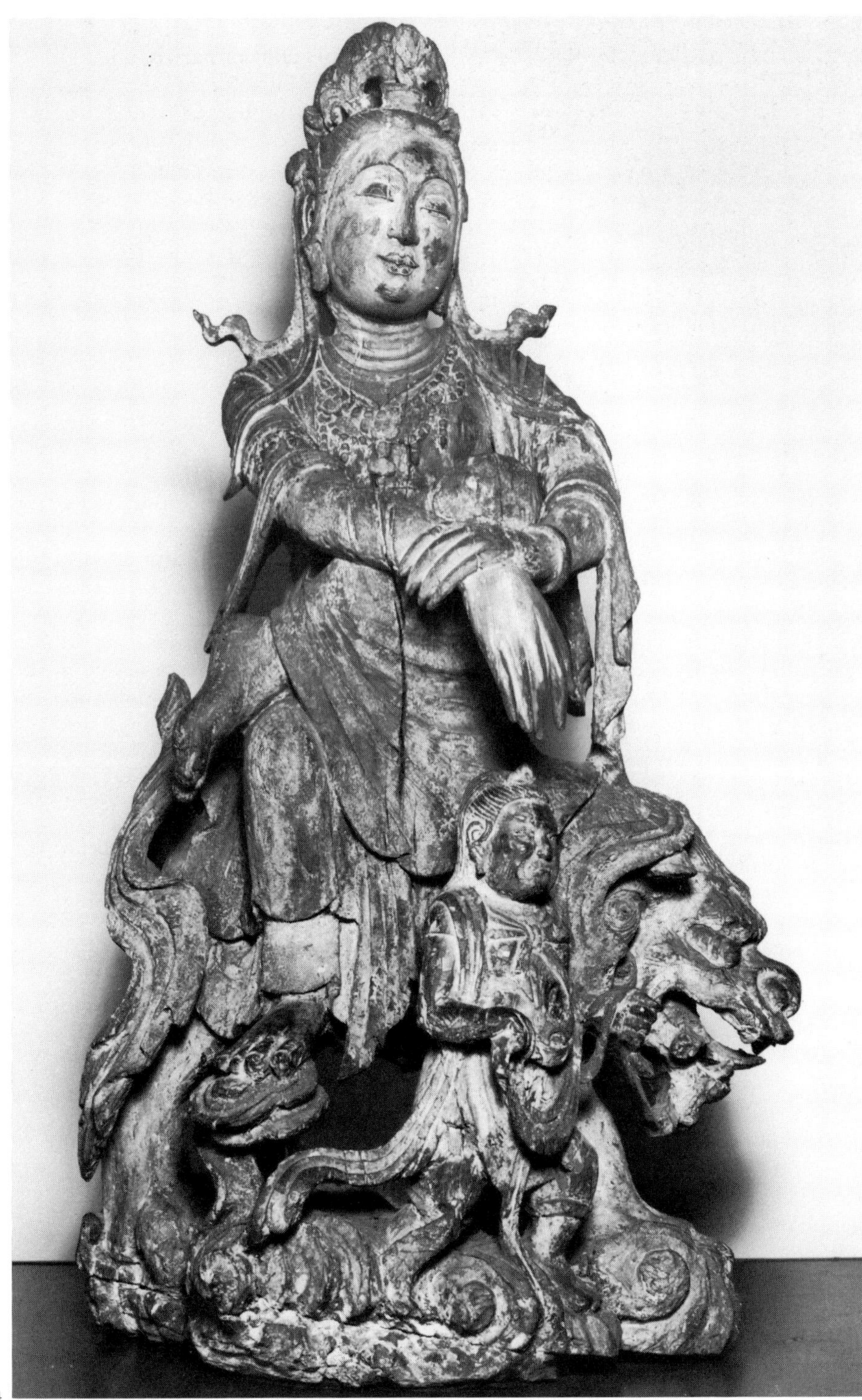
14

more formal style of the preceding Tang dynasty. The scarf draped round the Buddhisattva's neck flutters in the breeze, her face is a picture of serenity, and below her, on the billowing base, the lion and the attendant snarl fiercely. The pose is so relaxed that it avoids the standard positions and gestures: the legs are crossed in a position close to the attitude of meditation (*lalitasana*) while the left hand merely clasps the right one around the left knee. Her breast and upper arms are festooned with pendant jewellery, in standard Song dynasty style.

A comparable Wenshu in polychromed wood and on a lion is to be found in the Upper Temple, Guangshensi, near Zhaochengxian, Shansi province, and is dateable to *c.* 1150; a similar Guanyin, in the same material, is in the Muzeum van Aziatische Kunst, Amsterdam. None of the comparable pieces, however, adopt as informal and unusual a pose as that of the Manchester Boddhisattva.

15 *Narcissus Bowl*

Jun ware, grey stoneware with speckled lavender glaze with 'worm tracks', edged with copper crimson. Incised number *yi* (one) on green glazed base.
Chinese, Song (960–1279) – Yuan (1260–1368) dynasties, 13th century
Diameter: 22.8 cm (9 in)
G. Beatson Blair Bequest (1947.538)

Because of the wealth and patronage available in North China, particularly in the province of Henan, following the fall of the Tang dynasty (618–907), artistic life flourished. Pottery became so advanced that the northern wares of the subsequent Song dynasty (960–1279) are regarded as classics. *Jun* is a classic ware, and was produced in Henan; kilns where it was fired have been excavated in Yuxian.

Narcissus bowls, in Chinese *Shuixian pen*, were formed with the aid of complex moulds, and the three cloud-scroll feet added later. Along with a variety of flower pots and stands, they were produced in relatively standard sizes denoted by a number between 1 and 10 incised into the base. After an initial firing, the unglazed *Jun* ware was coated with white clay slip, and dipped in the final thick glaze. Fine copper filings were then blown onto rims and edges of the piece, producing patches of red copper oxide. This effect, and the lovely blue colour of the glaze itself were the result of 'reduction' firing, during which the amount of oxygen entering the kiln was skilfully controlled or reduced. This bowl has 'earthworm tracks' inside, which are faults in the glaze, often admired by connoisseurs. As the glaze is fired up to 1450°C, cracks appear, which fill with thin, pale blue glaze.

Jun and the other classic Song wares called *Guan*, *Ru* and *Northern Celadon*, were revered by later Chinese dynasties, and in the West. Production of *Jun* ware, especially numbered pieces, continued under the following Ming emperors (1368–1644). *Jun* ware was particularly popular at the Imperial court.

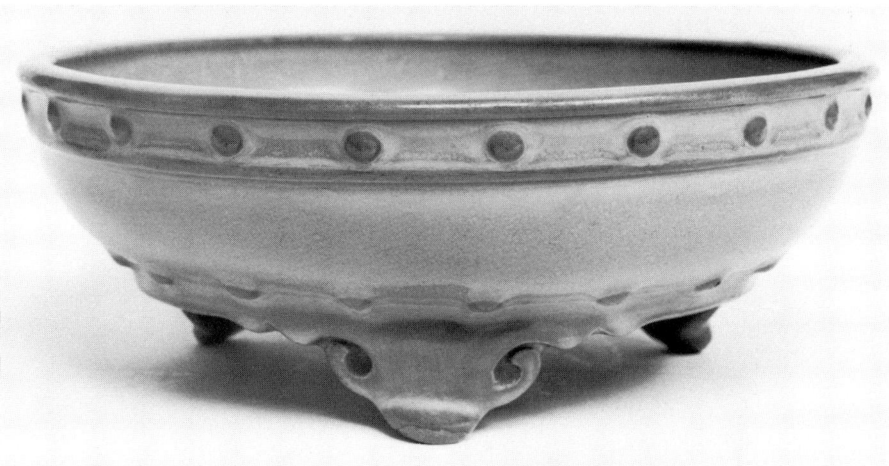

15

16 *Double Gourd Vase*

Porcelain decorated in underglaze cobalt blue with, on the upper gourd, a procession of animals, elephant, *qilin* (unicorn), lion and dog in a landscape, and on the square, lower gourd, landscape scenes (*shanshui*, literally mountains and water). One of a pair.
Mark: character *Jiajing* mark on base.
Chinese (Jingdezhen region, Jiangsi province)
Ming dynasty (1368–1644), Jiajing period (1522–66)
Height: 28.6 cm ($11\frac{1}{4}$ in)
Sir John Scurrah Randles Bequest (1953.192/2)

The manufacture of fine porcelain during the Yuan (1260–1368), Ming (1368–1644) and Qing (1644–1912) dynasties was concentrated in the region of Jingdezhen in Jiangsi province in south China. The most prolific and well-known type produced was 'blue and white', in Chinese *qinghua baidi* (blue ornament on white ground). The production of this type had been made possible during the Mongol Yuan dynasty by the import of cobalt oxide from the Kashan area of Persia. It was referred to by the Chinese as *huihuiqing*, 'Mohammedan blue', and during the Ming dynasty was mixed with inferior native cobalt from Yunnan province, called *shiqing*, or 'stone blue'. At first this porcelain was produced to be exported to the wealthy Islamic rulers of the Middle East, but during the Ming dynasty emphasis was shifted to the Chinese Imperial court.

The blue and white porcelain of the Jiajing period was characterised by a liking for very dark blue, and by its decoration, which attempted to imitate ancient silk brocades. This change is particularly noticeable from the Jiajing period onwards, when more popular subjects, for example children, scholars, animals, birds and flowers appear in natural surroundings, replacing the formalised high style of the 15th century.

This piece, a double gourd bottle (*huping*) is particularly unusual in having a square lower bulb. There is a comparable piece in the Victoria and Albert Museum, from the Rev. Bloxam Collection, decorated with playing children (*wawa*) and figures in a landscape, while a much larger example was formerly in the Clark Collection.

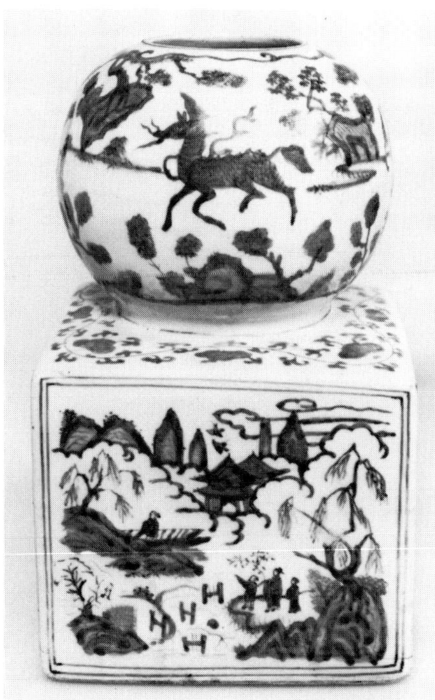

16

17 *Dragon Jar*

Grey stoneware with dragon and clouds painted in iron red under a clear glaze.
Korean, Yi dynasty (1392–1910) 16th–17th century
Height: 33.7 cm ($13\frac{5}{16}$ in); diameter: 39.2 cm ($15\frac{3}{16}$ in)
Purchased (1936.115)

Large jars of this sort painted with calligraphic vigour in abstract interpretations of natural subjects are some of the finest products of the provincial Korean peasant potter. The technique has its origins in the *Cizhou* wares of north China during the Song and Yuan dynasties, and is particularly associated with north east and central Korea, in the area around Pyong yang; particular kiln sites have not yet been identified. Iron brown was popular because of the scarcity and expense of cobalt blue, most of which had to be imported from China.

The dragon is depicted here above stylised cloud scrolls; this indicates that he is a 'fully fledged, heaven-called' dragon. Although in Chinese and Korean mythology dragons are essentially creatures of the ocean, after one thousand years a horned dragon will metamorphose into a flying dragon, who flies not with the use of wings but the exercise of will-power. This type of jar, not unlike the Chinese *guan*, is used for the storage of food, and this particular flattened spherical shape was in use from the 15th to the 18th century. Similar dragon jars are to be found in the Fitzwilliam Museum, Cambridge, and the Duskoo Palace Museum in Korea: other decorative motifs include tigers, bamboo and reeds. The free flowing brushwork, employing calligraphic technique, and the rich colours have evoked admiration from, and imitation by, modern artist-potters.

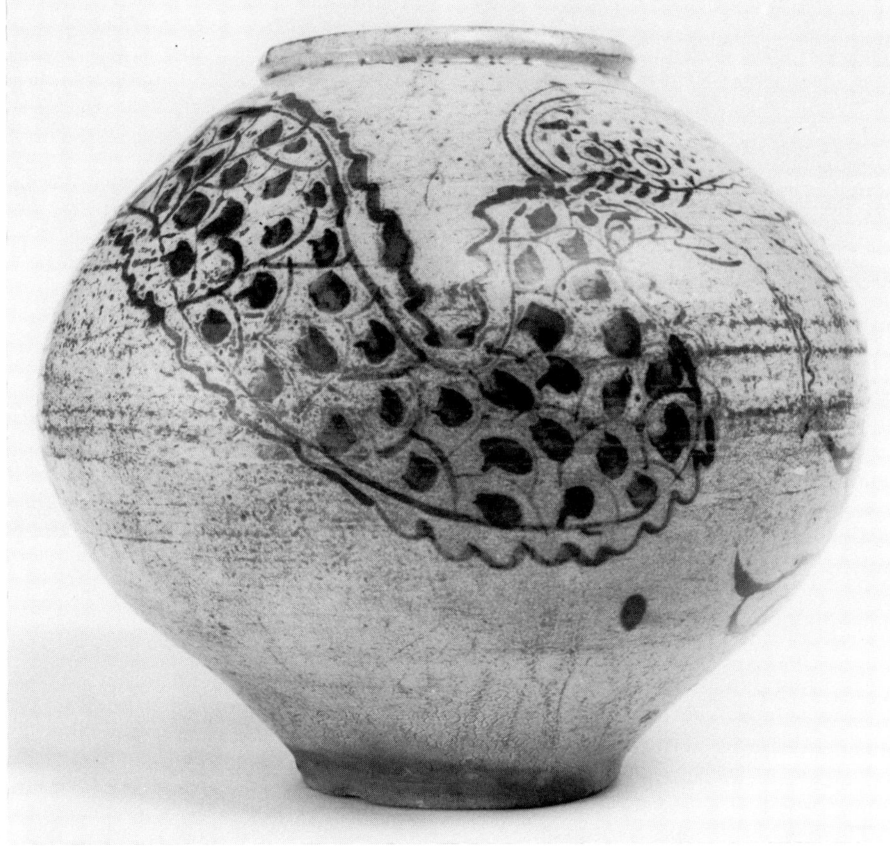

17

18 *Plate*

Porcelain, decorated in underglaze cobalt blue with European scene of an outdoor musical party, surrounded by landscape medallions.
Chinese (Jiangsi province, Jingdezhen region)
Qing dynasty, Kangxi period (1662–1721), *c.* 1700–10
Diameter: 35.6 cm (14 in)
Leicester Collier Bequest (1917.559/2)

This plate, one of a pair, belongs to an interesting group of porcelain, probably for the Dutch market, which took their decoration from fashion illustrations by the Parisian brothers Bonnart, active from *c.* 1675 in the rue St. Jacques. The engraving from which this design was copied, drawn by Robert Bonnart and engraved by Nicholas Bonnart, is entitled *Symphonie du Tympanum, du Luth et de la Flute d'Allemagne* and bears verses in which the pleasures of music are compared unfavourably to those of love.

A lady dressed in high fashion with piled hair is seated (in an armchair in the original) at a table, playing a dulcimer; she accompanies two men wearing frock coats and wigs, playing a lute and a flute. The scene in the original print is set on a paved verandah, edged with a low wall with columns, behind which trees may be seen, while the Chinese version places the group on grass with trees behind and overhanging them. Certain detail differences may indicate that the version presented at Canton for copying may have been a pirated Dutch copy of the French original.

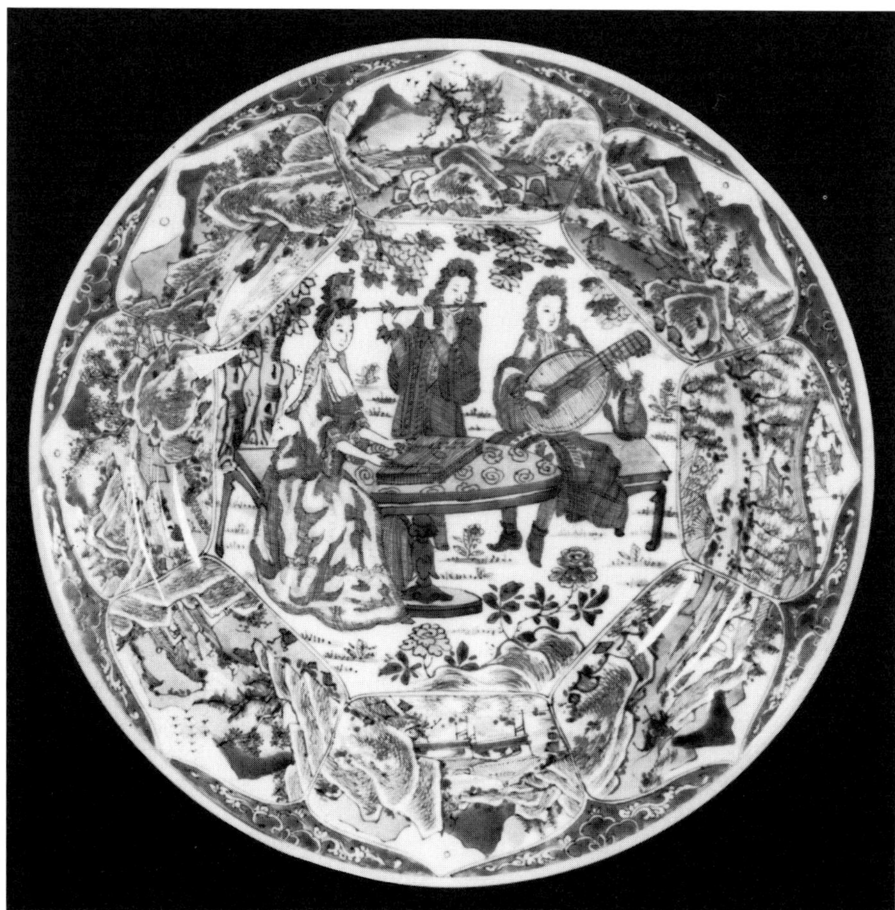
18

Similar plates are in the British Museum, Victoria and Albert Museum, London; the Princesshof Museum, Leeuwarden; the Chait Galleries, New York; and the Mottahedeh Collection.

19 *Jade Vase*

Pale 'mutton-fat' nephrite, decorated with a band of archaistic *taotie* ornament around the base, and four antlered dragon heads, their tongues holding ring handles.
Chinese, Qing dynasty, Qianlong period (1736–95)
Height: 33.9 cm ($13\frac{1}{3}$ in)
John Yates Bequest (1934.28)

Jade (in Chinese *yu*) has always occupied, in China, the position reserved in the West for gold and diamonds; from earliest times it was associated with immortality. The word covers a range of semi-precious hardstones, including jadeite, but the finest pieces have been made of nephrite imported from Turkestan. Nephrite consists of calcium-magnesium silicate, with iron (white Actinolite) or without (green Tremolite), and belongs to the mineralogical group of monoclinic amphiboles.

The Qing dynasty saw the highest technical achievements in jade carving, aided by the fact that the Manchu rulers' empire controlled the sources of supply. The Qianlong emperor was the greatest patron in the history of jade carving. A fanatical collector, he was particularly interested in ancient art. The form of this vase derives from the bronze wine jar, *hu*, of the Han dynasty (206 BC–AD 220), and similar pieces may be seen in Minneapolis Institute of Art and the Victoria and Albert Museum, London.

The so-called *taotie* decoration around the base was developed in Shang-dynasty China, and comprises, in stylised form, the face, with prominent eyes, and body of a mythical creature.

The Yates gift provided Manchester with one of the finest collections of Chinese jade of the 18th and 19th centuries, and of the Qianlong period in particular.

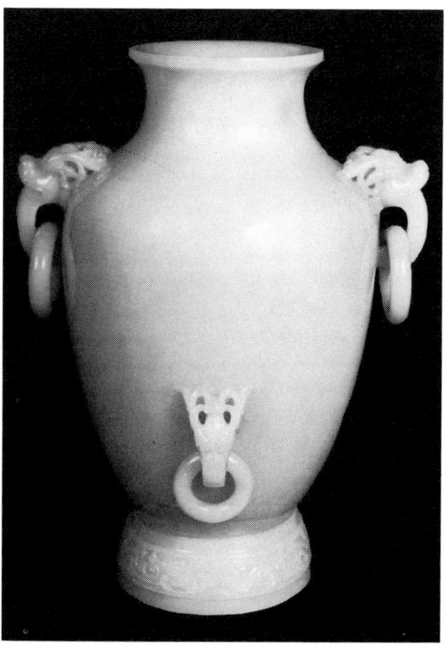
19

20 *Jar and Jar Stand*

Marble stand on four hoofed feet with hollow octagonal trunk and long basin. Alabaster jar with low relief decoration.
Egyptian, Fatimid (969–1171) – Ayyubid (1171–1250) period, probably *c.* 1200
Kilga 65 × 37.5 × 47 cm ($25\frac{1}{2} \times 14\frac{3}{4} \times 18\frac{1}{2}$ in), overall height 97 cm ($38\frac{1}{4}$ in)
John Yates Bequest (1934.235)

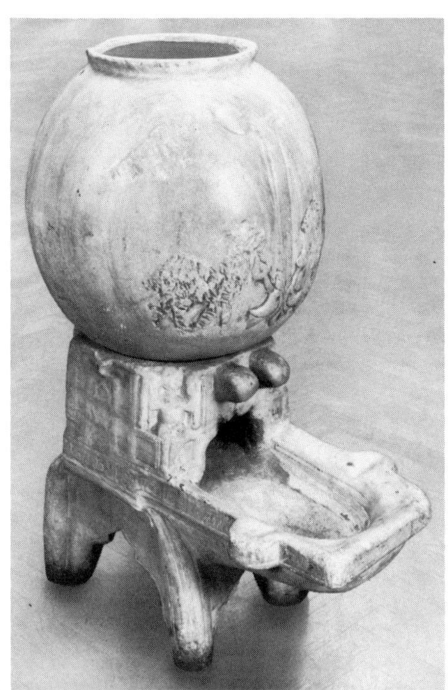

20

Jar stands (*Kilgas*) were used to support unglazed terracotta *habb* jars, through the porous bodies of which Nile water would seep into the basin below down the 'stair' (*salsabil*). Water was purified by the process and cooled by evaporation. The trunk is decorated with two abraided lions' heads above a tricusped arch through which the water flows, and the front diagonal faces with seated *orantes* (nude females with arms raised in prayer). The sides and rear contain framed *mihrab* niches, while the rear diagonals contain *mihrab* niches framed by columns. The *mihrab* is a niche in the wall of a mosque indicating the direction of Mecca. The basin has two overflow spouts, and around the medial band is an eroded *kufic* inscription.

Some sixty of these stands are known, most of them in Cairo, in the Museum of Islamic Art and the Coptic Museum. This appears to be the only example in Britain. The only *kilga* bearing a date within its inscription, albeit mutilated, can be dated to the decade between 1193 and 1203. Although the Manchester *kilga* is somewhat unusual, it is best associated with the group containing the dated stand.

Many of the surviving *kilgas*, like this one, now contain alabaster jars which date from the 15th to 17th centuries and which are purely decorative, since they cannot perform the function of the original terracotta jars.

21 *Suit of Armour*

Russet iron plates embossed in *uchidashi* style, blue, red and white silk lacing, and leather plates. Iron helmet with black lacquered plates.
Helmet signed: *Munemitsu saku*
Japanese, Momoyama period (1568–1616)
Earl Egerton of Tatton Bequest
(1910.15.185)

The Momoyama period (1568–1616) was one of dramatic civil war, in which the most powerful of the *daimyo* (feudal lords) attempted the re-unification of Japan. This task was started by Oda Nobunaga (1534–82), and continued by his successors Toyotomo Hideyoshi (1536–98) and Tokugawa Ieyasu (1542–1616). European influence, in particular the introduction of firearms by the Portuguese in 1543, combined with the intensification of warfare to impose radical alterations on armour. Equipment was simplified and lightened, and the old intricately laced lamellar armour was replaced in the 'modern armour' (*tosei gosuto*) by solid plate armour in hinged sections. This type is called *Yuki no shita*, after the armourer Myōchin Hisaie of Yuki no shita, Sogami province, by whom it was first produced in the late 16th century.

The Manchester example is supposedly from Osaka castle, destroyed in 1615 by Tokugawa Ieyasu. It is decorated by embossing (*uchidashi*) with a design of the powerful Buddhist deity Fudo Myō-ō bearing the sword of wisdom (*ken*) and surrounded by a halo of flames. This embossed style was practised by the Myōchin family of armourers during the 17th and 18th centuries. The signature of Munemitsu is frequently found on Myōchin armours and iron articulated animals, but does not appear in the Myōchin family records. Below the breastplate are laced leather *kusaziri*, and the shins are protected by *shino suneate*. The arms are covered with armoured sleeves (*kote*) in the *odagote* style, which combine mail (*kusari*) on silk brocade with black lacquered plates. The helmet (*kabuto*) is of *kōshōzan*, 'high victory mountain' type, and is fitted with a face guard (*mempo*) of iron lacquered red inside, with detachable nose piece.

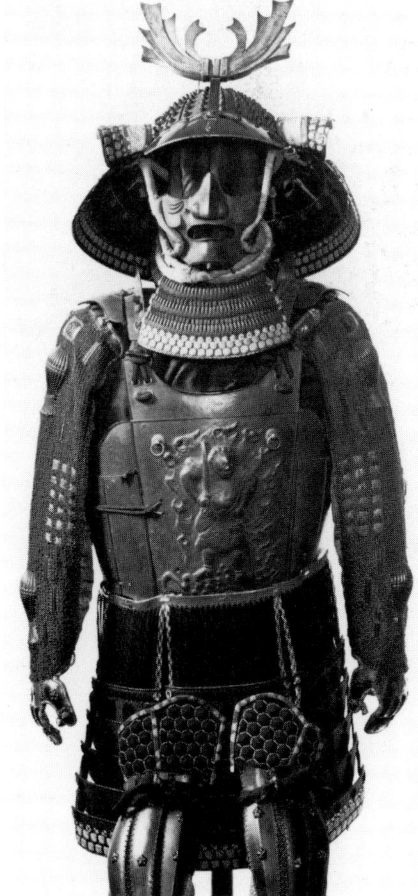

21

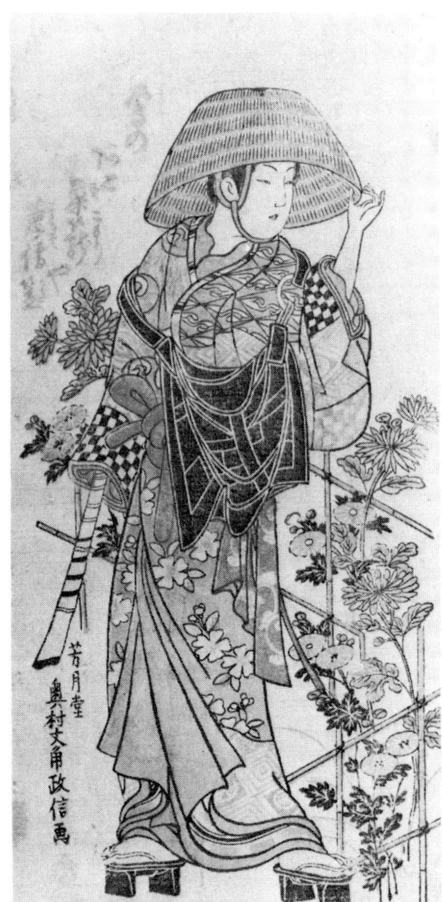

22

22 *Okumura Masanobu*
(1686 1764)

A WANDERING MONK, KOMUSO

Beni zuri-e (2-colour printed) woodblock print
Signed: *Hogetsudo Okumura Bunkaku Masanobu ga*
Sealed: Tanchōsai
Japanese, Edo (Tokyo) *c.* 1745
Hosoban, 29.3 × 13.7 cm ($11\frac{1}{2} \times 5\frac{3}{8}$ in)
Craven Moore Bequest (1978.324/8)

Masanobu was one of the most important and influential figures in the early history of *ukiyo-e* art. He was the proprietor of a bookshop in Edo, and began to illustrate books in 1701. From 1724 he published his own prints, and subsequently those of his pupil Okumura Toshinobu (fl. *c.* 1717–50), stamped with the gourd-shaped Tanchōsai trademark. He appears to have studied for a while with Torii Kiyonobu (1664–1729), but was largely self-taught. He was responsible for numerous innovations in *ukiyo-e* art; he invented the *hashira-e* (pillar print) format, and the *uki-e* (perspective picture), and was the first artist to use lacquer in the *urushi-e* (hand-coloured print). When the simple colour printing technique was invented in 1741, he may have been the first artist to use it; he was certainly responsible for the fashion for *bijin-ga* (pictures of beautiful women) which, along with actor portraits, dominated *ukiyo-e* art for the remainder of the century.

This print shows an itinerant monk (*komosu*) identifiable by his beehive hat which was intended to cover the face (this was hence a popular disguise for outlaws). He carries over his shoulders a black bag for the reception of offerings, given as a reward for his playing of the five-holed bamboo flute (*shakuhachi*), which he holds in his right hand.

23 *Katsushika Hokusai*
(1760–1849) *pl. 14*

KIRIFURI FALL, KUROKAMI MOUNTAIN, SHIMOTSUKE PROVINCE

Series: *Shokoku Takimeguri* (Around the waterfalls of the country) No. 1
Signed: *Zen Hokusai I-itsu hitsu*
Publisher: Eijudo
Japanese *nishiki-e* colour woodblock print
Edo (Tokyo) *c.* 1833
Oban tata-e, 37.2 × 25.8 cm ($14\frac{5}{8} \times 10\frac{1}{4}$ in)
Craven Moore Bequest (1978.324/31)

In the West, Hokusai is, justifiably, the best known of all Japanese artists. He was one of the most eminent masters of the Japanese graphic arts, in all the fields of painting, book illustration, drawing and print designing. Although for most of his life he was a recluse, Hokusai's work was intensely popular and he had numerous imitators. His *go*, or artist's name, *Hokusai*, means 'worker for the North', a reference to the boddhisattva Myōken. Hokusai was a member of the Buddhist sect of Nichiren, in which Myōken was an incarnation of the North Star. The signed name *I-itsu* was coined in 1820, when he passed into his second sixty-year cycle, the basis of the Japanese calendar.

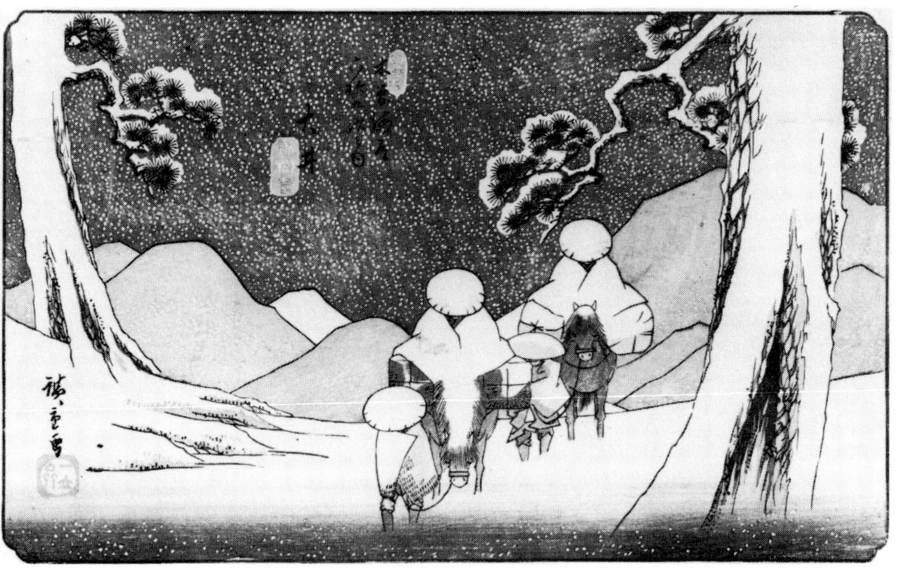

24

Hokusai's great work, *The thirty-six Views of Mount Fuji*, was first advertised in 1831, and was published shortly thereafter. Thus the *Shokoku Takimeguri* series belongs to the period of his finest work. It comprises eight views of famous waterfalls, in which the power and violence of the Japanese landscape, *sansui*, literally 'mountains and water', is rendered as a thing of beauty, with which man can live in peace and harmony. This was an approach quite alien to the contemporary Japanese, who regarded this beautiful scenery in the European sense, as something dangerous. Hokusai's humanistic approach is clearly expressed in *Kirifuri Fall* by the figures comfortably observing the scene.

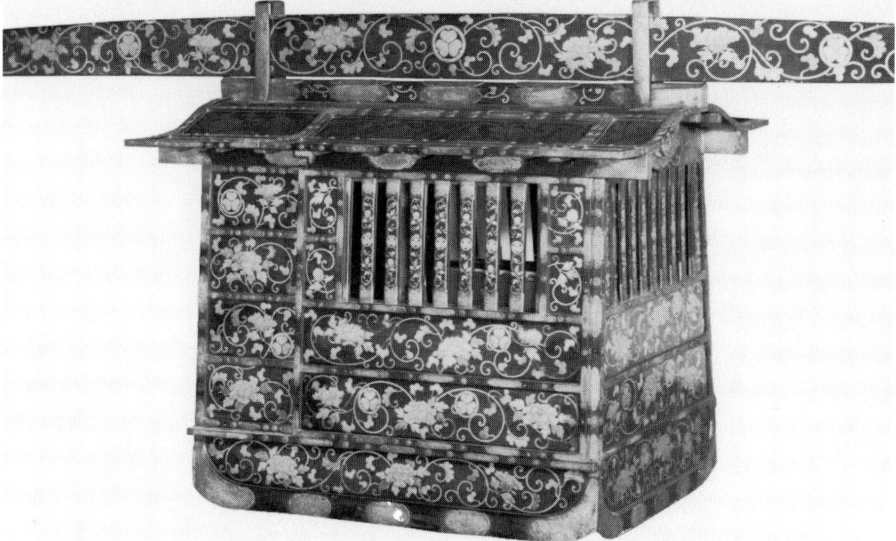

25

24 *Andō Hiroshige*

(1797–1858)

OĪ STATION

Series: *Kisokaido rokujuku tsugi* (Sixty-nine Stations of the Kisokaido) (no. 47)
Signed: *Hiroshige ga*; seal: Ichiryusai
Publisher: Kinjudo
Censor seal: Kiwamä
Japanese *nishiki-e* colour woodblock print 1st edition, Edo (Tokyo) *c.* 1839
Horizontal *oban* 22.5 × 35.5 cm (8⅞ × 14 in)
Craven Moore Bequest (1978.324/24)

Hiroshige's reputation as a designer of woodblock prints was established by the publication in 1834, by the influential publisher Hoeido, of the series *Tokaido gojusan tsugi* (Fifty-three Stations of the Tokaido) which comprised dramatic views of the posting stations on the coastal route from Edo, the capital, to Kyoto. This series of prints proved immensely popular, and Hiroshige, under the pressure of popular demand, produced at least twenty different versions of the Tokaido. In the face of such popularity, it was natural that Hiroshige should produce a comparable series of the sixty-nine stations of the overland route from Edo to Kyoto, the Kisokaido.

The subject of this print, *Oī* station, is one of the finest compositions in the series. Two travellers with bowed heads, and muffled in huge cloaks, ride on heavily-laden and equally depressed pack donkeys, led by attendants, through knee-deep snow. The scene is framed by two huge pine trees, their branches laden with snow, and the sombre white hills, on a grey day full of snowflakes. The grey and white of snow and sky is relieved only by the green of the pine needles and red-brown of the donkeys.

The fine quality of this impression can be judged by the freshness of the details in the woodblock. The sharpness of the bark on the trunks of the pine trees is particularly diagnostic of an early print. The provenance of the print is known not, in this case, from a collector's seal, but from an attribution on the original mount to the Kato collection.

25 *Palanquin (Norimono)*

Black lacquered wood, decorated with foliage and the *mon* (heraldic badge) of the Tokugawa family in *kirikane* (cut foil) gold leaf decoration, with gilt copper *kanemono* (edge-pieces).
Japanese, Edo period (1600–1868) *c.* 1850
Length (overall): 473 cm (172 in)
Gift of Councillor Philip Wyman (1982.714)

Early in the Tokugawa, or Edo, period, in which the family of Tokugawa Ieyasu held the *shogunate* and ruled Japan, it became fashionable for the nobility to travel in palanquins, carried by two or four coolies. These replaced the previously fashionable ox-drawn carriages, which were still used by the Emperor and Empress. The new palanquins came in two varieties; the simple, cheaper ones, made of bamboo, were called *kago*, and were often plied for hire by *kumosuke* (cloud fellows). The more elaborate type was the *norimono*, which, as in this example, had slatted doors and front window, and was lined with fine paintings of birds and flowers. These expensive and prestigious conveyances were limited by 17th-century law to people with an income of over 10,000 *koku* (units of rice by which wealth was measured) per annum; this precluded all but the *daimyos* (feudal lords) of whom there were less than three hundred. The presence in the decoration of the badge of three hollyhock leaves (*aoi*) encircled, shows that this example was made for the ruling Tokugawa family, possibly the last *shogun*, Keiki (r. 1866–67).

26 *Two Indian Daggers*

CHILANUM

The hilt and blade are forged in one piece; the curved double-edged blade with four fullers, symmetrical hilt with bulbed grip, horn-like quillons and pommel. This dagger is decorated with gold *koftgari* onlay in fine floral panels within borders.
Central Indian, possibly late 17th century
Length: 41.1 cm (16⅛ in)
Earl Egerton of Tatton Collection (1910.15.114)

The *Chilanum* is associated with the Mahrattas of the Deccan, and stylistically linked with another Mahratta dagger, the *bichwa* (scorpion). A comparable specimen in the Victoria and Albert Museum has Vizianagram, Andhra Pradesh, as a provenance.

KHANJAR

The blade is single-edged with a T-shaped back for part of its length and a heavily reinforced point. It was decorated with gold *koftgari* onlay beside the hilt, and is of finely watered mechanical damask steel. The hilt is of dark green nephrite jade, shaped as a pistol grip, with floral inlay in gold wire.
North West India (Punjab), late 17th to early 18th century
Length: hilt 12.7 cm (5 in), blade 24.1 cm (9½ in)
Earl Egerton of Tatton Collection (1910.15.107a)

This Mughal dagger is interesting for the combination of its elements: the jade pistol-grip Indo-Persian hilt, normally found with double-edged blades, here with the single-edged blade, heavily reinforced at tip and back for mail piercing, which is normally found with a quite different hilt, and called a *peṣhkabz*. This combination makes this weapon very unusual. It was probably made at Lahore, where the finest arms and armour of the Mughal empire were produced.

27 *Sikh Armour*

CAVALRY ARMOUR

Indo-Persian (Lahore), late 18th century comprising:

MAIL SHIRT, 'ZIRAH'

Fine butted steel and brass mail, worked in a lozenge diaper pattern. Part of a set including trousers and hood.
Indian (Lahore), 1885
Earl Egerton of Tatton Bequest (1910.15.1)

BREASTPLATES, 'CHARĀ'INA

Four rectangular steel 'mirrors', cut away under the arms, decorated with a vegetal band of gold *koftgari* inlay. Lined with crimson quilted silk.
Indian (Delhi), 1803, Hamilton Collection
Earl Egerton of Tatton Bequest (1910.15.7)

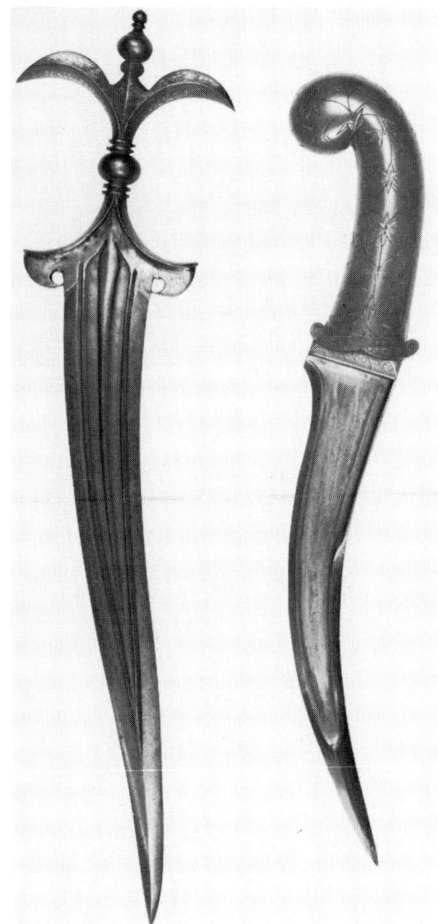

26

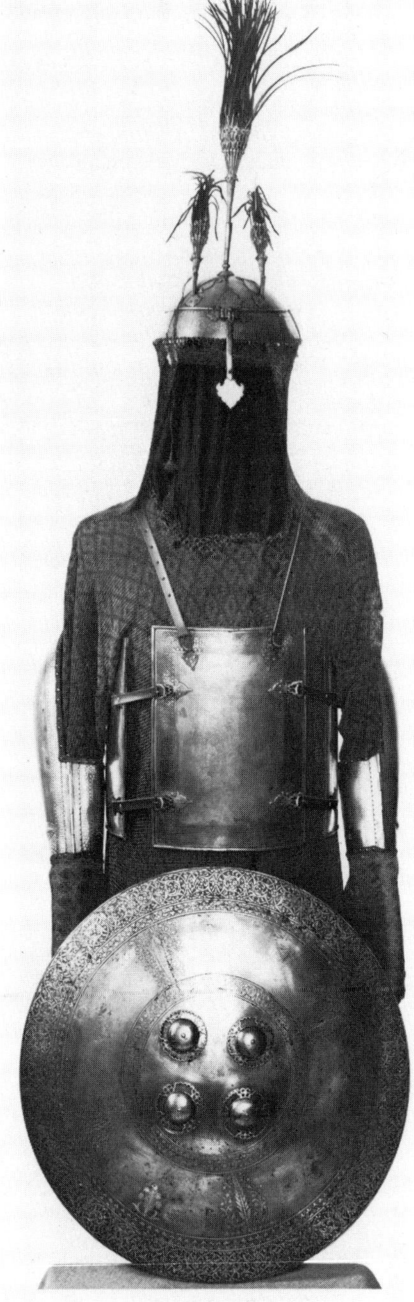

27

HELMET, 'TOP'

Steel bowl with gold *koftgari* inlay, nasal with link and hook to support, mail aventail of brass and steel links in lozenge diaper, and

three plumes of black heron feathers, *kalghi*, on wooden sticks wrapped with gilt thread.
Indian (Lahore), 1855
Earl Egerton of Tatton Bequest (1910.15.3)

VAMBRACES, 'DASTANA'

Steel decorated with gold *koftgari* inlay, with steel and brass mail gloves, lined with crimson silk over cotton padding, attached with a gimp band.
Indian (Delhi), 1803, Hamilton Collection
Earl Egerton of Tatton Bequest (1910.15.10)

SHIELD, 'SEPAR'

Steel, decorated with gold *koftgari* inlay, lined with crimson silk with embroidery of gold thread. The four bosses retain double hand loops and a quilted pad.
Indian (Delhi)
Earl Egerton of Tatton Bequest (1910.15.14)

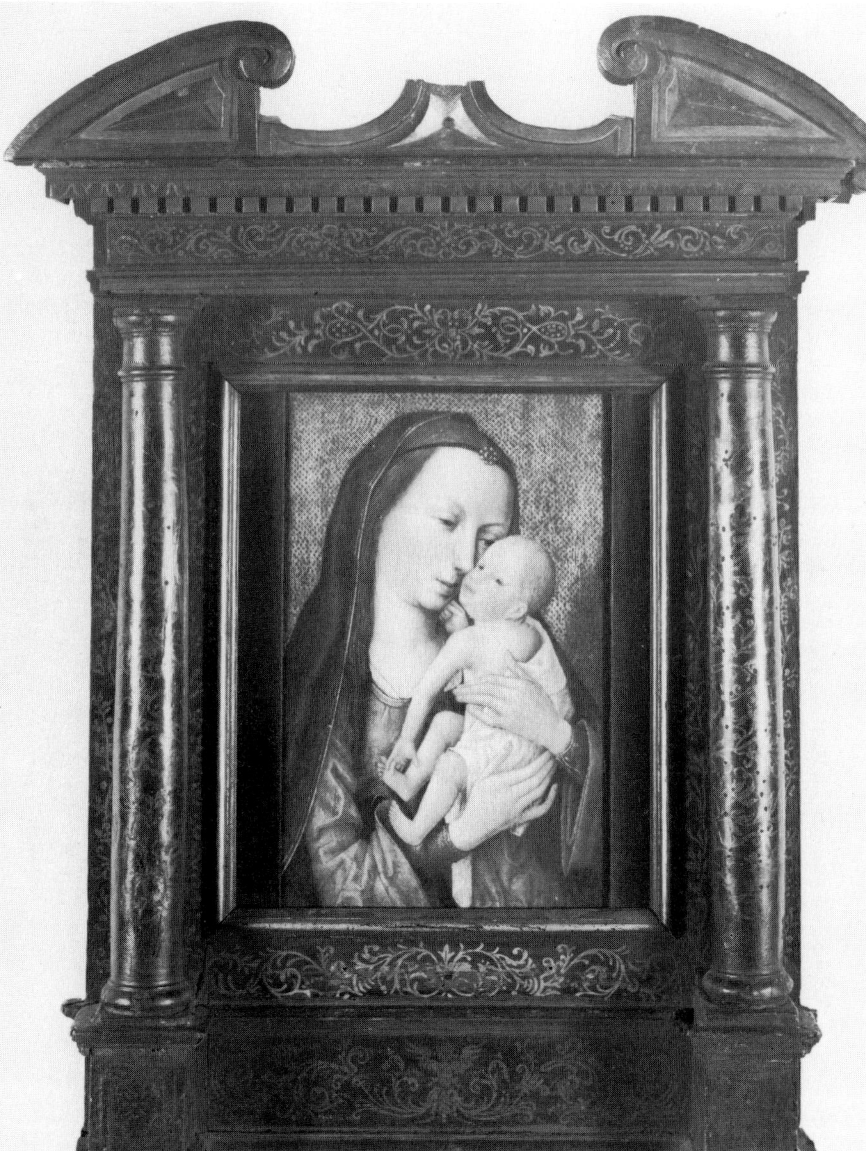

28

The collection of Wilbraham, 1st Earl Egerton of Tatton, of Tatton Park, Cheshire (1832–1909) is of great importance, since its owner was the first scholar to work in the field of oriental armour.

This piece, although composite, is typical of the armour of a cavalryman of the Sikh kingdom of the Punjab (1761–1849). Before the military reforms of Ranjit Singh (1780–1839), when infantry based on the European model were introduced, the Sikh army was composed primarily of cavalry. These were armed with a matchlock musket (*toradar*), sword (*talwar*) and lance (*neza* or *barcha*). The style of armour equipment was derived from that of the Mughal empire, and heavily influenced by Persian fashions and developments. Lahore was the centre of the Sikh kingdom following the Battle of Pānīpat (1761) between the Afghan Durrānīs and Indian Marathas. Under the Mughals, Delhi and Lahore had been the most important centres for the production of military equipment, and this excellence continued under the Sikhs. The mail is decorated in a typical Lahuri style, in the lozenge diaper called *Ganga-Jamini* after the confluence of the two rivers, where the white water of the Ganges meets the yellow of the Jumna.

28 Master of the Magdalen Legend

(active *c.* 1483–1527)

VIRGIN AND CHILD

Flemish; oil on panel
25.2 × 15.4 cm (9 × 6⅛ in)
Unsigned
Henry Boddington Gift (1911.27)

The painter of this panel is unknown, but he apparently worked in Brussels in the late 15th and early 16th centuries. He is named after an altarpiece depicting scenes from the legend of St. Mary Magdalen, now split up between

Budapest, Copenhagen, Philadelphia and Vienna.

The Manchester picture is closely derived from a type of Madonna by Rogier van der Weyden, an example of which is in the Houston Museum of Fine Arts. Rogier van der Weyden, in his turn, was following a much older prototype, a famous Italo-Byzantine painting of the Madonna brought from Rome in 1440 and preserved since 1450 in Cambrai Cathedral. The *Notre-Dame des Graces* of Cambrai was revered as the legendary portrait of the Virgin painted by St. Luke. It shows the Virgin holding the Christ Child up to Her face, whilst He twists His head round and grasps at Her chin.

The Manchester *Virgin and Child* may be the left hand side of a diptych, the other panel being a portrait of a donor in prayer. Both panels would have been in simple rectangular frames, hinged together so that they could stand on a table for daily devotions. The elegant classical frame of this panel is not original: the picture has been extended on either side to fit into it.

Rogier van der Weyden was responsible for introducing to late 15th-century Flanders both this type of portable altarpiece, and the intimate and tender half-length representation of the Virgin, so charmingly followed in this panel.

29 *Albrecht Dürer*

(1471–1528)

THE NATIVITY 1504

German; copper engraving
18.7 × 12.1 cm ($7\frac{3}{8} \times 4\frac{3}{4}$ in) plate size
Signed (on inn sign) in monogram:
1504 A D
Leicester Collier Bequest (1967.93)

Dürer's enormous *œuvre* consists of woodcuts and engravings, paintings and drawings, treatises on measurement, fortification, proportion and artistic theory, besides a detailed diary of his

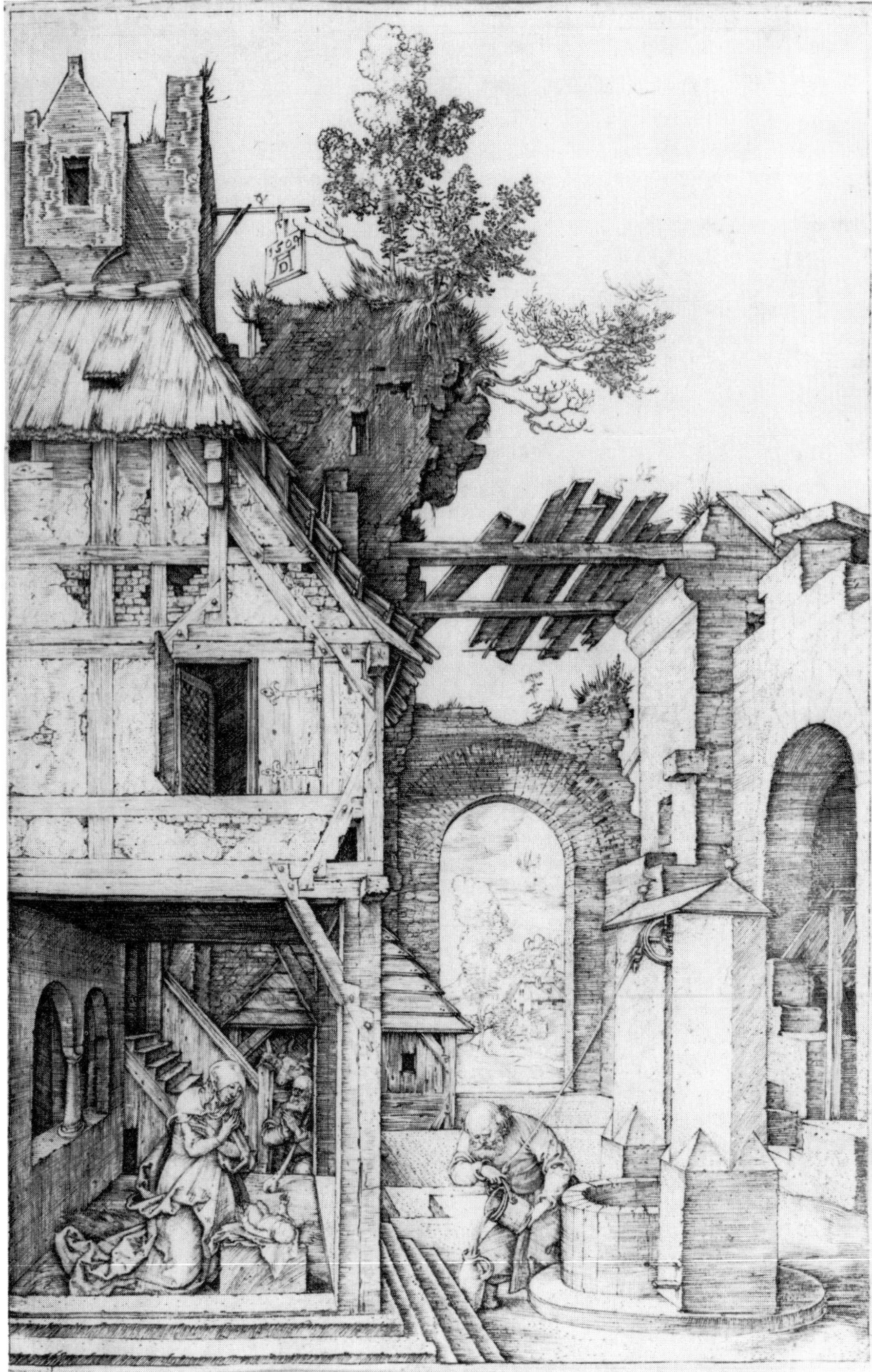

29

Netherlands journey. It was mainly through him that the ideas originated by the Italian Renaissance were introduced into Northern Europe. In Dürer's work, these ideas are combined with an individualism typical of the German Gothic tradition. His greatest influence was exerted through his graphic work, which was easily transportable and made his technique, subjects and style well known all over Europe.

The Nativity of 1504 combines Dürer's vivid imagery with masterly draughtsmanship and complex iconography. Dürer entitled the print 'Weihnachten' (Christmas) in the entry in his Netherlands Journal for 20 August 1520. Although the figures take up a small proportion of the whole composition, they are the dramatic focal point of their stage-like surroundings and are scaled considerably larger than the architecture. The extraordinary decaying buildings in differing styles, sprouting with clumps of vegetation, symbolise the decline of previous civilizations at the advent of Christianity. The well and unbroken pitcher represent the purity of the Virgin and the sacrament of Baptism. By 1504, Dürer had mastered the rules of perspective and all the vanishing lines converge on one point. Although *The Nativity* is a comparatively early work, it demonstrates that Dürer's sophisticated engraving technique was already fully developed to produce this timeless and compelling image.

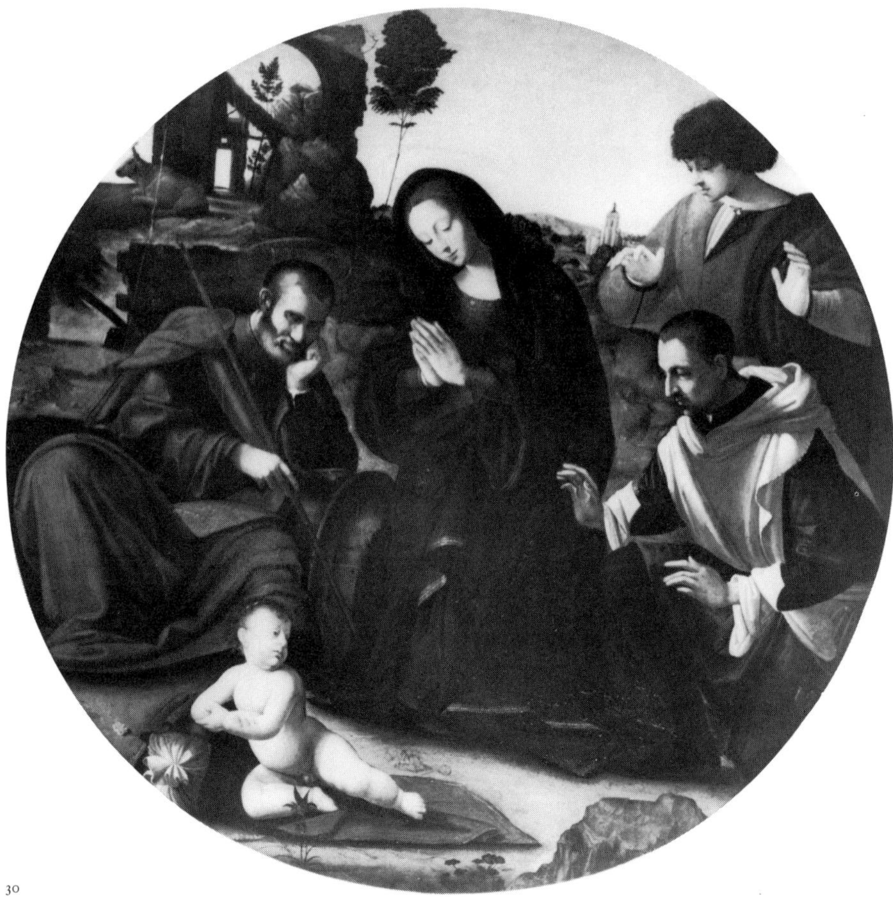

30

30 *Ridolfo Ghirlandaio*

(1483–1561)

ADORATION OF THE SHEPHERDS
c. 1505–10

Italian; oil on panel
Diameter: 114 cm (44⅞ in)
Unsigned
Purchased with the aid of the Sir John S. Randles Bequest Fund (1947.188)

Ridolfo, the son of the more celebrated Domenico Ghirlandaio (1449–94), became one of the leading painters in Florence in the first half of the 16th century. He had a large workshop with many pupils and was patronised by the Medici as a designer of temporary decorations and stage scenery. His elegant, linear style shows the influence of a number of contemporary artists, particularly Raphael.

This painting was formerly thought to be by Piero di Cosimo (1462–1521). The present attribution rests primarily on a comparison between the head of the kneeling shepherd and a very similar head in Ridolfo's *Way to Calvary*, painted after 1504 and now in the National Gallery, London. It is possible that the shepherds, who have no obvious attributes, may be portraits of donors. The painting displays an interesting stylistic transition from the purity of the Quattrocento to the greater artificiality of the Mannerist period. The delicate flower painting in the foreground and the background landscape are reminiscent of 15th-century Flemish painting. However, the vivid, almost harsh, colouring heightens the emotional intensity of the subject and the sharp highlighting draws attention to the exaggerated gestures. The figures are skilfully grouped around the Christ Child whose contrived pose echoes the circular composition. The picture suffers from some areas of damage and poor repainting, particularly the Virgin's face and hands and the face of the standing shepherd.

31 Giulio Pippi

called Giulio Romano (*c.* 1499–1546)

A CARYATID IN THE FORM OF A SATYR

Italian; pen and brown ink and brown wash
21.5 × 16.4 cm ($8\frac{1}{2} \times 6\frac{7}{16}$ in)
Inscr. in brown ink (verso): *Giulio Roman*
Purchased (1979.215)

Giulio Romano was the favourite pupil of Raphael (1483–1520), after whose death he completed the decorations in the Vatican left unfinished by his master. From 1524 he worked almost exclusively for the Gonzaga court at Mantua, where he designed and decorated the Palazzo del Tè. A leading exponent of the Mannerist style, Giulio was one of the most versatile artists of his generation, active as a painter, architect and designer of objets d'art.

This drawing is a study for a caryatid in the Sala de' Venti in the Palazzo del Tè, executed from September 1527 until about September 1528. The satyrs were modelled in stucco and support the pendentives of the room's ceiling. Swags and festoons trail from the figures more elaborately than in the drawing. It is a typically dynamic and forceful design, combining the grotesque and melodramatic qualities associated with Mannerism and displaying Giulio Romano's virtuoso skill as a draughtsman. The drawing is still pasted down to its ornamental blue and gilt mount provided by the great French connoisseur of drawings, Pierre-Jean Mariette (1694–1774), and it bears his collector's mark. It is one of three fine Giulio drawings in the Galleries' collection.

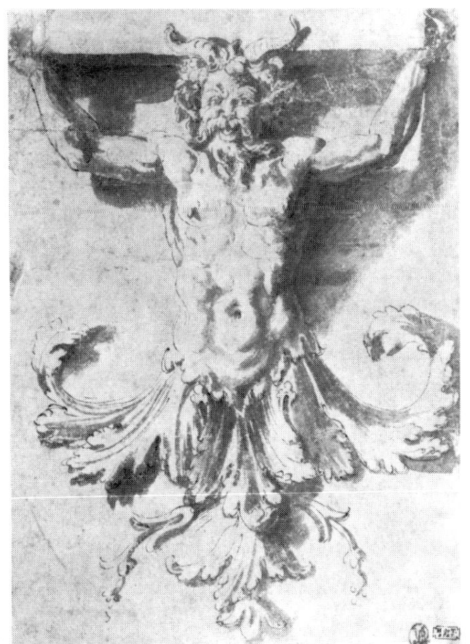

31

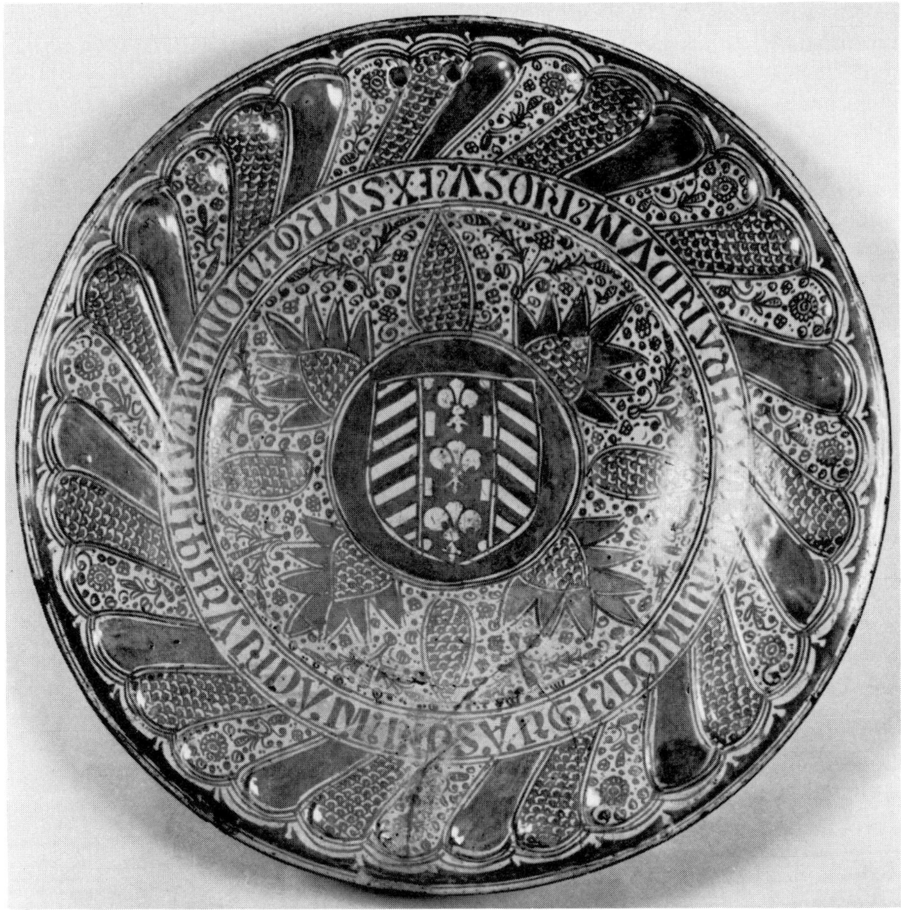

32

32 Dish

Tin glazed earthenware painted above and beneath with brown-gold lustre over a cream glaze.
Inscribed: EXSVRGE DOMINE AD LIBERANDVM NOS VRGE DOMINE AD LIBERANDVM NOS V. In the centre a coat of arms: *Chevronny, a pale embattled charged with three fleur de lys.*
Hispano-Moresque (Valencia, Manises), *c.* 1500
Diameter: 47.3 cm ($18\frac{5}{8}$ in)
Purchased (1982.118)

Hispano-Moresque pottery is characterised by its rich lustre decoration which simulates the sheen of precious metal. Earthenware decorated with lustre was introduced into Spain from the Moslem East in the 11th century. By the mid-13th century Malaga was the leading centre of production. A century later migrant Moslem potters from Murcia and Malaga settled in the Valencia area, particularly Manises. The political situation was conducive to artistic production, and Moslems, *mudéjares*, and Christians worked side by side. Large dishes of the style illustrated were introduced around 1480 and reflect the vogue in metalwork for elaborate ornament and Renaissance form. Characteristic of this period is the moulded spiral gadrooning with a shield of arms in the centre. Many of these large dishes also bear liturgical inscriptions in Latin, lettered in Lombardic capitals, encircling the central coat of arms. This particular inscription ('*Rise, oh Lord, to deliver us* . . .') was also, on occasion, shortened by the potters to the first two words. The dense patterns which decorate the gadroons were derived from Islamic metalwork and Spanish textiles.

33 *Italian maiolica*

PAIR OF DRY DRUG JARS ('ALBARELLI')

Maiolica painted in blue, inscribed in gothic black letters (to the left): *c°nenufarino* and (to the right): *v° rasino*.
Italian (Faenza), 1510–20
Height: 13.3 cm ($5\frac{1}{4}$ in)
Leicester Collier Bequest (1917.327 and 326)

Apothecary jars formed part of the stock in trade of Italian maiolica potters, and many workshops owed their prosperity to commissions for these vessels from pharmacies and monasteries. The form of the *albarello* came from the Middle East and, with a flange at the open end, a piece of parchment could be tied on to cover the contents. These jars were used for the storage of solid or dry materials and from the mid-15th century they were usually inscribed with the name of the contents. *c° nenufarino* was a water-lily conserve, used as a sleeping draught and to ease headaches; *v° rasino* was a resin ointment, used for ulcers and boils.

PLATE

Maiolica painted in enamel colours with the story of Perseus and Andromeda and bearing the arms, top centre, *checky argent and azure* surmounted by a cardinal's hat and augmented with banners for Cardinal Juan Alvarez de Toledo.
Inscribed on underside in underglaze blue: *Andromeda et persio/1542*.
Italian (Pesaro?), 1542
Diameter: 26.7 cm ($10\frac{1}{2}$ in)
Leicester Collier Bequest (1917.335)

Princess Andromeda, daughter of King Cepheus and Queen Cassiope, was unjustly chained to a rock by Jupiter Ammon. Menaced by a sea monster, she was watched in despair by her sorrowing father and mother. Perseus, who was the son of Jupiter and Dänae, killed the monster and freed Andromeda from her plight, on the understanding from the King and Queen that the hero was given the Princess's hand in marriage (Ovid, *Metamorphoses*, IV).

The painter of this narrative scene in the *istoriato* manner probably derived

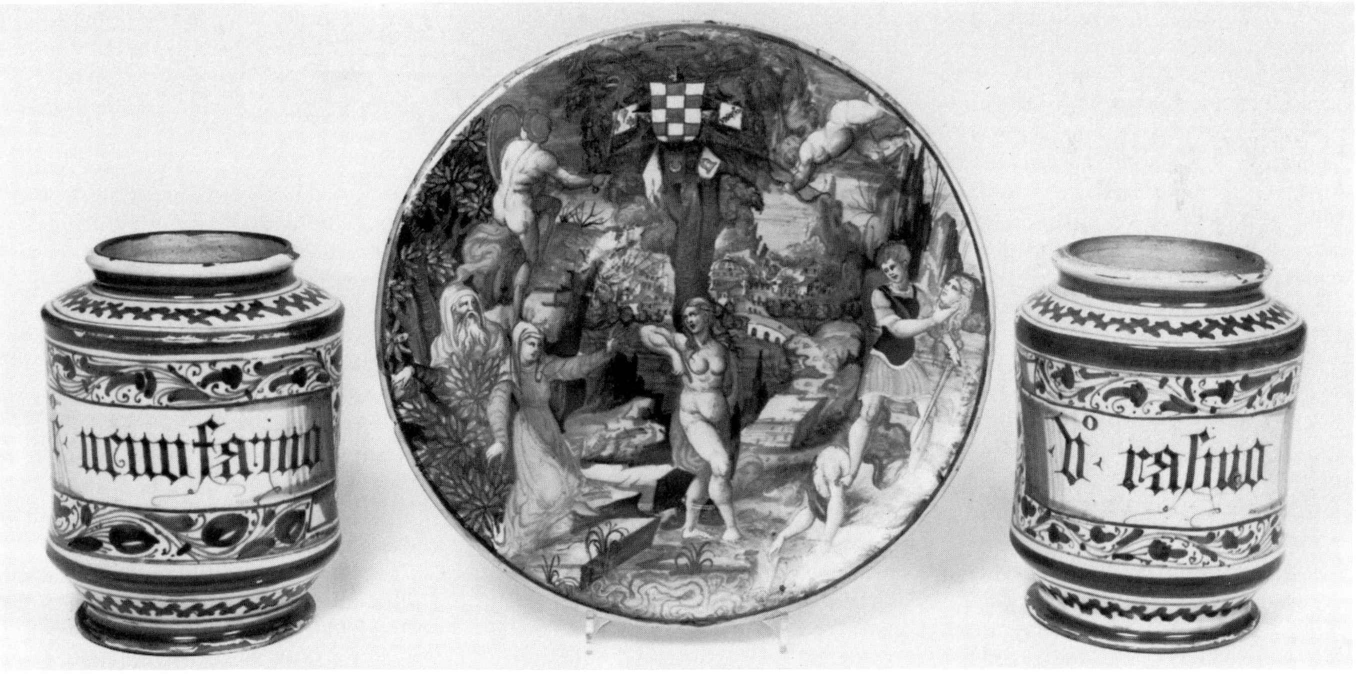

33

the figures' poses from contemporary engravings. Such plates, part of a service, were highly prized and only purchased by the rich and powerful. This example was made for Juan Alvarez de Toledo (1488–1557), who received the Cardinal's hat in 1538. He was the brother of Pedro de Toledo, Viceroy of Naples (1484–1553), Captain General of Charles V's troops in Italy, and uncle of Eleanora, wife of Grand Duke Cosimo de' Medici (1519–74), a famous patron of the arts.

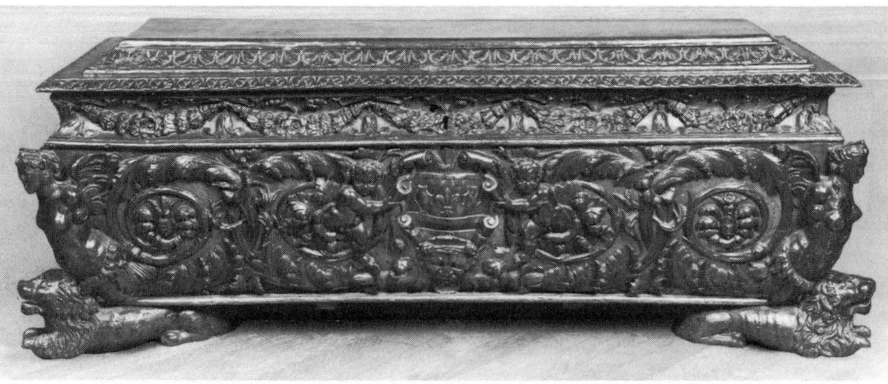

35

34 Roundel

pl. 2

Maiolica, painted with figures of three saints. Inscribed around rim: SANCTE·BONA·VENTURA·ORA·PRO·NOBIS—SANCTE·FRANCISCE·ORA·PRO·NOBIS—SANCTE·LVDOVICE·ORA·PRO·NOBIS.
In centre: MCCCCCL·AVG·XXX.
Italian (Venice), 1550
Diameter: 31.8 cm (12½ in)
Leicester Collier Bequest (1917.331)

Earthenware covered with an opaque tin glaze was first developed in the Near East and ultimately spread to Italy via Spain and Majorca, from where it acquired the name 'maiolica'. The white surface provided artists with a suitable ground for painted, mainly pictorial, decoration, a potential fully exploited during the Renaissance. The production of maiolica developed in many centres throughout Italy; in Venice it was made in several workshops from the early 16th century. This roundel shows a particular characteristic of Venetian maiolica, as it is painted *a berettino*: the tin glaze has been stained with cobalt to give a lavender blue ground. *A berettino* first appeared in Faenza and was probably an invention of the Casa Pirota, the foremost workshop there.

The subject of this roundel is taken from a painting by Vincenzo Catena (*c.* 1470–1531), *Three Franciscan Saints* (now in the Accademia, Venice), at the time in the Chapel of St. Francis, in the Frari, Venice. The three saints are depicted with their distinctive emblems: St. Francis of Assisi (1182–1226), the founder of the order, with the stigmata; St. Bonaventura (1221–1274), an Italian theologian, with a cardinal's hat at his feet; and St. Louis of Anjou, Bishop of Toulouse (1274–97), with the crown of Naples before him, which he renounced to take holy orders.

35 Cassone

Poplar, walnut, parcel gilt.
Italian (possibly Roman), mid-16th century
Length: 162 cm (63¾ in)
Gift of R. G. Tatton of Wythenshawe Hall (1926.44)

The *cassone* was the principal receptacle for a bridal trousseau in mediaeval and Renaissance Italy, and was often decorated by leading artists. Often made in pairs, they were always monumental and generally placed in the bedchamber. They were amongst the most impressive pieces of furniture in the household.

The sarcophagus form was used by carvers in marble and wood from the early Renaissance period onwards and can be seen on monuments, fountains, lavabos and on furniture such as this *cassone*. The rich acanthus leaf ornament carved on the front and sides is derived from architectural decoration to be found on antique Imperial buildings. Here there is also a suggestion of Mannerist strapwork surrounding the central cartouche (or *stemma*), which is supported by *putti* and incorporates the arms of the Caraffa (?) family.

36 Abraham Bloemaert

(1564–1651)

THE RAISING OF LAZARUS

Dutch; oil on canvas
194.2 × 156.4 cm (76½ × 61½ in)
Unsigned
Purchased with the aid of a Government grant (through the Victoria and Albert Museum) (1980.320)

The raising of Lazarus from the dead is a miracle from St. John's Gospel (ch. 11, vv. 38–45). The scene takes place by the graveside outside Bethany. Jesus 'cried with a loud voice, Lazarus, come forth. And he that was dead came forth, bound hand and foot with graveclothes; and his face was bound about with a napkin. Jesus saith unto them, Loose him and let him go.' The richly dressed Mary Magdalen, Lazarus' sister, kneels and offers supplication, whilst his other sister Martha holds her yellow robe up to shield herself from the stink of the corpse. Lazarus had been dead for four days, and representations of this scene often show figures holding their noses.

Bloemaert spent most of his life in Utrecht, a Catholic enclave in a predominantly Protestant country, and is one of the principal exponents in Holland of Mannerism, an aristocratic style which swept across Europe in the 16th century in reaction to the balance and fullness of the High Renaissance. Bloemaert has placed his figures in elegantly affected postures, leaning in and out of the picture to create a feeling of restlessness. The figure of Lazarus is in the centre, perversely in shadow. A glamorous frisson is created by the brilliant and unusually combined colours of the glossy silk and damask costumes. The palette is reminiscent of the great Italian altarpieces painted by Pontormo and Rosso Fiorentino some eighty years earlier.

This picture, the most distinguished Dutch Mannerist altarpiece in Britain, probably dates from just after 1600. There is another version of the subject in Munich, dated 1607, and preparatory drawings for the composition are in the Albertina in Vienna and in the Leipzig Museum. Several more are recorded in the artist's sketchbook, etched in facsimile in reverse by the artist's son Frederick and published in Amsterdam in 1740.

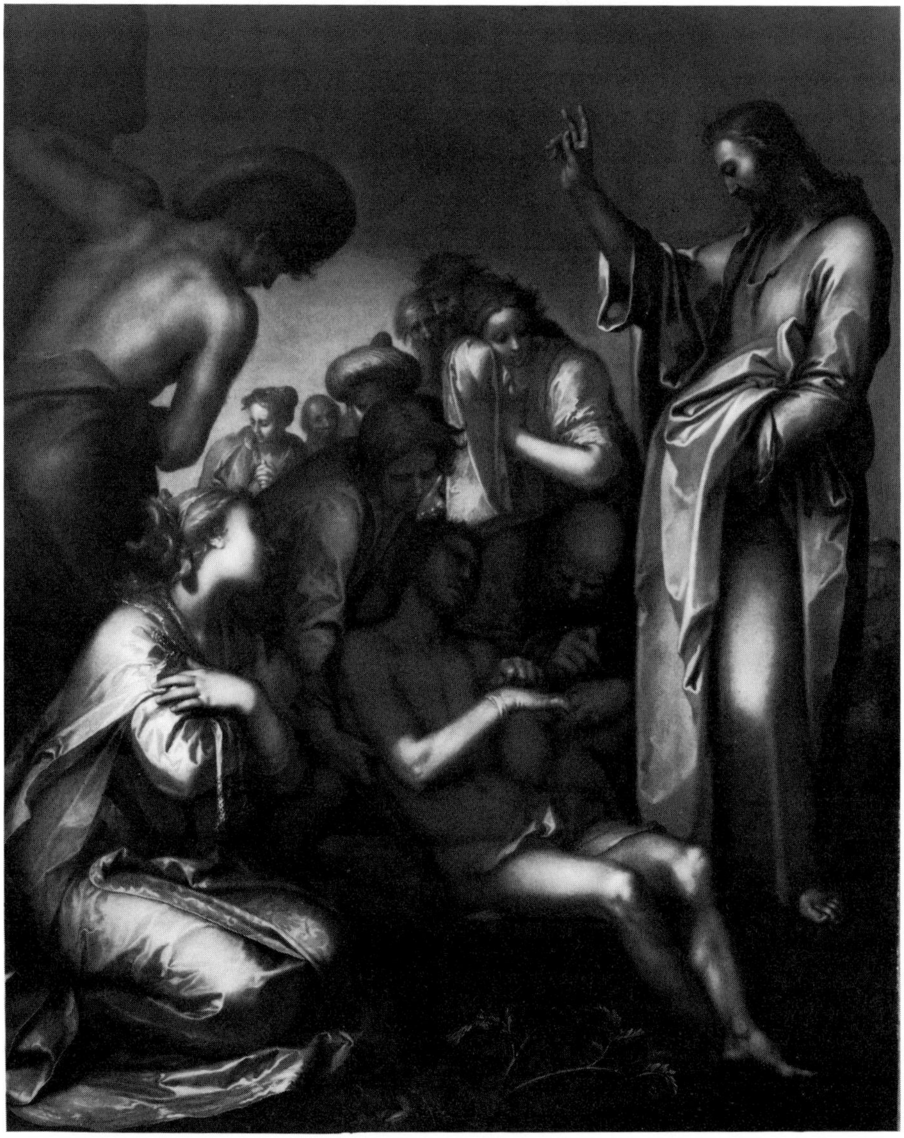

36

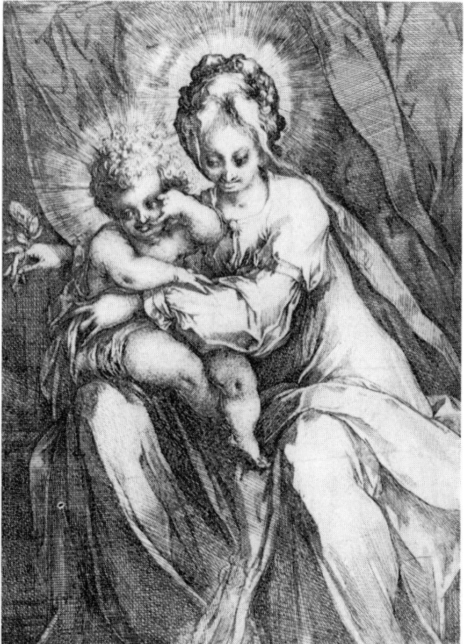

37

37 *Jacques Bellange*

(1575–1616)

THE MADONNA WITH THE ROSE

French; etching with stippling in the flesh areas

19.5 × 14 cm ($7\frac{11}{16} \times 5\frac{1}{2}$ in)

Purchased (1980.322)

Bellange worked mostly in Nancy where he executed decorations in the Ducal Palace for Charles III de Lorrain. He may have visited Italy in the 1590s, and this work is strongly influenced by Italian Mannerism. Drawings and prints by this rare artist survive, but only two oils are known. The remainder were destroyed in a fire at the Ducal Palace.

The figure drawing in this print shows the deliberate distortions typical of Mannerism. This was a self-conscious style, characterised by tall, elongated figures, elegant theatrical gestures and courtly grace, often expressed with witty ambiguity and paradox. In this print, a soft and delicate effect is created by the fluid line of the etching needle. The image is playful and intimate. The Christ Child sucks his finger while the smiling Virgin attracts his gaze with the rose she holds before him. The rose, sometimes a symbol of purity, is a flower particularly associated with the Virgin, who is often referred to as a rose without thorns.

38 Alessandro Turchi

called 'Orbetto' (1578–1649)

THE FLIGHT INTO EGYPT
Italian; oil on canvas
307.5 × 180 cm ($121\frac{1}{8} \times 70\frac{7}{8}$ in)
Unsigned
Purchased (1978.259)

This is a full-scale autograph replica of the altarpiece painted for the little church (now destroyed) of S. Romualdo, Rome, which belonged to the Camaldolese Order. It was probably commissioned by Cardinal Antonio Barberini the younger, protector of the order, in or before 1631. The S. Romualdo picture is now generally agreed to be in the Prado, Madrid, while a smaller scale version is in the Museo Nazionale, Naples. The composition was fully described and much admired by Giovanni Battista Passeri in his *Vite de' pittori, scultori et architetti*, 1677–79. The Manchester picture, which is probably the same as a version offered for sale and exhibited at the chemist's shop of Giuseppe Bartoli in Piazza Navona, Rome, in January 1794, later appears to have been acquired by the Sidebottom family of Harewood Lodge, Broadbottom. It was probably given by Mrs Mary Anne Sidebottom to St. Luke's, Cheetham Hill, Manchester, sometime before 1860. This fine gothic church (built by T. W. Atkinson in 1836–39) was sadly pulled down in 1978, when the altarpiece was purchased by the City.

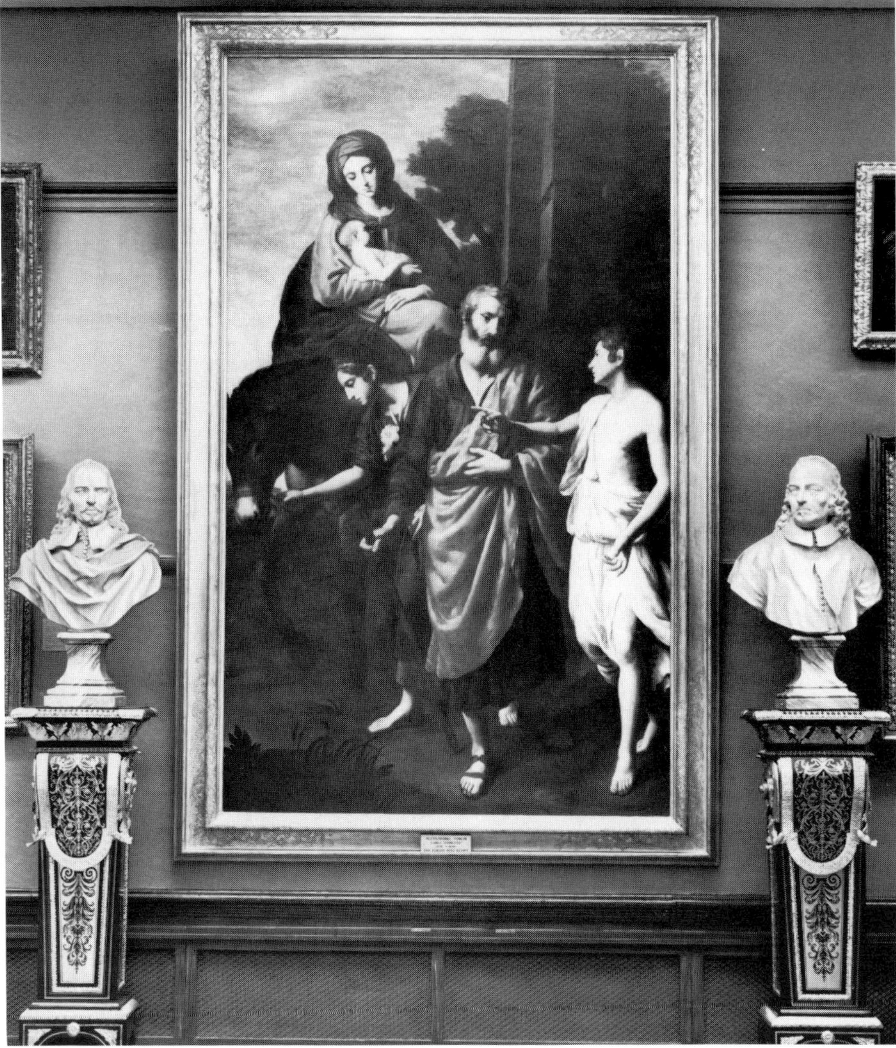

38

Turchi's painting is flanked by marble busts by Giovanni Battista Foggini (Florence, 1652–1725), carved *c.* 1700, of, to the left, Giovanni Alfonso Borelli (1608–79) and, to the right, Marcello Malpighi (1628–94). Both sitters were professors at the University of Pisa, respectively of Mathematics and Anatomy. They were commissioned as part of a series of busts of celebrated men by the humanist Lorenzo Bellini in 1692 for his own house. These two busts stand on buhl pedestals closely similar to those by Etienne Levasseur (1721–98) in the collection of the Duke of Wellington at Stratfield Saye. Foggini carved five other busts in the series, and these, with the two above, were allocated by H.M. Government 'in lieu' to Manchester in 1974 (1974. 157 and 156).

39 *Guido Reni*

(1575–1642)

ST. CATHERINE *c.* 1638–40

Italian; oil on canvas
102 × 83.6 cm ($40\frac{1}{8} \times 33\frac{7}{8}$ in)
Unsigned
Purchased with the aid of grants from the National Art-Collections Fund and the Government (through the Victoria and Albert Museum) (1974.88)

This is a very late work by Guido Reni, who was born in Bologna, studied briefly with the Carracci, worked intermittently in Rome, and in 1622 returned to his native town to become the leading Bolognese painter of his day. His work represents the classical, calm side of the Baroque (like Algardi, see no. 40), in contrast with the drama and intense realism of Caravaggio. In the 18th century he was regarded as one of the very greatest Italian artists, and his work was much sought after. Reni's figures are characterised by fresh colour, grace and breadth of technique.

St. Catherine is dateable *c.* 1638–40 on stylistic grounds. The lilac cloak and pale green robe show the typical delicate colour and silvery tone of Reni's late work. The painting may have been in the Palazzo Colonna, Rome, in 1678. It must have been in Paris in 1689, when an engraving by Bazin was published, and where, in 1769, the picture-dealer and engraver Sir Robert Strange bought it and brought it to England. His drawing of it is in the British Museum, but no copy of his engraving is known. St. Catherine holds a palm to signify her martyrdom, and at the bottom right is the spiked wheel, the instrument of her torture (the 'Catherine wheel'). Despite her crown denoting her rank as 'Queen' of Alexandria, she modestly gazes downwards. X-rays of the Manchester picture show that numerous changes took place while Reni worked on the picture, and some of these are visible to the naked eye.

40 *Alessandro Algardi*

(1598–1654)

MONSIGNOR ANTONIO CERRI

Italian; marble
Height: 65.5 cm ($33\frac{3}{4}$ in)
Unsigned
Purchased with funds from a national appeal, and grants from the Victoria and Albert Museum Special Fund, National Heritage Memorial Fund, National Art-Collections Fund, Patrons and Associates, and Friends of the Manchester City Art Galleries (1981.305)

The subject of this brilliantly realistic bust is Monsignor Antonio Cerri (1569–1642) from Pavia, who after the death of his wife became a prelate and was appointed Avvocato della Camera Apostolica. The Cerri family emblem of an uprooted oak tree is carved on the socle of the bust. He died in 1642 and was buried in the Cerri Chapel in the Church of the Gesú. Shortly before his death he was negotiating with the church authorities over the decoration of the Chapel, which includes a version of this bust in a circular niche designed

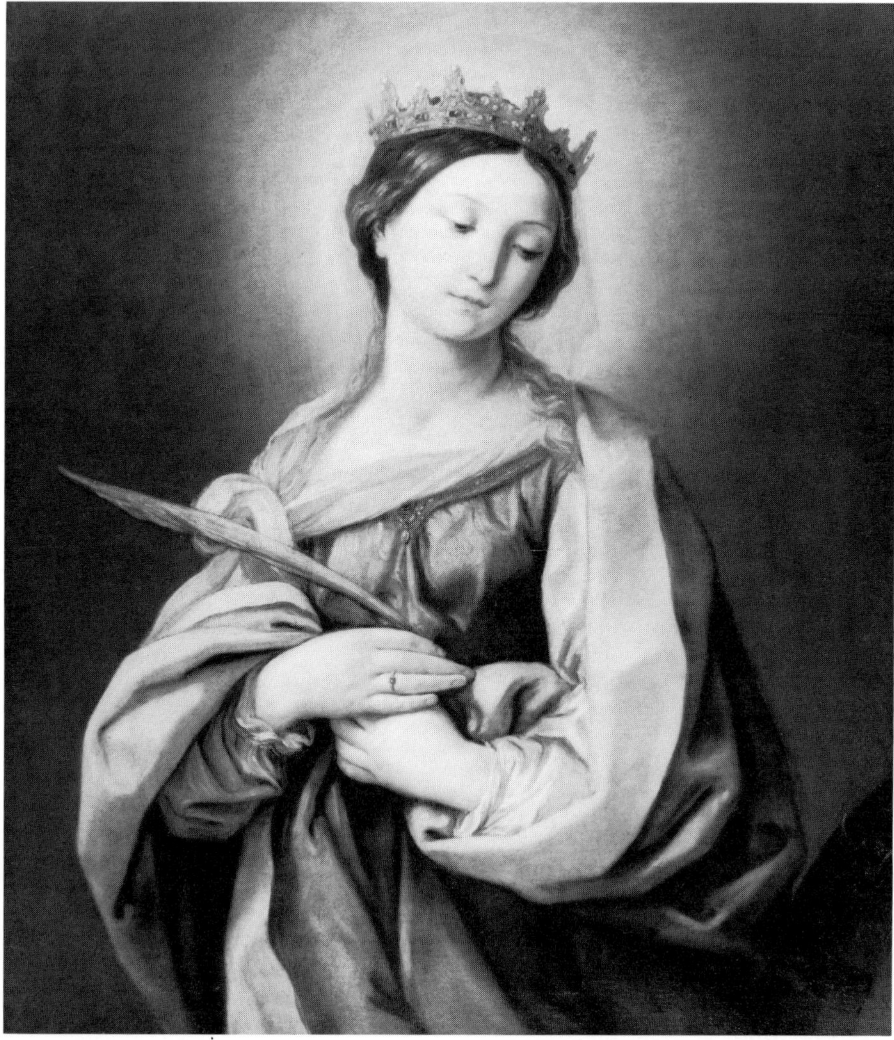

39

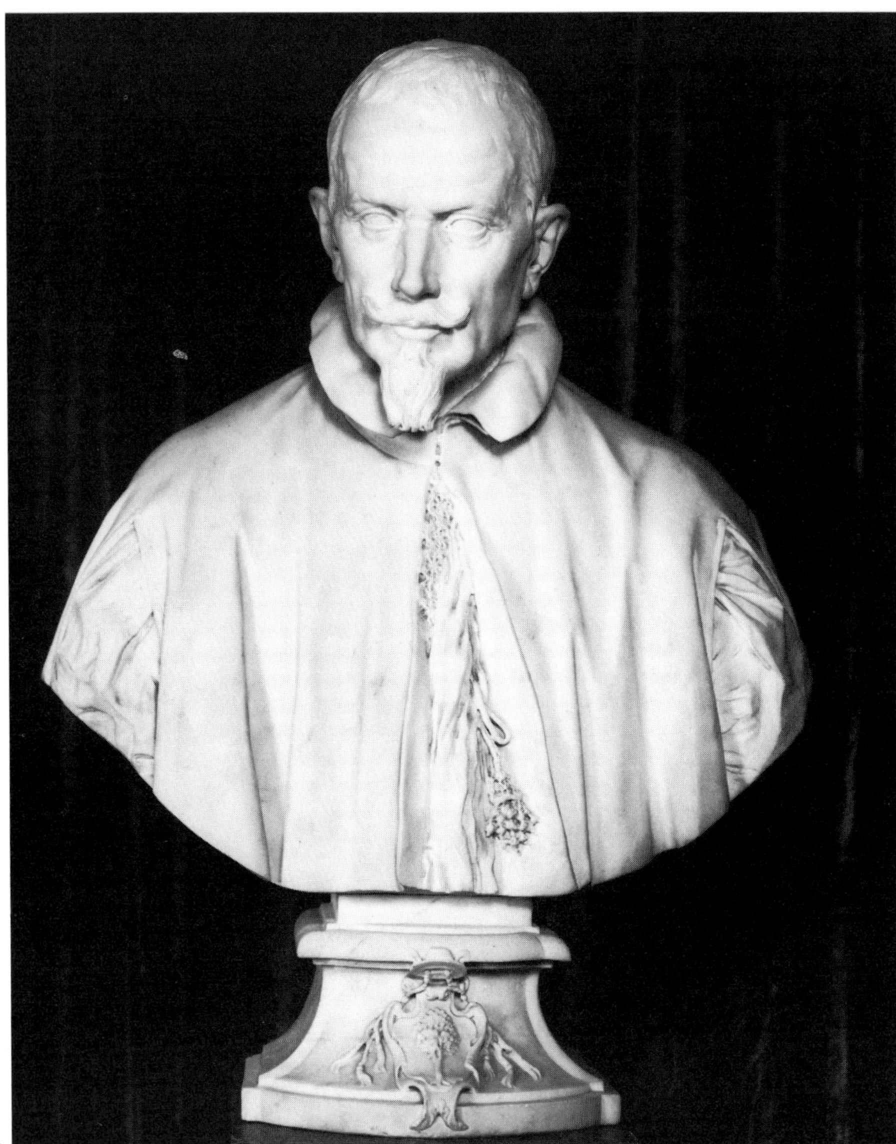

40

by Pietro da Cortona (1596–1669). But the present bust gives every appearance of being carved from the life and probably dates from the 1630s. The bust in the chapel seems to be a posthumous version from Algardi's studio.

Algardi's achievement in Baroque sculpture is second only to that of the better-known Bernini. Whilst Bernini's portrait busts emphasised vitality and movement, Algardi was supreme in re-creating the solidity and physical presence of his sitters by the most meticulous accumulation of detail. In the bust of Cerri, illusionistic carving is carried to the extreme in the differentiation between the hair, the flesh and the costume with its fall of lace and tassel. Particularly subtly textured are the wrinkles, veins and variations in surface on the forehead and temples.

Algardi's work is rare outside Italy. This bust was almost certainly in the collection of the early 19th-century connoisseur and collector Thomas Hope of Deepdeene, Surrey (see entry on Thorvaldsen's *The Shepherd Boy*, no. 104) or that of his son. In 1979 it was sold at auction, but its threatened export to the United States was prevented after a public appeal to buy it for Manchester.

41 *Claude Gellée*

called Claude Lorrain (1600–82) *pl. 5*

LANDSCAPE WITH THE ADORATION OF THE GOLDEN CALF

French; oil on canvas
112.8 × 156.6 cm ($44\frac{7}{16} \times 61\frac{5}{8}$ in)
Signed and dated (on base of altar):
CLAVDE GELLE F I (i.e., 'Fecit et Invenit')
ROMA 1660
Purchased with a Government grant (through the Victoria and Albert Museum), with assistance from the National Art-Collections Fund, the Wolfson Foundation, the Patrons and Associates of Manchester City Art Galleries, the Friends of Manchester City Art Galleries, the National Heritage Memorial Fund and the Assheton-Bennett Fund (1981.3)

A mature masterpiece by Claude, who was one of the most important of all landscape painters. Born in Champagne (Vosges), he spent most of his working life in Rome where he evolved a poetic and idealized style of landscape, distilled from a close study of the surrounding countryside and its description by Ovid and Virgil. Though Claude paintings often depict religious or mythological stories, his landscape settings are given such prominence that the real subject of his art is the landscape itself. Here, Claude has grouped trees and rocks in the foreground to frame an expansive vista closed in by soft blue mountains in the far distance.

The subject is taken from Exodus, though the Biblical story is transposed into an Italian landscape. Whilst Moses ascended Mount Sinai to receive the Ten Commandments from God, the Israelites became disenchanted and impatient, made a golden calf and began to worship it, thus disobeying the first commandment. When Moses returned with the stone tablets of the law, he was so angry he cast down the tablets and broke them. The two small figures of Moses and Joshua are just visible at the foot of the mountain on the left.

The painting is based on another version of the same subject, now at Karlsrühe, which Claude executed in 1653. It is not known for whom he painted this version, which is separately recorded by a drawing in Claude's *Liber Veritatis* (formerly at Chatsworth but now in the British Museum). This was a sketchbook compiled by Claude to note down what he had painted and for whom, partly in an attempt to stop fakes of his paintings in his own lifetime. By the mid-19th century the Manchester painting had entered the celebrated collection of James Morrison of Basildon Park, from whose descendants it was acquired in 1981.

Claude profoundly influenced the course of landscape painting in England in the 18th century, when his work was avidly collected by English connoisseurs and admired by English artists, particularly Richard Wilson, and later by J. M. W. Turner. The oil painting by Turner, *Thomson's Aeolian Harp* (see no. 105), also from the Morrison collection, is a kind of homage to Claude.

42 G. B. Gaulli

called 'il Baciccio' (1639–1709)

ST. JOHN THE BAPTIST

Italian; oil on canvas
183.5 × 118.5 cm ($72\frac{1}{4} \times 46\frac{11}{16}$ in)
Unsigned
Purchased with the aid of a Government grant (through the Victoria and Albert Museum) (1968.104)

St. John the Baptist is seen with his attributes, the lamb and the banner 'Ecce Agnus Dei'. He points to a small figure of Christ in the landscape behind, according to the text from St. John (ch. 1, v. 29): 'John seeth Jesus coming unto him, and saith, Behold the Lamb of God, which taketh away the Sin of the World.'

The painting is a reduced variant of an altarpiece of *c.* 1670–71 in the church of S. Nicola da Tolentino, Rome. The fluid modelling, languidly expansive gesture and flamboyant draperies are derived from Gaulli's chief mentor and friend, Bernini (1598–1680). Such broad effects, designed to tell from a distance,

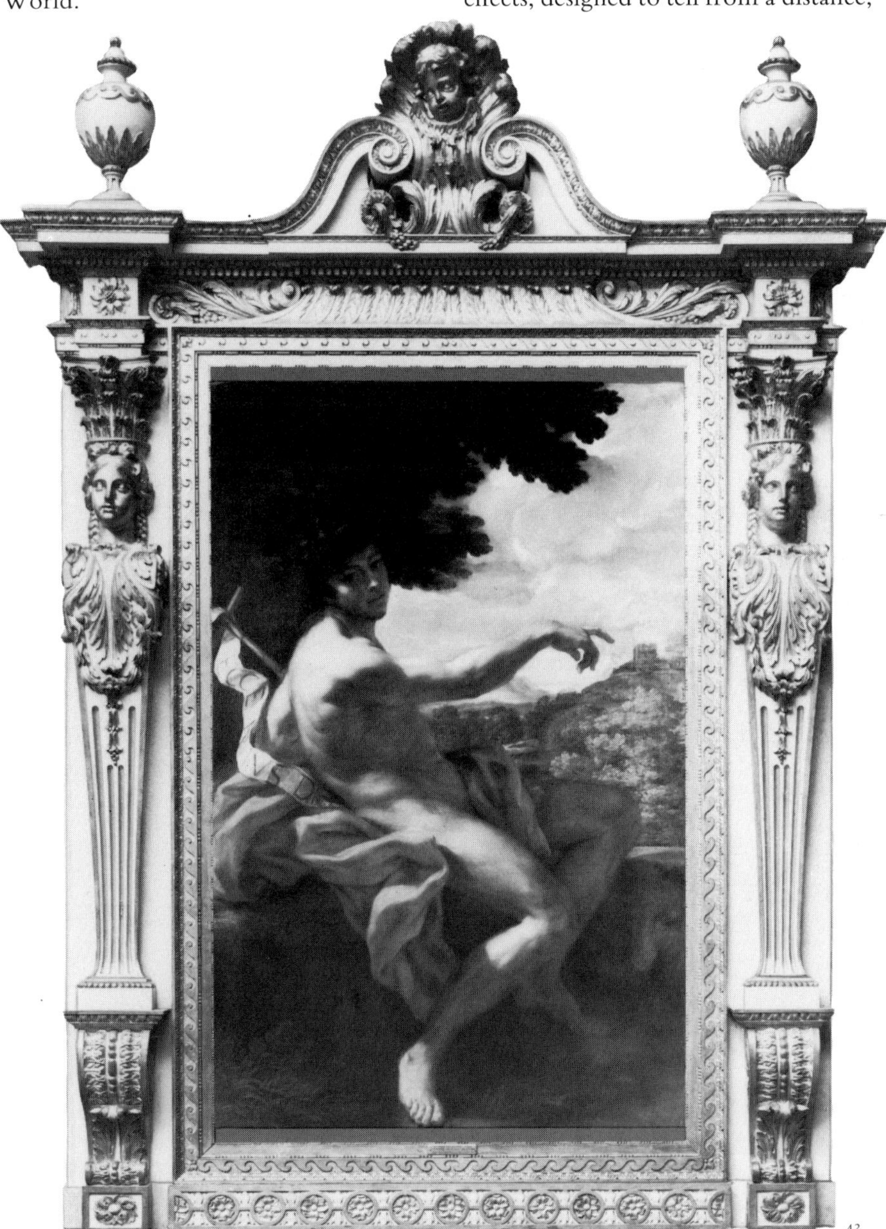

42

often in dimly lit interiors, came naturally to Gaulli. He was born in Genoa, and his most celebrated work is the ceiling of the Gesù, Rome, a magnificent celestial vision of many figures floating amongst clouds and adoring the Name of Jesus.

Though this is a devotional picture, it was not unusual in the Baroque period to represent the ascetic St. John as a beautiful naked young man. His pose is similar to another St. John by Caravaggio (now in the Capitoline Museum, Rome) where the treatment is even more sensual. The position is ultimately derived from two motifs on Michelangelo's Sistine Chapel ceiling, one of the *ignudi* (nude youths) combined with the pointing finger of God from *The Creation of Adam*.

The Manchester painting was at Redlynch, Somerset, in the 18th century, when it was remarked upon by the connoisseur Horace Walpole (1717–97) as hanging on the stairs. It later hung at Melbury, Dorset, the seat of the Earls of Ilchester, where it remained until 1967.

The picture is now exhibited in a white and gold frame (purchased with the aid of a Government grant through the Victoria and Albert Museum, 1980.260), designed by the Palladian architect, painter and garden designer William Kent (*c.* 1685–1748). The frame was designed for Devonshire House, London, built in 1733–40 for the 3rd Duke of Devonshire, and later transferred to St. James' Church, Buxton, near the Devonshires' country seat at Chatsworth, Derbyshire.

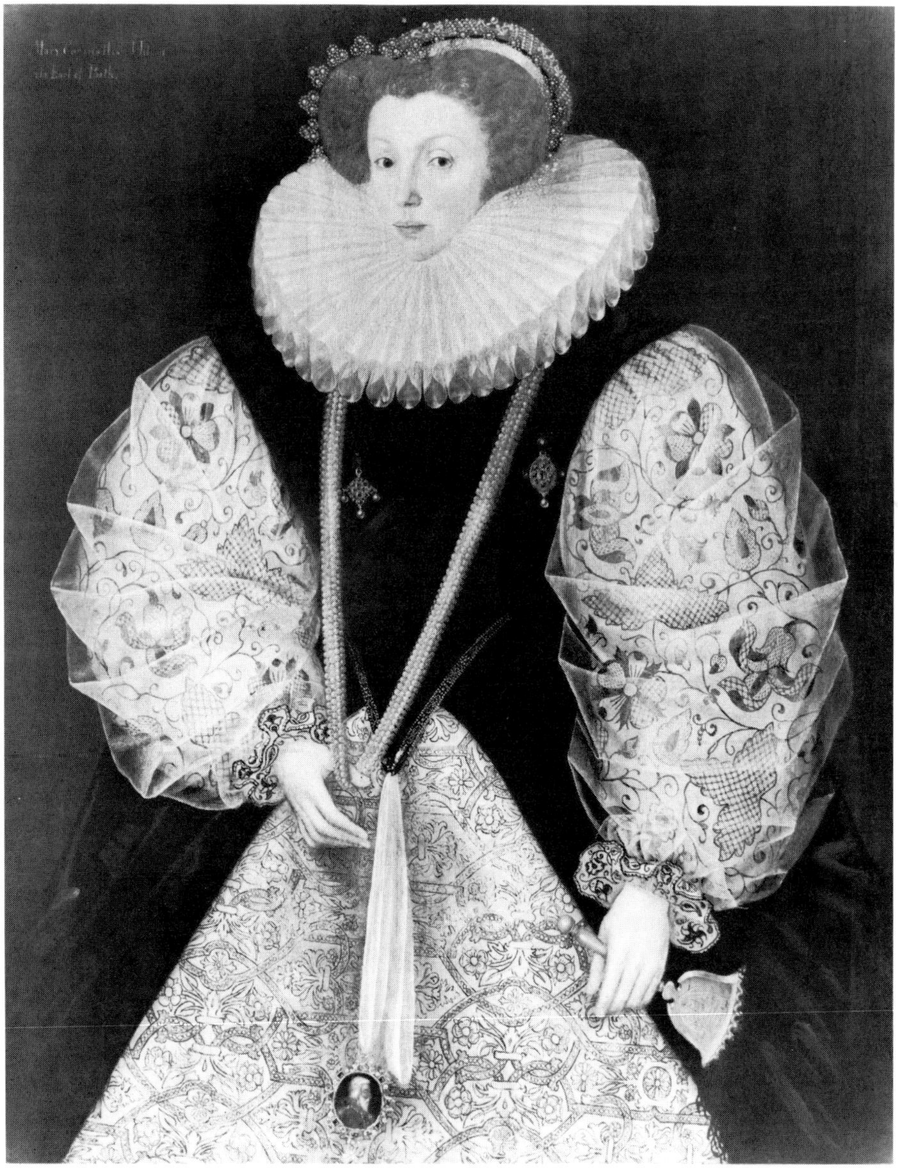

43

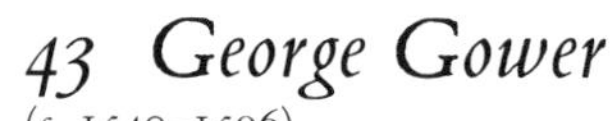

43 George Gower

(*c.* 1540–1596)

MARY CORNWALLIS *c.* 1580–85

English; oil on panel
117.2 × 94 cm ($46\frac{1}{8}$ × 37 in)
Unsigned
Inscr (t.l.c): *Mary Cornwallis, Wife of / the Earl of Bath*
Purchased (1953.112)

In portraits of the high Elizabethan age, a realistic likeness was secondary to the creation of a glamorous and decorative image. The shadowed faces and spatial solidity introduced by foreign artists to England were abandoned in favour of a two-dimensional, patterned style in which the faces were often reduced to expressionless masks. The emphasis was on a display of status, through rich costume, jewellery and heraldry.

Mary Cornwallis's costume, which helps to date the portrait to the 1580s, is predominantly black and white. She wears a large ruff, and her linen sleeves, decorated with blackwork embroidery, have semi-transparent oversleeves of silk or lawn. A flat strapwork pattern is embroidered on the skirt. Her plain black velvet gown sets off the five ropes of pearls, and the brooches pinned to her bodice. Pearls also decorate her head-dress and girdle, from which hangs a white silk ribbon and a jewelled cameo or miniature of a bearded man. In her left hand she holds a gold fan-handle, engraved with the arms of Cornwallis of Brome. This helps to identify her as the daughter of Sir Thomas Cornwallis of Brome, Suffolk, for the inscription giving her name was added to the portrait later. She was secretly married to William Bourchier, Earl of Bath (1557–1623); after pressure from his family, the marriage was annulled.

The attribution to Gower was made on the basis of similarity to his documented works. This portrait came from Hengrave Hall, where a series of Gower's portraits are recorded. He was born a gentleman from a Yorkshire family and, unusually for someone from such a background, became an artist. By 1573 he was one of the most fashionable portrait painters in London, and in 1581 he became Serjeant Painter to Queen Elizabeth I, with the role of supervising the decorative painting in all the royal palaces. Gower was a friend of the miniaturist Nicholas Hilliard, and in 1584 the two painters attempted to obtain a monopoly on royal portraits.

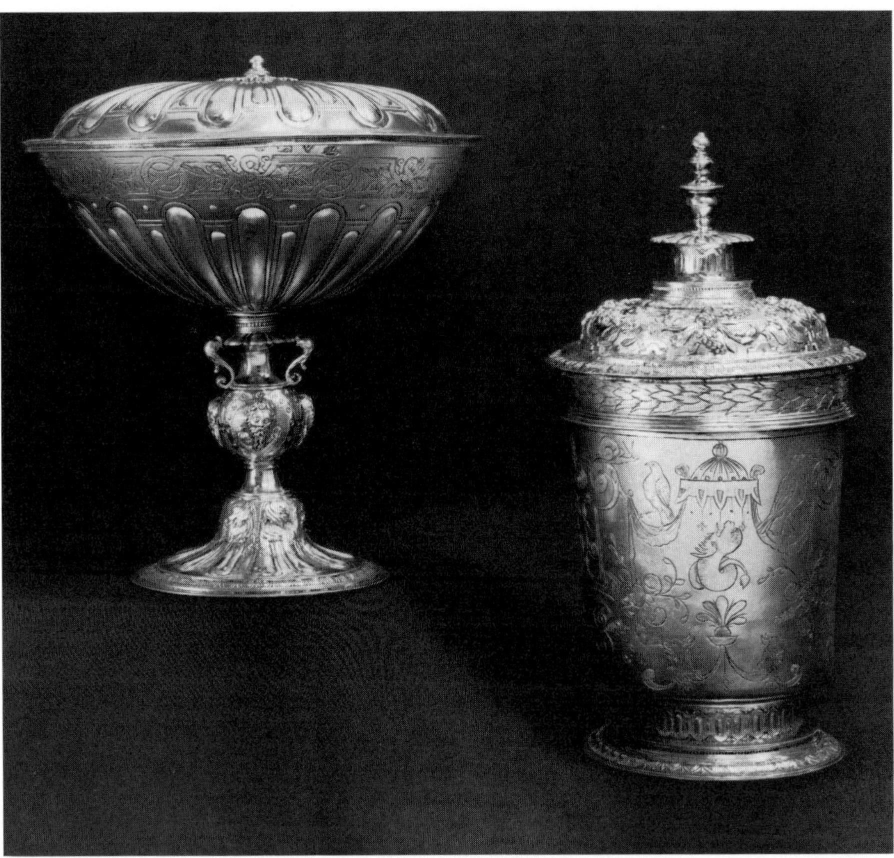
44

44 *Two Silver Cups*

THE WATERBEACH CUP (left)

Silver gilt
English (London), hallmark for 1557–58, maker's mark: W over a crescent
Height: 16.2 cm ($6\frac{3}{8}$ in)
Assheton-Bennett Bequest (1979.266)

THE MAGDALEN CUP (right)

Silver gilt
English (London), hallmark for 1573–74, maker's mark: MH in monogram
Height: 19.3 cm ($7\frac{3}{4}$ in)
Purchased with the aid of grants from the Government (through the Victoria and Albert Museum), the National Art-Collections Fund and the Worshipful Company of Goldsmiths (1956.257)

These two cups present fine comparative examples of English Renaissance ornament. The former, once at Waterbeach, Cambridgeshire, is derived in shape from Venetian glass *tazze*. It has a baluster stem, ornamented with bearded mask heads and cast dolphins, and unusual deep gadrooned ribbing. Around the top of the bowl is an early example of Renaissance interlaced ornament which, within a few years, was to become the standard decoration of Elizabethan communion cups. The Magdalen Cup is so-called from its beaker shape, the iconographic symbol of St. Mary Magdalen. The cover is ornamented with repoussé swags, the foot has a chased fillet and the bowl is covered with grotesque engraved decoration. This latter form of ornament, originating in antique wall painting and revived by Raphael (1483–1520), enjoyed a fruitful life in Northern Europe before it was superseded by Mannerist strapwork. It was described in Henry Peachum's *Graphice; or the most auncient* [sic] *and excellent art of drawing and limming . . .* (London, 1612) as 'an unnatural or unorderly composition for delight's sake, of men, beasts, birds, fishes, flowers etc without (as we say) Rime or Reason.'

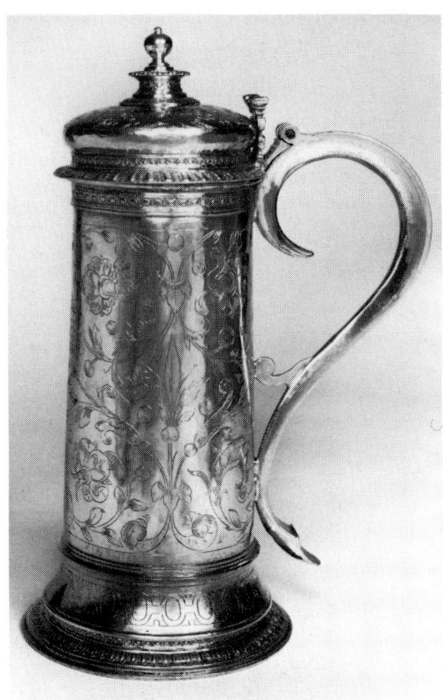

45

45 *The Mostyn Flagon*

Silver gilt
English (London), hallmark for 1601–02
maker's mark IA in a plain shield.
Engraved with the arms of the Mostyn-Gloddeath family
Height: 34 cm ($13\frac{3}{8}$ in)
Purchased with the aid of a Government grant (through the Victoria and Albert Museum) with assistance from the National Art-Collections Fund and the Assheton Bennett Bequest Fund (1978.1)

The Mostyn Flagon, or 'livery pot' as it would have been known, is among the finest recorded pieces of Elizabethan silver. The massive form of the body contrasts with the elegant double scroll of the handle while the cast work of the lid and base set off the superb engraving of the body. Its rich gilt surface gives a sense of opulence entirely characteristic of the age of Elizabethan expansion. Its chief function would have been to adorn the sideboard of Sir Richard Mostyn of Flintshire, Wales (d. 1617).

The highly distinctive engraved ornament illustrating plant forms and imaginary monsters on the body of the piece is almost certainly the work of a specialist engraver, Nicaise Roussel, a Huguenot refugee active in London from *c.* 1573 to *c.* 1617. His designs were published by John Barr under the title *De Grotesco Perutilis atq. omnibus pertinebit valde necessari Liber* (London, 1623) with plates illustrating grotesques with human masks, animal and bird monsters attached to plant forms. This flagon and its pair at Temple Newsam are therefore among a rare group of pieces of this date which can be attributed to a known engraver.

46 *Man's Nightcap* *pl. 9*

White linen, embroidered in silver and silver gilt thread, with coloured silk, in a variety of looped, chain and interlaced stitches and couchings.
Design of phoenix enclosed in scrolls forming shield shape, with oak leaves, acorns and flowers, and two obelisk shapes
English, 1590–1625
Height: 20 cm (7.9 in)
Purchased (1971.50)

Although called a 'nightcap', this elaborate example would not have been worn for sleeping, but for informal wear at home. Such work was often carried out by the women of the household, according to their own design or one obtained from a professional pattern designer.

Needlecraft was considered an essential part of a girl's education: by the turn of the 17th century, English embroidery had reached a high pitch of excellence. Its technique and style are said to be derived from the ecclesiastical tradition of church embroiderers, forced to earn a living in the outside world following the Dissolution of the Monasteries.

The main design of a phoenix and obelisks was taken from printed books of emblems, popular throughout the 16th and early 17th centuries. The best known was produced by Andrea Alchiati in 1531. Riddles, emblems and devices were much appreciated by the Elizabethans and Jacobeans. The books, with their attractive illustrations accompanied by an explanatory verse, were particularly useful as sources of patterns for embroidery. Many emblems can be identified not only on nightcaps, but also, for instance, on gloves and bodices; examples of which can be seen at the Castle Museum, Nottingham, and the Victoria and Albert Museum, London.

The obelisk, depicted here according to popular usage as a spire, was generally associated with monarchy. G. Whitney, in his *Choice of Emblems* of 1586, specifically identifies it with Elizabeth I, representing the strength which supports state and church, in a rhyme following the motto 'Te Stante, Virebo'. Whitney also includes an illustration and rhyme on the phoenix. Elizabeth adopted the phoenix, an image of eternal youth, as her particular emblem: for instance, it is seen on *The*

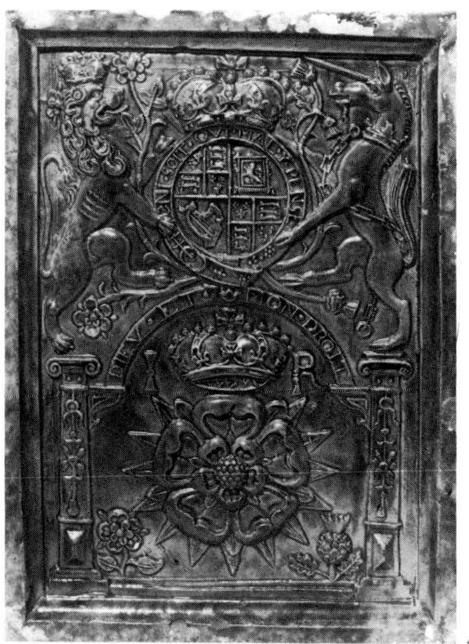

47

Phoenix Portrait of *c.* 1575, attributed to Hilliard (National Portrait Gallery).

The Platt Hall cap was designed as a compliment to Queen Elizabeth. Although the style of cap was worn well into the 1620s, it is unlikely that this example, because of its clear associations, would have been worked very much after Elizabeth's death in 1603.

47 *Tile*

Light red earthenware, press-moulded and covered with a green glaze. A design in relief within a rectangular border with the Arms of King James I of England and the mottoes DIEV.ET.MON.DROIT and HONI.SOIT.QUI.MAL.Y.PENSE, and IR also in relief.
English, 1603–25
Width: 24.5 cm ($9\frac{5}{8}$ in)
Thomas Greg Collection (1923.153)

Those who appreciate the robust simplicity of English earthenware, which did not change significantly from the Middle Ages until the 17th century, are struck by the extraordinary finesse of this 'Tudor' green tile. It is painstakingly constructed from three different clays, and moulded (an unusual technique for this date) with an heraldic design. Probably made for the Royal Household at Greenwhich Palace, it belongs to a rare group of moulded green glazed wares, decorated with the Royal Arms of the Tudors (1485–1603). The group consists of tiles, candle sconces and a fine, early cistern in the British Museum collection, showing the arms of Henry VII of England and Elizabeth of York.

At Greenwich Palace, Inigo Jones (1573–1652), appointed Surveyor of the King's Works in 1615, partially demolished and rebuilt the old Tudor apartments and laid the foundations for the so-called 'Queen's House'. Fragments of an identical tile to the Manchester piece, from the same mould, were excavated at Greenwhich in 1970–71 by the University of Nottingham. The fragments also have the arms of James I, and were probably from the pre-1615 buildings at Greenwich, as was the Greg tile. Green tiles would, in the reigns of Elizabeth and James, have been particularly appropriate for interiors. Writing in 1560, Levinus Lemnius said no nation more than the English '. . . trim up our parlours with green boughs, freshe herbes and vine leaves; . . .' (Reported in W. B. Rye, *England As Seen By Foreigners*, London, 1865).

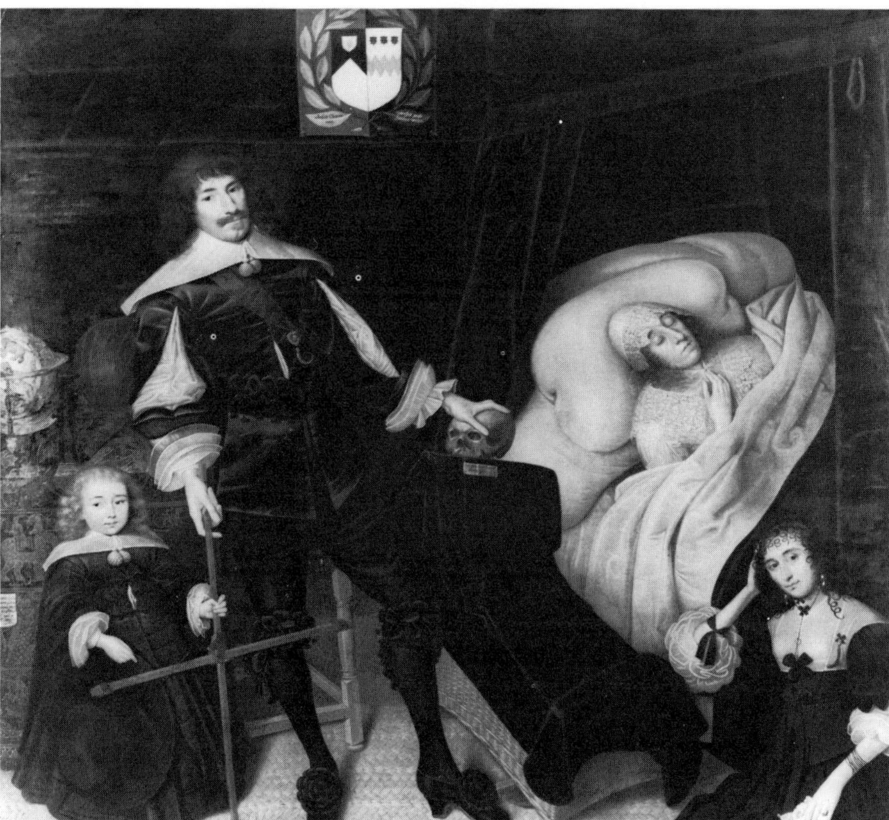

48

48 *John Souch*

(active 1616–36)

SIR THOMAS ASTON AT THE DEATHBED OF HIS WIFE 1635
English; oil on canvas
203.2 × 215.1 cm (80 × $84\frac{11}{16}$ in)
Signed (b. centre): *Jo:Souch* / *Cestren*(s) / *Fecit*
Peter Jones gift through the National Art-Collections Fund (1927.150)

This is a memorial picture of Magdalene, Lady Aston. Death, grief and the vanity of the world are the themes of the symbolic language of gestures and objects, and these themes are also given in Latin quotations painted into the picture. 'The griefs of death surround me; in the year of grief September 30, 1635, aged 35. Though I walk through the valley of the shadow

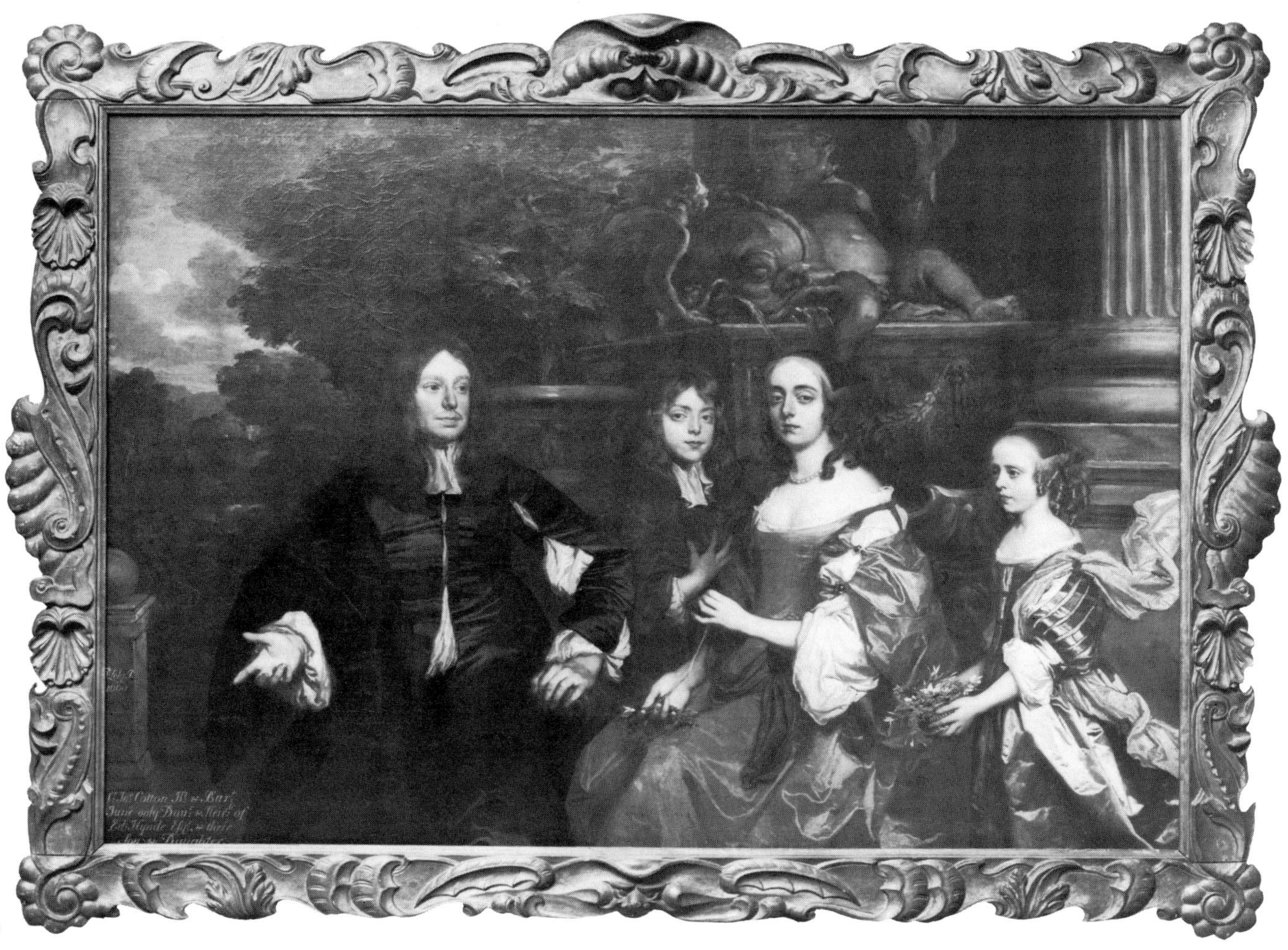

49

of death, I fear not, I will be consoled.'

The bereaved Sir Thomas, dressed in black, rests his hand on a skull, placed on a cradle draped in black velvet. This indicates that Lady Aston died in childbirth. Lady Aston herself is shown both on her deathbed and as in life, a medieval type of representation, old fashioned for this date. Beside Sir Thomas stands their son, holding a cross-staff, a navigational instrument. This refers to the crucifixion, but also gives point to the Latin inscription on it, 'The seas can be defined, the earth can be measured, grief is immeasurable.' The globe and unstrung lute are symbols of the passing of worldly pleasures. 'He who sows hope in flesh reaps bones' is the meaning of the Latin on the parchment beneath the skull.

The artist, John Souch, who signs himself 'of Chester', is known from a very few signed portraits of Cheshire, Shropshire and North Wales sitters. He was apprenticed to an heraldic painter and so was familiar with the language of symbols. This is an ambitious, large scale work for a provincial painter and although its tilted figures are clumsy by the standards of contemporary court painting (Van Dyck was working in London at this time), it is nevertheless a moving and impressive piece of allegorical imagery.

49 *Sir Peter Lely*

(1618–1680)

SIR JOHN COTTON AND HIS FAMILY
1660

English; oil on canvas
157.4 × 225.3 cm (62 × 88 11/16 in)
Signed (b.l.): *P. Lely. P./1660*
and inscr(b.l.c.): *S[r]: Jn:[o] Cotton K:[t] & Bar:[t]/ Jane only Dau:[r] & Heir:[ss] of/Ed. Hynde Esq:[r]*

& their/Son & Daughter
Purchased with the aid of the National Art-Collections Fund (1966.344)

Born in Westphalia of Dutch parents, Peter Lely arrived in England some time between 1641 and 1643. By the Restoration he was considered the finest portrait painter 'in large' in England. Lely's reputation, in his day, surpassed that of Van Dyck to whose position he succeeded as Principal Painter to the King in 1661, a year after Charles II's accession to the throne. His studio was frequented by many notable figures, including Pepys who records visits to 'Mr. Lilly's, the painter's' in his Diary.

This richly-coloured group portrait from Lely's finest period is a development on a grander scale of a Van Dyck design such as *The Family of Endymion Porter*, a painting which Lely owned.

Sir John Cotton (1615–89/90) of Landswade, Cambridgshire, was High Sheriff and Deputy Lieutenant of the county. He is seen with his wife Jane, his son John, later MP for Cambridge, and his daughter Jane, who brings flowers for her mother to bind into a wreath, a motif also from Van Dyck. The group is set in a landscape against an imaginary dolphin fountain.

During the Civil War Sir John brought the University Plate to the King at Oxford. For this he was fined £350 by the Parlamentarians but at the Restoration he was rewarded for his loyalty by being appointed Keeper of the King's game on Newmarket Heath.

The handsome auricular frame is of the 'Sunderland' type, an English variety of the Dutch 'Lutma frame', named after the Dutch goldsmith Jan Lutma the Younger (1624–85). The 'Sunderland frame' was so called after the second Earl of Sunderland who reframed many of his portraits in this manner for the Gallery at Althorp, when it was rebuilt and decorated in the late 1660s.

50 *Slipware dishes*

DISH

Red earthenware with a trailed dark and light red slip design on a white slip ground, lead glazed.
English (Staffordshire), *c.* 1670, by Thomas Toft
Signed: THOMAS TOFT
Diameter: 42.5 cm ($16\frac{3}{4}$ in)
Thomas Greg Collection (1923.147)

Toft, the most famous of the English *plattermakers* in the 17th century, was living in the Staffordshire hamlet of Stanley in 1663–66. Only two of the thirty-five dishes which bear his name are dated, one to 1671 and the other to 1674.

The portrait is probably that of Catherine of Braganza, married to Charles II in 1662. A Toft dish in the Glaisher Collection at the Fitzwilliam Museum, Cambridge, shows an almost identical but smaller portrait, crowned and posed beside a monarch in ermine robes, said to be Charles II.

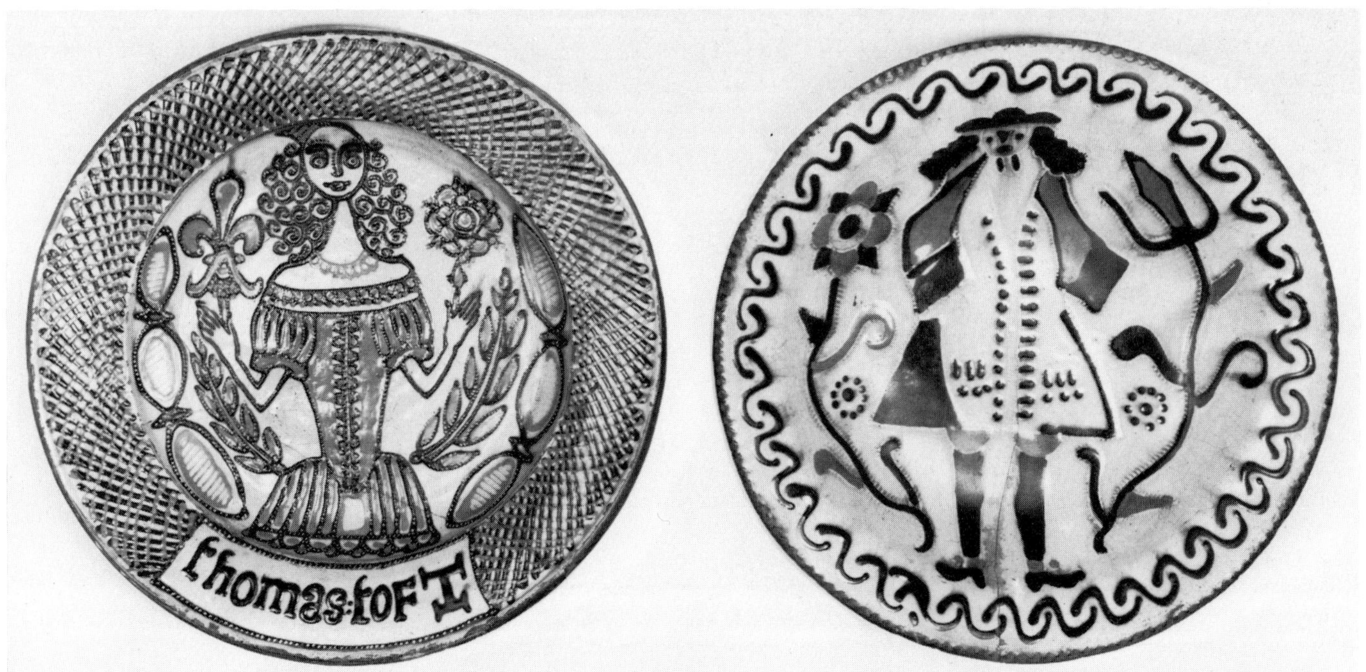

50

Contemporary portraits by D. Plaats and Huysman reveal that Catherine, the daughter of the Queen Regent of Portugal, had a distinctive, full hairstyle with ringlets. It was in the Spanish fashion of the day, supported with wire to make it stand out from the head. A 1664 portrait of the Infanta Maria by Velazquez, now in the Prado, shows this type of hairstyle, with a typically Spanish side parting.

DISH

Buff-coloured earthenware with a relief design, covered with a white slip ground embellished with trailed light and dark red slip, lead glazed.
English (Staffordshire or Shropshire), 1751 or later, from a mould by William Bird
Diameter: 41.5 cm ($16\frac{3}{8}$ in)
Thomas Greg Collection (1923.196)

This type of 18th-century slipware dish was pressed from a convex *hump* mould, carved with a basic design which appeared in relief on the dish. They were also made by Samuel Malkin of Burslem, Staffordshire. The mould for this dish, which is in the British Museum collection, is inscribed: *William Bird / made this mould / In the year of / Our Lord / 1751*. The more common Malkin pressed dishes often have the initials 'SM' in the design, but the Bird dish and mould are initialled 'RG'.

Daniel Bird, 'potter', and at least three William Birds are recorded in the Parish of Stoke in 1753. However, a 'William Bird of Broseley, Plattermaker' is recorded in the Borough Archives of Much Wenlock, Shropshire, in 1739.

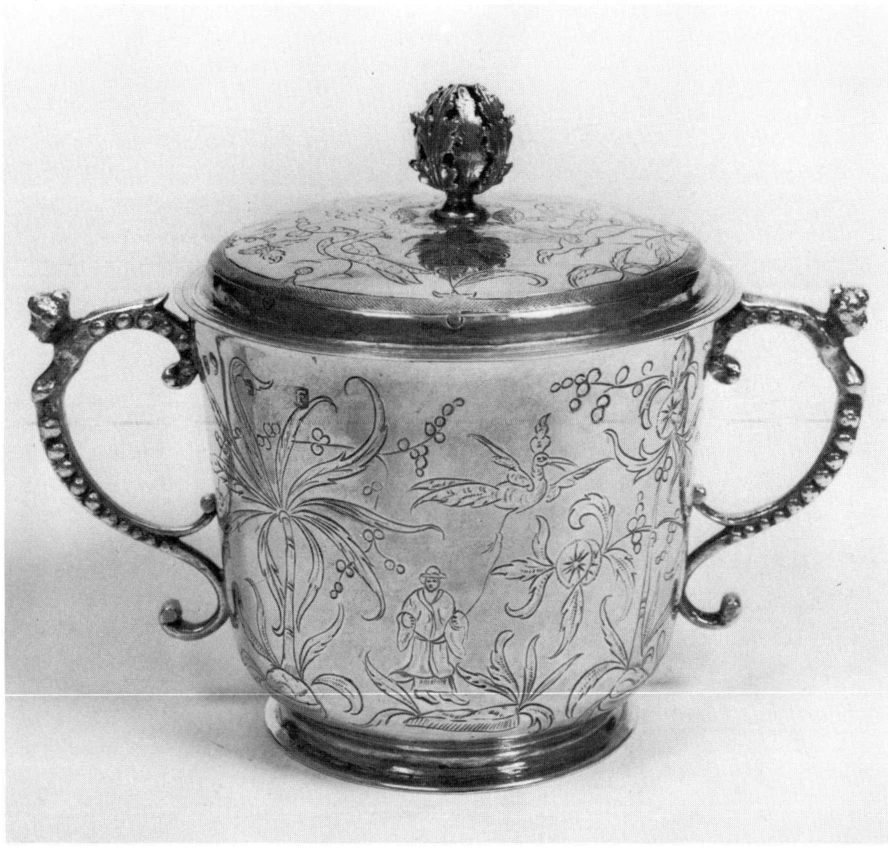

51

51 *Porringer*

Silver
English (London), hall mark for 1683–84, maker's mark S crowned (probably for Robert Smythier)
Height: 18.4 cm ($7\frac{1}{2}$ in)
Purchased (1957.87)

The porringer is one of the most characteristic objects of English Restoration plate. It was often given by the king for official New Year gifts through the Jewel House and the Royal Goldsmith. The maker of this piece, whose mark *S crowned* has now been identified as belonging to Robert Smythier (fl.1660–88), is closely associated with the period when Sir Robert Viner was the Royal Goldsmith. The same mark is found on large quantities of luxurious items made for state occasions and the magnificent plate produced for the newly reconstituted Chapels Royal.

The 1680s saw a brief vogue for flat-chased chinoiserie decoration. The sides of this porringer are decorated with exotic flora and fauna, a fountain in the shape of a dragon and a vague chinaman with a ho-ho bird on a lead. It reflects the rage for all things oriental which swept through Europe at this time, based on the flimsiest evidence of true oriental art. The publications of travellers were illustrated with particularly distorted ideas of Chinese and 'Indian' topography and customs. Possibly the most whimsical designs were those of Stalker and Parker's *Treatise of Japanning, Varnishing and Guilding* (1688) which was intended as a source book for cabinet makers (both professional and amateur) specialising in lacquer. One of its plates depicts children with game fowl on leads and is inscribed 'Several figures to be plased as Occassion serveth in Jappan Worke' [sic].

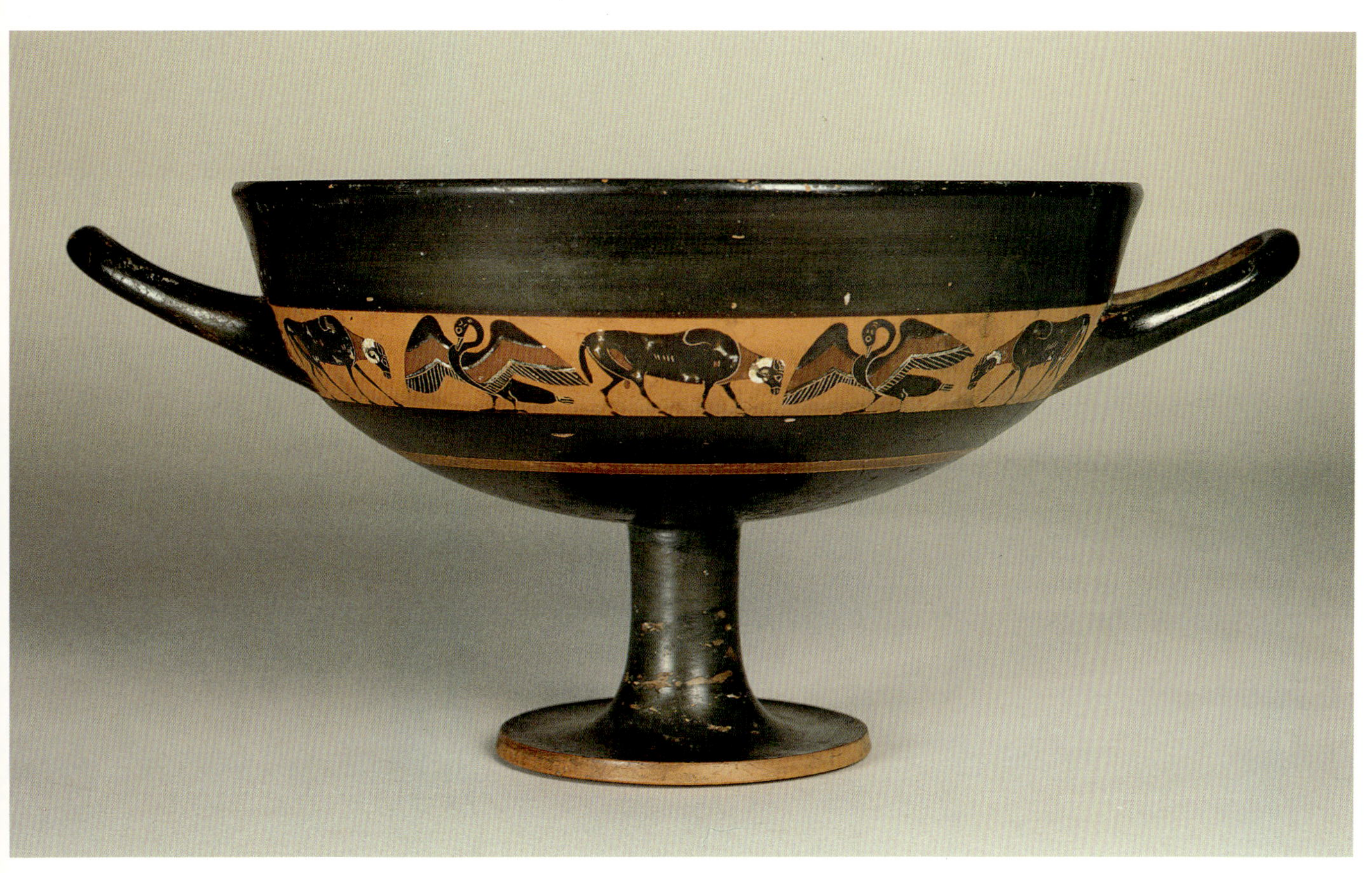

1. Greek stem cup (entry no 5)

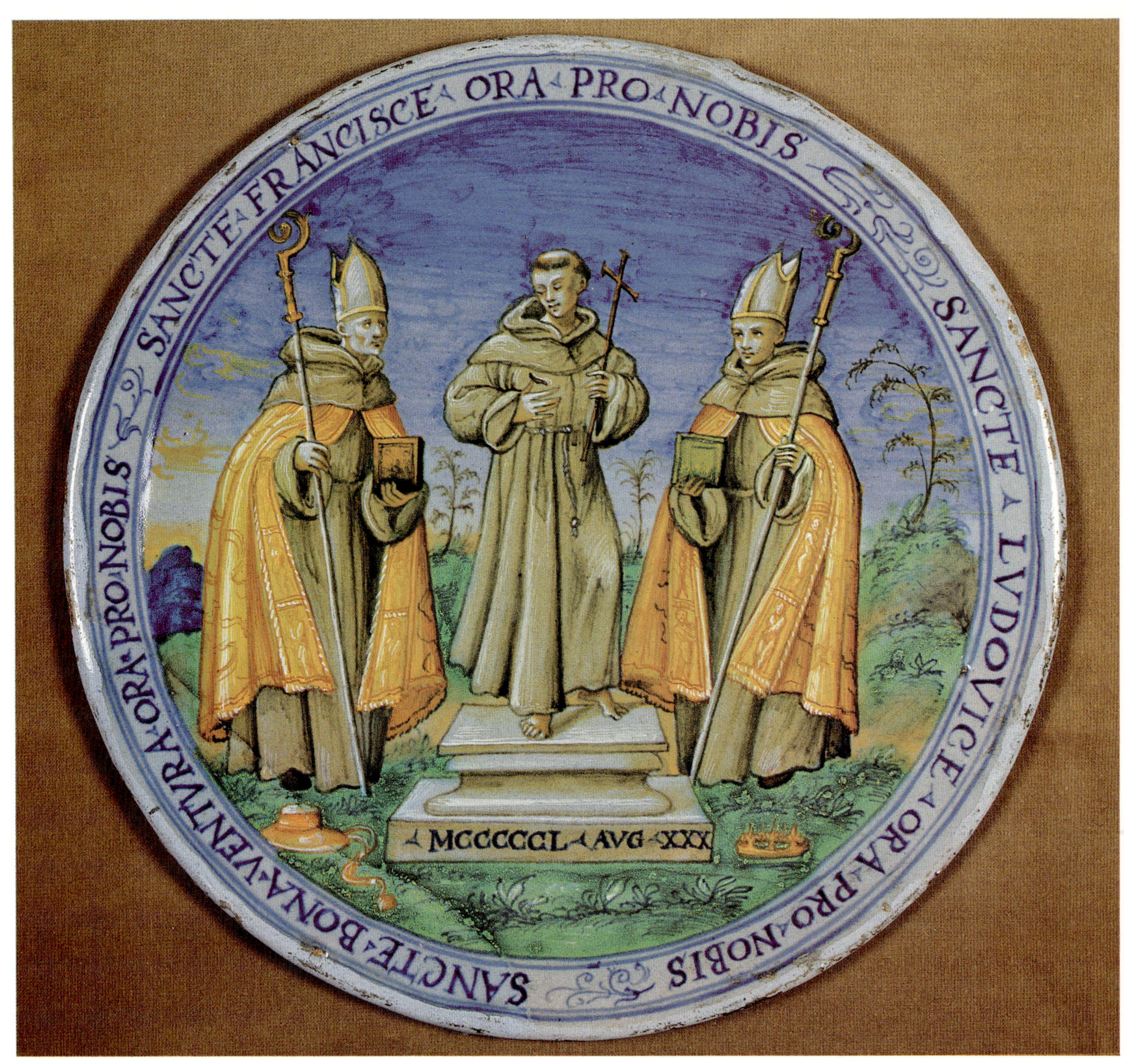

2. Italian maiolica roundel (entry no. 34)

3. The Tatton cup (entry no. 64)

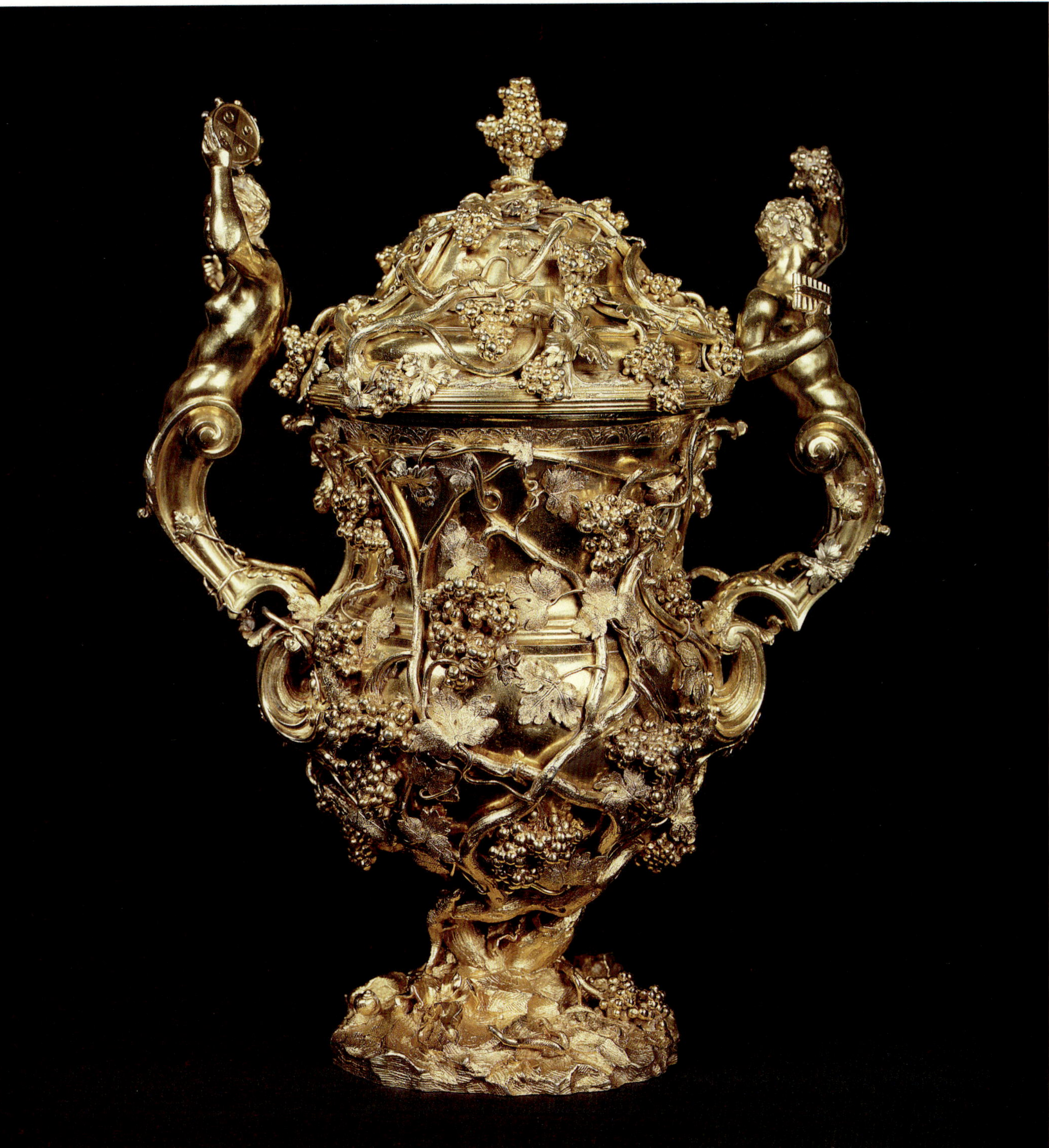

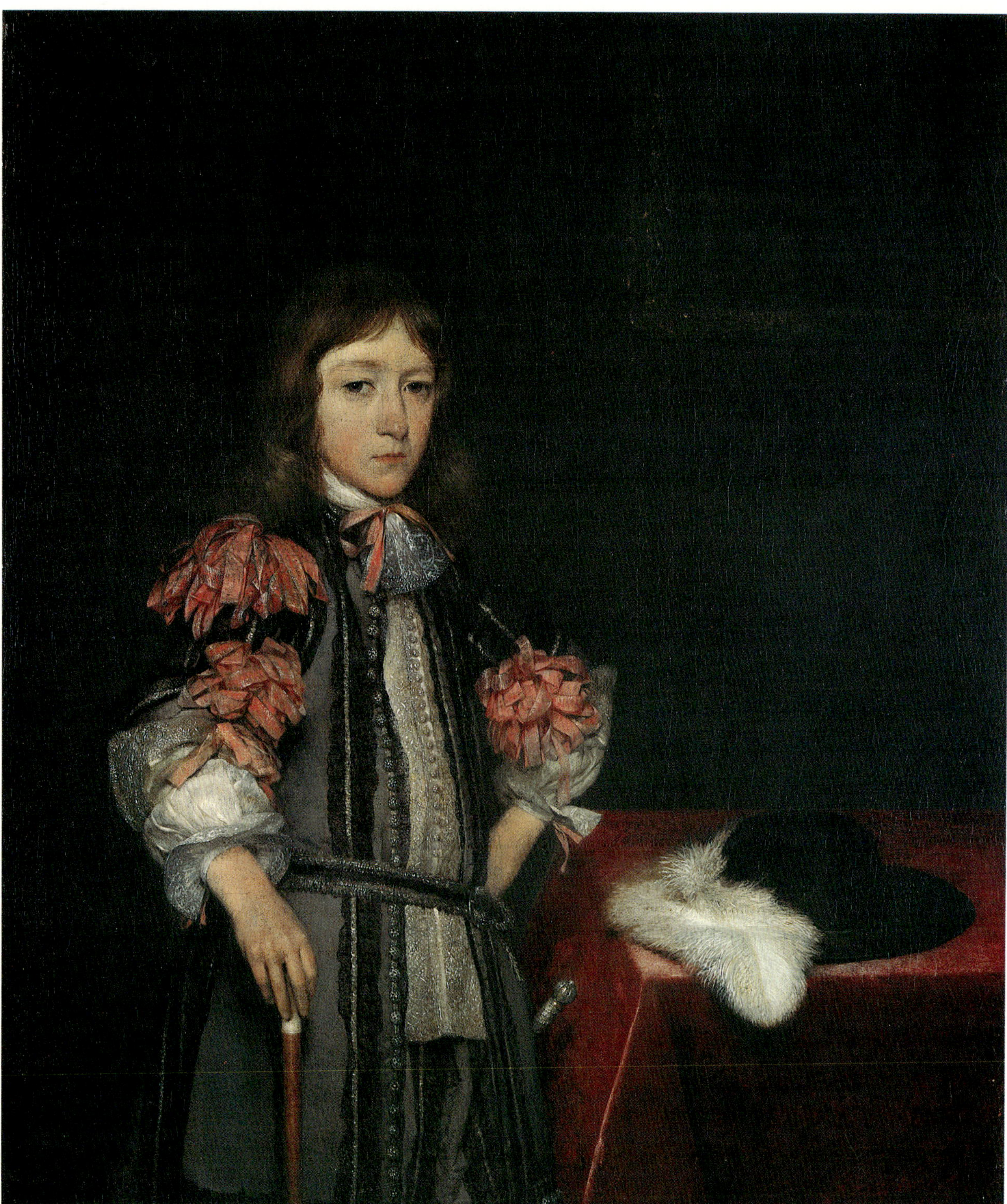

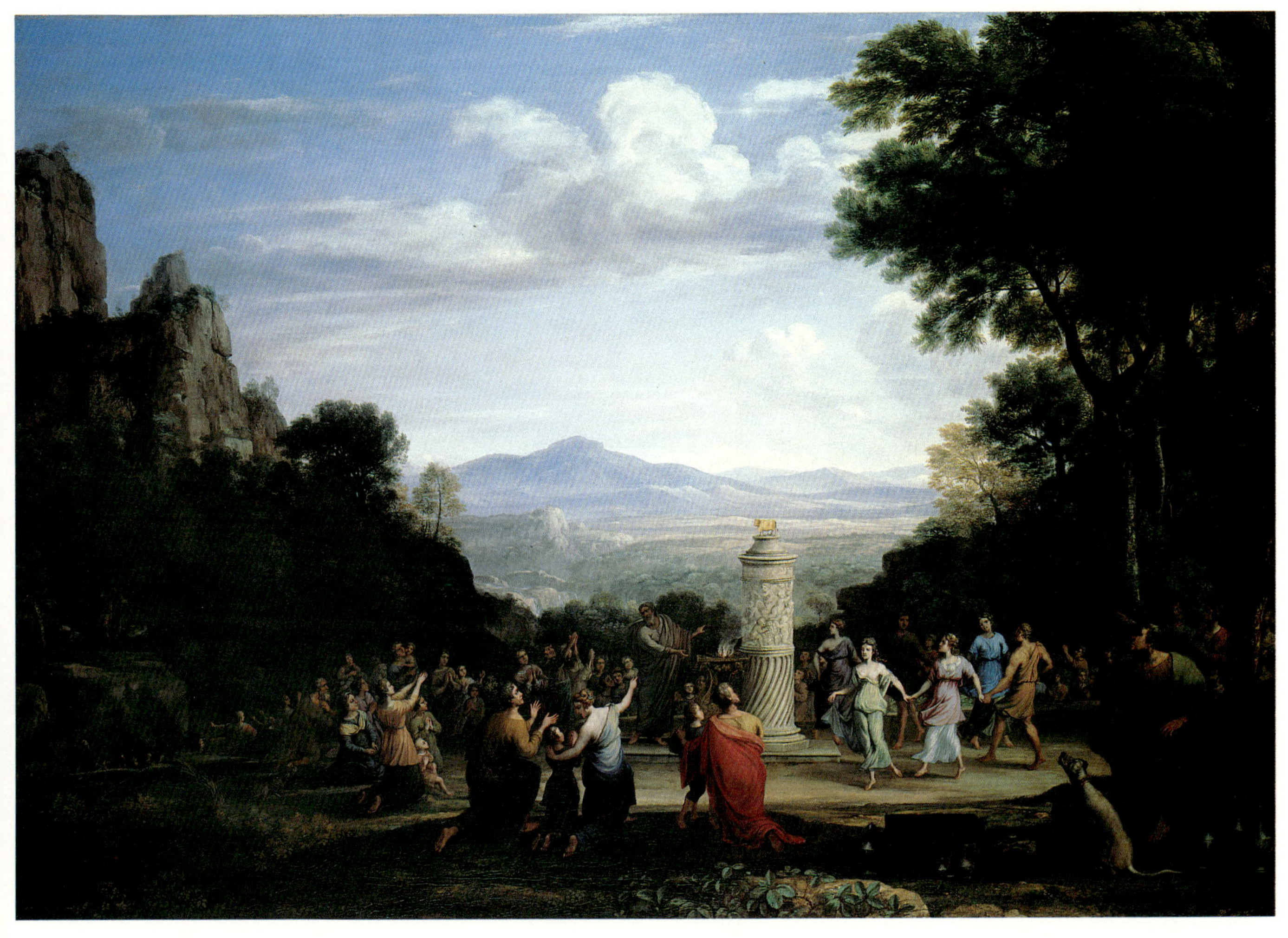

5. Claude Lorrain: *Landscape with the Adoration of the Golden Calf* (entry no. 41)

4. G. Ter Borch: *Hendrik Casimir* II (entry no. 57)

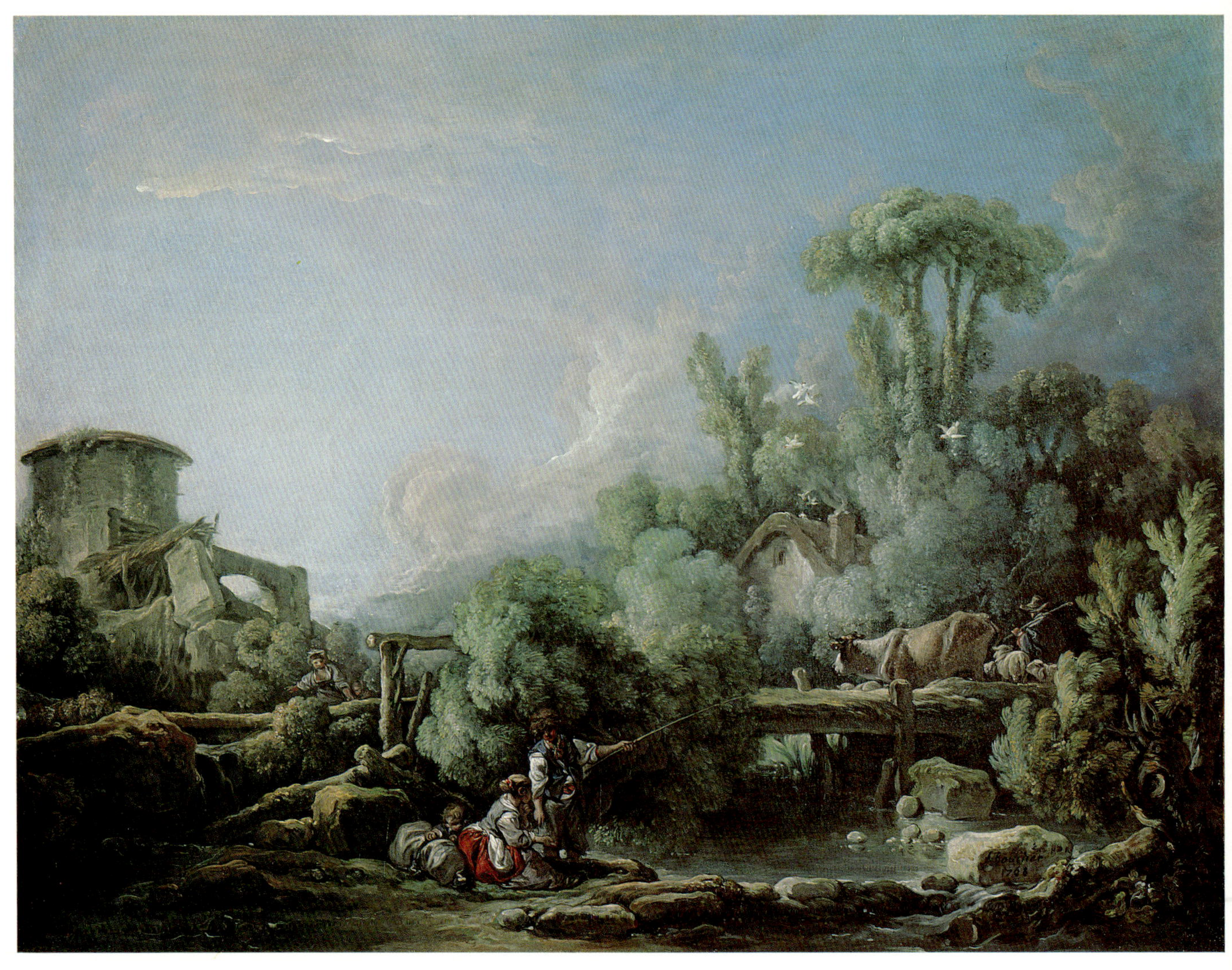

6. F. Boucher: *Le Galant Pêcheur* (entry no. 79)

7. Gainsborough: *A peasant Girl gathering Faggots in a Wood* (entry no. 96)

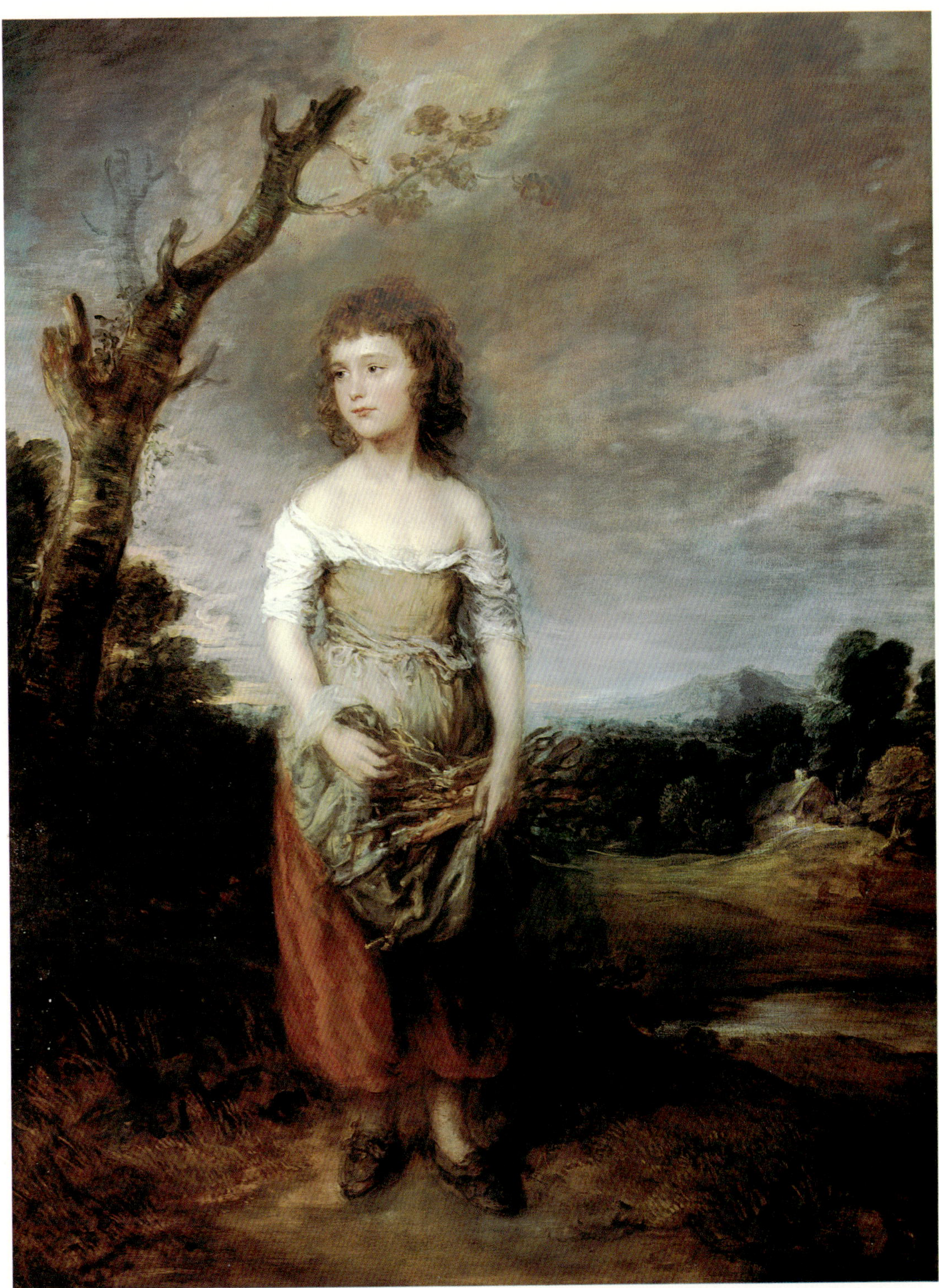

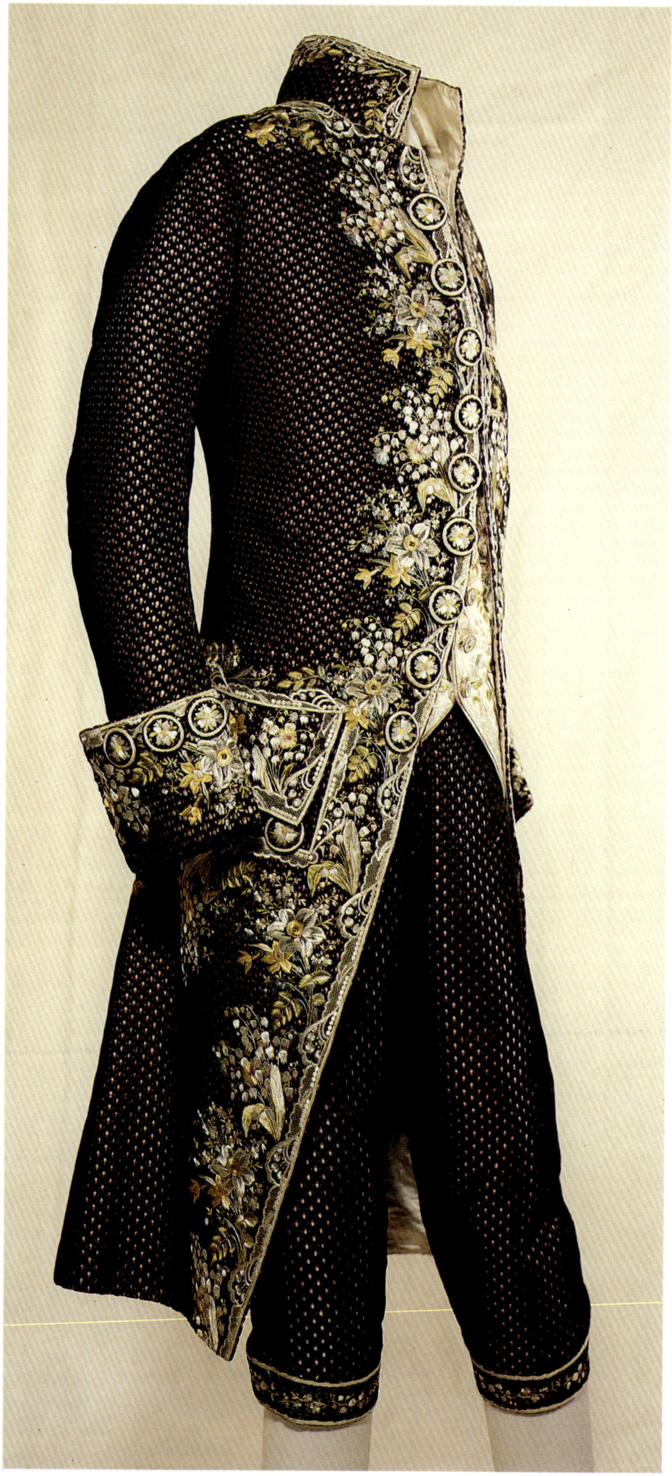

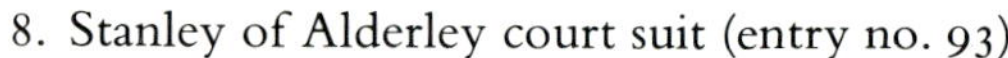

8. Stanley of Alderley court suit (entry no. 93)

9. Man's nightcap (entry no. 46)

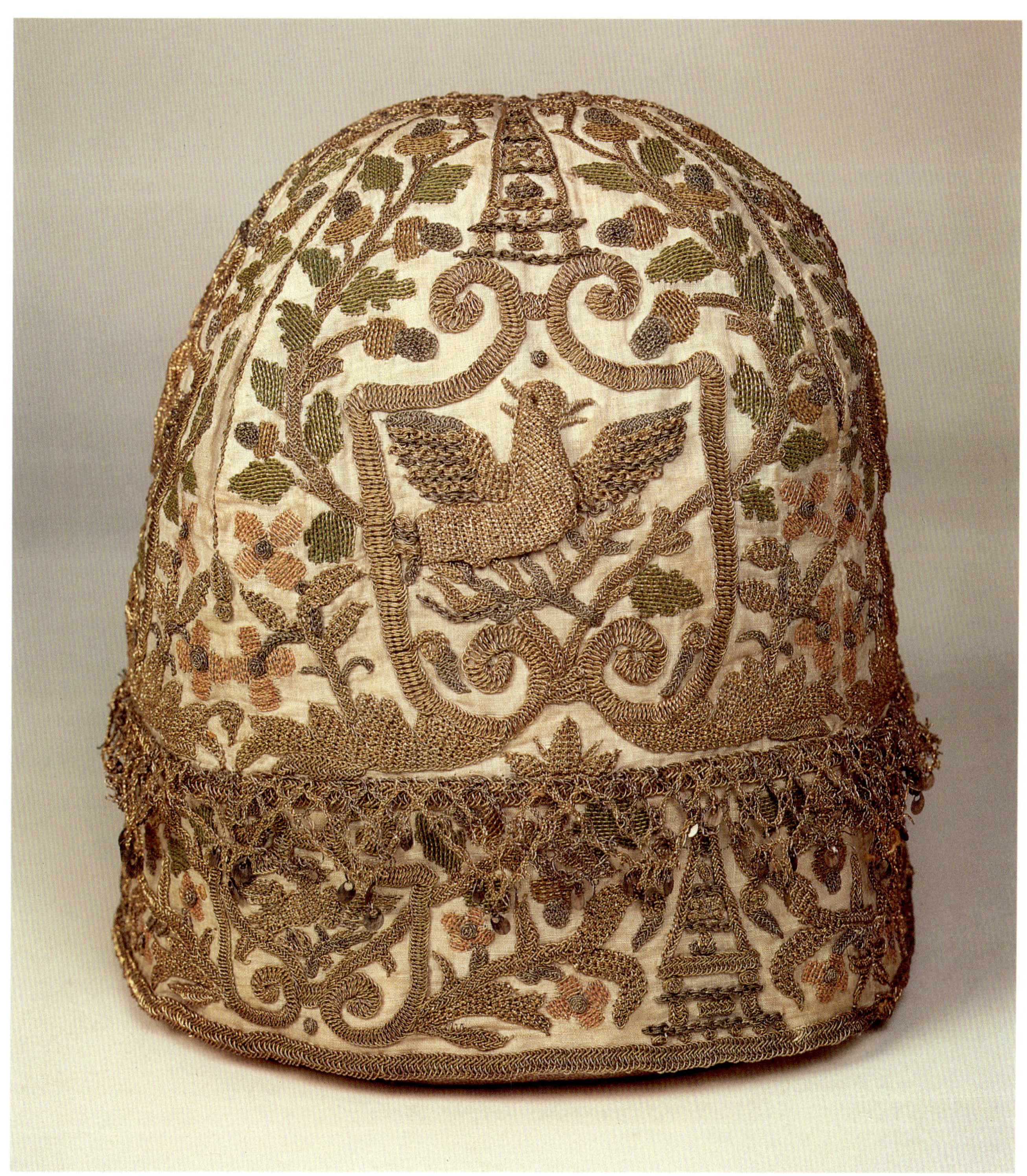

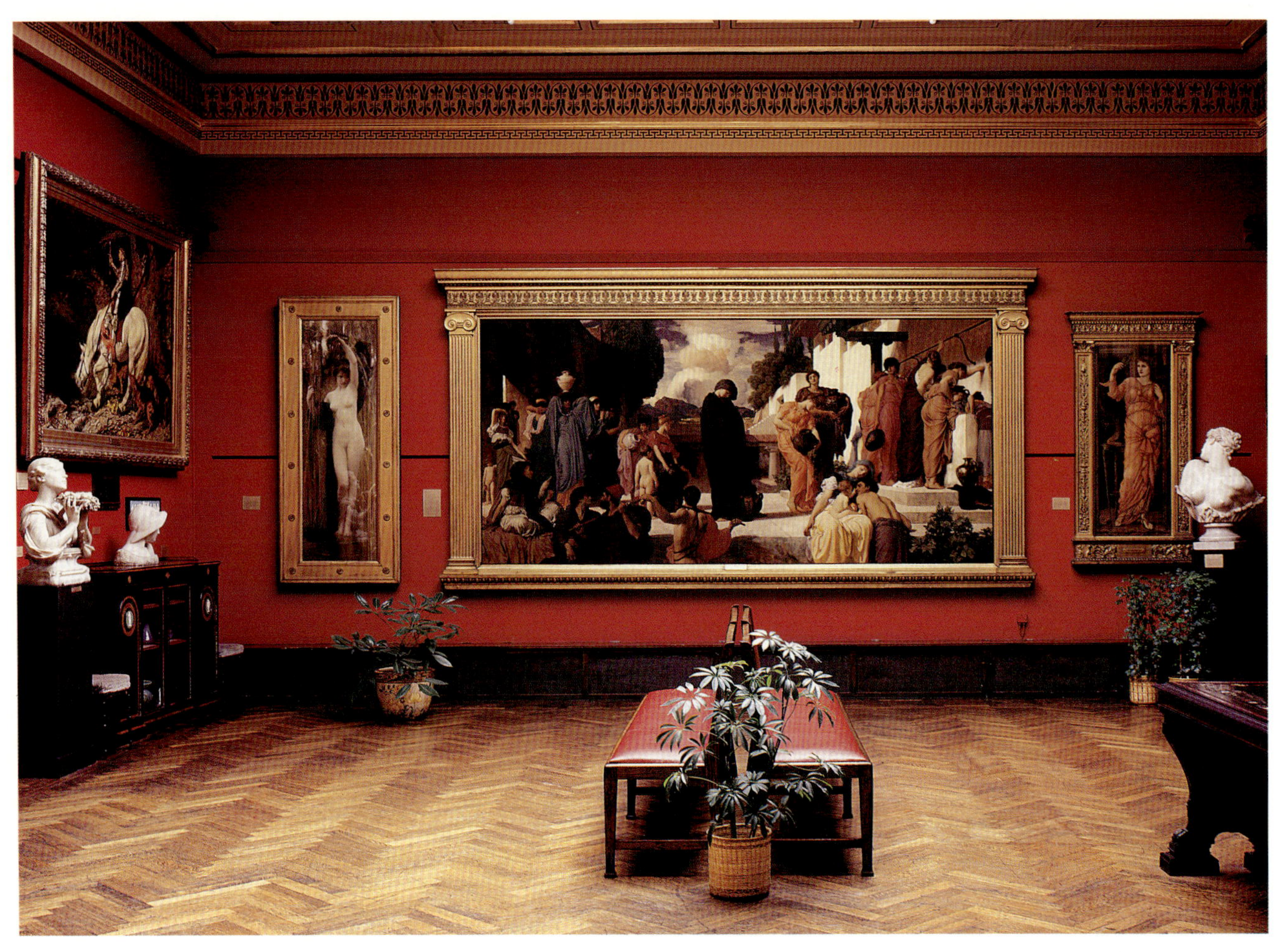

10. Frederic Lord Leighton: *Captive Andromache* (entry no. 144)

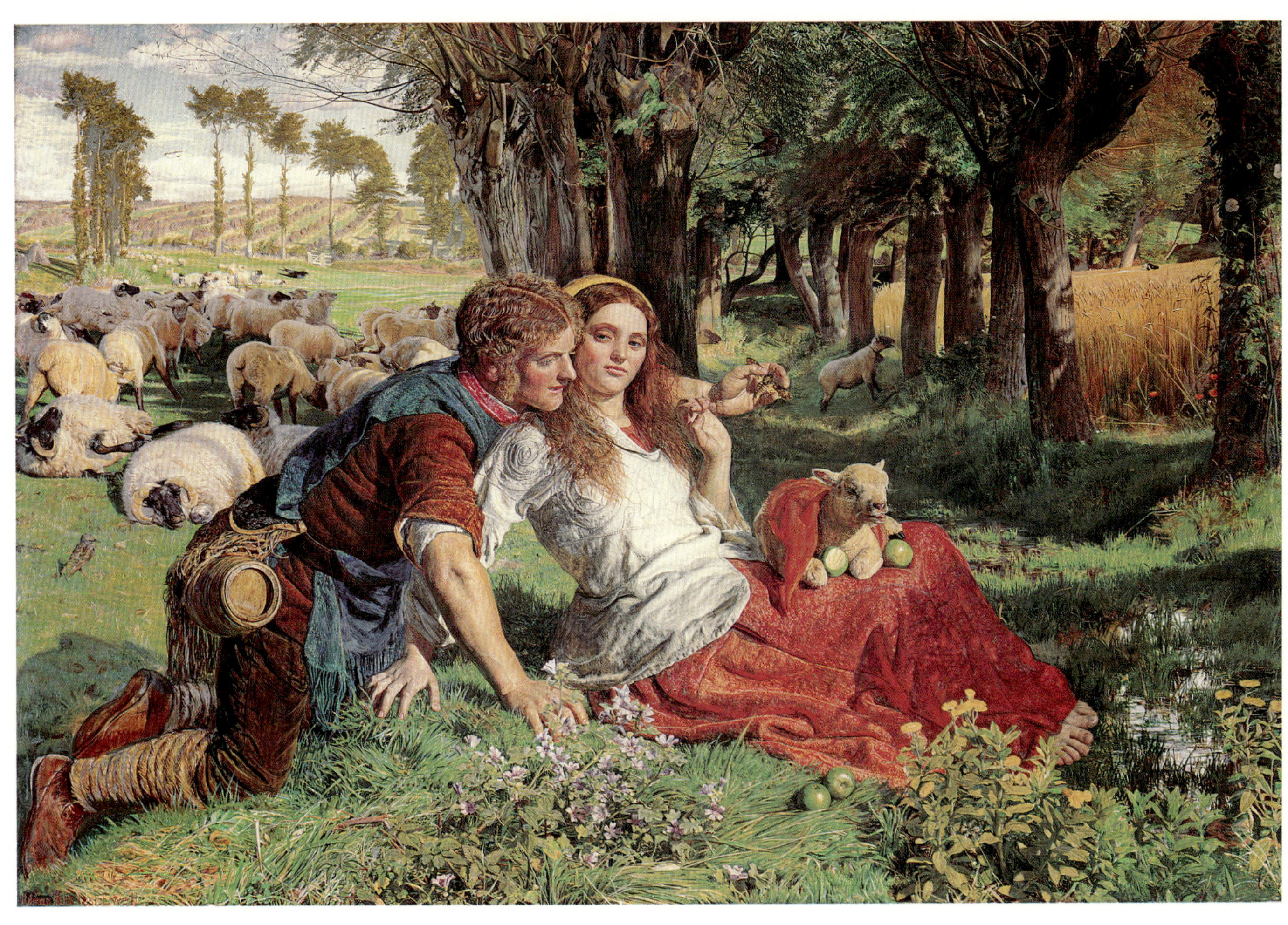

11. W. Holman Hunt: *The Hireling Shepherd* (entry no. 121)

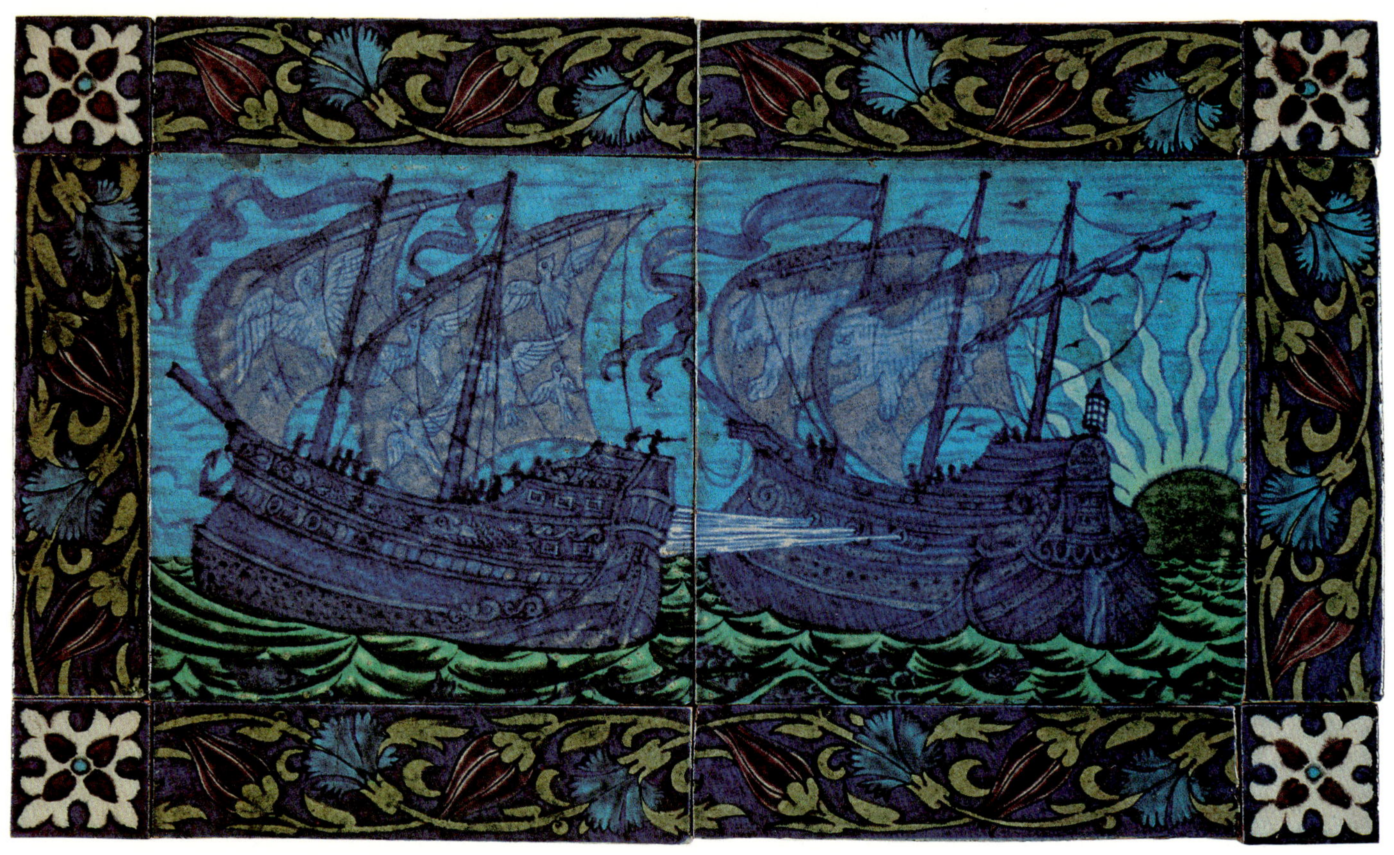

12. De Morgan tile panel (entry no. 132)

13. Burges escritoire (entry no. 131)

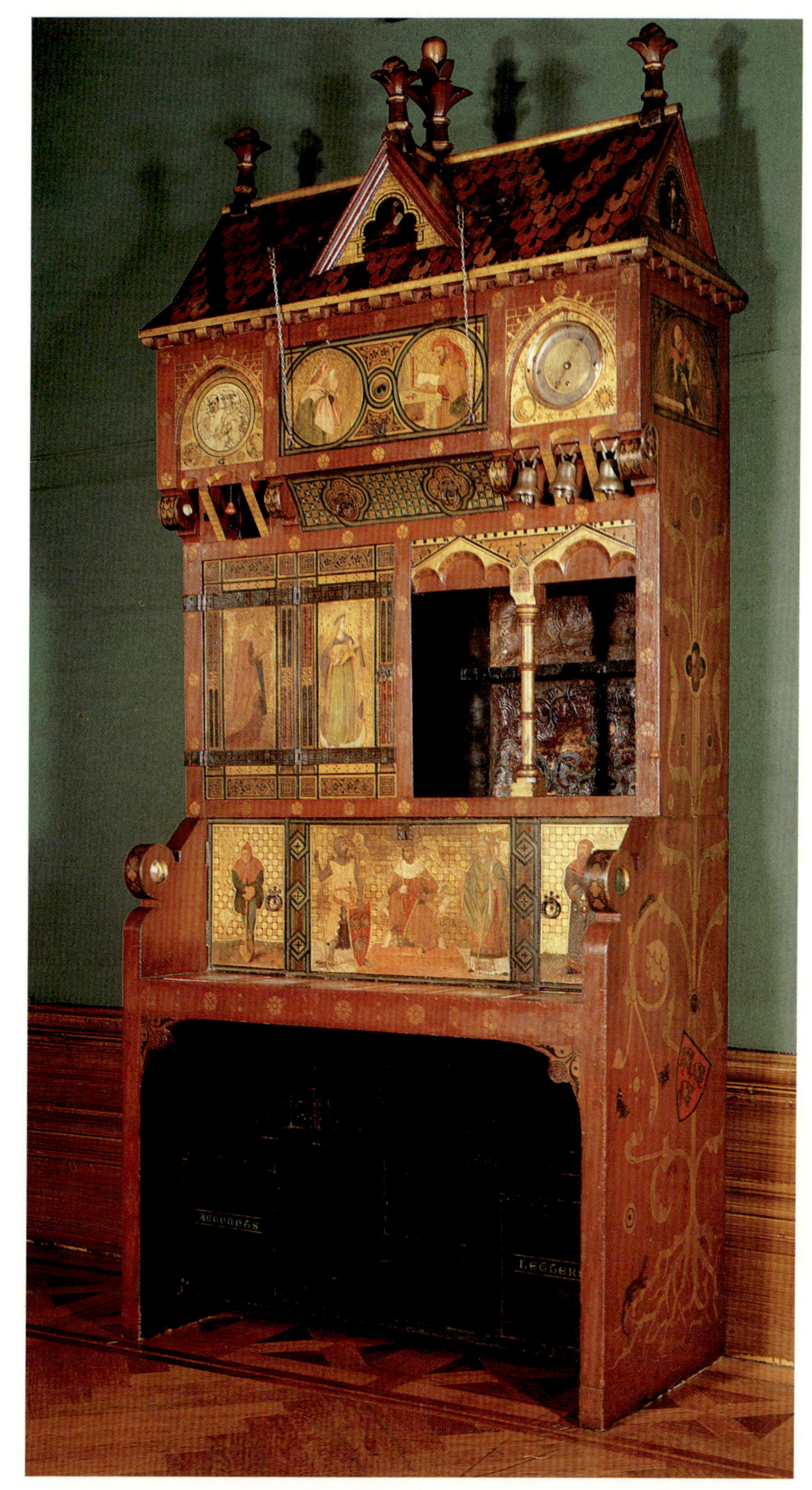

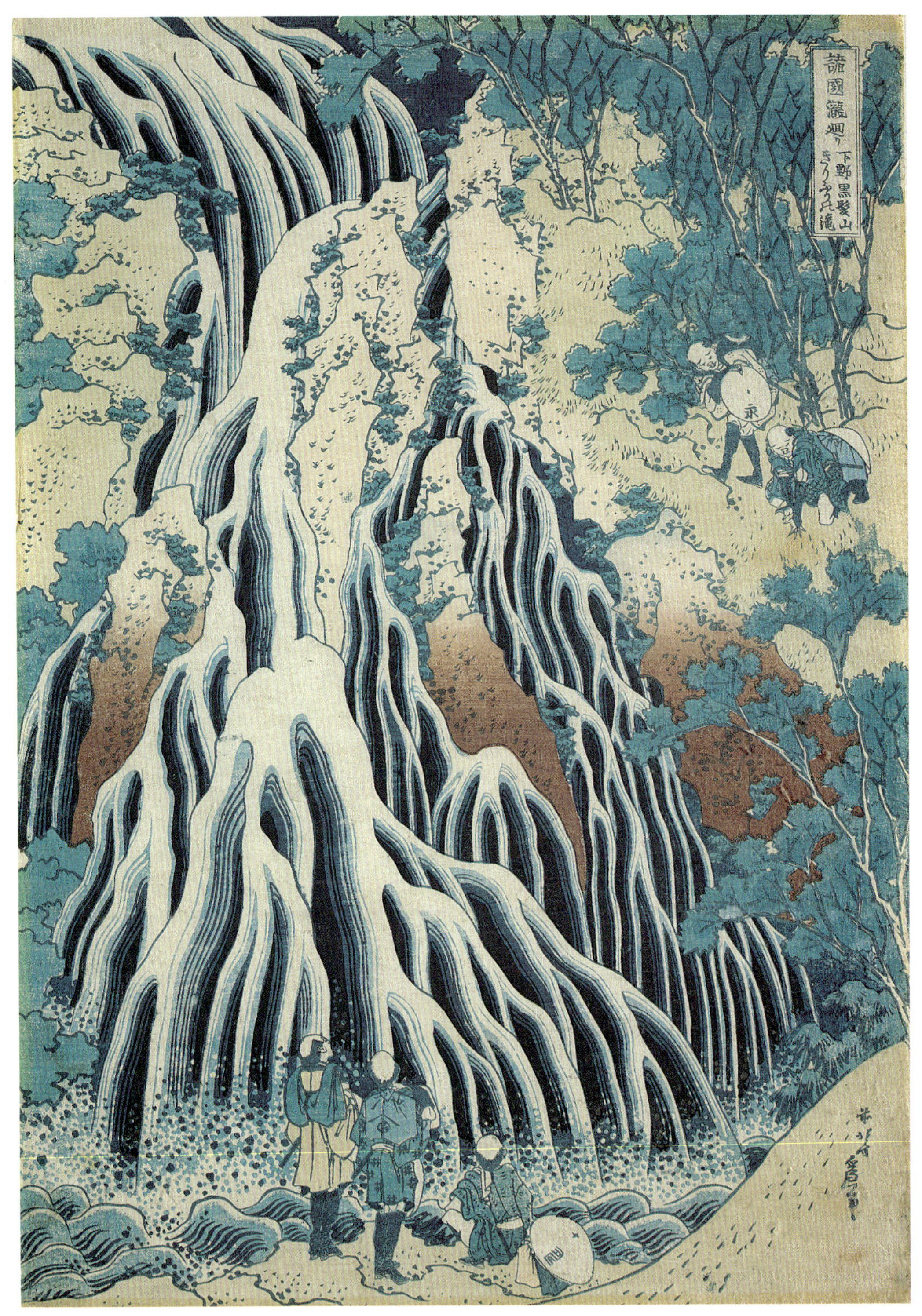

14. Katsushika Hokusai: *Kirifuri Fall* (entry no. 23)

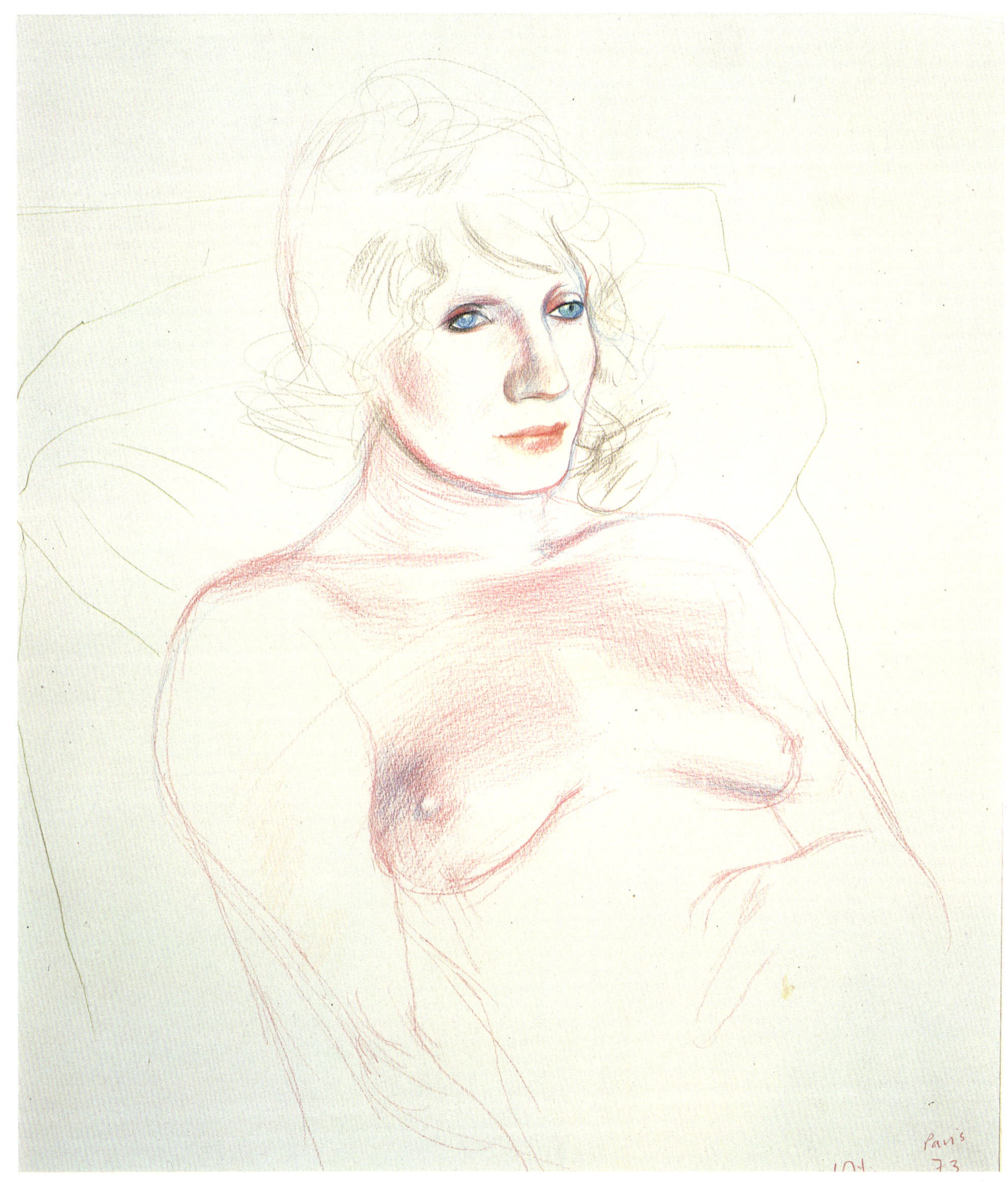

15. D. Hockney: *Celia* (entry no. 175)

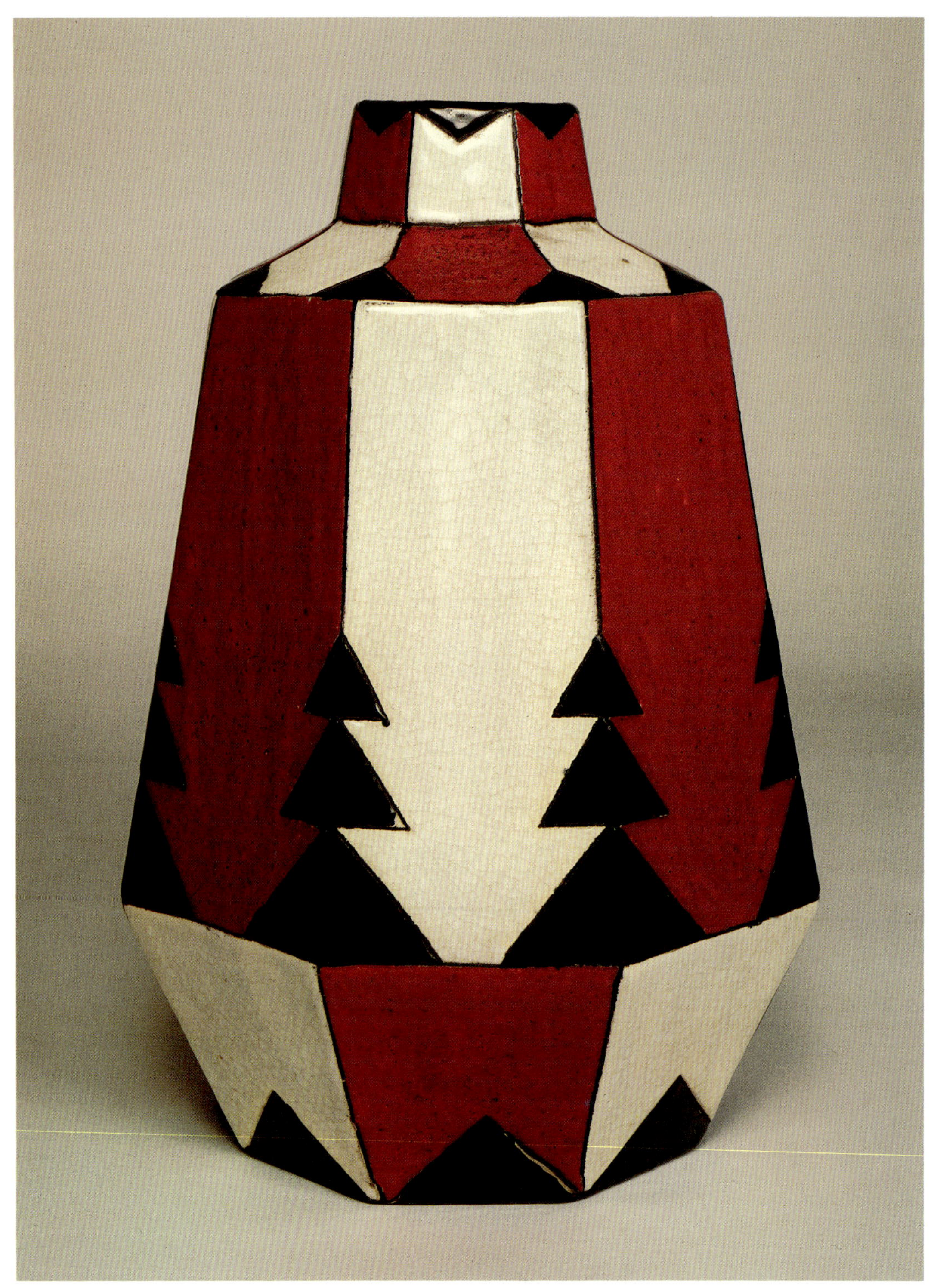

16. Boch Frères Keramis vase (entry no. 163)

52 'La Fécondité' Dish

Tin-glazed earthenware, moulded and painted in blue, with green, yellow and brown.
English (London), *c.* 1660
Diameter: 50.2 cm (19¾ in)
Purchased (1964.256)

London 17th-century potters making tin-glazed earthenware ('delftware') were influenced by French earthenware made by Bernard Palissy (1509–89) and his followers in the late 16th century. There was presumably a market for French pottery in London about 1600, when a merchant called Bauls is known to have been trading with Jean Barthélémy, a Fontainebleau potter and contemporary of Palissy's. London potters copied Palissy's *La Fécondité*. This was a very handsome, polychrome-glazed moulded dish, showing at the centre in relief a naked woman with five children. Examples are now in the Louvre and the Victoria and Albert Museum.

La Fécondité is thought to have been taken from a metalwork original. Other Palissy items have known counterparts in metalwork, such as a basin by the pewterer Briot of *c.* 1585, in the Louvre. A reclining female nude similar to *La Fécondité* in Palissy ware, known as *The Nymph of Fontainebleau*, was copied

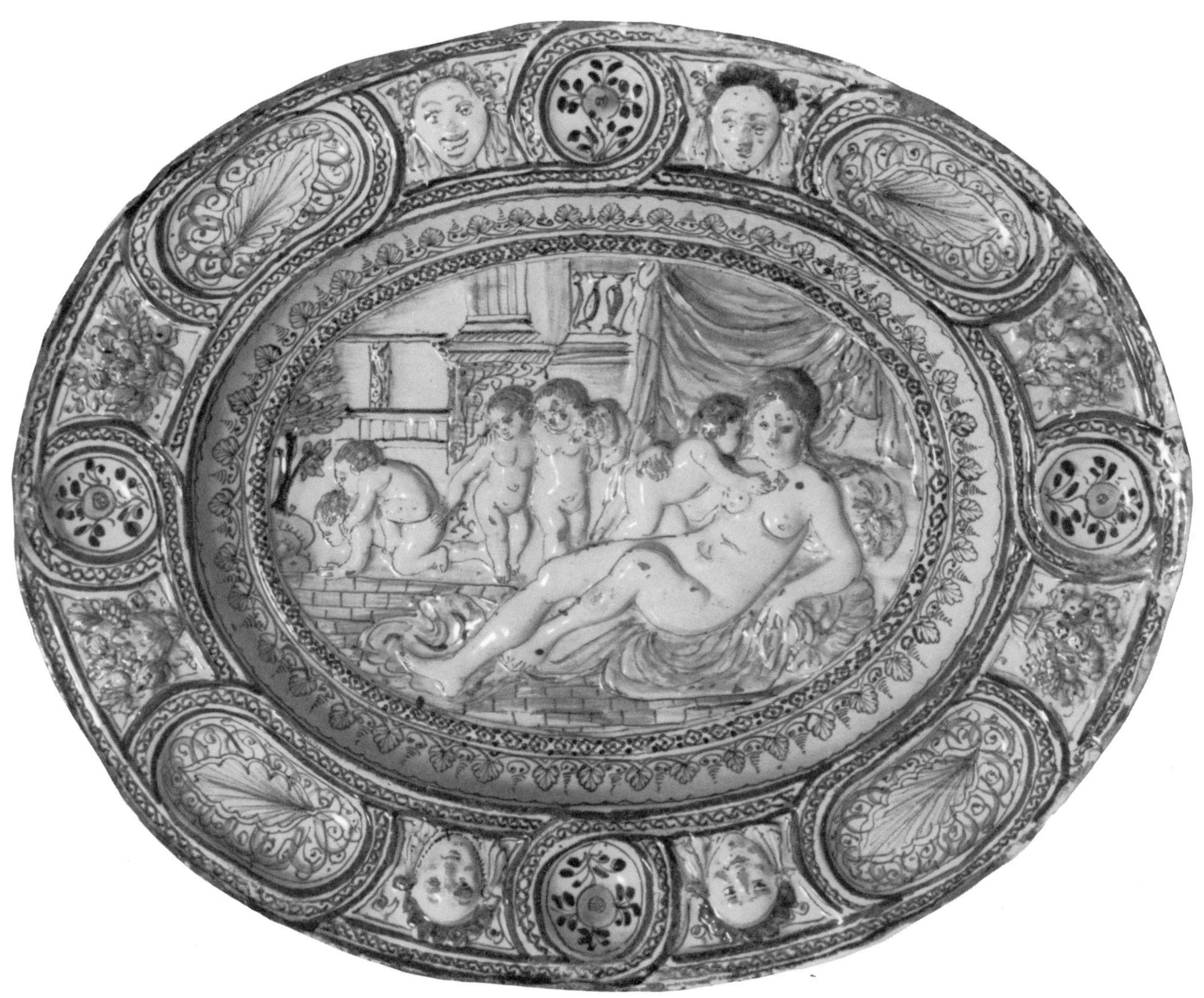

52

from a fresco by Rosso in Francis I's palace at Fontainebleau.

The tin-glazed copies of *La Fécondité* bear dates between 1633 and 1697. They are either painted in blue, or blue touched with yellow, green and brown in recurring styles and patterns. Seascapes and landscapes painted in a fine 'pencilled' style occur in the concave border panels, as do a variety of fruits and flowers, painted in a pseudo-Ming style. The Manchester dish, formerly in the Garner Collection, has flower panels, as does a similar dish now in the Fitzwilliam Museum (Glaisher Collection). The 'pencilled' style occurs again on a London posset pot in the Manchester collection, with the poignant inscription:
WILLIAM·CARTER·AND·ANN / THE·LOVE·I·O·AND·CANNOT·SHOWE·1651

53 *Rembrandt*
(1606–69)

HEADS OF TWO ACTORS *c.* 1635
Dutch; pen and brown ink
10.5 × 12.2 cm ($4\frac{1}{8} \times 4\frac{13}{16}$ in)
Unsigned
Assheton-Bennett Bequest (1979.494)

In 1631–32 Rembrandt moved permanently to Amsterdam and set up as a portrait painter establishing his reputation with the *Anatomy Lesson of Dr. Tulp*. His output was prodigious and, in the course of a long career, he produced 1500–2000 drawings over and above his many paintings.

The speed with which the pen touched the paper can be sensed in this vivid sketch, probably done on the spot. It is datable *c.* 1635 and is probably one of a series of studies of actors, possibly members of an English troupe who frequently performed in Amsterdam. Rembrandt often depicted himself and his sitters in exotic costumes and was no doubt attracted by the actors' theatrical and flamboyant garb.

54 *Jan van Goyen*
(1596–1656)

WINTER SCENE WITH A SLEDGE IN THE FOREGROUND AND FIGURES GATHERING ROUND A TENT ON THE ICE 1653
Dutch; oil on panel
27.9 × 43.1 cm (11 × 17 in)
Signed (b., in centre): *VG 1653.*
Assheton-Bennett Bequest (1979.459)

Van Goyen, born at Leyden but working from *c.* 1632 chiefly in the Hague, was one of the leading exponents of the 'tonal' phase of Dutch landscape painting which began in the late 1620s and 1630s. In such paintings, variegated local colours and individual details were subordinated to an almost monochromatic colour scheme and a broad handling: the landscape was treated as a whole, to create a unified atmosphere, with simple compositions dominated by large areas of sky.

This is a late work by van Goyen, painted only three years before his death. It is a magnificent example, in excellent condition. Using a colour scheme restricted to browns, greys and creams, he achieved the effect of a dull winter afternoon, with pale light breaking through grey clouds, and reflections glinting in the ice beneath the huddled figures. The effect of veiled shifting cloud was conveyed by the use of thin paint, letting the ground of the panel shine through the brushstrokes. On the trees at the right the paint has been trailed casually on to the surface, and throughout one can follow the movement of the artist's brush. Van Goyen was also a prolific draughtsman and made hundreds of drawings from nature in a similar vivid and rapidly executed style.

Though a successful and respected artist, he was constantly travelling, often to avoid financial troubles. He died insolvent, having speculated in land and tulips as well as in art dealing.

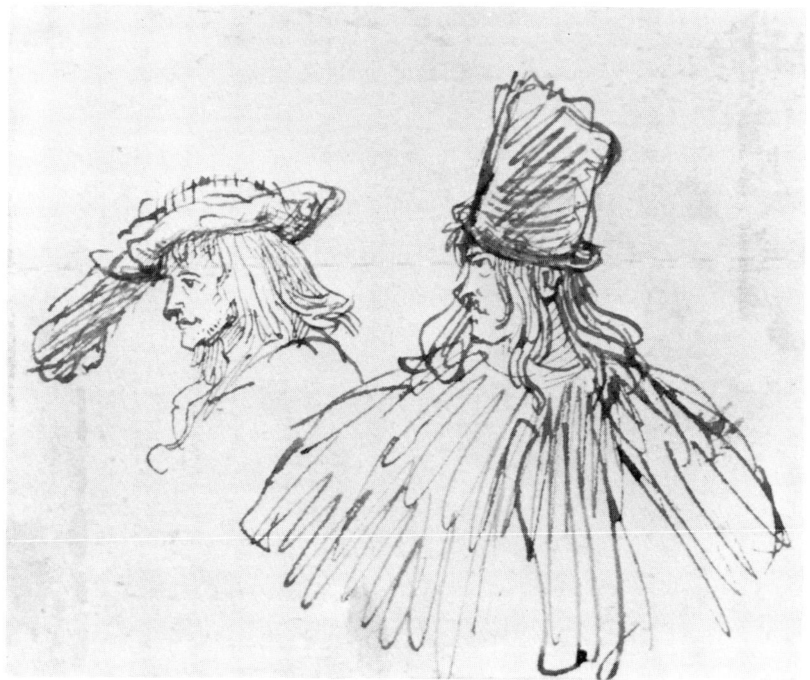
53

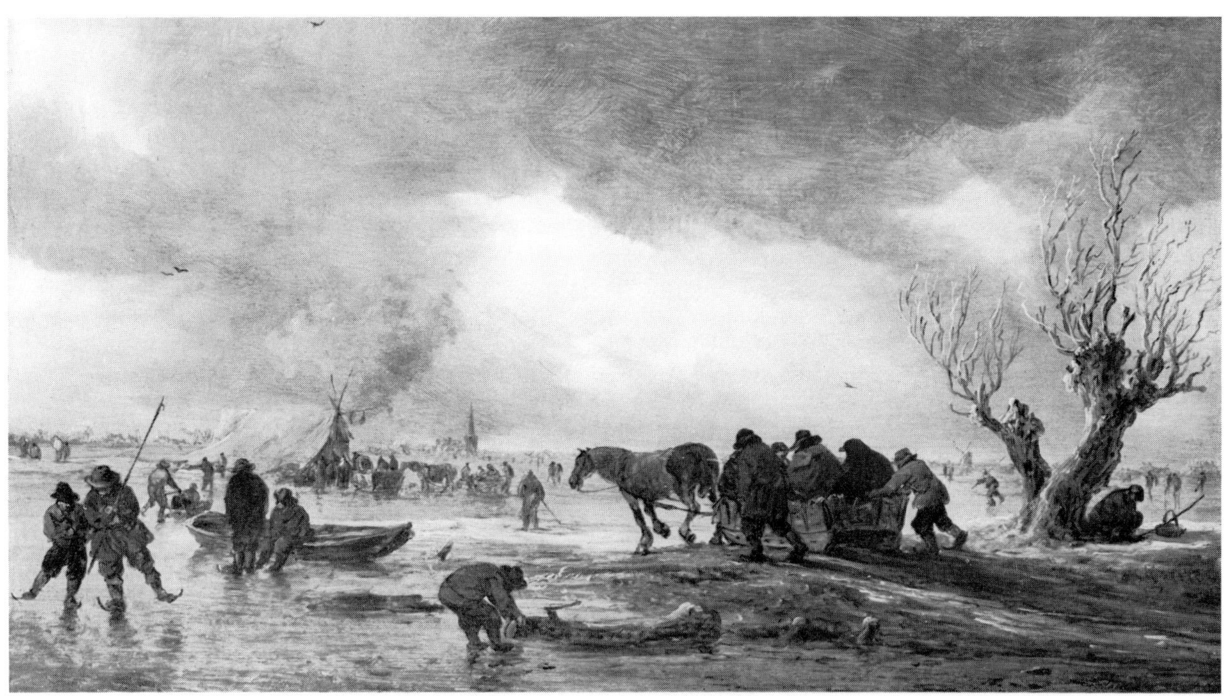

54

55 *Jacob van Ruisdael*

(1628/9–82)

A STORM OFF THE DUTCH COAST

Dutch; oil on canvas
85.3 × 100.4 cm ($33\frac{5}{8} \times 39\frac{9}{16}$ in)
Signed (b.r.c.): *Ruisdael*
Presented by the National Art-Collections Fund from the E. E. Cook Collection (1955.124)

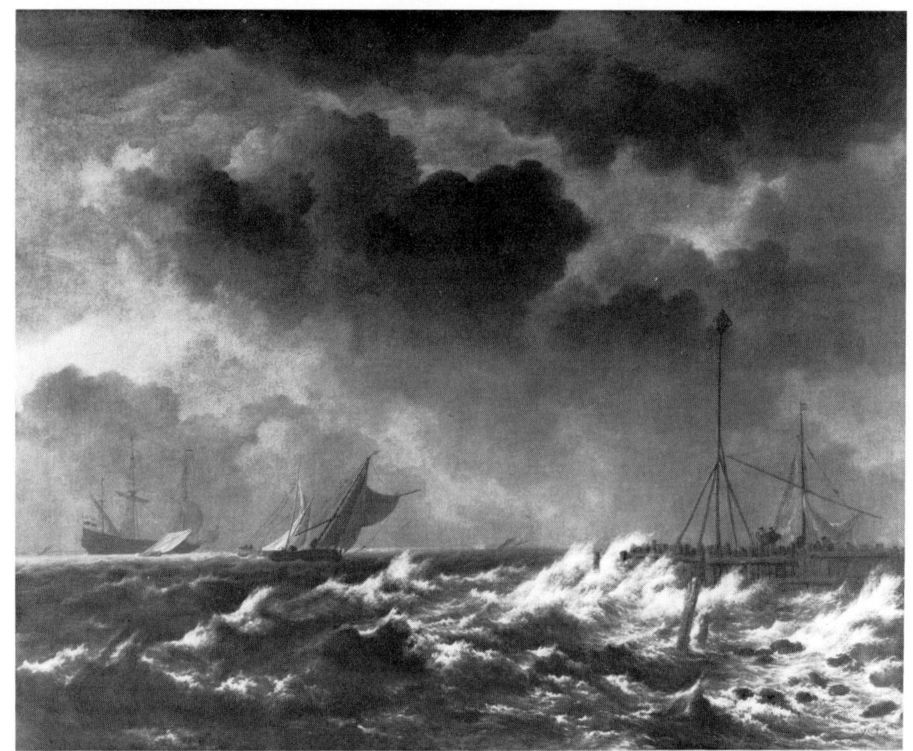

55

Ruisdael's contribution to Dutch landscape painting was to invest it with heroic, dramatic qualities, and his later works are dominated by a mood of melancholy grandeur. Born at Haarlem, he was at first taught by his father and uncle Salomon. He first worked at Haarlem and from *c.* 1657 in Amsterdam. He painted beach and river scenes, forests, waterfalls and the sea. About thirty of his seascapes are known today. None of them are dated, but they all seem to have been painted after 1660, late in his career. There are no calm seas among them.

This stormy sea is one of a group

sharing similar elements: a large area of sky with threatening clouds, waves breaking against a jetty or wooden posts, sailing boats leaning over at perilous angles, and sometimes in the background a distant view of land or, as here, a stately man-of-war. Others are in the Boston Museum of Fine Arts, the National Gallery, London, the National Gallery of Ireland, and the Staatliche Museen, Berlin. In the Manchester picture, there are tiny figures on the jetty at the right, pointing at the sailing boats, but the ships and figures occupy a relatively small area: the scene is dominated by the dark clouds moving across the sky and the light catching the surf of the waves as they crash against the jetty. Apart from the brown sail in the centre, the palette is restricted to sombre blues and greys. In its mood of foreboding, Ruisdael's storm anticipates the romantic movement of the early 19th century, with its concern for the powerlessness of man, confronted with the forces of nature.

56 *Willem Kalf*

(1619–93)

STILL LIFE: FRUIT, GOBLET AND SALVER

Dutch; oil on canvas
58.9 × 50.7 cm ($23\frac{1}{8}$ × $20\frac{1}{16}$ in)
Signed (b.l.): *W. KALF.*
Assheton-Bennett Bequest (1979.468)

Willem Kalf was master of the *pronk* still life (*pronk* is Dutch for ostentation). The taste for showy pictures of tables loaded with precious silver and glass came naturally to rich Amsterdam merchants, and in the mid-17th century succeeded in vogue the more frugal 'breakfast pieces'.

This is a work from Kalf's later period. The crowded opulence of his early pictures has been toned down to create an impression of discreet luxury, and the eye is concentrated on a small number of choice objects. On a silver platter of half-peeled fruit is a fruit-knife with a mother-of-pearl handle and a *roemer* (a Dutch wine glass of the period) of red wine, its broad stem decorated with raspberry *prunts* (impressed relief motifs). The tall glass holding white wine is known as a flute. A Turkish carpet is thrown casually on the table, with an orange and a lemon resting on it. The fruit on the plate, with the orange leaf and the twist of lemon peel, give an impression of immediacy. Despite the seemingly casual asymmetry, the objects are carefully arranged, and the deliberately placed accents of light set against a dark background create an air of mystery like that in a Rembrandt. Though the surface textures are beautifully realised—the softness of the carpet, the glitter of precious materials and the almost tangible lemon peel—Kalf, foreshadowing Chardin, captures the essence of the objects, transforming the material world into something spiritual.

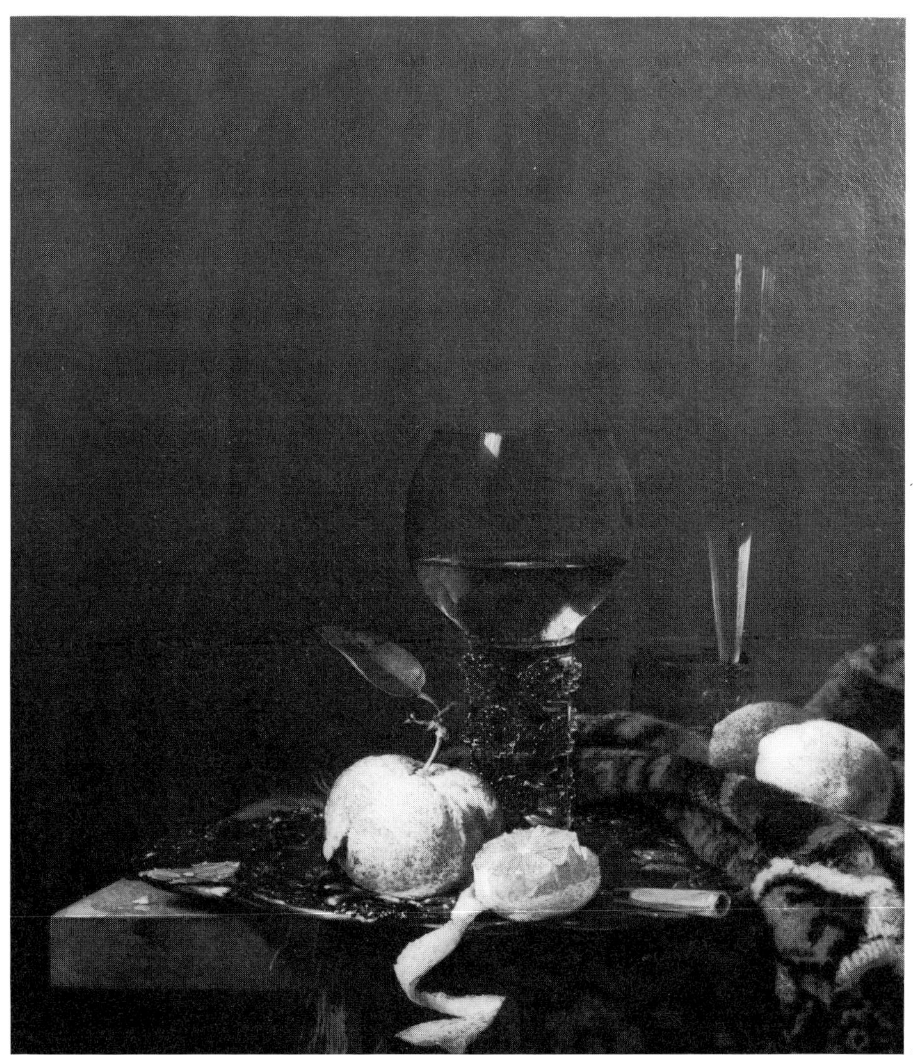

56

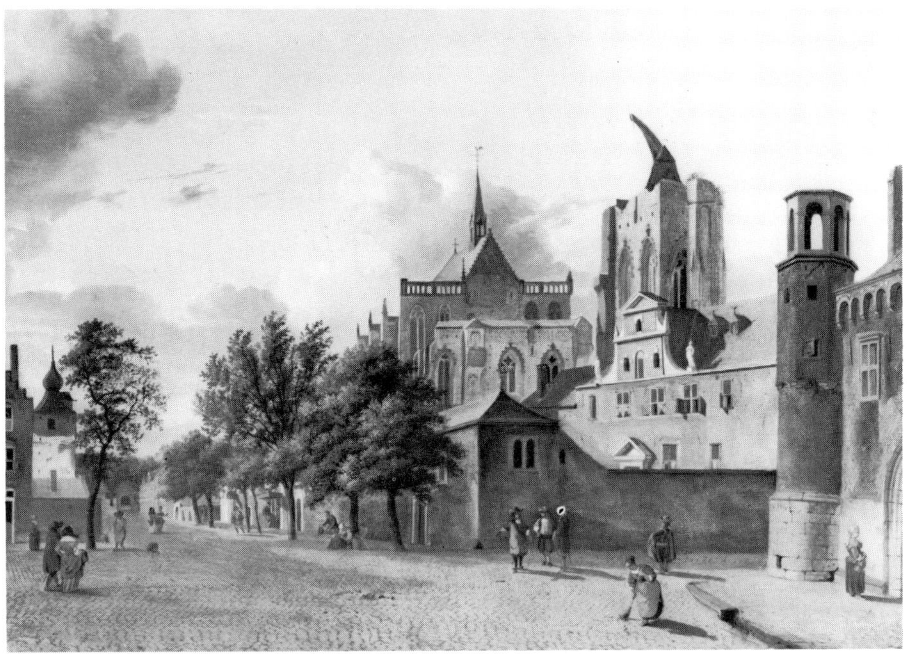

58

57 *Gerard Ter Borch*

(1617–81) *pl. 4*

HENDRIK CASIMIR II, PRINCE OF NASSAU-DIETZ (1657–96) 1670

Dutch; oil on canvas
33.4 × 27.8 cm (13⅛ × 10 15/16 in)
Signed (r. below painting): *GTB* (mon)
Inscr: *AETATIS 12 / 1670.*
Assheton-Bennett Bequest (1979.447)

Prince Hendrik Casimir II of Nassau-Dietz was twelve when he had his portrait painted in 1670, according to the inscription. He was thirteen on 18 January 1670, so the portrait must have been painted just before his birthday. Responsibility had come early to him, for in 1664, whilst still a small child, he had become governor of the provinces of Friesland, Groningen and Drente, under the guardianship of his mother. When he grew up, he became jealous of his cousin, Prince William III of Orange, who was captain-general of the Dutch armies and later became King of England. During the 1672 war with France they quarrelled violently. It is remarkable how Ter Borch has brought out in the portrait of the youth the extremely difficult character of the future ruler. He does not look as if he enjoyed posing for the artist.

Ter Borch's work is distinguished for its exquisite nicety in the painting of rich stuffs, and he has beautifully realised the little prince's elegant costume, with its elaborate bows of salmon-pink ribbon, its silver embroidery and the ostrich feathers of his hat resting on the red velvet tablecloth.

This Dutch artist is best known for his genre scenes, but he also advanced the art of portraiture. In the 1640s he achieved fame with his miniature portraits, and in the 1650s developed a new type of small full-length portrait, as well as the kind of three-quarter length seen here; these achieve a delicacy of psychological penetration rare in many full-size portraits.

58 *Jan van der Heyden*

(1637–1712)

A STREET IN COLOGNE WITH THE UNFINISHED CATHEDRAL IN THE CENTRE 1694

Dutch; oil on panel
31.7 × 40.5 cm (12¼ × 16 in)
Signed (b.r. on base of gate tower): *I V Heyden f. 1694.*
Assheton-Bennett Bequest (1979.463)

Van der Heyden, described by John Constable's friend Archdeacon Fisher as 'the man who painted brick buildings so minutely', was renowned for his street scenes, which combine crisp detail with a sense of space remarkable for such a small format. In this view of Cologne, seen in the clear morning sunshine, figures stroll beneath the trees, whilst a woman with a broom sweeps the cobblestones. The scene is dominated by the cathedral, begun in the 13th century but left half-finished in the mid-16th century. The Gothic tower, with a large crane on top of it, was left incomplete in about 1450 and the crane remained a Cologne landmark until 1868. Van der Heyden has even painted the weeds growing from the ragged stonework.

The panel is one of several variants of the same subject, others being in the Hermitage, Leningrad, the National Gallery, London, and the Wallace Collection, London. The Manchester picture, which is signed and dated 1694, is a simplified version of the Wallace picture, with different figures, and is probably the last of the group. The figures in the variants may be by different painters: those in the Manchester picture are probably by Eglon van der Neer (1634–1703). In all the paintings, not only do the figures differ, but there are minor changes in the detail of the Cathedral, and the surrounding buildings are completely altered. Though van der Heyden sees without prettification, he embellishes the truth: he painted several architectural fantasies which deceptively combine in one picture buildings from different places. Van der Heyden's interest in streets and buildings was extremely practical, for he was involved in projects to improve street-lighting and fire-fighting in Amsterdam.

59 *Jan van Huysum*

(1682–1749)

STILL LIFE: FLOWERS AND FRUIT

Dutch; oil on panel
88.9 × 67.5 cm (35 × 26⅝ in)
Signed (b.l. on table, each side of fallen carnation): *Jan van Huysum f.*
Assheton-Bennett Bequest (1979.467)

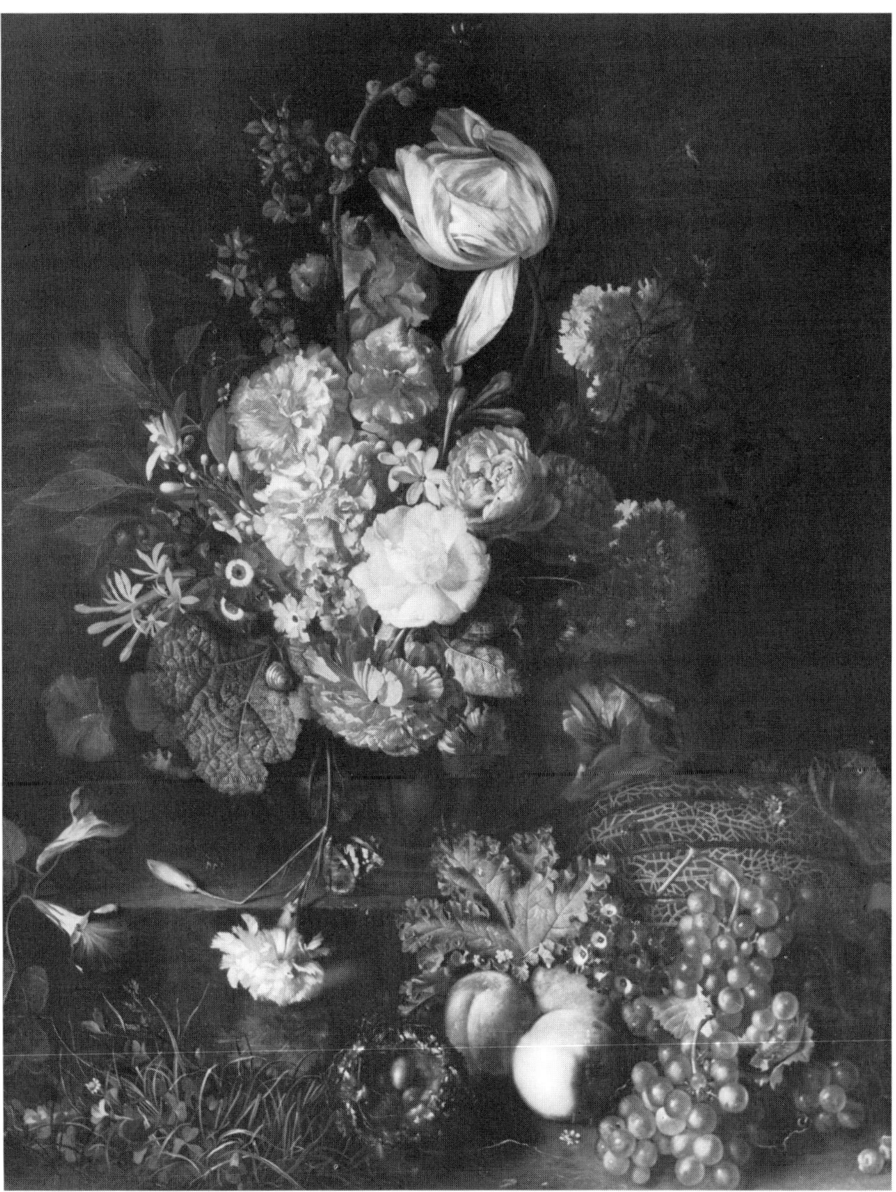

59

Van Huysum was called by his contemporaries 'the phoenix of all flower painters' and his work was sought after by collectors and commanded high prices. Born in Amsterdam in 1682, his art clearly belongs to the 18th century; his asymmetrical compositions have a rococo grace and freedom, unlike the stiffer bouquets of the earlier 17th-century painters. Though he shared the Dutch passion for botanical accuracy, in common with many Dutch flower painters he included in the same picture plants which flower at different seasons.

Here, the flowers and fruit are highlighted against a dark green background and painted with an almost metallic touch. The fruits in the right foreground include grapes, peaches and a melon, with a spray of primulas and forget-me-nots. A clump of grasses to the left of the bird's nest includes clover leaves and a daisy, and a convolvulus creeps in at the left. But the eye is drawn to the luxuriant bouquet in the centre, consisting of white and pink old-fashioned roses, with, at the top, a large white tulip streaked with scarlet. Around are arranged stephanotis, gentians and hollyhocks. Closer inspection reveals Peacock, Red Admiral and Small Tortoiseshell butterflies, snails, beetles and caterpillars crawling on the blooms, while some of the leaves glisten with dewdrops.

60 *Bowl*

Tin-glazed earthenware decorated in blue, yellow and brown, in the centre a lion fighting a leopard, outside a landscape with classical buildings.
Spanish (Talavera de la Reine), *c.* 1660
Diameter: 37 cm (14½ in)
Leicester Collier Bequest (1917.323)

Pottery made in the 16th and 17th centuries at Talavera de la Reine in the province of Castile was very different in style and treatment to the lustred Hispano-Moresque wares. By the mid-

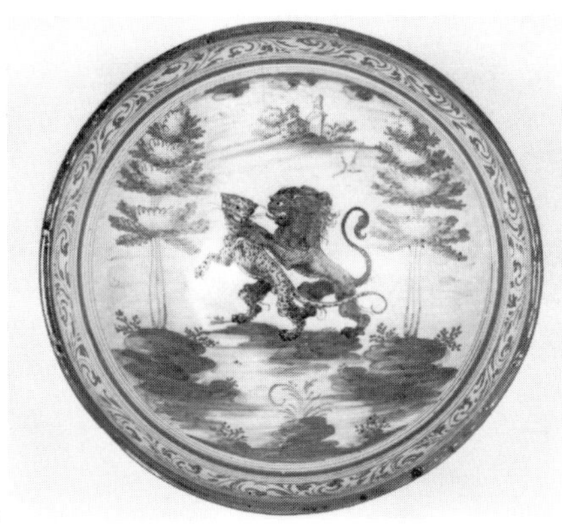

60

16th century there were over 200 workers employed at eight potteries in Talavera. The products won the approval of Philip II (1556–98); in 1572 he presented 359 pieces to the monastery at the Escorial, especially designed for the refectory and pharmacy.

This large bowl is characteristic of the products from the mid-17th century, when birds, animals and hunting scenes were favourite types of decoration. Talavera pottery was frequently referred to in 17th-century Spanish literature, especially in the writings of Lope de Vega (1562–1635). Large quantities of it were exported to the Spanish colonies in the New World, especially Mexico, where it influenced the native ceramic industry.

61 *Bowl and Cover*

Lead crystal glass
English, 1725–50
Height: 22.5 cm ($8\frac{7}{8}$ in)
Lloyd Roberts Bequest (1920.1007)

Manchester's European glass collection well illustrates the best of English late 17th-, 18th- and early 19th-century lead crystal, and contains some unusual pieces. The finest of these is this two-handled sweetmeat bowl and cover, blow-moulded (including the rib ornament) into eight compartments, each engraved with a different flower. The bowl's shape is unlike that of German engraved and covered cups of the early 18th century, and places it conveniently between them and English blow-moulded pieces of the same date; the latter have a robust baroque quality and derive from glass attributed to George Ravenscroft (1632–83), the leading English glassmaker of the 17th century who perfected the process of making lead glass. The decoration is exceptionally precise, clearly influenced by contemporary German wheel-engraving and not usually found on a moulded glass of such quality. The choice of engraved motifs is quite English, since German and Bohemian engraving consisted of heraldic, religious and landscape scenes.

62 *Bread Basket*

Silver
English (London), hallmark for 1731–32, maker's mark for Paul de Lamerie.
Length: 38.5 cm ($15\frac{1}{4}$ in)
Assheton-Bennett Bequest (1979.561)

Silver bread or cake baskets had been known since the early 17th century, but only became a more frequent, albeit somewhat extravagant, piece of domestic plate in the second quarter of the 18th century. This fine early example is based on a subtle rococo conceit, whereby the semi-precious metal is made to resemble humble basket work. The base is decorated with

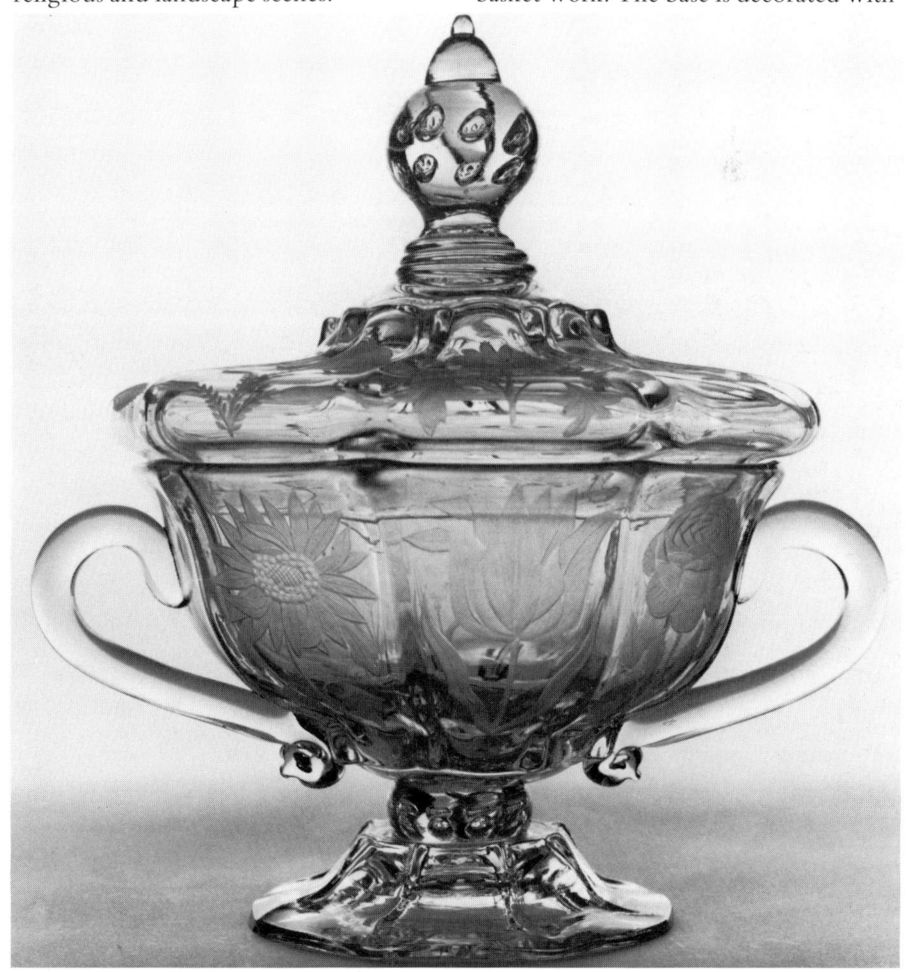

61

an engraved coat of arms surrounded by chased wicker trellis work, *rocaille* and scrollwork, while the sides and rim consist of interlacing curved and grooved strands with cast rosettes and *faux* string handles. The existence of a small number of identical examples made by de Lamerie in the 1730s suggests that this was a highly successful model.

Paul de Lamerie (1688–1751) is often considered the finest English rococo goldsmith, on account of his technical brilliance and great sense of design. At this period his clients were charged approximately eight shillings per ounce for the silver, making this basket (56 ozs) about £22, with perhaps an additional £3 3s for engraving a coat of arms. His client was Thomas, second Baron Southwell, whom Doctor Johnson described as 'the highest man without insolence that I was ever in company with; the most *qualitied* I ever saw.'

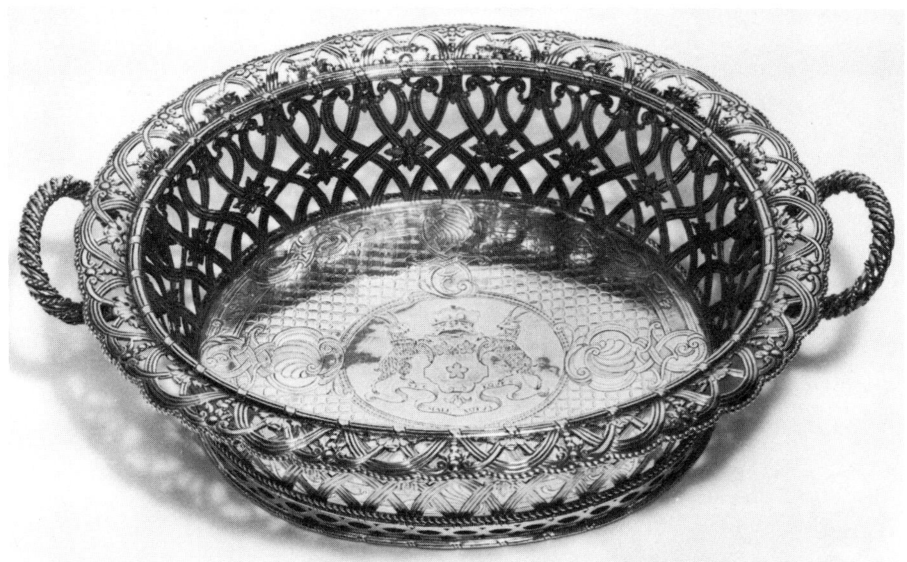

62

63 *Two Teapots*

KER TEAPOT (left)
Gold
Scottish (Edinburgh), hallmark for 1736–37, maker's mark for James Ker.
Height: 14.6 cm (5¾ in)
Assheton-Bennett Bequest (1979.562)

WILLAUME TEAPOT (right)
Silver
English (London), hallmark for 1706–7, maker's mark for David Willaume.
Height: 15.6 cm (6⅛ in)
Assheton-Bennett Bequest (1979.328)

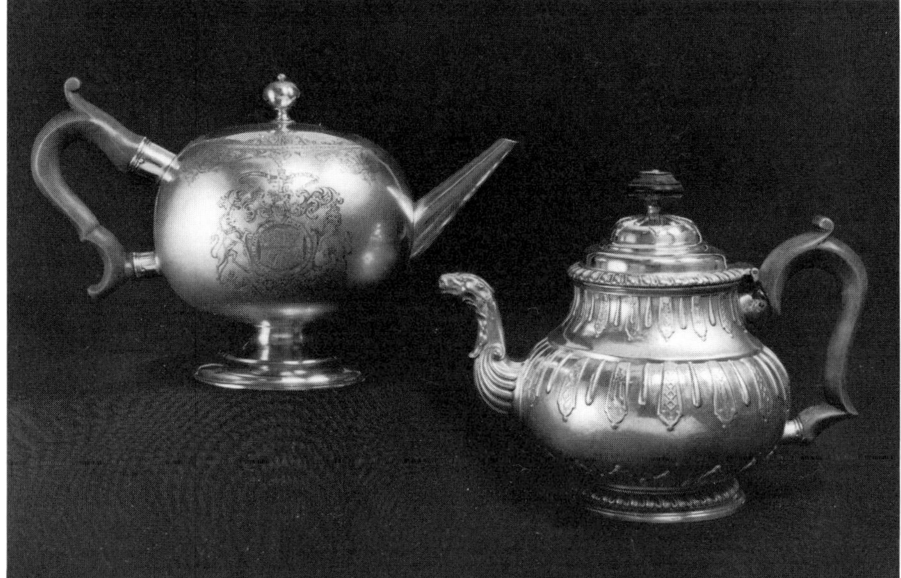

63

The early years of the 18th century saw a vigorous revival in silver design and production, led by the emigré Huguenot goldsmiths, forced to leave France after the Revocation of the Edict of Nantes (1685). They brought with them new techniques and designs which forced British workers to follow their lead, although this was not achieved without a struggle. One of the first to become 'free' of the Goldsmiths' Company was David Willaume (1658–*c.* 1741). His teapot (right) displays some of the most characteristic features of Huguenot plate: the monumental scale, the applied cut card work in the form of three rows of alternate lambrequins and straps, and the spout cast in the shape of an animal's head.

Although Queen Anne teapots are generally pear-shaped or octagonal, spherical and ovoid designs followed slightly later and were particularly favoured in Scotland. The gold teapot by James Ker (fl. 1723–*c.* 1748) was won as a prize in the Royal Race at Leigh near Edinburgh by *Legacy* in 1736. It was not particularly unusual at this period for teapots to be offered as trophies instead of the more usual two-handled cup and cover. The austere shape of this piece is offset by the flamboyantly carved handle and its magnificent engraving with, on one side, the Royal Arms used by George II in Scotland, and, on the other, a racehorse with jockey up. Another Ker piece of the following year is in the collection of the Earl of Rosebery.

64 *The Tatton Cup*

Silver gilt *pl. 3*
English (London), unmarked, *c.* 1760
Engraved with the arms of the Tatton family of Wythenshawe.
Height: 37.5 cm (14¾ in)
Purchased with the Assheton-Bennett Bequest Fund (1978.139)

This unmarked cup has been conclusively shown to be the work of the royal goldsmith Thomas Heming (fl. 1745–83). The arms and crest are those of the Tatton family of Wythenshawe Hall, near Manchester (now part of Manchester City Art Galleries). The cup probably came into their possession some considerable time after having been made, as the family were then known for their parsimony.

The naturalistic details and the use of asymmetrical lines, so characteristic of the exuberance of the rococo style, are employed here to display the virtuosity of the goldsmith's technique and his ingenuity of design. Cast trailing vine tendrils and fruits had been used as part of the decorative repertoire of leading goldsmiths since the 1730s, notably by Paul de Lamerie (1688–1751), George Wickes (1698–1761) and Paul Crespin (1694–1770). The rocky naturalistic ornament of the base, deriving from French sources, was also used by these earlier goldsmiths. The brilliantly-cast figures of Pan and a Bacchante on the handles, which also appear on a number of similar cups by Heming, are derived from those on the massive wine cistern by Charles Kändler (fl. 1725–50) commissioned in 1734 for Empress Anne of Russia and modelled by J. M. Rysbrack (1694–1770).

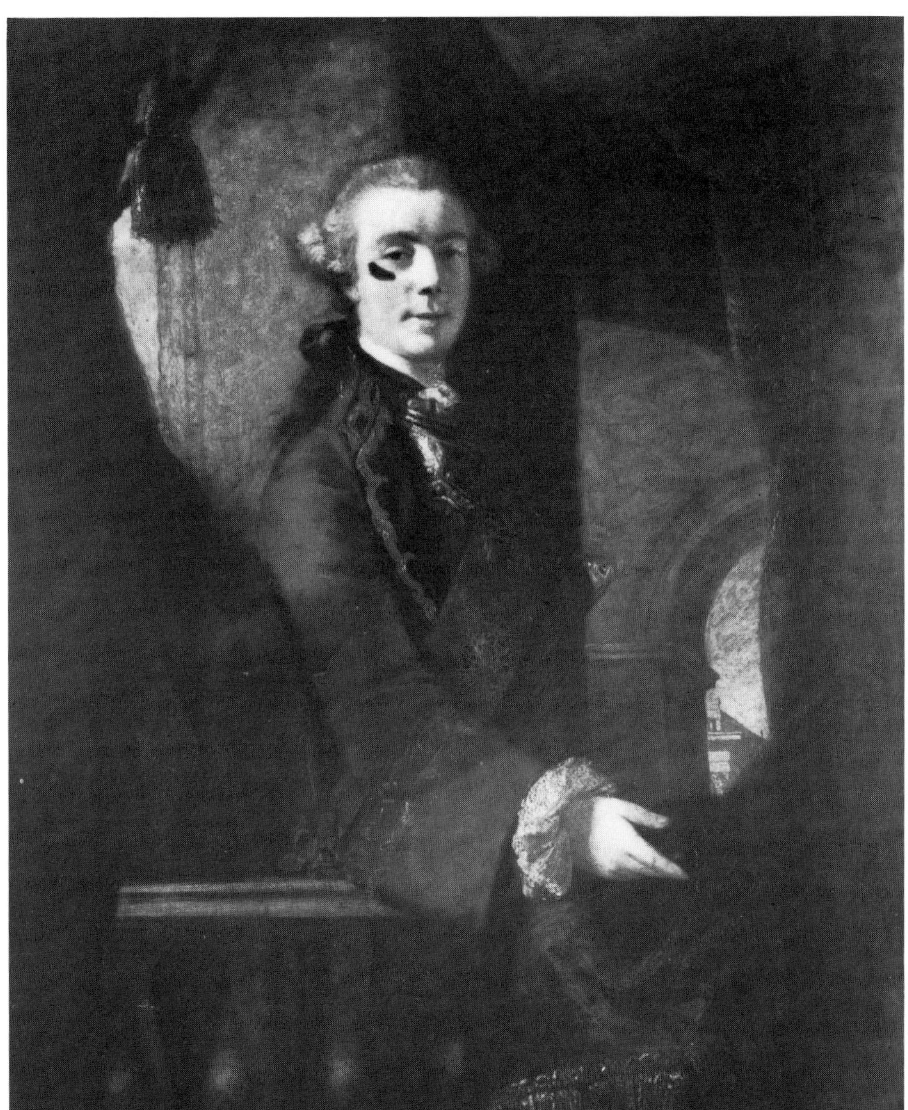
65

65 *Sir Joshua Reynolds*

(1723–92)

CHARLES, 9TH EARL CATHCART
1753–55
English; oil on canvas
124 × 99 cm (48$\frac{13}{16}$ × 39 in)
Unsigned
Purchased from Major General The Earl Cathcart with the aid of a Government grant (through the Victoria and Albert Museum) and the National Heritage Memorial Fund (1981.36)

Charles, 9th Earl Cathcart (1721–76), the eldest son of his father, succeeded in 1740. He began a distinguished military career serving under Lord Stair and later

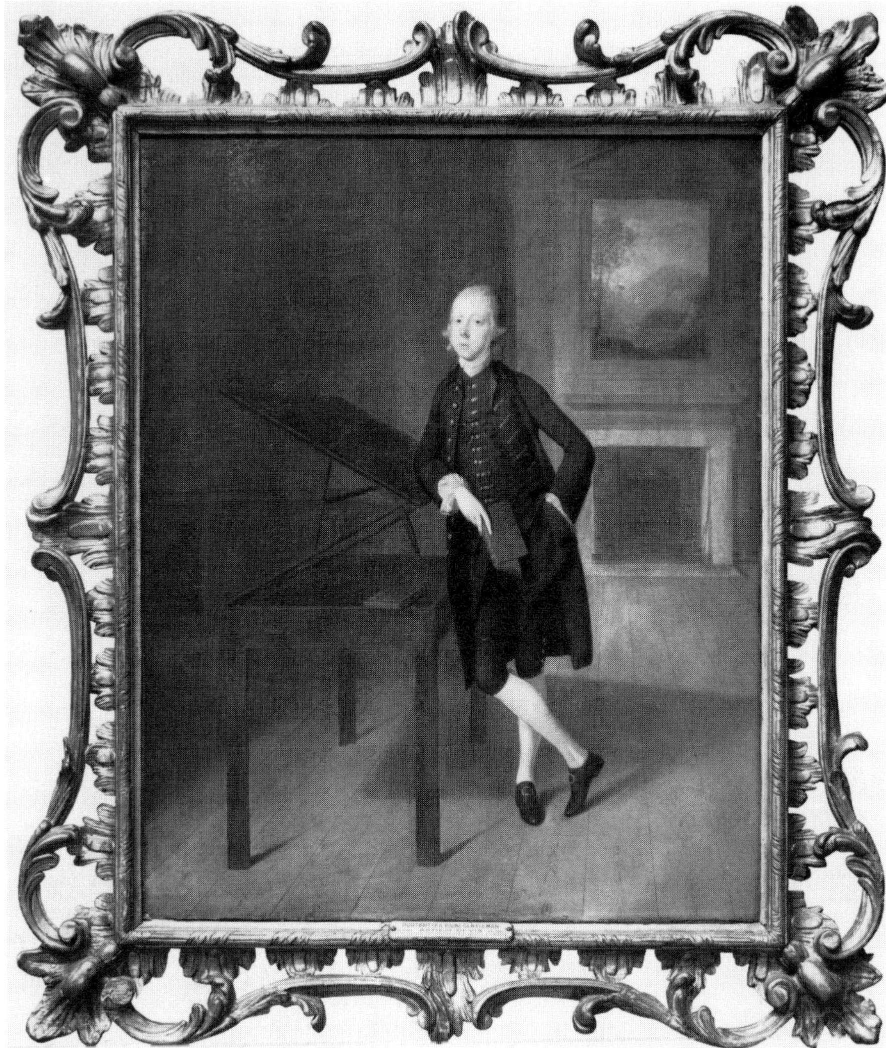

66

was aide-de-camp to the Duke of Cumberland. He fought at the battle of Fontenoy in 1745 where he was shot through the face. Fontenoy, near Tournai in Flanders, was the scene of a great battle between France and the allied troops of Austria, Saxony and England during the Wars of the Austrian Succession. The English were defeated and Lord Cathcart's only brother was killed. Subsequently, the Earl became popularly known as 'Cathcart of Fontenoy' and is portrayed wearing a black silk lunette patch on his right cheek covering his Fontenoy scar, in which he took great pride. In 1763 he was made a Knight of the Thistle and from 1766 to '71 he served as Ambassador to the Russian Imperial Court.

In October 1753 Lord Cathcart wrote: 'Again with Mr. Reynolds, and was disagreeably surprised with the figure. After some reasoning he came to the opinion that it would not do, I breakfasted with him and stood to him a good while. I thought it was much improved, and he was extremely satisfied with the alterations so we parted in great good humour.' The portrait appears to have taken two more years to complete, as Reynolds' sitters book for 1755 shows that Lord Cathcart sat to the artist on 25 February and 9 April.

The portrait is a pair to that of *Jane Hamilton, Countess Cathcart (1726–1771) with her daughter Jane (1754–1791)*, signed and dated 1755 (also owned by Manchester City Art Galleries). The source for Lord Cathcart's distinctive pose is probably a mezzotint engraving of 1739 by John Fowler after Hudson's portrait of *Henry Clarke*. The pose is closely paralleled by Alessandro Longhi's portrait of *Carlo Goldoni* in the Museo Correr, Venice.

The Galleries also possess Reynolds' portraits of *Lady Anstruther* (*c.* 1763) and *Admiral Lord Hood* (*c.* 1783).

66 *Arthur Devis*

(1711–87)

A YOUNG GENTLEMAN AT A DRAWING TABLE 1761

English; oil on canvas
63.5 × 50.9 cm (25 × $20\frac{1}{16}$ in)
Signed (b.l. on skirting board): *Ar . . .* [illeg.]/*1761*
Purchased (1928.89)

Devis came from Preston and is thought to have been a pupil of the Antwerp-born artist Peter Tillemans. He specialised in portraiture, either single figures or conversation pieces, and his patrons came mostly from the country gentry. Devis's work has a distinctive charm but is not innovatory. It follows the portrait tradition of Francis Hayman and Bartholomew Dandridge.

The figure in this portrait is treated in Devis's characteristic stiff and doll-like manner: it is known that he used miniature lay figures to help him paint the poses of his sitters. The clothes for such a figure, which belonged to Devis, survive at the Harris Museum and Art Gallery, Preston. The drawing table in the picture probably belonged to Devis, as it appears again in his portrait of the Rev. Edward Foyle. These popular pieces of furniture were introduced early in the century and used by draughtsmen, architects and amateur artists. The unusual sparseness of the room suggests that it is imaginary.

Devis's delightful naive paintings have an immediate appeal. He seems always to have painted on a small scale. The size of his pictures suited the more modest houses of the gentry and squirearchy who commissioned his work. His group portraits never achieved a sense of communication, and his single portraits are often more successful. This example is enhanced by a finely carved contemporary gilt frame.

67 *Richard Wilson*

(1714–82)

A SUMMER EVENING 1764

English; oil on canvas
123.5 × 105.9 cm ($48\frac{5}{8} \times 41\frac{11}{16}$ in)
Signed (b.l. in mon.): *RW 1764*
Purchased from Mrs Clementia Tindal-Carill-Worsley with the aid of a Government grant (through the Victoria and Albert Museum) and the National Art-Collections Fund (1969.182)

A Summer Evening was commissioned in 1764 by John and Deborah Lees for the overmantel in the dining room at their newly-built house, Platt Hall, Manchester. This is confirmed by a letter in Wilson's hand to Mr Lees' agent, James Massey. It reads:

London Dec.r 18. 1764

Dear Sir,

This Day the Landskip was very carefully packt up and sent according to your order directed to Your friend M.r Lees – The Picture represents a Summer Evening, and is Esteemed by the first painters here to be my very best *performance, and have kept a Drawing of it in order to do another for our next exhibition – The Case packing and Carriage to the Inn comes to 12.s which twenty five Guineas makes £26 = 17 = 0. The receipt of Which I leave to my good friend M.r Massey, returning you my hearty thanks for y.r kind remembrance of*

Dear Sir

Y.r Most Obliged
Affectionate Ser.t
R. Wilson.

The Complem.ts usual to the Season attend.

Wilson does not seem to have carried out his intention, as there is no record of a second version being exhibited, and the drawing is now lost. Joseph Farington (1747–1821) referred to both the painting and the letter in his diary for 1 November 1796, reads:

Mr. Carils Worsleys I dined at, at Platt.

An upright landscape of Wilsons is over the chimney piece in the dining room. Mr. Worsley shewed me a letter written by Wilson to Mr. Massey who ordered the

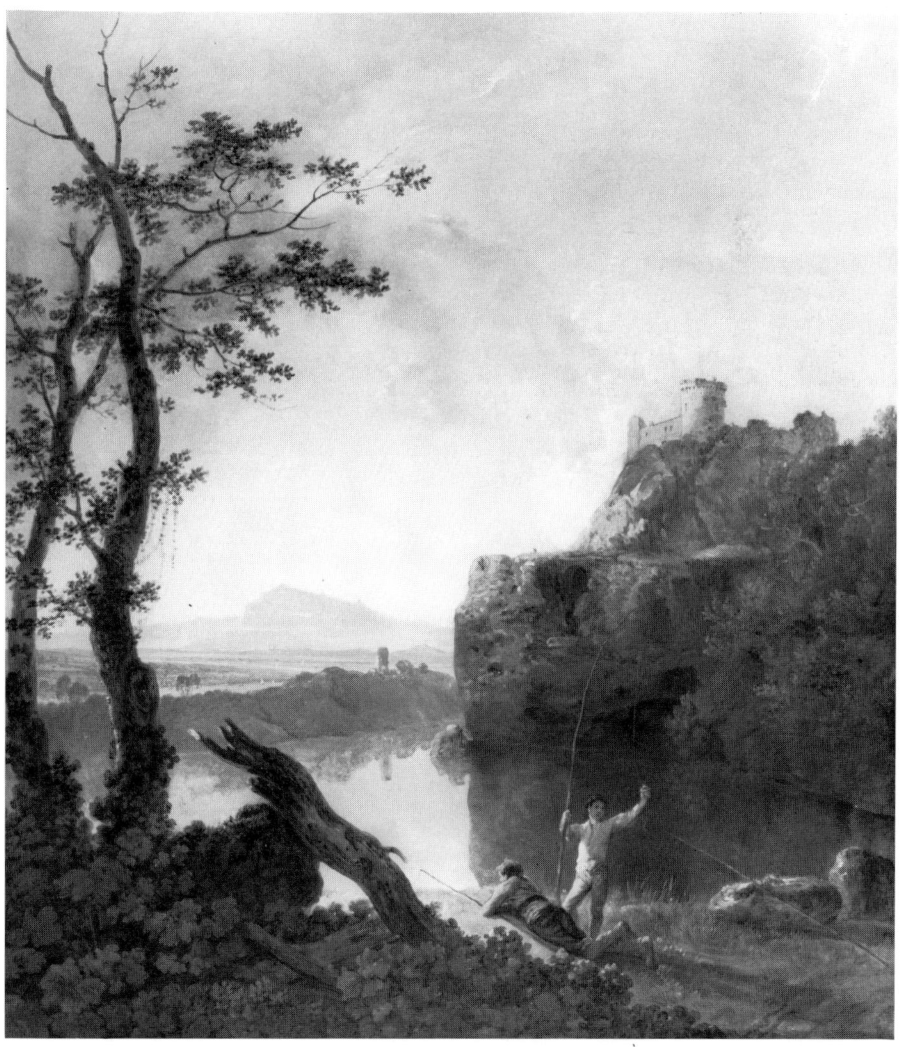

67

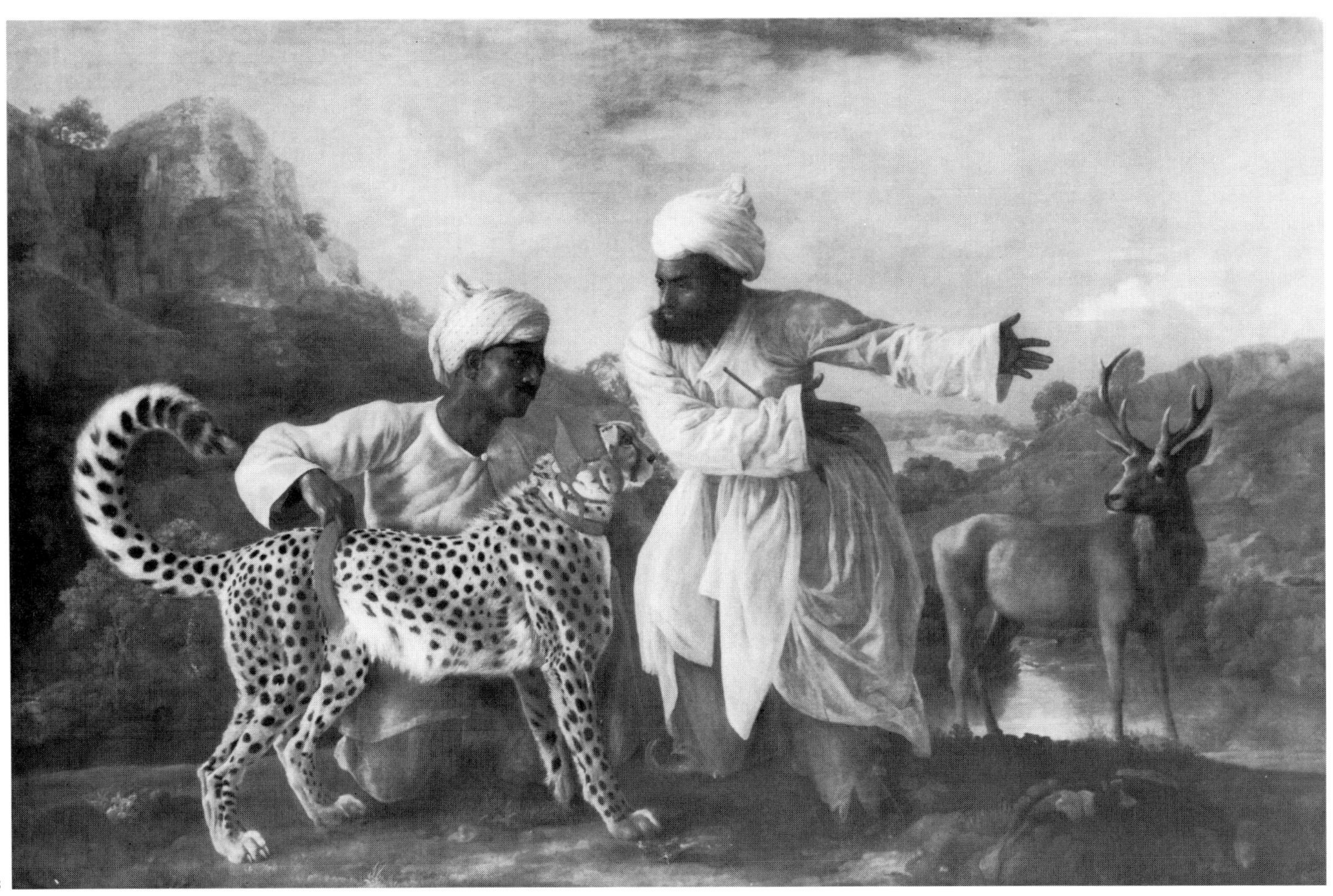

68

picture for Mr. Lee. – The picture is equal to a half length in size, yet Wilson had only 25 guineas for it & the Case & porterage 12s. – This was considerably less than Wilsons price, but Mr. Massey proposed the Commission and between him & Wilson the price was settled. – The picture is slight, but the eye of it beautiful. – Town, a Liverpool Artist, at the desire of Mr. Blundell, has been lately permitted to copy it. Wilsons letter is dated Dec. 28th 1764.

The copy by Charles Towne (1763–1840) does not appear to have survived, although a watercolour copy, probably by one of the Worsley family, is in the Galleries' collection.

A book of designs for the interior of Platt Hall, signed T. Lightoler, shows the dining room, virtually as it is today, with a decorative landscape over the fireplace. The designs are probably by the carver-architect, Thomas Lightoler (fl. 1755–75). The size of the space on the drawing coincides to within a fraction of an inch with *A Summer Evening* and with the wall space in the decorative plasterwork. The source of sunlight in the painting (from the left) corresponds with the daylight in the dining room at Platt, while the rococo plasterwork echoes the asymmetrical flowing lines of the trees to the left. The original colouring of the room (walls textured grey blue, with relief plasterwork in buff parcel gilt) is carefully orchestrated to set off Wilson's palette.

The view in *A Summer Evening* is probably imaginary. The rocky outcrop surmounted by a castle and the flat receding plain suggest that Wilson used ideas taken from his sketches of Italian landscapes. The golden haze pervading the scene evokes the warmth and stillness of a summer evening, accentuated by the unruffled surface of the water and the long shadows cast by the fisherboys. The Gallery boasts four other oil landscapes by Wilson.

68 *George Stubbs*

(1724–1806)

CHEETAH AND STAG WITH TWO INDIANS *c.* 1765

English; oil on canvas
180.7 × 273.3 cm ($71\frac{1}{8} \times 107\frac{5}{8}$ in)
Unsigned
Purchased from the Art Fund with grants from the Government (through the Victoria and Albert Museum) and from the National Art-Collections Fund, Eugene Cremetti Fund (1970.34)

George Stubbs, the animal painter, was a scientist as much as an artist, and made a profound study of animal anatomy. He dissected horses for his book *The Anatomy of the Horse*, and was interested in portraying exotic animals such as monkeys and lions, as well as the horses which were the staple of a sporting painter. Here, the cheetah's sleek body quivers with life, its tawny fur vividly suggested, contrasting with the white silk drapery and turbans of its dark-skinned keepers.

This is an unusual painting for Stubbs on account of both its large size and its subject, with the exotic beast and its native keepers set in a very English 'sublime' landscape, reminiscent of Dovedale. In 1764 the Duke of Cumberland, uncle of George III and Ranger of Windsor Forest, was sent two cheetahs for the menagerie at Windsor. They were a gift from Lord Pigot, Governor of Madras. To demonstrate its hunting skills, one of the cheetahs was confronted with a stag. At the cheetah's third attempt to attack, the stag tossed it some distance. The cheetah at once fled, escaped to the woods and killed a deer. When the Indians eventually retrieved the cheetah, they covered its eyes with a hood and led it to its cage.

The composition is curious, and perhaps not entirely successful, with the figures, gesturing flamboyantly, grouped uncomfortably in the foreground as in a neo-classical low relief. They are set against a very naturalistic three-dimensional landscape. The awkwardness of the image's construction is made up for, however, by the superbly realistic painting of the animals.

69 *Fan*

'Chicken-skin' (fine vellum) leaf with blonde tortoiseshell sticks and guards.
Probably French, *c.* 1750
Height: 28.4 cm ($11\frac{3}{16}$ in)
Purchased (1983.25)

The eighteen sticks are *clouté* (inset) with red gold, in a design of dolphins and grotesque sea-creatures; the guards are *clouté* with foliage, masks, birds and allegorical figures. The leaf is painted in the *trompe l'œil* manner, with a profusion

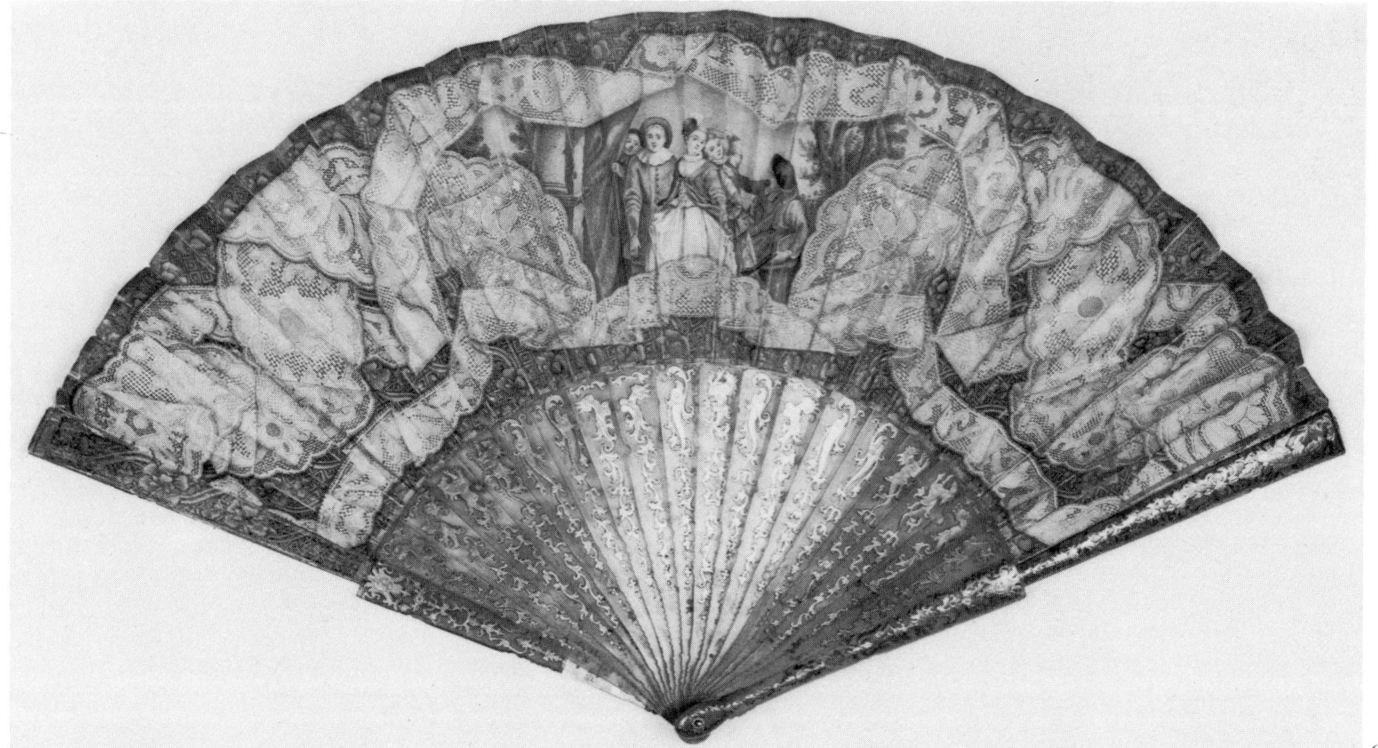

69

of lace spread on a background of purple and gold figured silk. It is possible to identify the lace as a Mechlin or Antwerp bobbin lace of the mid-18th century.

The central vignette is taken from an etching by Jean Antoine Watteau (1684–1721), finished with the burin by Charles Simonneau the elder (1645–1728), who added two quotations, beginning, 'Les habits sont Italiens . . .' This print is also sometimes called *Five Characters from the Commedia dell'arte*. Ettore Camecasca (*The Complete Paintings of Watteau*) suggests that this scene represents the start of a performance, though it may equally well show a moment of stage 'business' being overheard by the eavesdropper behind the curtain. The etching is in reverse from the painting on the fan. Watteau's oil original is in the Rosenheim Collection, Paris, with the (later) title, *Masquerade*.

Characters of the Commedia dell'arte, or, more precisely, players of the Comédie-Italienne, were frequently depicted by Watteau and his follower Nicolas Lancret (1690–1743). The troupe were granted the right to perform in French by Louis XIV, and had their theatre in the Hôtel de Bourgogne, Paris. They became celebrated for their performances of the comedies of Marivaux, in a style said to combine Italian robustness and stagecraft with an elegant wit more suited to the French taste.

The figures on the fan would have been familiar to a theatre-going Parisienne: the *innamorata* in her rakish little hat; Columbine in her Harlequin patterned costume; the clown musician (Le Mezzetin); the old man in a false nose spying behind the curtain (the lawyer, Dr Balanzone, Pantaleone's friend). Most haunting is the melancholy clown, Gilles, a recurrent image in Watteau's work. Gilles and Pierrot are often confused, Gilles being

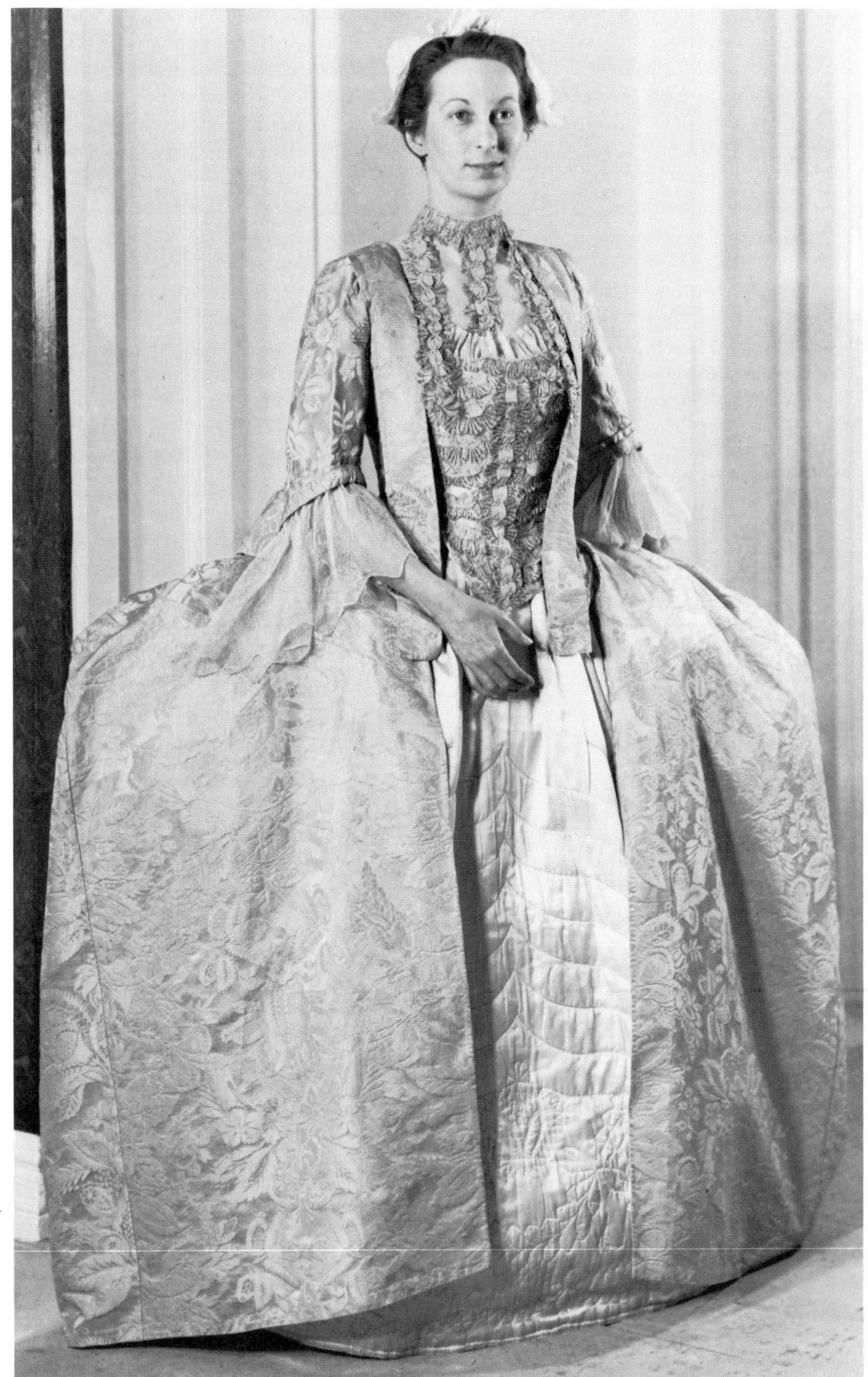

70

seen as a prototype of Pierrot. At this period, Pierrot was the clown of the rival Comédie-Française. It is best to imagine them as aspects of the same stock character, who has come down to us as the sentimental Pierrot, and to reserve the name 'Gilles' for the actor of the Comédie-Italienne.

As is usual, the reverse of the fan is less skilfully painted. The lace appears again, this time on a blue figured silk ground, with reserves of white vellum. A trail of lilac and yellow *ombré* striped ribbon frames a vignette of an Italianate landscape with ruins, painted in blue on white.

The Comédie-Italienne declined in popularity in the mid-18th century, merging with the Opéra-Comique in 1762. Watteau's painting probably dates from *c.* 1717–19, and it is unlikely that it would have been a fashionable subject much later than 1750. This is therefore a relatively early example of the *trompe l'œil* style, which became universally popular in Europe in the 1760s.

Platt Hall has a good representative collection of some 240 fans.

70 *Dress*

Open robe and petticoat, with stomacher and neck ornament. Pink silk damask.
English, reputedly a wedding dress, 2 May 1743
Width of fabric: 51 cm (20 in); 42 cm (16½ in) deep
Purchased (1951.281/5)

The damask, originally of a vivid rose colour, now faded to salmon pink, has a design of leaves, fruits and flowers with trailing vines, all framed by arches. Such formal patterns, symmetrically composed about a vertical axis and today known as 'lace patterns', were in vogue around 1685 to 1730. By the 1740s such designs were largely confined to furnishing fabrics and would have been rather out-of-date for fashionable dress. In today's terms, it had become a design classic, and its formality would have been a prudent choice, suitable for a solemn occasion such as a wedding, especially in a provincial town. The mantua-maker has been careless in cutting the silk; in the right front panel of the skirt the pattern is upside-down.

A dress of this date, complete with its accessories, is extremely rare. The robe has the fashionable form of the 1740s with its skirt supported by the oblong side-hoops which were in vogue throughout the 1740s to '60s, and which are familiar from many portraits by Gainsborough and his contemporaries. The back of this dress is made with the pleats stitched down to a point at the waist, with the waist seam running all round the dress. A more usual form would be the sack, with pleats forming an unbroken line from neck to hem. It is possible that this dress has been altered, but there are no marks of previous pleats.

The robe is worn open, over a white satin quilted petticoat associated with the dress, but not necessarily worn with it originally. Deep pleated wing cuffs are in the fashion, and are shown here with contemporary bobbin net ruffles. Wide turned-back pleats frame the bodice opening, which is filled by a matching stomacher decorated with pink ribbon and silver lace. A ribbon neck ornament (solitaire) with three hanging ribbons, all edged with silver lace, completes the dress.

The model wears a linen cap with bobbin lace trimming, worn as a 'pinner', the lappets pinned to the top of the cap making a charming frame for the face. This fashion, general for indoor use, is often seen in 'conversation pieces'; a frequent subject is the lady of the house taking tea with her family. For a wedding or other great occasion, a more elaborate 'head' of lace might have been worn.

This dress is said to be the wedding dress of Elizabeth Bethall, who married Captain Charles Medcalf (or Metcalf) of the Royal Horse Guards on 2 May 1743 at York. She is supposed to have worn the dress at the York Assembly Rooms in the year after the wedding.

If this is the case, it is the oldest wedding dress in a British collection by exactly one year and twelve days, though it is not as fine as the magnificent embroidered wedding mantua of 1744 in the Victoria and Albert Museum.

71 *Watches and chatelaines*

REPEATER WATCH AND CASE (above)
Gold, the case back in blue enamel set with a cluster of diamond brilliants, the border in green and pink enamel.
English (London), *c.* 1750; the movement by Higgs and Evans (fl. 1780–1822)
Diameter: 4.8 cm (1¾ in)
Lloyd Gift (1947.511)

REPEATER WATCH AND CASE (below)
Silver, the case back with embossed rococo decoration. Verge escapement.
English (London). *c.* 1760; the movement possibly by P. Charleson (fl. 1764)
Diameter: 6.1 cm (2⅜ in)
Lloyd Gift (1947.516)

CHATELAINE
Base metal, gilt, with cast rococo decoration, the equipage consisting of étui, thimble container and bloodstone egg.
English (London), *c.* 1755–60
Overall length: 22.2 cm (8¾ in)
Purchased (1953.357)

The movement and case of the upper watch are consummate examples of the London watchmakers' and jewellers' art; they were made in the last quarter of the 18th century by Higgs and Evans, expressly for the Spanish market. The rich case of the lower watch is embossed, in a rococo reserve, with an allegorical figure of the City of London standing before St. Paul's Cathedral displaying an oval portrait medallion of a hero to the seated Britannia. In the centre background is a palm tree, which may be a reference to the unidentified hero's associations with the Indies.

The chatelaine consists of a serpentine shaped hook-plate cast with a sphinx and putti enclosed by rococo scrolls, three hanging plaques and an étui, all chased with figures, flowers, rococo 'S' and 'C' scrolls on a matted ground. The étui contains scissors, a bodkin, an ivory writing tablet, and a silver pencil of later date. The thimble case, of more symmetrical form, appears to be a little earlier and to date from *c.* 1740. Chatelaines were important daytime jewellery, worn by ladies at the waist.

Such virtuoso examples of the rococo as the silver watch case and gilt chatelaine are reminiscent of the manner of George Michael Moser (1706–83), a German Swiss who came to England and, with a few other artists and craftsmen like the Frenchman H. B. F. Gravelot (1699–1773; in England 1733–46), was responsible for popularising this fantastical alien style. Sir Joshua Reynolds referred to Moser as 'the first gold chaser in the Kingdom'.

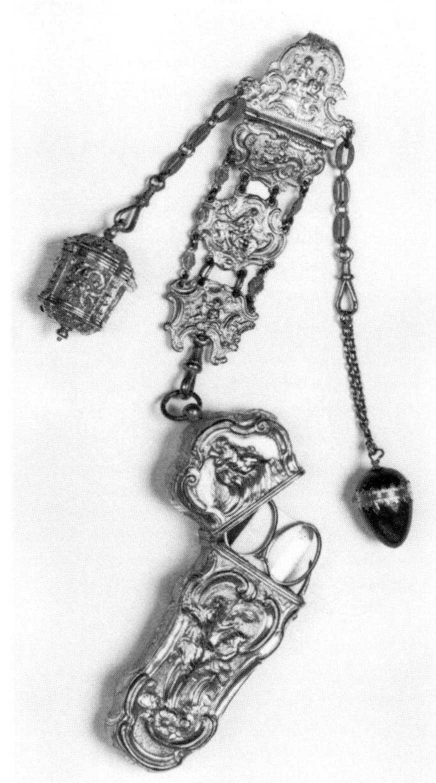

71

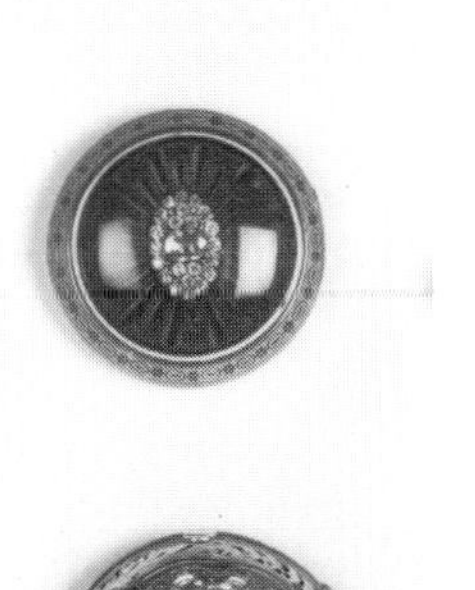

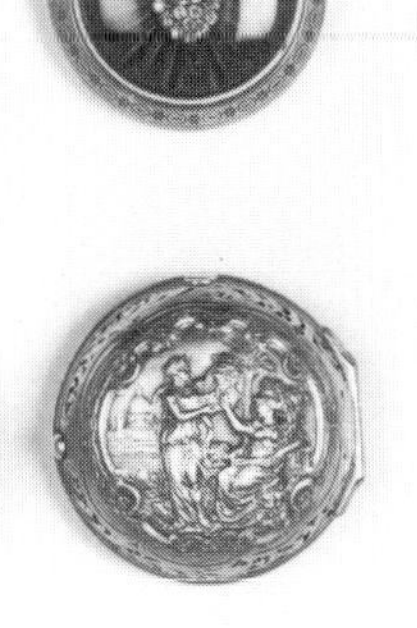

71

72 *Plate*

Soft paste porcelain printed in brick red with *Aeneas and Anchises Fleeing from Troy.*
English (Bow), 1756–58
Diameter: 19.7 cm ($7\frac{3}{4}$ in)
Dykes Bequest (1948.216)

Prints on Bow porcelain were usually executed in black or brick red, and most are in the distinctive style of Robert Hancock (1730–1817) who went on to work at the Worcester factory in 1757. This particular plate shows a print probably engraved by Hancock after a drawing by Hubert Gravelot (1699–1773). The Frenchman Gravelot was instrumental in introducing the rococo style into England. This drawing was one of a series engraved to illustrate John Theobald's translation of the *Aeneid*, Book II, published in 1736.

73 *Casket*

Enamel, decorated with landscapes; inside, two tea caddies and one sugar box, set in chased copper gilt rococo mounts.
English (South Staffordshire), *c.* 1770
Length: 21 cm ($8\frac{1}{4}$ in)
Raby Bequest (1958.470)

Enamels were first made on a commercial scale in England during the 1740s, inspired by French richly jewelled and enamelled gold boxes. The use of copper instead of gold as the base metal gave rise to a flourishing industry producing a wide variety of enamel objects.

The largest area of enamel production was South Staffordshire, centred on Bilston and Wednesbury. Already noted for its metalwork products, by 1745 the region had attracted many French Huguenot craftsmen refugees. Characteristic products were small boxes bearing inscriptions and animal-shaped *bonbonnières.* This richly decorated casket, fully fitted inside, shows the lavish ornament and colours which were often used on larger items or on delicate snuff or patch boxes. The subject matter was often derived from prints and popular books of engravings, such as Robert Sayer's *The Ladies Amusement* (1758–62). In this case the lid appears to derive from a composition by Nicolaes Berghem (1620–83), while the front and sides are taken from Adam Perelle (1638–95).

This is one of a collection of 461 English enamels in the Gallery, bequeathed by Harold Raby, who was also a distinguished numismatist.

74 *English Teapots*

TEAPOT

Salt-glazed stoneware, with moulded crabstock handle and a cannon spout. Applied relief and painted enamel decoration in black, blue, pink and green.
Inscribed: *Fred. Prussiae Rex, Semper Sublimis.*

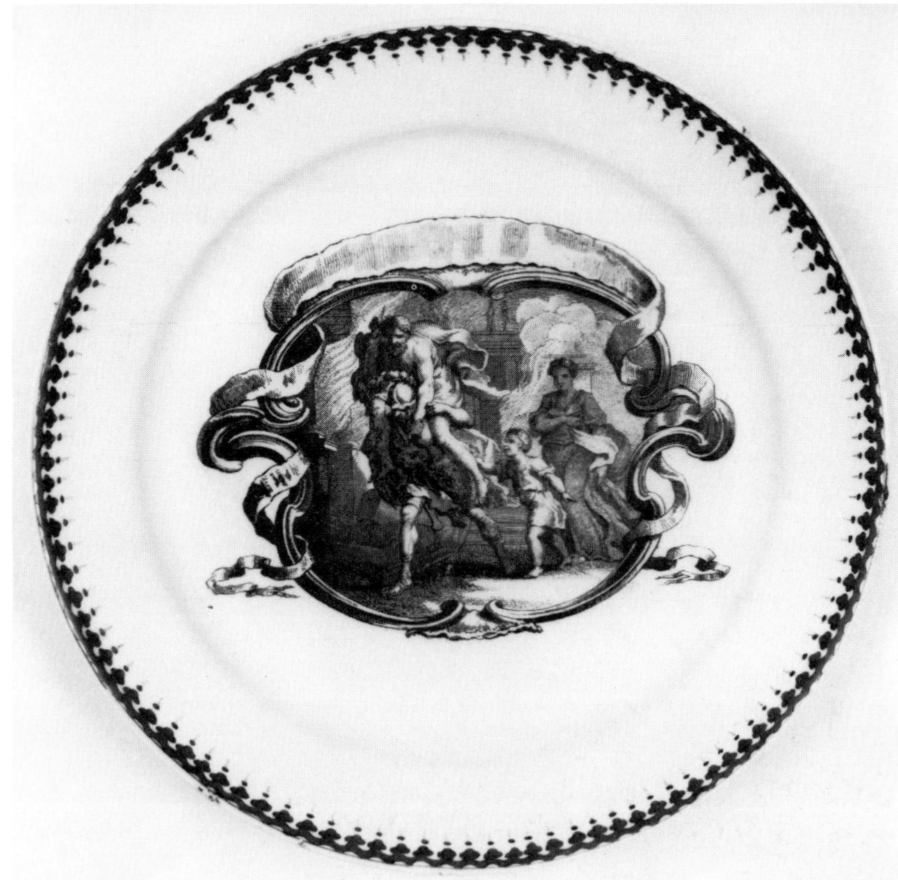

72

English (Staffordshire), *c.* 1760
Height: 13.3 cm ($5\frac{1}{4}$ in)
Thomas Greg Collection (1923.558)

The decoration alludes to England's ally during the Seven Years War (1756–63), Frederick II of Prussia (1740–86), known as 'Frederick the Great'. He was a popular hero, whose campaigns on the Continent enabled the British army and navy to concentrate on the Colonial campaigns. Indeed, Frederick was said at the time to be 'winning Canada on the Banks of the Elbe'. The body is ornamented with cartouches of Frederick the Great in relief on one side, and the Prussian Eagle on the other.

TEAPOT

Lead-glazed earthenware, with moulded leaf handle and cabbage leaf spout. Six rectangular panels with Chinese figures moulded in relief and stained with green, yellow, manganese purple and blue/grey oxides.
English (Staffordshire, Fenton), William Greatbach, after 1764
Height: 13 cm ($5\frac{1}{8}$ in)
Thomas Greg Collection (1923.717)

This chinoiserie piece has decoration showing three different figures: a figure at a table, with a small boy and beneath a tree; a figure with a parrot on a stick;

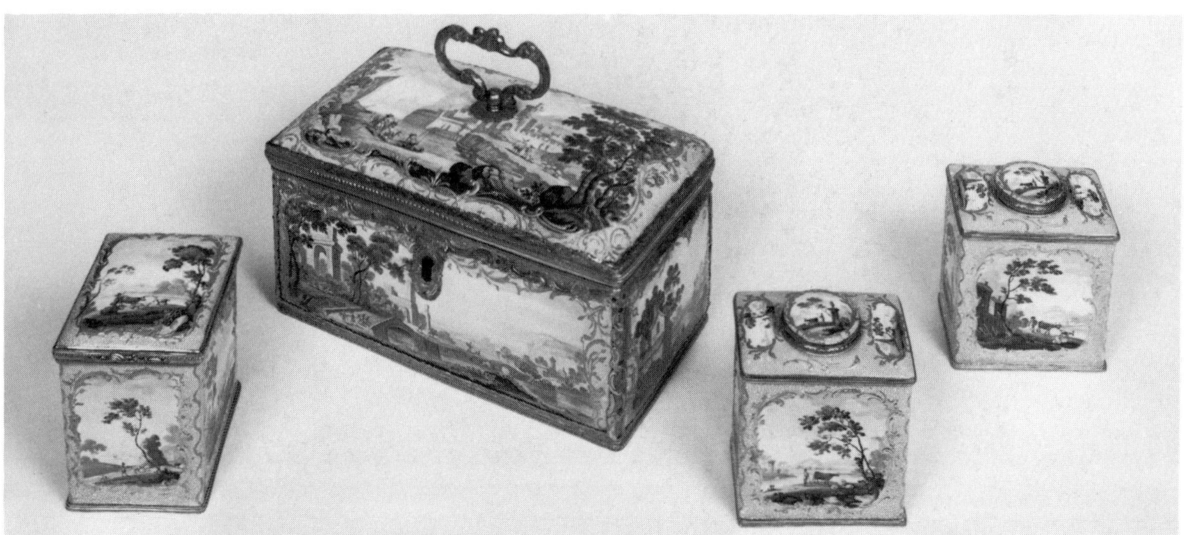

73

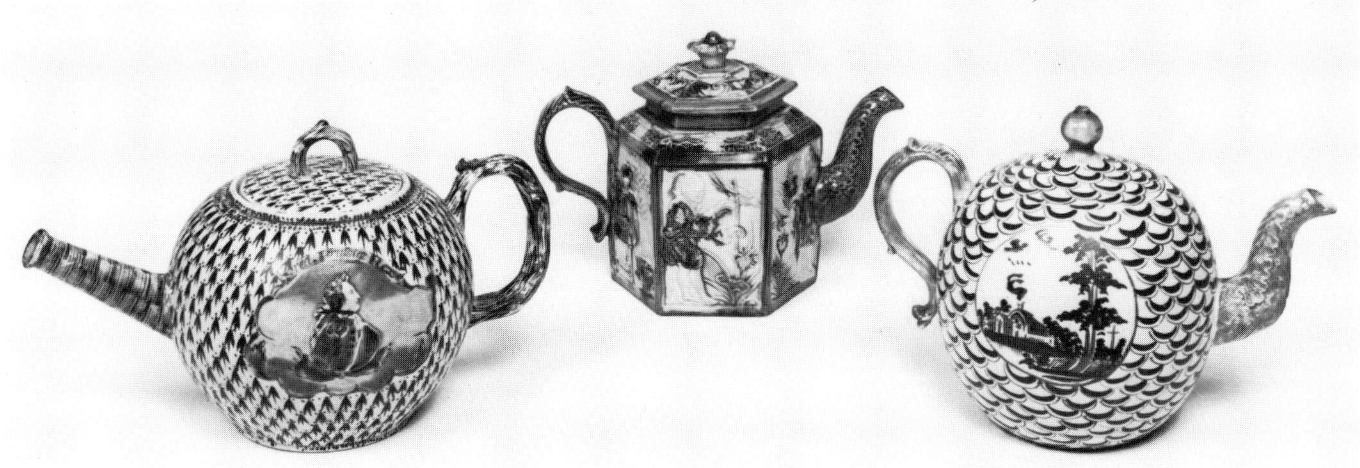

74

and the same figure with a parrot perched on his arm. The same relief design occurs on lead-glazed and salt-glazed tea-caddies in the Greg Collection (1923.715, 1923.416) and on a similar teapot in the Zeitlin Collection, in enamelled creamware. 'China tps' are referred to in a letter from Greatbach to Josiah Wedgwood (May 1764), apparently supplied by Greatbach in quantity. Fragments of a teapot such as the Manchester piece have been excavated by Stoke-on-Trent Museum Archaeological Society on the site of Greatbach's factory waste dump in Fenton. Teapots and caddies were made from a salt-glaze mould, of identical pattern, such as the one in the Victoria and Albert Museum Collection.

TEAPOT

Creamware, with moulded leaf handle and cabbage leaf spout, glazed green. Painted with a fish-scale pattern surrounding two landscape cartouches, in black and red enamel.
English (probably Josiah Wedgwood), *c.* 1768
Height: 14 cm (5½ in)
Thomas Greg Collection (1923.895)

Similar creamware teapots impressed WEDGWOOD are known, including a green glazed piece in the Fitzwilliam

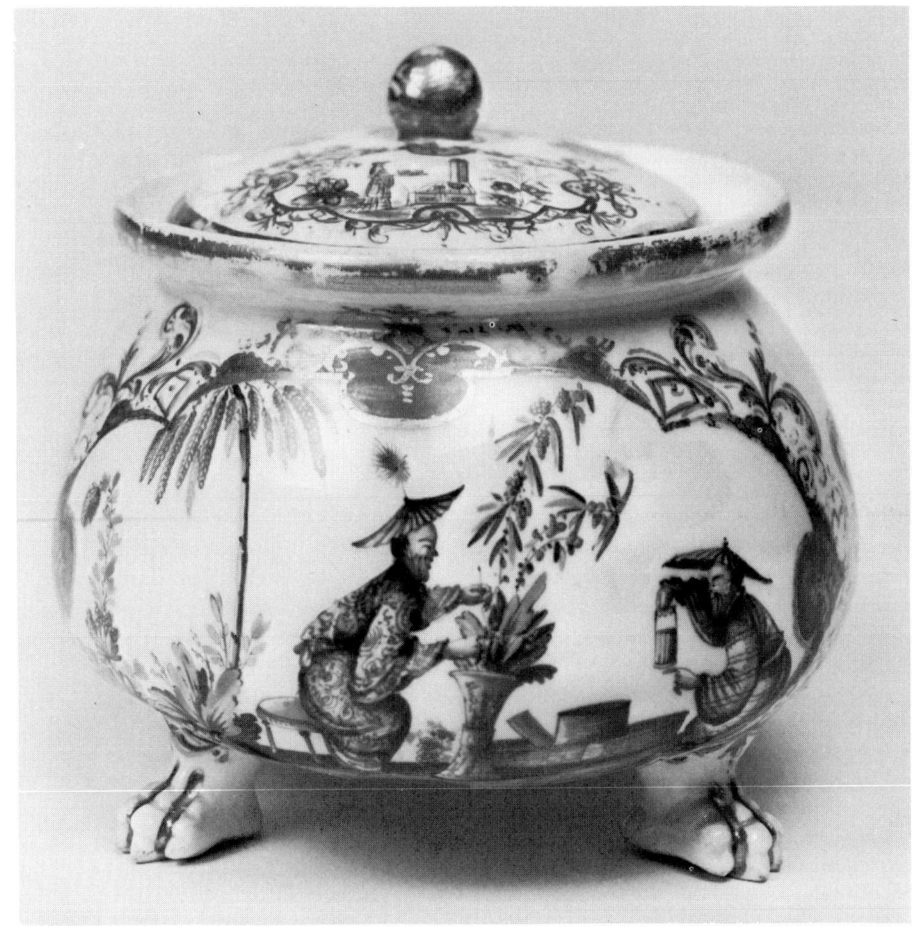

75

Museum, Cambridge. Virtually identical forms, attributed to Wedgwood, are in the Norwich Castle Museum, and at Temple Newsam House, Leeds. The decoration, especially the two landscapes, is probably the work of the Leeds enamellers, Robinson and Rhodes. David Rhodes wrote to Wedgwood in December 1764 asking for 'Cream Coloured teapotts' and, moving to London in the spring of 1768, was sending Wedgwood bills amounting to £178 10s 1d for pottery 'to be enamelled at D. Rhodes and Co.' (Correspondence now at Keele University Library.)

75 *Cream Pot and Cover*

Hard paste porcelain painted in enamel colours and gilt.
Mark: [mark] in gilt and red enamel
German (Meissen), *c.* 1725
Height: 9.3 cm ($3\frac{5}{8}$ in)
Lacks Collection (1981.372)

The cream pot and cover, of globular shape with a scrolled handle, is set on three paw feet. It is decorated with two seated Chinamen set in a shaped cartouche, surrounded by elaborate scrollwork, painted in iron red, mauve, brown and green enamel colours, *perlmutter* lustre and gilt. A miniature chinoiserie scene in a similar cartouche decorates the cover and there are scattered *indianische Blumen* over the body.

The chinoiserie decoration on the cream pot is characteristic of the period at Meissen when Johann Gregorious Höroldt (1696–1775) was in charge of the painting. The first hard paste porcelain in Europe was made at Meissen in 1709 by Johann Friedrich Böttger (1682–1719), but it was Höroldt, who came to the factory in 1720, who improved the quality of the material. He extended the range and quantity of shapes produced and perfected and developed the use of enamel colours. The factory's fame increased and consequently the growth in its markets.

Chinoiserie scenes in endless variations were used to decorate Meissen porcelain from 1723 for about ten years. The delicate painting was appropriate for the material and was in keeping with the fashion for the orient. These chinoiseries were not copied or adapted from original work, but were purely imaginary scenes illustrating Chinese life and customs. The style was not Höroldt's own invention, but was probably originally adapted from illustrations in Dutch travel books. Höroldt soon extended these to produce his own charming fantasies in infinite variations.

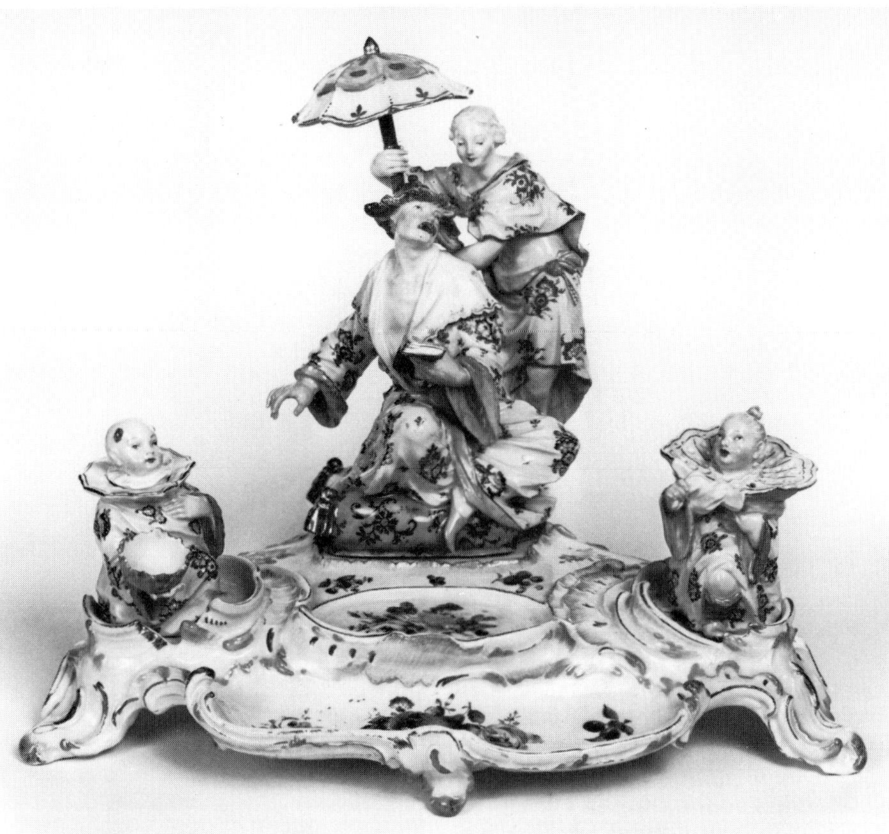

76

76 *Rococo Inkstand*

Hard paste porcelain, painted in enamel colours and gilt.
Mark: crossed swords in underglaze blue
German (Meissen), *c.* 1760
Height: 27.8 cm ($10\frac{7}{8}$ in); width of tray: 34.3 cm ($13\frac{1}{2}$ in)
Purchased with the aid of a grant from the National Art-Collections Fund (1979.246).

This rococo inkstand in the chinoiserie taste is composed of four figures set on a shaped tray. In the centre a Chinaman, holding a book, is seated on a padded stool; an attendant stands behind him, holding a parasol. On the right the sander is modelled as a kneeling Chinese girl with pierced holes in her ruff, while on the left, forming the ink, with his head removable for the purpose, is a kneeling Chinese boy, holding a bowl.

The original model for the inkstand may have been made around 1760 by Johann Joachim Kaendler (1706–75), chief modeller at Meissen from 1733 until 1775 and the creator of all the major figure models which earned Meissen its high and influential reputation. A mention is made in the Meissen factory archives of a similar chinoiserie inkstand made in 1762 for Frederick the Great, King of Prussia: 'A writing stand, in which a Chinese man sits on a padded stool, lifting his head up as if singing, behind him a nymph holding a sunshade over his head, in a listening attitude.'

A few complete inkstands such as this survive. Similar ones are in the Bayerisches Nationalmuseum, Munich, and in the Fitzwilliam Museum, Cambridge. In the Wadsworth Atheneum, Hartford, Connecticut, there is just the central group of Chinaman and attendant, mounted on an ormolu base. On the base is the monogram *CA* for Clemens August, Elector of Cologne and Duke of Bavaria (1736–61), who was a regular customer of the Meissen factory.

77 *Wine Glass*

Lead glass, with a double knopped stem and stipple engraved bowl.
English, *c.* 1775. Engraved in Holland, probably by David Wolff
Height: 18.4 cm ($7\frac{1}{4}$ in)
Lloyd Roberts Bequest (1920.989)

Nine glasses with stipple-engraved decoration are signed *D. Wolff* and dated between 1784 and 1796. Wolff (1732–98), of Swiss parentage, was married in the Hague in 1762, apparently in a state of poverty. The nine signed glasses are almost all of a distinct form, dated after 1780, with polished, faceted stems.

In the Stedelijk Museum of Leyden is an earlier glass with a knopped stem, stipple-engraved with three figures,

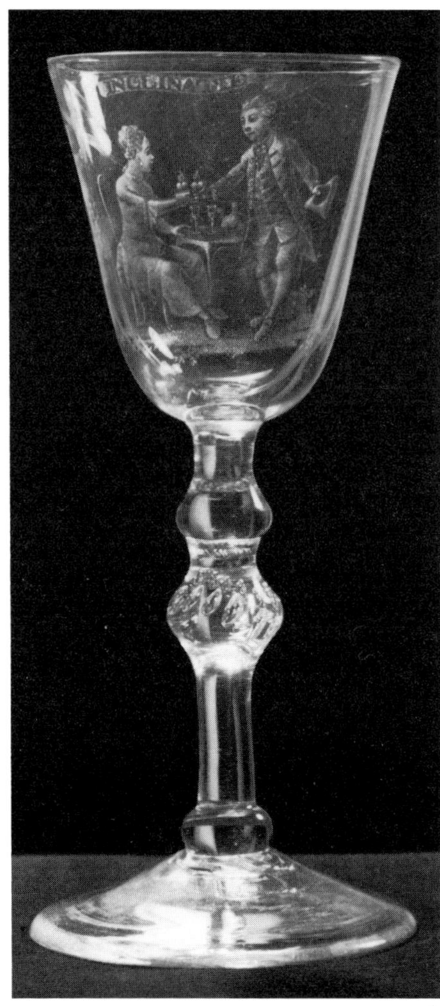
77

which is well documented by a bill dated 1775. The decoration was designed by Abraham Delfos (1731–1820), and delivered by Wolff, who was paid for the glass.

The Manchester example shows a betrothed or married couple, the woman seated at a table and the gentleman approaching her with his hat removed. On the table are two glasses of similar form to the glass itself, and the couple each clasp a flaming heart which is warmed by Cupid catching the sun's rays in a magnifying glass. Above the scene is an engraved ribbon showing the word INCLINATIE (desire).

Stipple engraved marriage glasses from the first Wolff period, (*c.* 1760–80) are known dated 1762, 1763, 1775 and 1778, which all bear the curious 'hearts aflame' device. Fourteen 'Wolff' glasses appear in the catalogue of the J. Van Buren collection sale (7–12 November, 1808, Scheuleer, The Hague). They include Lot 107, 'One, two young people and a Cupid, with the device of desire (inclinatie). Price 12 guilders 5 stivers. Buyer H. Voogt.'

The subtle effects of Dutch stipple engraving ('stippelen' means pricking) called for English lead glass, which was incomparably brilliant during the 18th century. The design, which is virtually impossible to see in normal light, appears as a soft white chiaroscuro effect when the glass is filled with red wine.

78 *François Boucher* *pl. 6*

(1703–70)

LANDSCAPE WITH A YOUNG FISHERMAN (LE GALANT PÊCHEUR) 1768

French; oil on canvas
51.2 × 66.1 cm ($20\frac{1}{4}$ × 26 in)
Signed and dated (l.r.) *F. Boucher PDR* 1768
Purchased with the aid of the National Art-Collections Fund and a Government grant (through the Victoria and Albert Museum) (1981.60)

Boucher, friend and protégé of Mme de Pompadour, is the artist *par excellence* of the French Rococo, the style of the sophisticated urban and courtly society of mid-18th-century Paris. His pictures echo the prettiness and gaiety of the rococo interior. Many of Boucher's paintings were intended as part of decorative schemes, and he also designed for tapestries and for the theatre.

This is an example of Boucher's late landscape style. He had in his younger days studied nature and painted models from the life, but had 'left off them for many years' according to Reynolds,

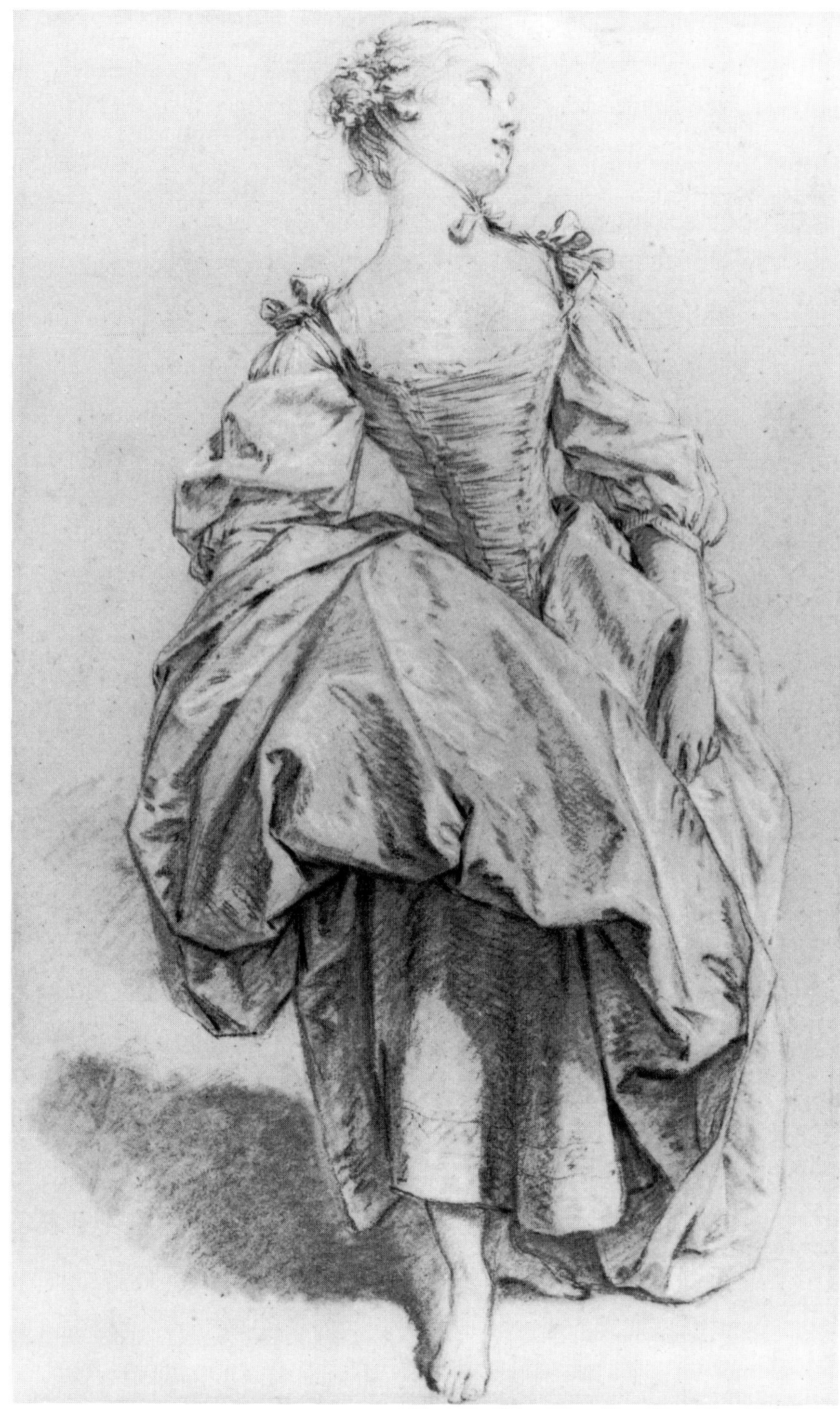
78

who did not approve. The fat cow of the herdsmen introduces a touch of realism derived from the Dutch 17th-century painters of idyllic pastoral landscapes, but in the Boucher all is fresh, light-hearted and deliberately contrived. The fisherman inhabits a sunlit world of artfully picturesque tumbledown buildings and contented rustics, where love-birds fly overhead. The trees are painted with the frothy elegance of touch of which Boucher was a master, and the delicious palette of blues and greens conjures up a seductive world of the imagination, an artificial view of nature distilled from reality.

After his signature Boucher has written the initials PDR for 'Peintre du Roi', an honour given him by Louis XV in 1763. The painting is first recorded in the sale of the Duc de Caylus in 1773. Later it belonged to the Paris branch of the Rothschild family, great connoisseurs of French 18th-century art.

79 *François Boucher*

(1703–70)

A SHEPHERDESS LOOKING UPWARDS

French; black chalk, touched with red chalk, heightened with white on buff paper
48.1 × 29.4 cm ($18\frac{15}{16} \times 11\frac{9}{16}$ in)
Bequeathed by G. Beatson Blair, 1941
(1947.126)

This charming drawing of a shepherdess is not related to any of Boucher's recorded paintings, but is stylistically close to a number of finished studies, including one in the Louvre dated 1750. The artist's delightful vision of rustic simplicity greatly appealed to his sophisticated, aristocratic audience, used to the formal magnificence of the French court. Shepherds and shepherdesses frequently people Boucher's idyllic and sentimental vision of Nature. The young barefoot shepherdess in this drawing is dressed in a simplified version of fashionable costume. She is far removed from the

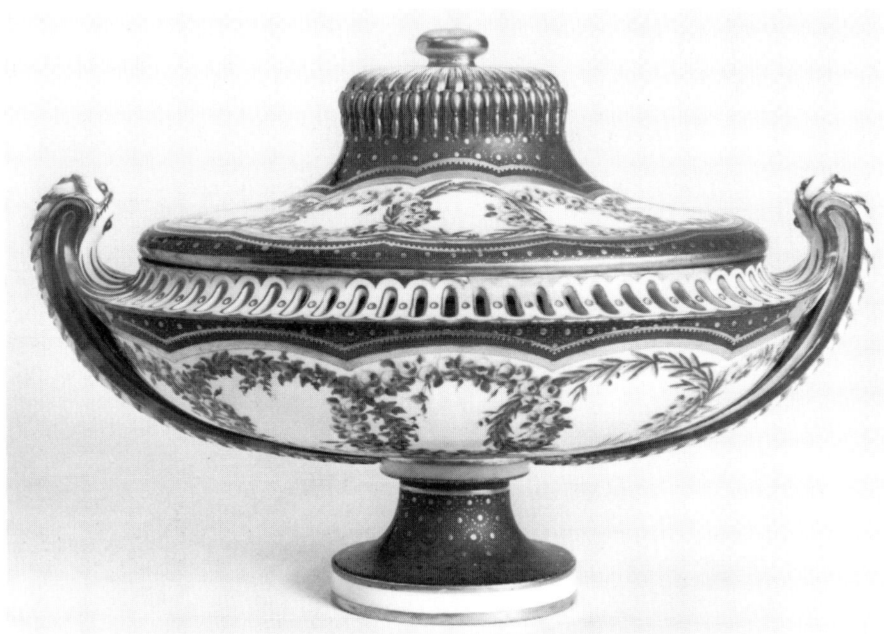

80

reality of rural life in 18th-century France and is closer to the rustic fantasies created by Marie Antoinette in her miniature farm at Versailles.

80 *Cassolette Duplessis*

Soft paste porcelain painted in enamel colours and gilt
Mark: interlaced *Ls* in underglaze blue with date letter *N*; three dots in blue enamel for the painter J. B. Tandart.
French (Sèvres), 1766
32.5 × 21.7 cm (12¾ × 8½ in)
Purchased with the aid of a Government grant (through the Victoria and Albert Museum) (1980.182)

The *Cassolette Duplessis*, or pot-pourri vase and cover, is of oval shape with the body and domed lid pierced. The vase is painted with garlands of flowers on a white ground within borders of *bleu nouveau* and gilded with *oeil de perdrix* (partridge eye).

A vase of this form was first recorded in the sales registers of the 1760s, but it was not until the 19th century that it was registered under the name '*vase cassolette Duplessis*' when the design was attributed to Jean-Claude Duplessis (active 1745–74). Duplessis, the Royal Goldsmith, was originally appointed at Vincennes to design the forms of the factory's new productions; he later became artistic director and was probably responsible for nearly all the great models produced at Sèvres during the Louis XV period. The garlands of flowers were painted by Jean Baptiste Tandart (1731–1803) who had been a fan decorator before he was employed at Vincennes to become a specialist flower painter. A *Cassolette Duplessis* of identical form is in the Wallace Collection, London; another, with the addition of gilt bronze, is in the Detroit Institute of Arts.

81 *Pascal Candlestick*

Copper, parcel gilt
Italian (Roman), mid-18th century
Embossed with the royal (Stuart) arms surrounded by a Prince's closed coronet and a Cardinal's hat.
Height: 176 cm (69¼ in)
Purchased with the aid of a Government grant (through the Victoria and Albert Museum) (1980.262)

The arms embossed on the plinth, with crescent for difference, are those of Prince Henry Benedict, Cardinal Duke of York and Bishop of Frascati (1725–1807). He was the grandson of King James II and younger brother of Prince Charles Edward, the Young Pretender. They indicate that the candlestick must have been made

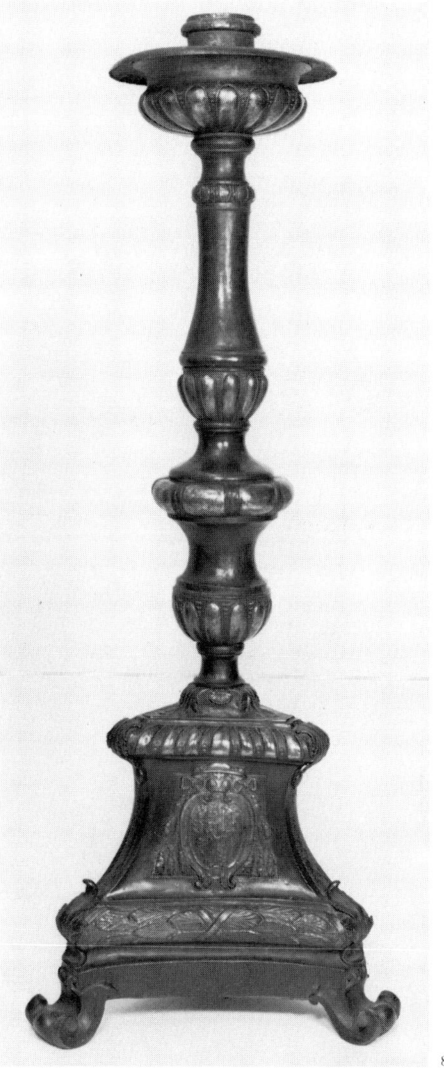

81

between 1747, when he received his Cardinal's hat, and 1766 when his father, the Old Pretender, died. On his brother's death in 1788, the Jacobites proclaimed him King Henry IX of Great Britain and Ireland. He was the last of the male line of the Stuart dynasty and one of the leading celebrities of 18th-century Rome.

The pascal candlestick, used during liturgical celebrations in Eastertide, is a superb example of 18th-century Italian metalwork. The beaten copper with alternately gilded mouldings, strongly resembles cast and chased bronze work of this period. Its provenance is uncertain, but it may have formed part of the liturgical equipage of Frascati Cathedral or of Santa Maria in Campitelli, Rome, of which the Cardinal was protector. His library at Frascati is still extant but the Cathedral was despoiled by the French in 1797.

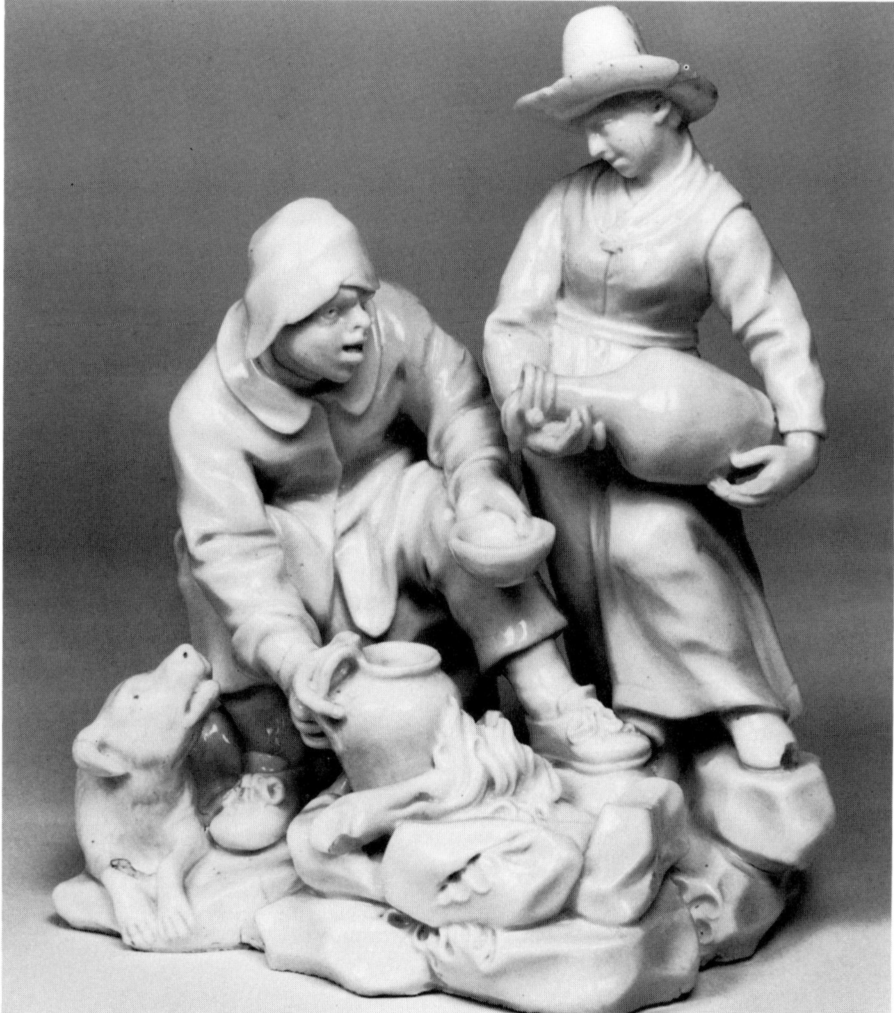

82

82 *Group of Peasants*

Soft paste porcelain
Mark: a fleur-de-lys in underglaze blue
Italian (Capodimonte), 1745–50
Height: 23.9 cm ($9\frac{3}{8}$ in)
Leicester Collier Bequest (1917.412)

The Capodimonte porcelain factory was founded by Charles III, King of Naples (1734–59) in June 1743. Charles was encouraged to make porcelain after his marriage in 1738 to Princess Maria Amalia of Saxony, who was the granddaughter of Augustus the Strong, the founder of Meissen, the first porcelain factory in Europe. As part of her dowry she brought seventeen sets of Meissen tableware.

The broad and lively modelling of this figure group suggests that it is the work of Giuseppe Gricci (d. 1770), chief modeller at the factory. Gricci's most important commission came from the King in 1757, the *gabinetto di porcellana*, a room in the palace of Portici which was to be completely covered in porcelain and embellished with porcelain figures, vases and other ornaments. Left in the white this figure group admirably displays the beautiful quality of the Capodimonte paste. The subject matter probably derives from prints after paintings of Neapolitan low life.

In 1759 Charles left Naples to become King of Spain. He took all that was transportable of the porcelain works with him and set up another factory in the gardens of his palace of Buen Retiro, near Madrid.

83 *Bernardo Bellotto*

(1720–80)

THE COURTYARD OF THE CASTLE OF KÖNIGSTEIN FROM THE WEST
c. 1756–58

Italian; oil on canvas
133.9 × 238 cm ($52\frac{11}{16}$ × $93\frac{3}{4}$ in)
Unsigned
Purchased with the aid of a Government grant (through the Victoria and Albert Museum), the National Heritage Memorial Fund, the National Art-Collections Fund, the Patrons and Associates, and Friends of Manchester City Art Galleries (1982.712)

83

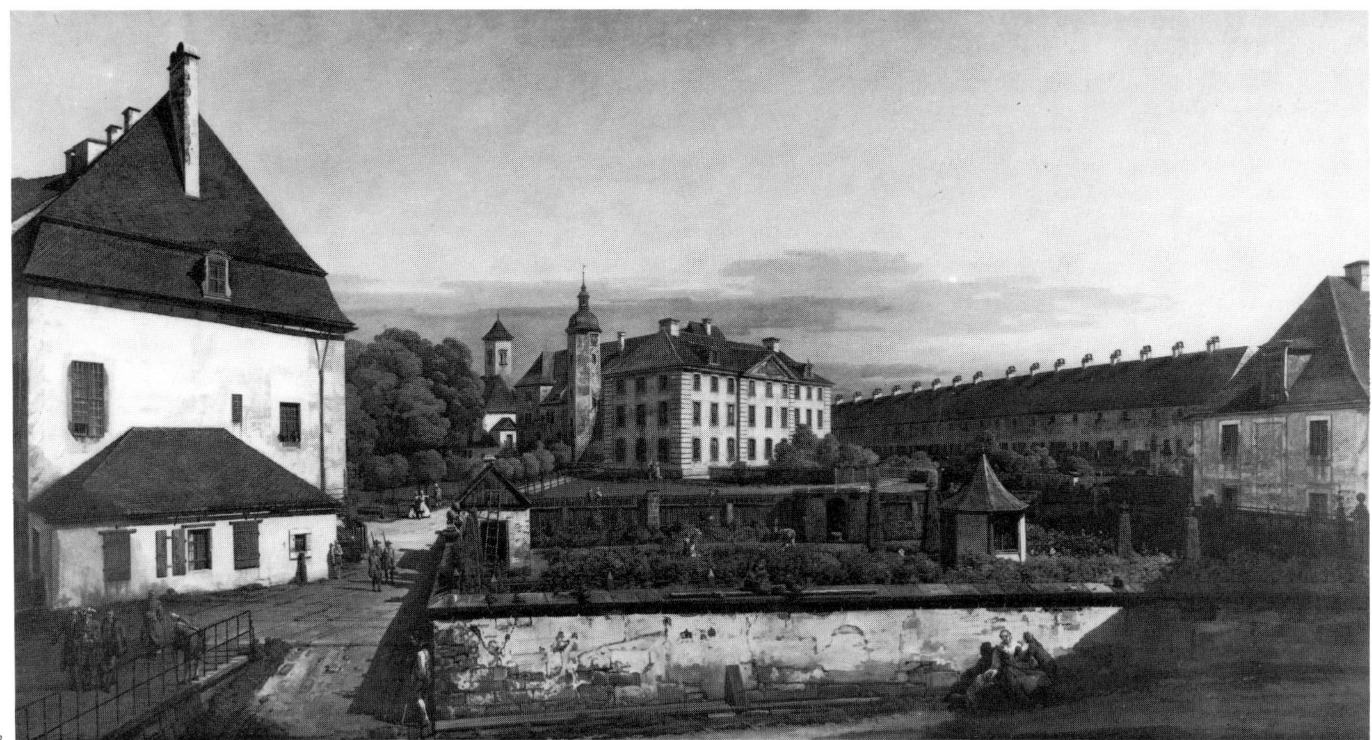

Bellotto was nephew, pupil and collaborator of the famous Venetian view painter Antonio Canaletto (1697–1768). In clarity of atmosphere, he follows his uncle, but his colours are generally cooler, and he takes perhaps even greater pleasure in depicting the activities of the figures in his townscapes. Bellotto left Venice in 1747 and went to Dresden, where he was appointed Court Painter to the Elector of Saxony, Augustus II. In 1767 he moved to Warsaw, where he remained for the rest of his life. This view was painted for Augustus as part of a large series showing castles in his domains. The picture was apparently never delivered because of the outbreak of the Seven Years War, but was eventually taken to London and put up for sale at Christie's in 1788, where it was bought by an ancestor of the Marquis of Londonderry, from whom this picture was acquired.

The castle of Königstein in Saxony is on the top of a rocky eminence. The buildings seen here, the Georgenburg, the Brunnenhaus and the Old Arsenal, are inside a ring of fortifications. In the centre is a walled garden with delightful topiary obelisks. Bellotto also painted a companion picture of the castle buildings from the south, and views of the castle from the river below. Some of these views exist in several versions.

84 G. D. Tiepolo

(1727–1804)

THE FLIGHT INTO EGYPT: JOSEPH KNEELS IN ADORATION OF THE CHRIST CHILD 1752

Italian; etching
24.6 × 18.9 cm ($9\frac{11}{16} \times 7\frac{7}{16}$ in)
Removed from Bryan's *Dictionary of Painters and Engravers*; immediate provenance unrecorded (1982.675)

The Venetian Giovanni Domenico Tiepolo was a pupil and follower of his father, Giovanni Battista (1696–1770). This etching, dated 1752, is No. 19 in a series of 24 plates published in 1753, showing variations on the theme of the *Flight into Egypt* and entitled *Idee Pittoresche sopra La Fuga in Egitto*. The set is dedicated to Carl Philipp von Greiffenklau, Prince Bishop of Würzburg. Three other etchings from the set are in the Gallery's collection.

The circumstances concerning this set's dedication are diverting. Tiepolo father and son were working at Würzburg, decorating the Residenz for the Prince Bishop. Giovanni Domenico Tiepolo, who had been asked to furnish his patron with a design, provided one idea only and not, as was then customary, several alternatives. The Prince Bishop was apparently greatly disappointed by this lack of inventiveness, so, to display virtuosity in design, the younger Tiepolo etched twenty-four variations on the theme of the *Flight into Egypt*, dedicating them to the Prince Bishop.

A major source of the Gallery's Old Master prints is a grangerized copy of Bryan's *Dictionary of Painters and Engravers* rebound in 21 volumes. The expansion into so many volumes is caused by the insertion of no less than 2,062 prints. The volumes first belonged to Benjamin Gott (fl. 1790–d. 1840) of Armley Hall, a Leeds mill-owner who was a friend and patron of Sir Thomas Lawrence, Sir Francis Chantrey and John Flaxman. Many of the prints were probably purchased by Gott from P. & D. Colnaghi in the 1820s and 1830s when he was building up a fine collection of Old Master paintings.

85 *Armchair*

Giltwood with later cut velvet upholstery
Italian (Venetian), *c.* 1745, one of a pair
Height: 123 cm ($48\frac{1}{2}$ in)
Purchased (1982.114/2)

The rococo style flourished in mid-18th-century Venice with a flamboyance and extravagance rivalling even France and Germany. The Republic was enjoying its last years of existence in a spirit of decadent sophistication before its final extinction. It was in vain that the Doge and Senate enacted sumptuary laws in order to curb the dissipation of the Serenissima's lean resources. Large sets of chairs carved with rocaille, C and S scrolls, and covered in luxurious cut velvet were required for the *saloni* and *ridotti* of the aristocracy, whose

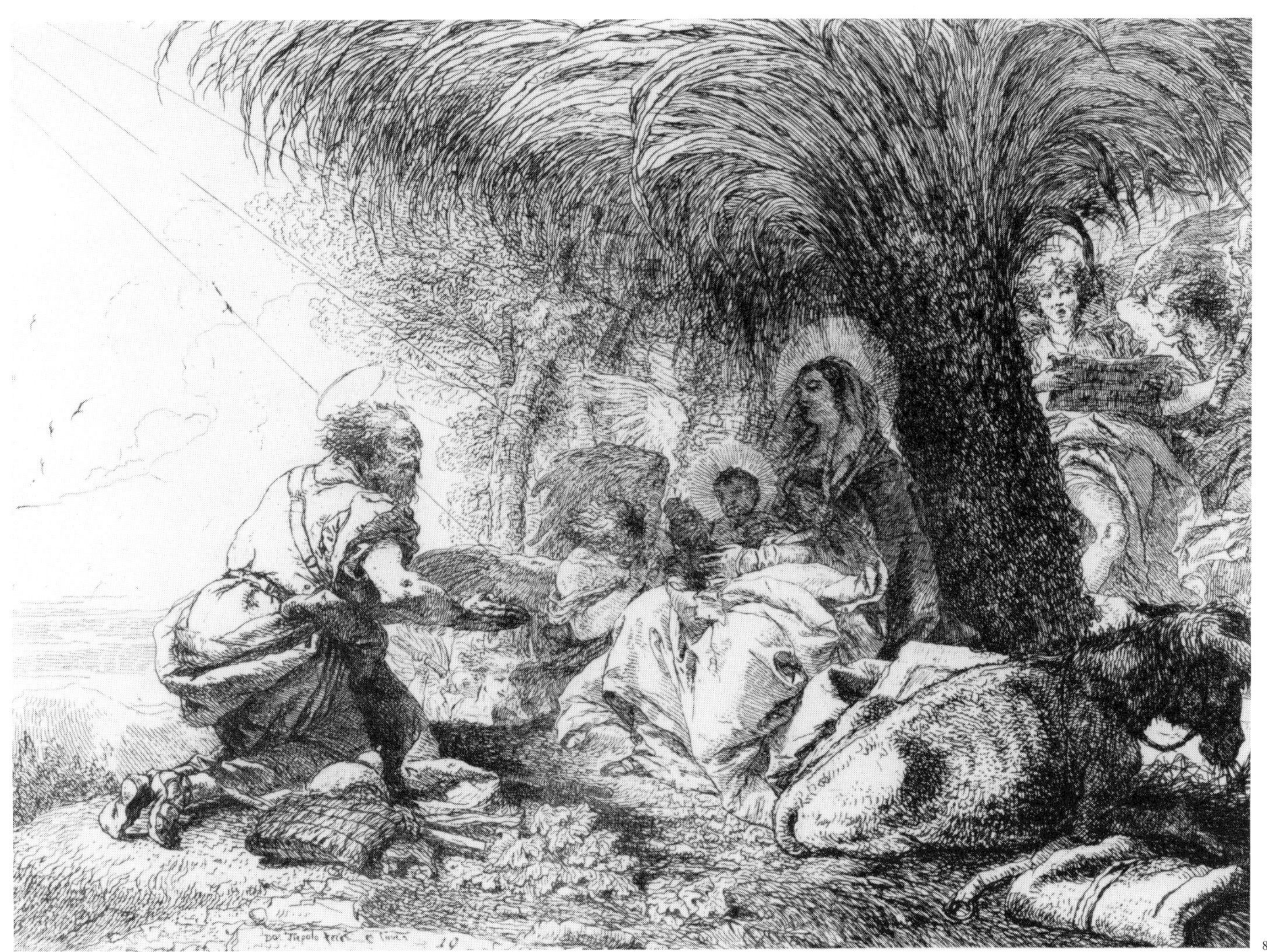

84

prodigality had made Venice the playground of Europe.

Venetian 18th-century furniture compensates in liveliness of form and decoration for what it often lacks in technical proficiency. The sculptural tradition reached new heights of virtuosity in the great suites of furniture by Andrea Brustolon (1662–1732) and Antonio Corradini (*c.* 1700–52). Its exuberance and vitality reflect the festive gaiety of the carnival, when it was said that 'the Venetians do not taste their pleasures, they swallow them whole'. Closely similar chairs are in the Ca' Rezzonico on the Grand Canal.

86 *Pompeo G. Batoni*

(1708–87)

SIR GREGORY PAGE-TURNER
(1748–1805)
1768

Italian; oil on canvas
134.6 × 99 cm (53 × 39 in)
Signed (on base of pillar): P. BATONI PINXIT ROMAE/ANNO 1768
Purchased (1976.79)

From the 1740s until his death, Batoni made his reputation and fortune as the most fashionable portrait painter in Rome at a period when English aristocrats on the Grand Tour were flocking to the city and made eager patrons.

Sir Gregory Page-Turner was the eldest surviving son of Sir Edward Turner. He succeeded to the fortune and estates of his great-uncle, Sir Gregory Page, second and last Baronet of Wricklemarsh, Kent, and succeeded his father as third Baronet of Ambrosden, Oxfordshire in 1766. By 1768, when this portrait was painted in Rome, Sir Gregory had developed a taste for extravagant living and fine clothes and is shown here wearing an exquisitely embroidered red silk suit.

The portrait is one of the finest of Batoni's Grand Tour pictures of his

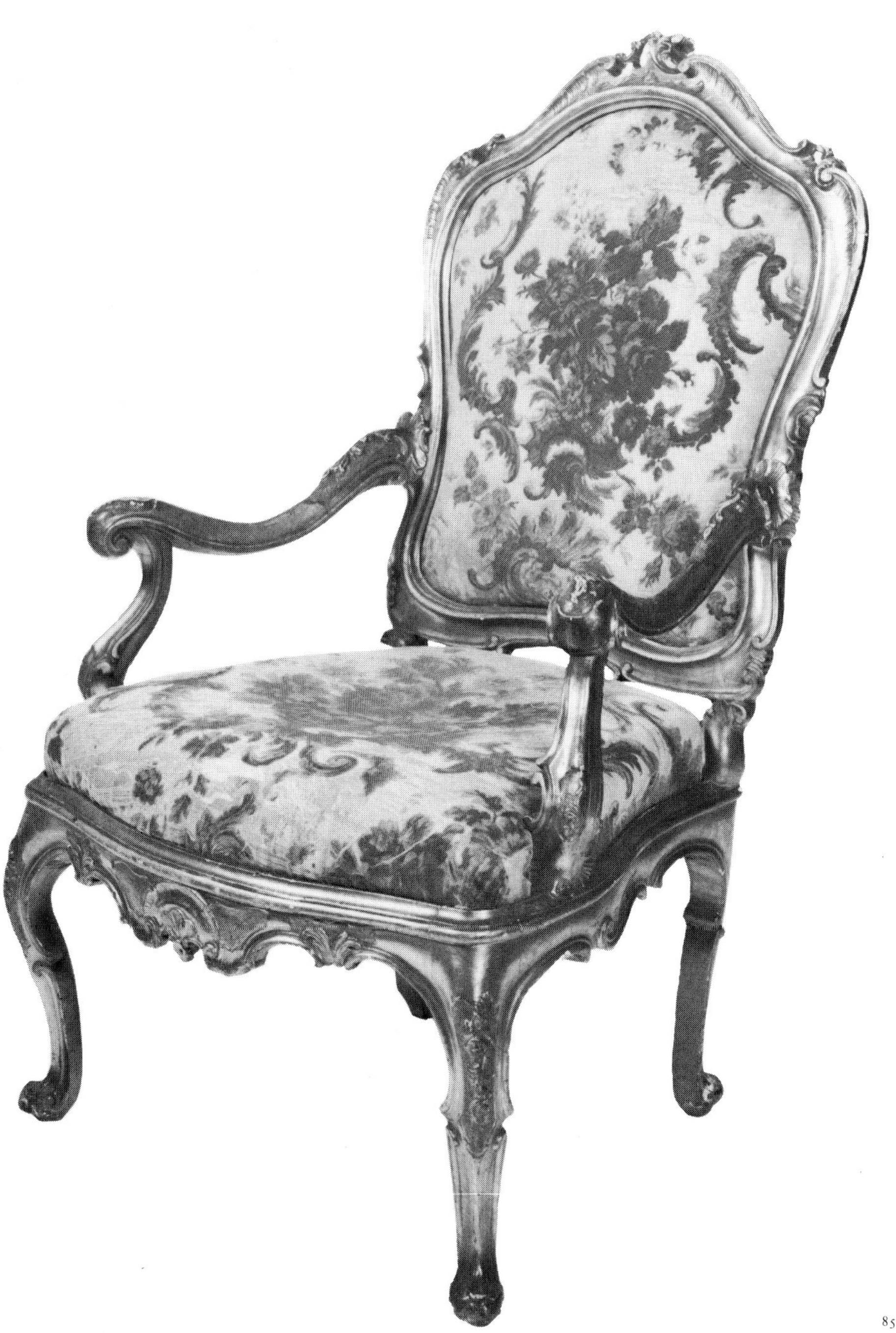

85

middle years. The swagger pose is loosely based on the Apollo del Belvedere whilst the map of Rome and view of the Colosseum are intended to show the sitter's familiarity with the city. On the left is a multi-coloured marble bust of Minerva, a studio prop that appears in at least four other Grand Tour portraits of English sitters. The canvas conforms to Batoni's regular size of 54 × 39 inches for three-quarter length portraits.

Despite owning estates said to be worth £24,000 a year, Sir Gregory later pulled down two of his great houses, Ambrosden and Wricklemarsh, for reasons of economy, and also sold the fine Wricklemarsh collection of paintings. He lived at the remaining family seat of Battlesden and is said to have died with 16,700 golden guineas in his secretaire and as much more in his strongbox. Despite his avarice he bought, in the year of his death, Titian's *Perseus and Andromeda* now in the Wallace Collection.

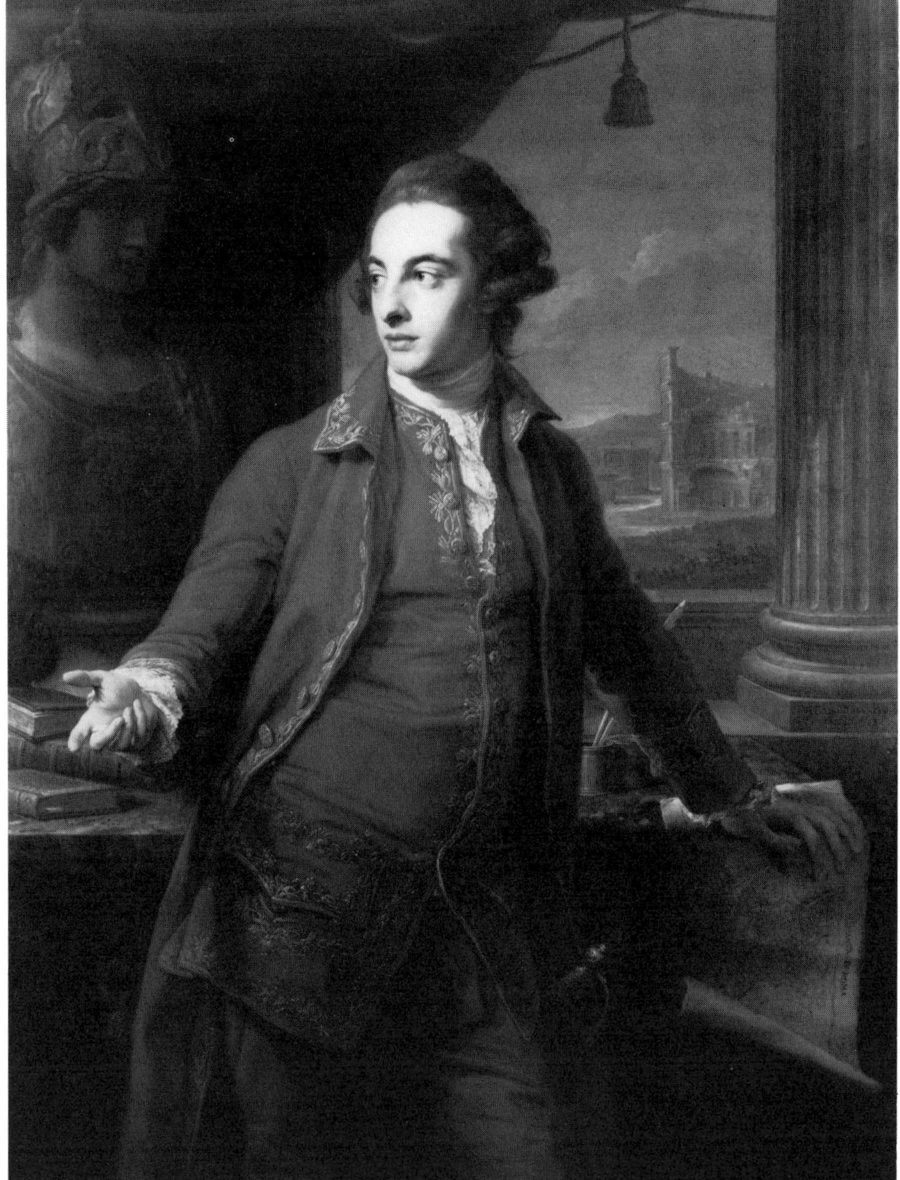

86

87 *Angelica Kauffman*

(1741–1807)

MISS CORNELIA KNIGHT 1793

English School; oil on canvas
90 × 80 cm ($37\frac{3}{4} \times 31\frac{1}{2}$ in)
Signed (b.r.): *Angelica Kauffman. / Pinx. Rome / 1793* and (on belt clasp): *ANGELICA KAUFFMAN*
Purchased (1901.9)

Cornelia (1757–1837) was the daughter of Sir Joseph Knight, Admiral of the Blue. She was a talented amateur artist and a writer. Brush in hand, she has drawn a rostral column, a monument to celebrate naval victories. Her novel of ancient Rome, *Marcus Flaminius*, is prominent amongst the books on the table. She wears the fashionable loosely curled hairstyle of the 1790s, a 'Grecian' high waisted dress with a lilac cloak and, at her waist, a cameo. This was originally a head of Minerva, the goddess of Wisdom, another allusion to the sitter's accomplishments, but Angelica Kauffman was persuaded to alter it into a self-portrait in profile, lettered with her name. For this was not a routine commissioned portrait, but a portrait of one friend by another. In her records, the artist wrote, 'this portrait was done by the artist out of friendship.'

Angelica Kauffman was of Swiss birth, but spent much of her life in Rome painting commissions for Englishmen on the Grand Tour. From 1766–81 she lived in England, carrying out decorative paintings in country houses, and in 1768 became a founder member of the Royal Academy. It was in England that she first met the Knights, but the portrait was painted in Rome whilst Cornelia and her mother were travelling. This prolonged Continental journey was forced on them by the grave financial circumstances they found themselves in after the untimely death of the Admiral. They travelled down to Naples, where they were befriended by the King and Queen of the Two Sicilies, and by Lord Nelson and Emma Hamilton. Later Cornelia returned to England and eventually became Lady Companion to Princess Charlotte.

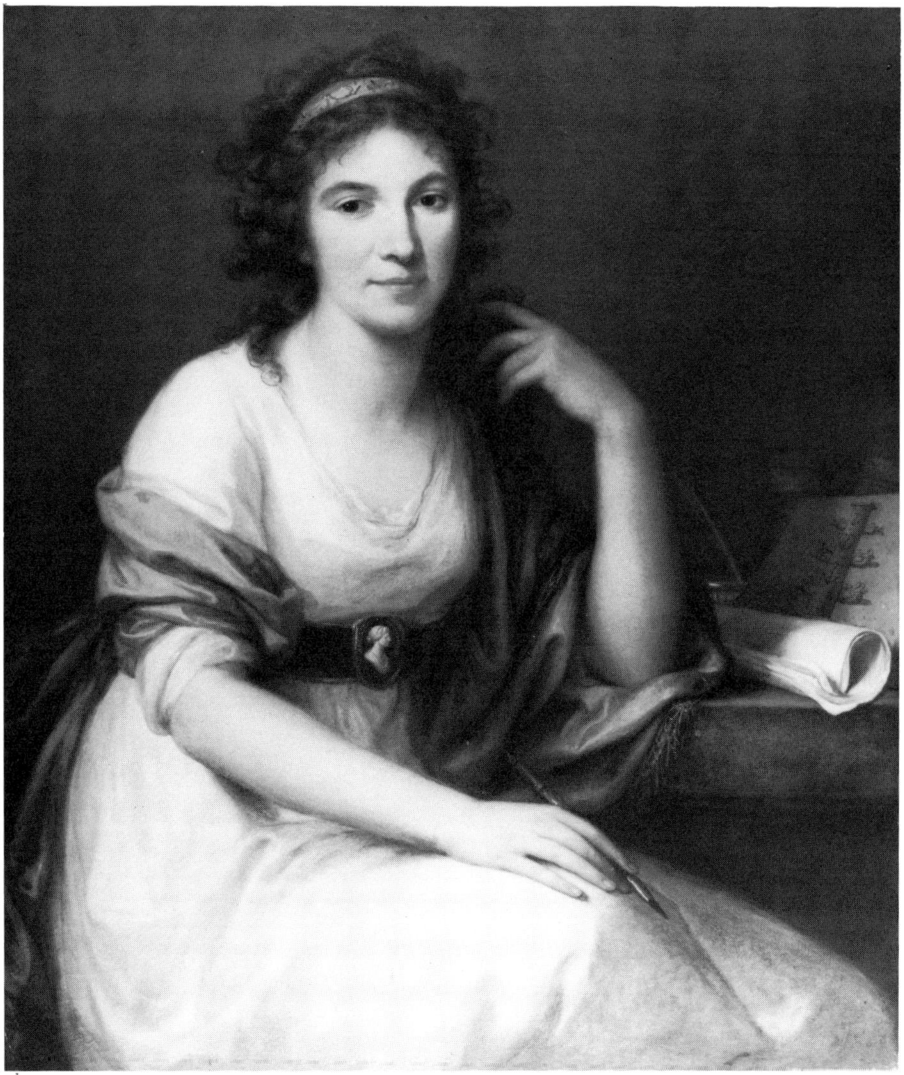

87

88 Cup and Cover

Gold
English (London), hallmark for 1772–73, makers' marks for John Parker and Edward Wakelin.
Height: 24.5 cm ($9\frac{5}{8}$ in)
Purchased with the aid of a Government grant (through the Victoria and Albert Museum) with assistance from the Assheton-Bennett Bequest Fund (1978.311).

This solid gold cup was made for the Honourable John Smith-Barry (1725–84), of Marbury Hall and later Belmont, Cheshire, youngest son of James, 4th Earl of Barrymore. In 1746 he had married the heiress Dorothy Smith of Weald Hall, Essex, and had assumed her surname in addition. The cup incorporates the arms of the Barry family. There is only one other English gold cup of this period in existence. The decoration of this one is strongly neo-classical and is characteristic of the early period of this style. The alternating enclosed anthemion on the cover, the floriate band and the festoons draping the central roundel find close parallels in the decorative work of the leading architects of this period, notably Sir William Chambers (1723–96).

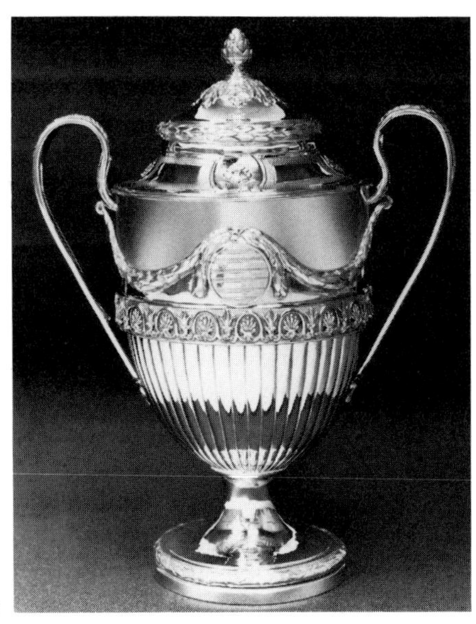

88

The cup cost £166 10s 6d and it was invoiced on 27 March 1772 (MSS Wakelin and Taylor Ledgers, Victoria and Albert Museum). It was made by melting four gold tumblers already in the Smith-Barry collection. John Parker and Edward Wakelin were leading London goldsmiths who inherited the business from George Wickes (1698–1761). It later became the firm of Garrard and Co.

89 *Mirror/Chimneypiece*

OVERMANTEL MIRROR

Giltwood
English (London), 1774, designed by Robert Adam (1728–92)
Height: 197 cm (78 in)
Purchased by the Friends of Manchester City Art Galleries (1980.162)

The revolution in taste so closely identified with Robert Adam was largely based on his rejuvenated form of classicism derived from a wider variety of sources than previously employed by architects and designers. His achievement was to create some of the most graceful and elegant buildings ever conceived, with a system of interior decoration in which the decorative arts were united to form consistent and harmonious ensembles. One of his most successful London interiors was Derby House, Grosvenor Square, for which this mirror was designed. It originally stood in the Countess's Dressing Room for which Adam meticulously planned every piece of decoration and furniture, later describing it (incorrectly) as the first 'Etruscan' room in England. The features employed on this piece, trailing rainceaux, caryatid figures, swags, palmettes, are highly characteristic of his mature style. The cresting has been recently restored by reference to the original drawing in the Soane Museum.

CHIMNEYPIECE

Marble
English, 1790–91, carved by John Bacon RA (1740–99)
Height: 169 cm ($66\frac{1}{2}$ in)

The chimneypiece was carved by John Bacon RA in 1790–91 for the Music

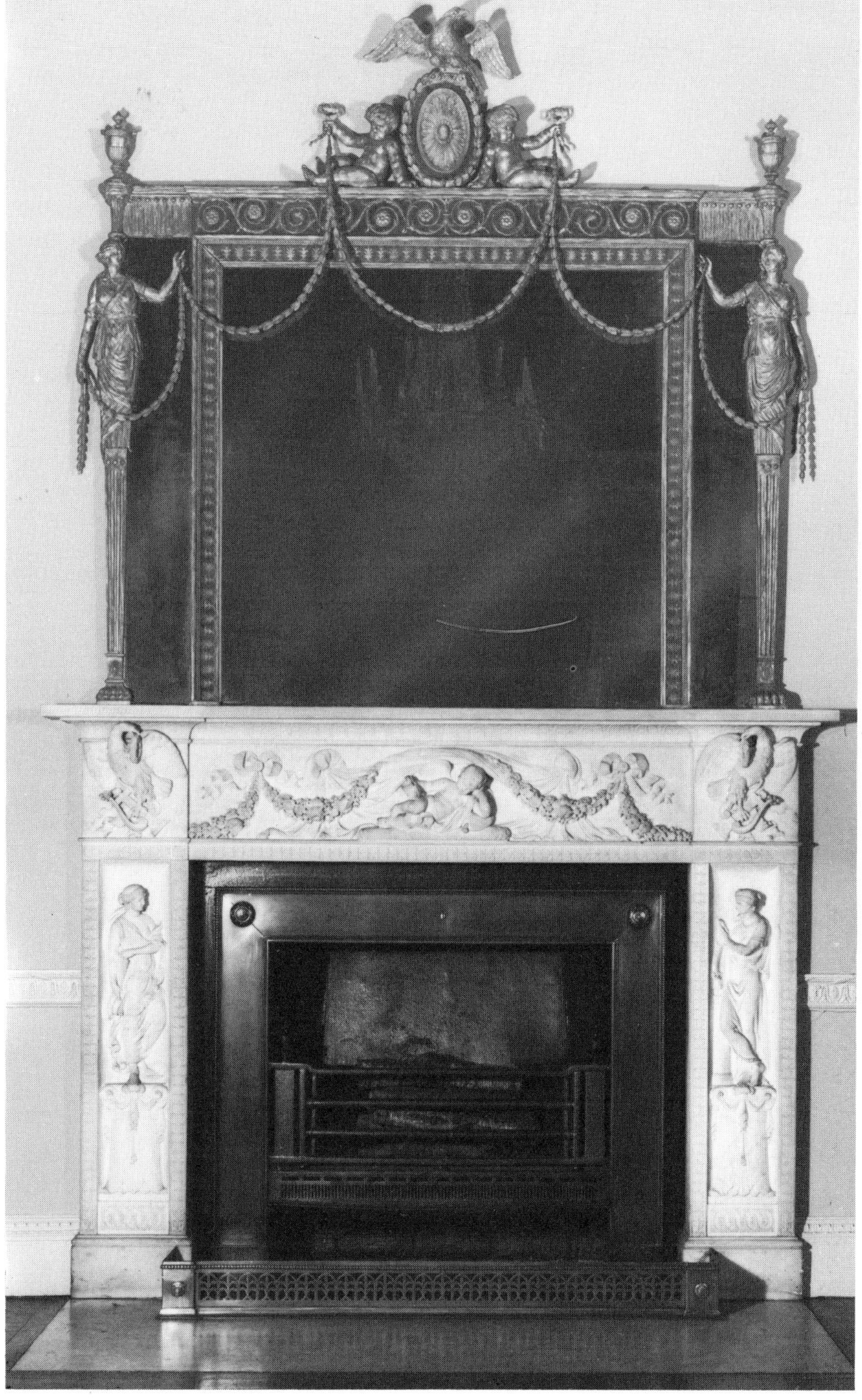

89

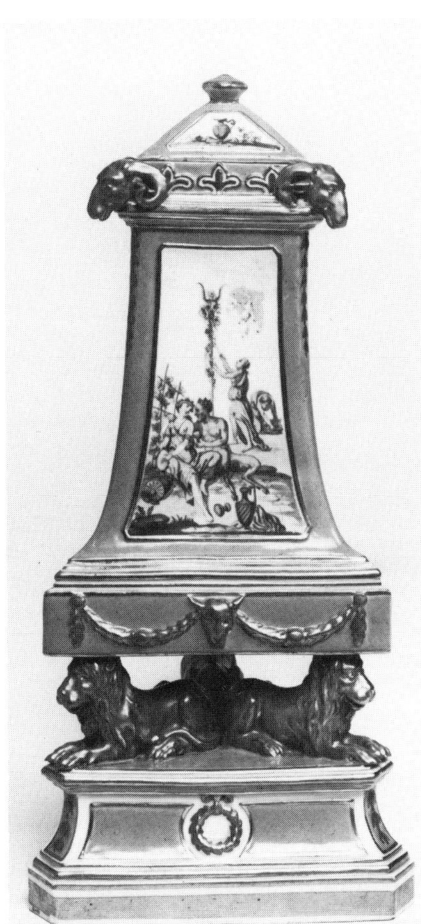

90

Room of Lord Grey de Wilton (created 1st Earl of Wilton in 1801) at Heaton Hall, Manchester, at an overall cost of £216 13s. Bacon's model, derived loosely from a plate in G. B. Piranesi's (1720–78) *Diverse Maniere d'Adornare i Cammini* (1769) is probably taken from a drawing by James Wyatt RA (1746–1813), who frequently collaborated with the sculptor. The design of the room, however, was by James's older brother Samuel (1737–1807). The 2nd Earl of Wilton married Lady Mary Stanley, daughter of the 12th Earl of Derby, who commissioned the Adam looking glass.

90 *Vase and Cover*

Soft paste porcelain painted in enamel colours and gilt
Mark: an anchor in gilt
English (Chelsea-Derby), *c.* 1780
Height: 37.4 cm (14¾ in)
Purchased (1979.19)

This neoclassical-style altar-shaped vase and cover is three-sided and is supported by three seated lions on a pedestal. It was made during the Chelsea-Derby period: William Duesbury, owner of the Derby factory, purchased the Chelsea premises and working materials in 1770 and kept up production until 1783. On each of the three sides of the vase are panels depicting bacchanals in grisaille, reserved on a ground of turquoise blue enamel. This colour is an example of the new 'blue celeste' mentioned in Duesbury's sale catalogue of 1771, clearly an imitation of the Sèvres ground colour, *bleu celeste*.

The actual form of the vase is faithfully copied from an etching in Comte de Caylus' *Receuil d'Antiquités égyptiennes, étrusques, grecques, romaines et gauloises*, first published in Paris in seven volumes in 1752–67 (Vol. VII, Supplément, pl. xliii). Chelsea-Derby vases of this curious shape were offered for sale by Christie and Ansell on 29 March 1773 and 17 April 1780. The description in the 1780 sale catalogue reads: 'An altar-shaped vase supported by three lions on a pedestal, enamel'd in compartments with figures and richly gilt.' The vase realised a price of £2 9s. Vases of this particular model are extremely rare; only one other example, lacking a cover, has been recorded.

91 *Wedgwood*

VASE

Black basaltes, painted in red 'encaustic' with a woman bearing grave offerings.
English (Josiah Wedgwood, Staffordshire), *c.* 1780
Height: 21.8 cm (8⅝ in)
Anna M. Philips Gift (1906.62)

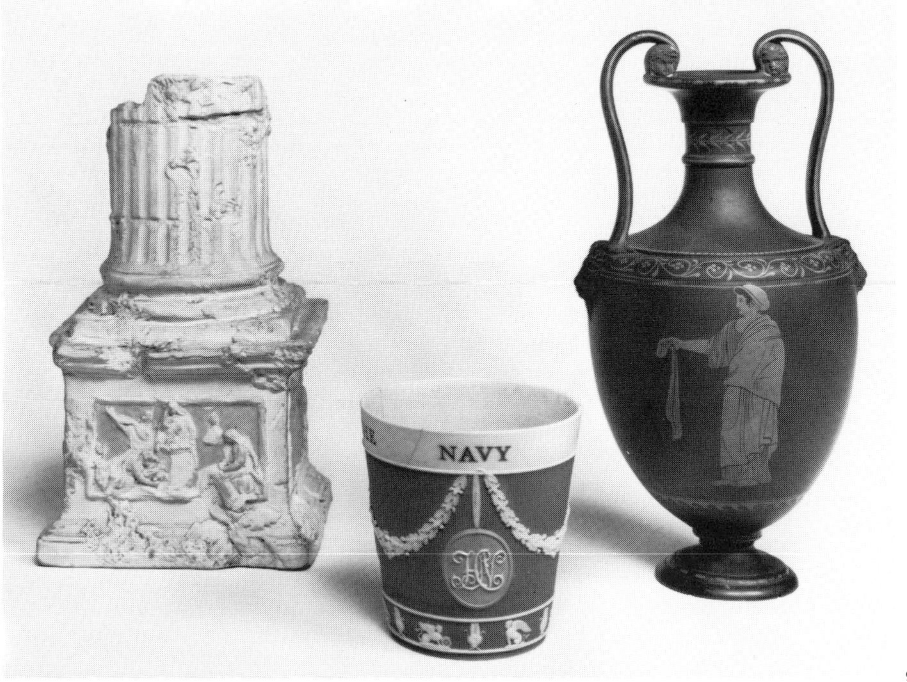

91

RUINED COLUMN

Jasperware, white with blue dip on low relief panels, two ornamented with sacrifice scenes, two imitating worn inscriptions.
Mark: WEDGWOOD
English (Josiah Wedgwood, Staffordshire), *c.* 1790
Height: 20 cm ($7\frac{7}{8}$ in)
Anna M. Philips Gift (1906.52)

BEAKER

Jasperware, white with dark blue dip and white relief, three medallions in lilac, one with monogram *HN*, the two others with figures of Hope and Neptune.
Inscribed around rim: THE NAVY OF BRITAIN.
Mark: WEDGWOOD.
English (Josiah Wedgwood, Staffordshire), 1798
Height: 8.5 cm ($3\frac{3}{8}$ in)
Anna M. Philips Gift (1906.63)

Josiah Wedgwood (1730–95) first produced black basaltes in 1768; this body was used, when painted in red 'encaustic', to imitate Greek red figure vases of the 5th century BC. The figure painted on the illustrated example is taken from an original vase in the collection of Sir William Hamilton (1730–1803), British Minister to Naples in 1764–72. Hamilton's collection was catalogued by P. F. Hugues, called D'Hancarville (1719–1803) and published in 1766–67. Wedgwood acquired a copy, and it was a constant source of inspiration to him.

After years of experiments, Wedgwood perfected his new ceramic body, jasperware, by 1775, a fine stoneware which could be coloured and so show up relief decoration in white. Jasperware was admirably suited to the current neo-classical style. The ruined column illustrates the fashion for depicting ancient ruins, inspired by excavations at Herculaneum and Pompeii. Columns such as this served as spill vases in a *garniture de cheminée*. Jasperware was also used to commemorate contemporary events.

The very rare beaker, bearing the monogram of Horatio Nelson (1758–1805) and Egyptian motifs, celebrates the Battle of the Nile in 1798.

The Galleries house a large and distinguished collection of Wedgwood.

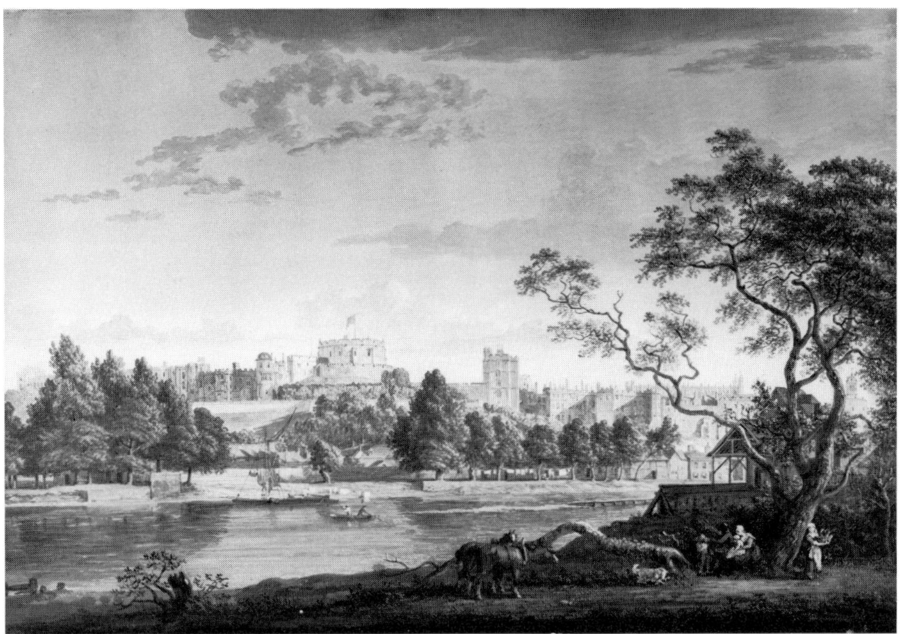

92

92 Paul Sandby

(1730–1809)

WINDSOR CASTLE 1780

English; bodycolour
49 × 70 cm ($19\frac{5}{16} \times 27\frac{9}{16}$ in) sight
Unsigned
Bequeathed by William Arnold Sandby (1905.8)

Sandby's long and successful career began as a draughtsman in the Military Drawing Office at the Tower of London. Both Paul and his brother, the architect Thomas Sandby (1723–98) established considerable reputations, enhanced by royal connections when Thomas was appointed Deputy Ranger at Windsor Great Park. Sandby first began to exhibit views of Windsor Castle at the Society of Arts in 1763. This example may have been bought by W. A. Sandby, a direct descendant, at Christie's on 23 May 1876 from a large folio of Windsor drawings, formerly in the collections of Sir Joseph Banks and Sir Wyndham Knatchbull, many of which are now in the Royal Collection at Windsor.

Windsor Castle is painted entirely in bodycolour (powdered colour mixed with size or isinglass jelly and honey), Sandby's preferred method for exhibited works. The rich colouring and detailed finish of Sandby's bodycolour technique meant that these works could hang at the Royal Academy side by side with oil paintings to more effect than the delicate watercolours or tinted drawings of the period. *Windsor Castle* is still in its original wide gilt frame, and is close-framed, without a mount, like an oil. Bodycolour was in common usage on the Continent but Sandby was one of the first native born artists to employ the medium. Sandby's friend Colonel Gravatt noted in his diary that Sandby would begin his bodycolours by covering the whole paper with a pure azure blue ground. The colonel wrote:

'I particularly remarked he did not, even in the nearest lights, allow the azure (previously painted as a ground) to appear, so that the whole landscape was of a lower tone than the sky, which is what gives such admirable clearness to his skies.'

93 *Man's Court Suit* *pl. 8*

Coat and breeches: black silk velvet with purple satin figure in small diaper pattern.
Waistcoat: ivory satin.
All copiously embroidered with a floral border pattern in pastel silks.
British or French, 1775–90
Coat length: 111.7 cm (44 in)
Purchased from Lord Stanley of Alderley (1952.359/3)

Close fitting coat with tight sleeves and high collar, the fronts curving back to the narrow skirt. The ten large embroidered self-fabric buttons are for decoration: it fastens with two hooks and eyes. The hip pockets with large shaped flaps, and the cuffs, are also embellished with buttons. The skirts are held in double pleats at the back with buttons top and bottom.

The whole is embroidered with a deep floral border in satin stitch, including lily of the valley, narcissi and forget-me-nots, interspersed with appliquéd net.

The breeches are plain except for the embroidered knee-bands. They have horn buttons for braces.

The waistcoat fastens with twelve small embroidered self-fabric buttons. It has pockets with deep flaps at the hips, and the front is cut in steep points. Its embroidery was designed to match that on the coat, but with the large narcissi worked in pink rather than cream. Its ground is dotted with forget-me-nots. This type of embroidery was made in specialised workshops, worked on the piece before the garment was cut out. It is likely that the embroidery was made in France, and the piece exported to England. The suit follows the typical line of late 18th-century male dress. The silhouette was becoming narrower, with the once full skirts now reduced to tight pleats drawn to the centre back of the coat as the fronts curved away from the chest. At the same time the waistcoat was becoming shorter and less important. By the 1770s such highly decorated garments were worn infrequently: men were beginning to prefer the more subtle pleasures of broadcloth and plain linen. Suits like this one were reserved for the grandest occasions, and in particular for use at court.

In the same way that modern official dress for men has become a type of uniform, derived from styles of evening dress no longer generally worn, so too were these gorgeous embroidered suits to remain the accepted dress for court long after they had been abandoned for any other occasion. The decoration gradually became more stylised until by the mid-19th century just a few flowered sprigs remained on the waistcoat.

This suit is said to have been worn by Sir John Stanley of Alderley (1735–1807), who was a Gentleman of the Privy Chamber to George III. It is not only of importance as a fine example in itself, but also because it is associated with no less than five similar suits, belonging to the same person. Because the wearer was evidently very slim, and fashion conscious, it is possible that they were worn by Sir John Stanley's eldest son, John Thomas Stanley, born in 1766, who was to become a well-known writer and traveller, and Fellow of the Royal Society.

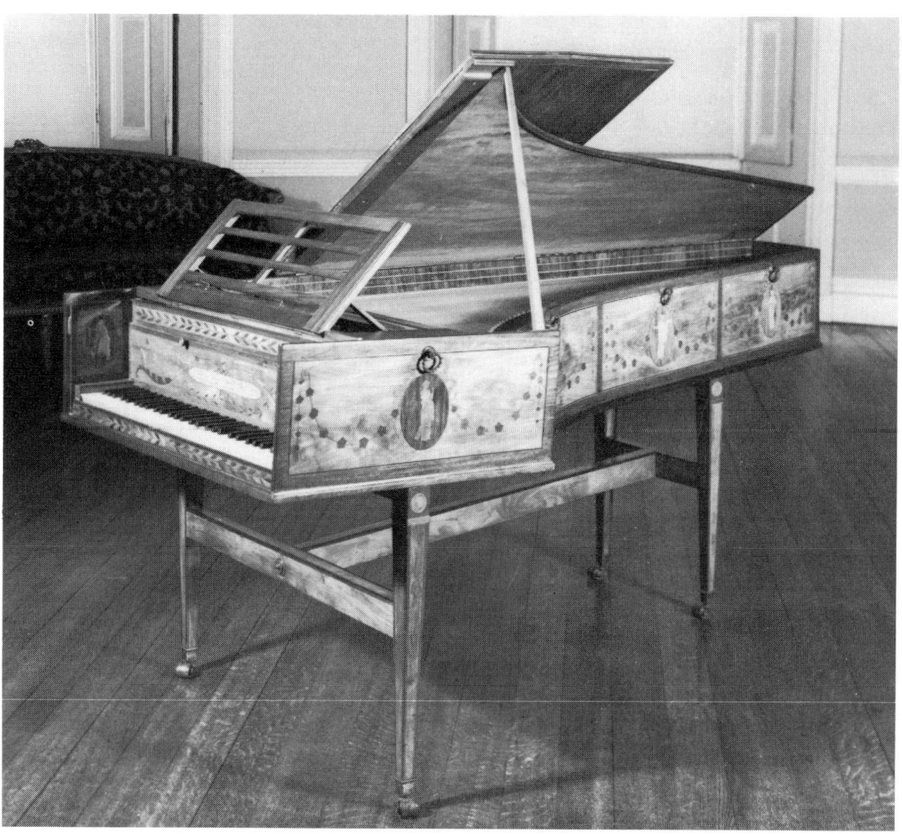

94

94 *Grand Pianoforte*

Pine, veneered in satinwood with rosewood bandings and marquetry panels
English (London), inscribed: *Robertus Stodart, Londini fecit 1784, Wardour Street Soho*
Length: 223 cm (87.75 in)
Purchased (1955.110)

The late 18th century was a transitional period in the evolution of keyboard musical instruments. Robert Stodart (fl. *c.* 1770–96) was one of the inventors of the 'English' pianoforte action with Americus Backers and John Broadwood. The action of this 'forte piano', as it would have been known, is of five octaves with an undivided, single pinned, harpsichord-type bridge and three metal gap spacers to reinforce the gap between the soundboard and the wrest plank.

The case is in the traditional harpsichord shape with a stand and stretcher. It was undoubtedly the work of a specialist cabinet maker who had made a special feature of the five marquetry panels on the outside of the case and two additional ones flanking the keyboard. These would have been supplied by a further specialist *marqueteur* whose sources for the former are the highly influential, red-figure Greek vases published by Sir William Hamilton in his *Collection of Etruscan, Greek and Roman Antiquities* (*c.* 1766–69), with illustrations by Pierre Hugues (1719–1805), better known as d'Hancarville (especially Vol. II, plate 45, and Vol. III, plate 65). The latter pair of figures probably represents Odysseus and Penelope. The identity of these specialist marquetry cutters remains a mystery. The same hand was probably responsible for similar panels on a pair of console tables at Temple Newsam, Leeds. A slightly earlier group of furniture and pianoforte cases made for Frederick Beck have marquetry attributed to the Swede, Christopher Fuhrlogh (fl. 1767–97), taken from engravings after Angelica Kauffmann.

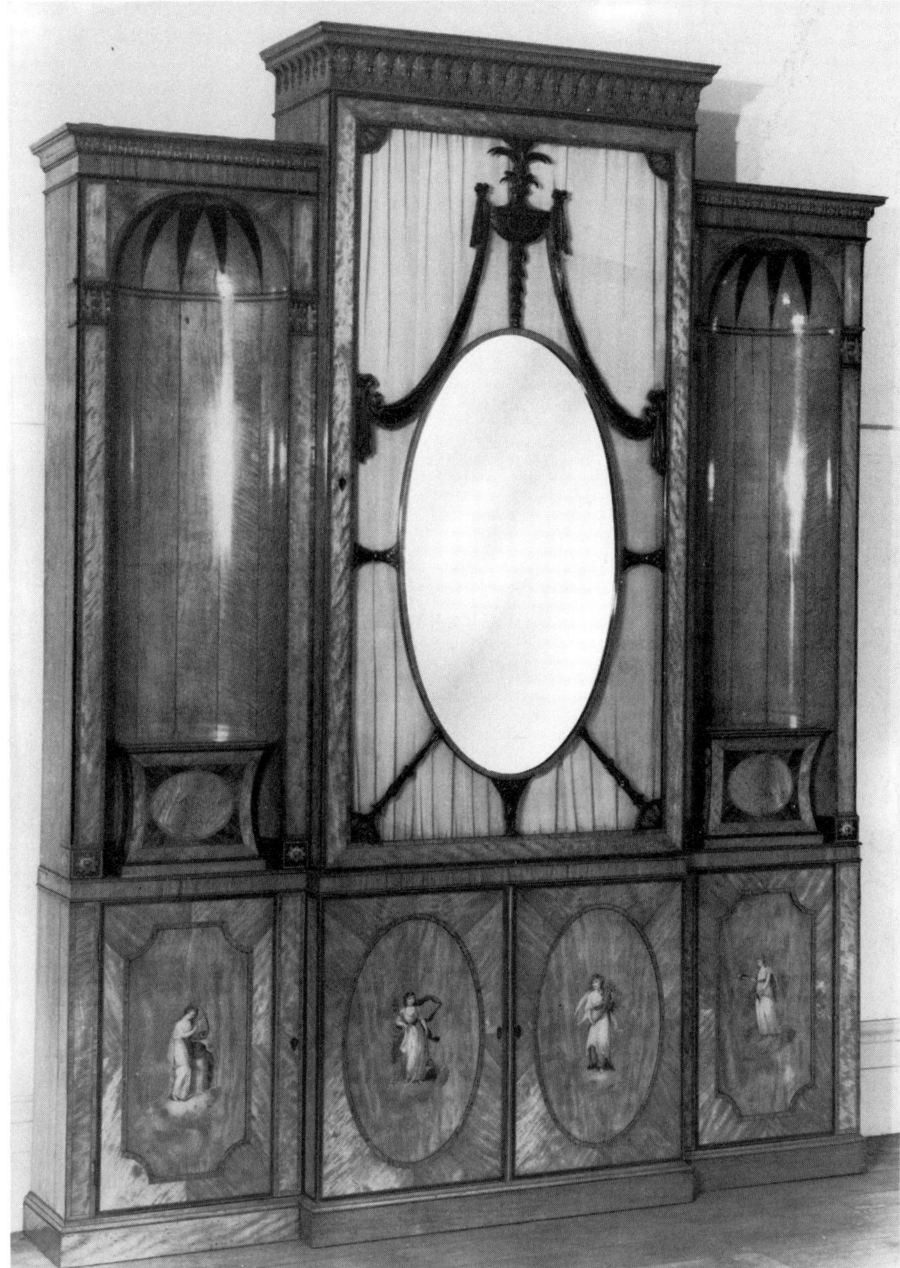

95

95 *Library Bookcase*

Deal, with satinwood veneer, tulipwood, rosewood bandings and painted decoration
English, *c.* 1800
Height: 274 cm (108 in); width: 147 cm (84 in)
Purchased (1960.339)

One of the most characteristic features of the elegant and delicate furniture of the last years of the 18th century is the use of light-coloured veneers with strong patterns and linear decoration. On this large and unusual bookcase (formerly in the collection of the late Viscount Boyd of Merton), the areas which in an earlier period might be expected to have carved details (in the pilaster capitals, the bases and friezes) are instead decorated with charming neo-classical painted paterae and palmettes. The painted figures of antique muses on the cupboard doors, derived from engravings after Angelica Kauffmann (1741–1807) and Michael Angelo Pergolesi (d. 1801), are alternatives to marquetry decoration.

The inspiration behind this piece is the most influential designer of the 1790s, Thomas Sheraton (1751–1806), whose *Drawing Book* (1791–94), *Dictionary* (1803), and *Encyclopaedia* (1806) aimed at acquainting cabinet makers with the most up-to-date designs. An illustration for a similar bookcase was included in his *Dictionary* (Vol. II, plate 54): it also contained niches in the lower cupboards, for which he recommended busts, 'which may be those of persons famed for literature and genius; and the figures in the upper part may be suited to the chief subjects of the books contained in the library case' (p. 260). The evidence of two filled-in peg holes at the top of the niches would support the suggestion that they originally contained figures in the manner suggested by Sheraton.

96 *Thomas Gainsborough*

(1727–88) *pl.7*

A PEASANT GIRL GATHERING FAGGOTS IN A WOOD 1782

English, oil on canvas
169 × 123 cm ($66\frac{1}{2} \times 48\frac{1}{2}$ in)
Unsigned
Purchased with the aid of Government grants (through the Victoria and Albert Museum) and the National Art-Collections Fund (1978.138).

In the last years of his career, tired of portraiture, Gainsborough experimented with a series of romantic, rustic scenes, inspired by the 17th-century Spanish painter Murillo. Few of these so-called 'fancy' pictures survive.

The first known example, *A Shepherd* (destroyed 1810), was exhibited at the Royal Academy in 1781 and engraved by Richard Earlom in that year. *A Peasant Girl* followed in 1782 together with *Girl with Pigs* (Castle Howard, Yorkshire) which was exhibited at the Royal Academy and bought by Sir Joshua Reynolds.

A Peasant Girl was not exhibited in the artist's lifetime and was sold by Mrs Gainsborough in 1797 as 'unfinished', presumably meaning that the work was not sufficiently tightly painted by Royal Academy standards. The face is the most highly worked part of the picture and the focal point of the composition. The hands and feet still remain unresolved. This may partly explain why the picture was sold for only five guineas. At the turn of the century, the 'fancy' pictures were considered to be the artist's best work, and Gainsborough himself charged greater prices for these than for other paintings.

A Peasant Girl was owned for many years by the Abdy family and there is a family tradition that one of the Abdy children modelled for the picture. This seems unlikely although Gainsborough did use models for his 'fancy' pictures. Jack Hill, a London beggar boy, modelled for at least two paintings included *A Shepherd. A Peasant Girl* has the same melancholy beauty that is seen in Gainsborough's portraits of fashionable, aristocratic women. It is a mature work displaying the artist's vibrant, fluid brushwork and shimmering, silvery colour.

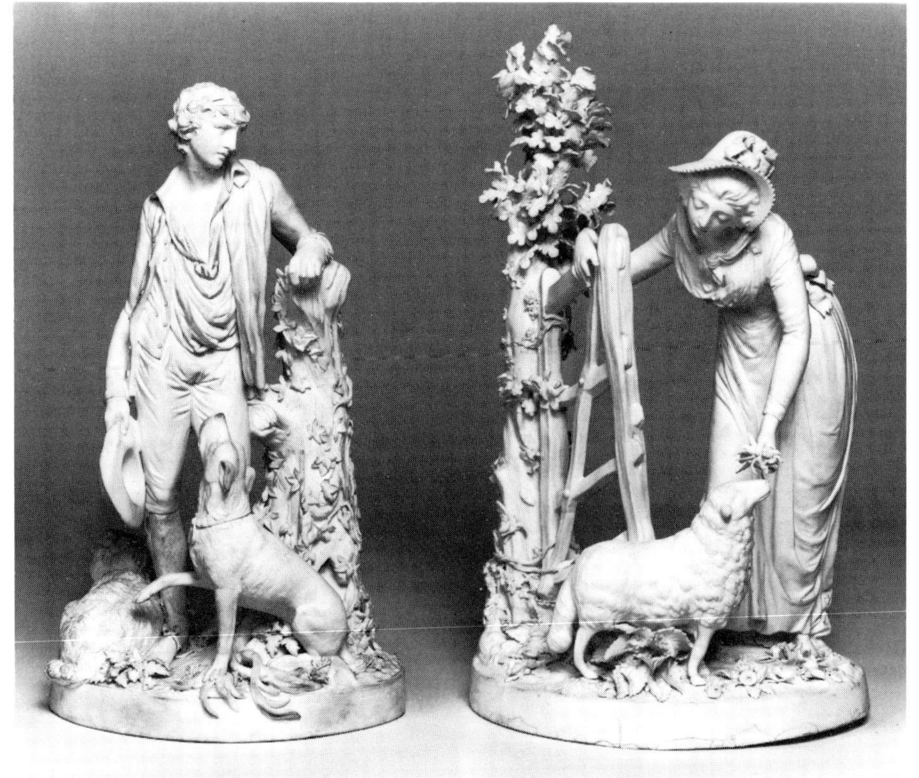

97

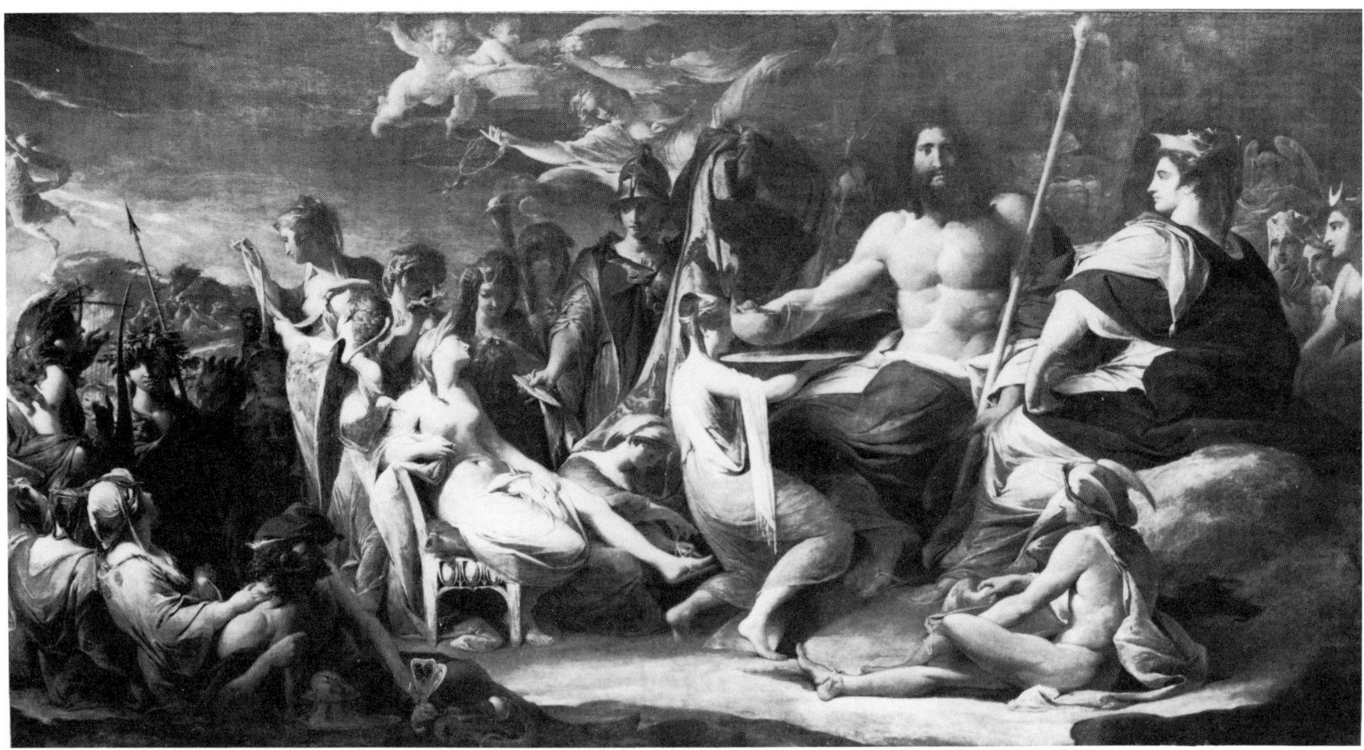

98

97 *Derby Porcelain*

FIGURE OF A SHEPHERD

Soft paste biscuit porcelain
Incised mark on base: *No. 396*
English (Derby), 1790–95
Height: 30.8 cm ($12\frac{1}{8}$ in)
G. Beatson Blair Bequest (1947.706)

FIGURE OF A SHEPHERDESS

Soft paste biscuit porcelain
English (Derby), 1790–95
Height: 34.9 cm ($13\frac{3}{4}$ in)
Purchased (1982.121)

These two figures are modelled in biscuit porcelain, a body first developed at Sèvres by 1753 and in use at Derby by 1771. The *Shepherdess* is taken from an engraving of *Adelaide* by J. Hogg after Francis Wheatley, published on 21 July 1787. It was modelled by J. J. W. Spängler (b.1755) and shows his characteristic fine attention to detail. The *Shepherd*, based on a cast of the antique in the collection of Joseph Wright of Derby, was also modelled by Spängler.

Spängler was a highly talented Swiss modeller who spent an ill-disciplined five-year period in England in 1790–95, working on and off for the Derby factory. During the 1770s he had probably worked as a modeller at the Zürich porcelain factory, where his father was technical director. There he met the Swiss sculptor J. V. Sonnenschein (1749–1828) whose graceful neo-classical style was to become the basis of Spängler's own. Spängler came to London in 1790, already a sophisticated modeller with an understanding of the Antique. He signed agreements with William Duesbury, proprietor of the Derby porcelain factory, which he continually broke. He tried to leave the country, got into debt, stole money and had two spells in prison. He eventually worked 'by the piece' for Derby, modelling a number of biscuit figures, until he was given notice in July 1795.

98 *James Barry*

(1741–1806)

THE BIRTH OF PANDORA (also called PANDORA OR THE HEATHEN EVE)

English School; oil on canvas
279 × 520 cm (110 × 205 in)
Unsigned
Transferred from the Royal Manchester Institution (1882.12)

The Irishman James Barry, a close friend of Edmund Burke, was the most ambitious exponent of history painting of his generation in Britain. In 1775 he exhibited at the Royal Academy a drawing of *Pandora*, now known only from an etching by Schiavonetti. Barry's drawing was conceived during his stay in Rome from 1766 to 1770, and was a conscious attempt to rival Raphael's *Council of the Gods* at the Villa Farnesina. His subject was Pandora brought before the Gods on Mount Olympus. According to Hesiod, she was modelled in clay by Vulcan, presented with the gifts of the Gods and sent by Jupiter to earth. His gift was the box or urn which she was forbidden to open. When she disobeyed, she released evil into the world. The Greek myth was seen as the pagan equivalent of the Biblical Fall of Man, hence Barry's alternative title, *The Heathen Eve*.

Barry took up the idea again later in his career and by 1791 was at work on this oil painting, which was complete in 1804. The main figures are Jupiter and Juno seated on the right, with Mercury below and Hebe kneeling with the cup. Pandora reclines to the left, with Venus and Cupid behind her holding a girdle, two of the Graces anointing and dressing her hair, whilst a third ties her sandal. Hymen with the marriage torch looks on, whilst in the centre Minerva, goddess of Wisdom, presents a shuttle and tapestry to instruct her in the arts. The figures on the far left include Apollo and Bacchus, whilst in front Vulcan guards a bird emerging from its shell, and releases a butterfly, symbolishing Pandora's soul. Behind Jupiter's torch are the three Fates, one of whom advances with the urn.

Though Barry was attempting to re-create the heroic figure style as well as the instructive allegory of the Antique, he has introduced a much richer *chiaroscuro* and variety of grouping which derive from the Baroque.

The painting was unsold at the artist's death. After he died it was auctioned, realising 11½ guineas, but it was unclaimed. In 1856 it was purchased by the Royal Manchester Institution. It is the largest painting in the collection.

99 Cruet Set

Silver and silver-mounted cut glass.
English (London), hallmark for 1791–92, maker's mark for Daniel Pontifex.
Height: 26.7 cm (10½ in)
Lloyd Roberts Bequest (1920.1205)

The elongated forms of this piece suggest the supreme refinement of taste in the closing years of the 18th century. The classical sources of the vase-shaped bottles and the fluted decoration on the feet are reduced to the merest suggestions. It is hardly surprising that within a very few years there was to be a strong reaction in favour of bolder forms and more archaeological sources. Cruet sets had first appeared in the late 17th century and by this period generally consisted of a boat shaped base with cut glass containers. A drawing in the Victoria and Albert Museum indicates that the bottles were used as receptacles for 'oil, soy, mustard, lemon, vinegar, ketchup, pepper and cayan', giving an interesting insight into 18th-century culinary embellishments.

Daniel Pontifex (fl. 1791 onwards) is best known for his fine gilt dessert dishes and baskets. The existence of at least two other identical models by John Schofield (fl. 1776–96) and Paul Storr (1771–1844) suggests either that a specialist worker would supply leading goldsmiths with these items for stock, or alternatively that the various mass produced cast pieces, from which they were made, were supplied by specialists (possibly in Birmingham or Sheffield) to be assembled and subsequently submitted for assay by the London goldsmiths.

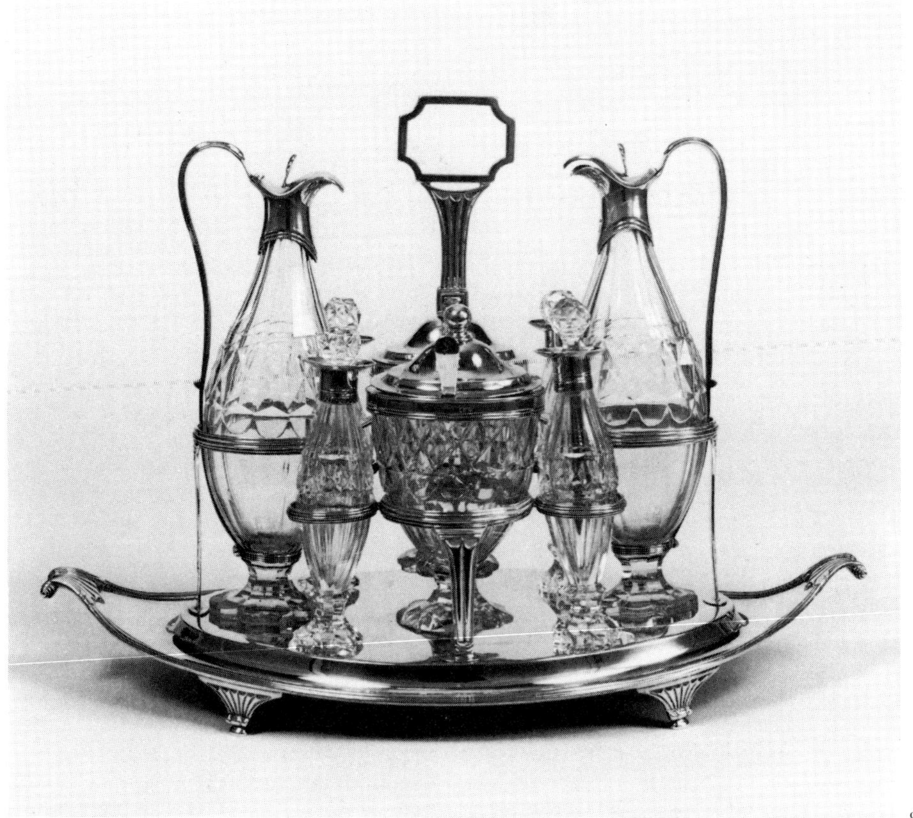

99

100 Louis Gauffier

(1761–1801)

PYGMALION AND GALATEA 1797

French; oil on canvas
67.5 × 51.2 cm ($26\frac{9}{16} \times 20\frac{3}{16}$ in)
Signed (b.r.c.): *L. Gauffier. Flor.ce 1797*
Purchased with the aid of a grant from the National Art-Collections Fund (1979.546)

The subject is from Ovid's *Metamorphoses*, X, 243–297. Pygmalion, the King of Cyprus, fell in love with an ivory statue he had made of the sea-nymph Galatea. In answer to his prayers, Aphrodite, goddess of love, breathed life (here symbolised by a butterfly) into the statue.

Louis Gauffier won the Grand Prix awarded by the French Royal Academy of Painting in 1784, sharing first prize with Jean-Germaine Drouais. The prize enabled him to become a *pensionnaire* at the French Academy in Rome, where he remained until 1793. In January of that year, Gauffier fled from Rome to Florence to escape the reprisals taken against the French after the execution of Louis XVI. In Florence, where this picture was painted, he was chiefly patronised by cultural circles of expatriate Englishmen and Russians.

Gauffier specialised in small-scale paintings in the Neo-classical style with subjects drawn from Roman history and Ancient mythology. Neo-classicism originated in Rome in the mid-18th century and was a conscious imitation of antique art inspired by the discoveries at Herculaneum and Pompeii. This was particularly true of sculpture, which survived in greater quantity and in better preservation than either painting or architecture. The antique objects in this picture were probably based on items in the Medici collections in Florence. The statue of Galatea was inspired by the Venus de' Medici, discovered in Rome and sent to the Uffizi in Florence in 1688, where it was revered as the most beautiful Venus and one of the finest antique statues to have survived. For the figure of Aphrodite and her drapery, Gauffier drew elements from both Adam and God the Father in Michelangelo's *Creation of Adam* in the Sistine Chapel, Rome. For Pygmalion, he drew from the famous Neo-classical painting, *The Oath of the Horatii* by Jacques-Louis David (now in the Louvre, Paris).

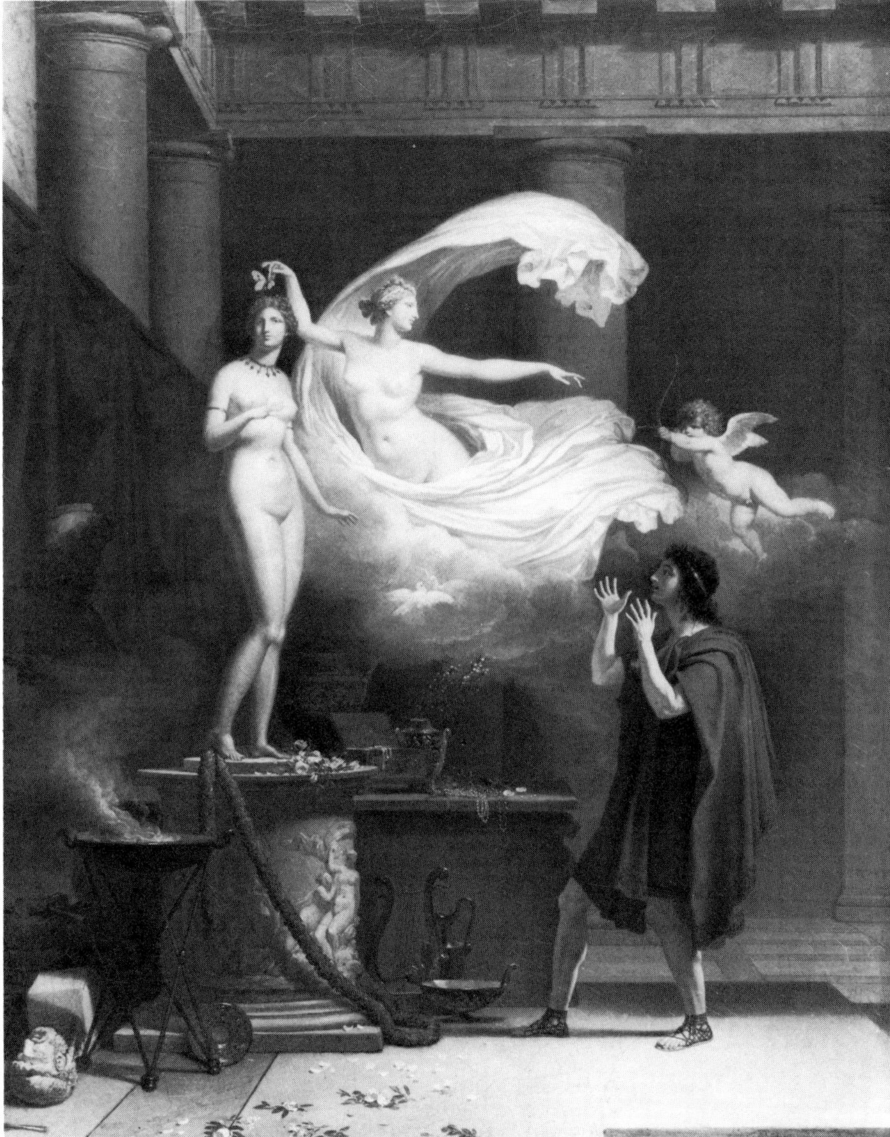

100

A preparatory drawing in black chalk is also in the Gallery's collection. It shows numerous variations on the final version. Pygmalion has clasped hands, indicating that Gauffier may have been influenced by Bronzino's oil of the same subject in the Palazzo Vecchio, Florence.

101 *Wine Jug*

Lead glass, cut and polished, with matt engraving.
French, *c.* 1810
Mark: signed QUIRIN GRAVEUR.
Height: 37 cm (14½ in)
Leicester Collier Bequest (1917.687)

Inscribed *AUSTERLITZ*, this Empire piece commemorates the victory of Napoleon's Grand Armée over the Russians and Austrians in December 1805, familiar from the account in Tolstoy's *War and Peace*. The jug, for which the stopper is lost, is also inscribed with the arms of Napoleon, *orbi et sibi imperat* (he rules the world alone) and *VICIT ET PEPERCIT* (he has conquered and spared).

The cutting and engraving is wonderfully deep, detailed and rich, and the jug is blown from comparatively thick metal. The source of the engraved scene is a mystery. A bowing hussar holding a letter before the Emperor may be a reference to an imperial proclamation, drafted for the French troops on the plain of Pratzen where the battle was won. Thévenin's picture, *The Surrender at Ulm, October 1805* from the Versailles Grand Trianon, refurbished by the Emperor in 1805, shows Roustram, Napoleon's Mamluk valet, restraining his rearing white charger Marengo, as does the engraving on the jug. However, the glass engraving is closer in style to the strict neo-classicism of David's pupil, J. B. Debret (1768–1848), who is known to have engraved three other incidents in Napoleon's European campaigns. In front of Napoleon there is also an altar, replete with Russian trophies, symbolising the 180 guns and 45 flags captured at Austerlitz by the French.

The design is an extraordinary prototype for the English claret jugs and decanters of the 1850s and '60s. Often of severe neo-classical form and decoration, these pieces were similarly wheel-engraved with superb skill. The celebrated 'Neptune' jug by J. G. Green shown at the 1851 Great Exhibition preceded a number of English engraved jugs, sometimes incorporating Greek or Egyptian form and decoration.

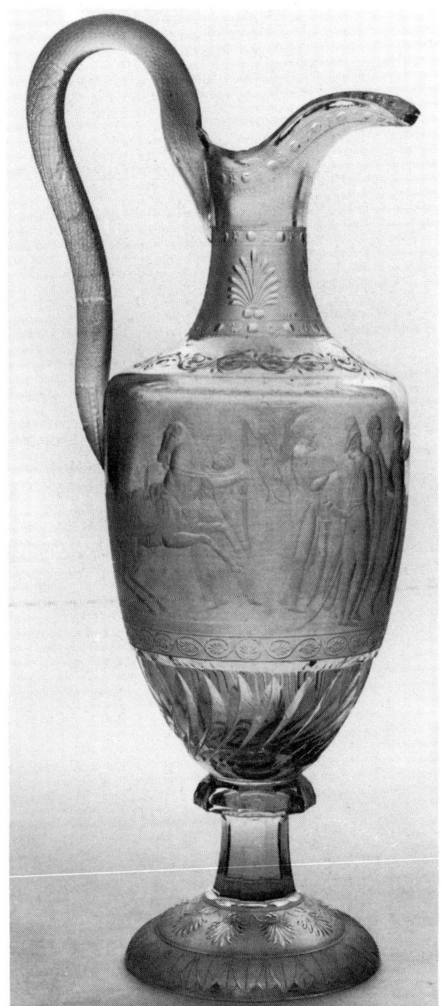
101

102 *Double Salt*

Silver with silver-gilt salt liners.
French (Paris), maker's mark of Jean-Baptiste-Claude Odiot, 1809–15
Height: 30 cm (11¾ in)
Louisa Mary Garret Bequest (1936.233)

The decorative arts of France under the first Napoleonic Empire are characterised by monumental neo-classical forms in sharp contrast to the delicacy of the preceding period. This double salt is supported by classical vestals, bearing sacrifices to an altar. Behind them stands a richly decorated classical column surmounted by a vase. They stand on a base embellished with trailing rainceaux and honeysuckle, supported on cast lion feet. Althogether the piece is in deliberate emulation of the Roman period of Augustus with which the Empire identified itself so closely.

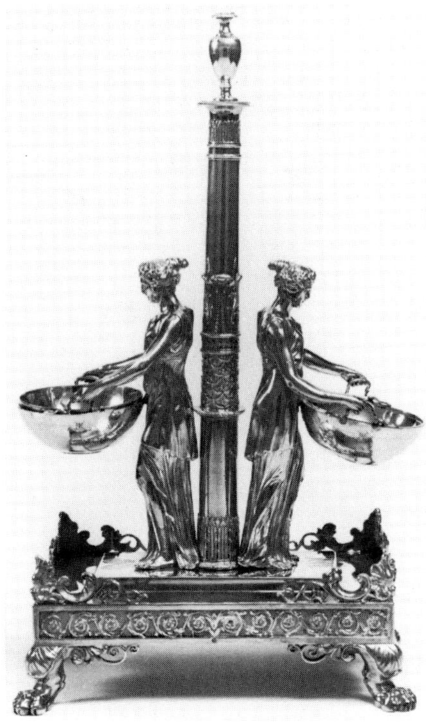
102

Jean-Baptiste-Claude Odiot (1763–1850) was one of the leading goldsmiths of this period and had a powerful clientèle, which included several members of the Imperial family (Madame Mère, Princess Borghese, and the ex-Empress Josephine), and later Louis XVIII. He collaborated with Martin-Guillaume Biennais (1764–1843), the Emperor's official *orfèvrier* who received orders worth 100,000 *livres* per year. This salt, which would have formed part of a large *surtout de table*, is engraved with two oval conjoined shields of arms as yet unidentified. Similar silver gilt examples are in the Rijksmuseum, Amsterdam. Odiot employed some of the finest designers of the period, including the most influential figures, Charles Percier (1764–1838) and Pierre-François-Leonard Fontaine (1762–1853), as well as the *Ciseleur de l'Empereur*, Pierre-Philippe Thomire (1751–1843).

103 Bureau à Abbatant

Pine, veneered in mahogany with ormolu mounts
Possibly South German (Stuttgart), *c.* 1815
Height: 232.5 cm (91.5 in)
Purchased (1961.276)

The monumental neo-classicism of the first French Empire rapidly became an international style, both within the subject nations and beyond. This bureau incorporates many characteristics of the best furniture of the period: finely figured mahogany veneers, elegantly designed and nicely chased ormolu mounts, and a monumental scale. The mounts here include many of the favourite motifs of the Empire style – sphinx heads, lyres, bees, stars, laureated torches and a central panel of two putti. The clock surmounting the design is encased in the form of a classical temple.

This example does not closely correspond with French, Italian or Swedish pieces, and equally lacks the *gemütlich* quality of the slightly later Biedermeier style, let alone the idiosyncratic character of the furniture designed by Karl Friedrich Schinkel (1781–1841) or made by Josef Danhauser (fl. 1804–30). Two bureaux in the Württembergisches Landesmuseum, Stuttgart, attributed to the designs of the architect and painter Nikolaus Thouret (1767–1845), have remarkably similar mounts and disposition of panels.

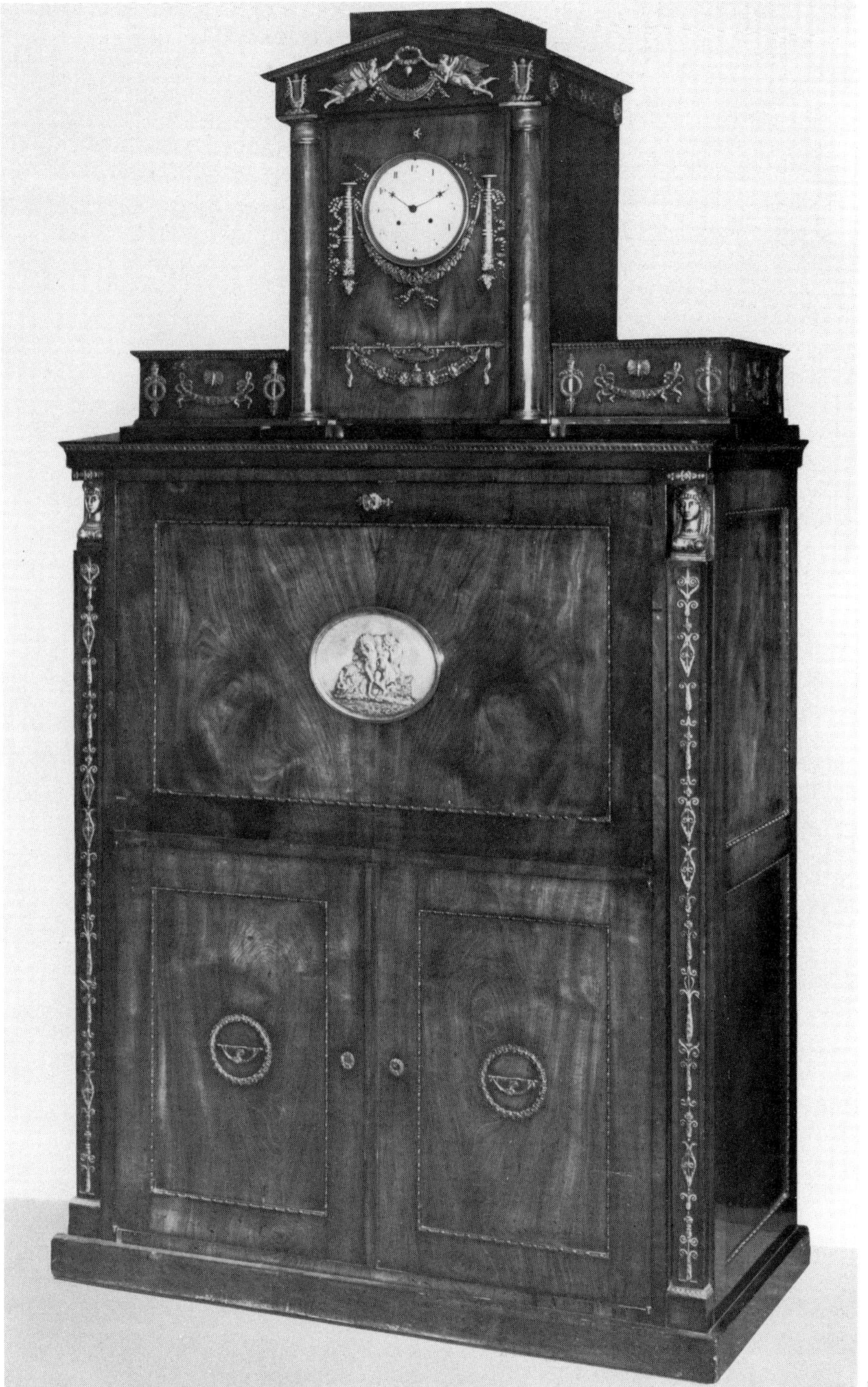

103

104 Bertel Thorvaldsen
(1770–1844)

THE SHEPHERD BOY 1825–26

Italian School; marble
Height: 149 cm ($58\frac{3}{4}$ in)
Signed: THORVALDSEN / FECIT
Bequeathed by Mrs McGrigor Phillips (the writer Dorothy Una Ratcliffe) (1937.672)

The fine group of *The Shepherd Boy* was carved by Thorvaldsen in Rome, where the Danish sculptor spent most of his life, working on commissions from all over Europe. In chaste white marble, the sculpture bears all the hallmarks of Thorvaldsen's style: serene harmony, graceful outline, and a gentle fusion of nature with the Antique.

It was originally conceived in 1817, when Thorvaldsen's young model, resting in the studio after posing for a group entitled *Ganymede and Jove's Eagle*, casually took up this position. The face of the boy is idealised, but the dog is a portrait of the sculptor's dog, called Teverino. The original sketch model in plaster, together with a sheet of pen and ink studies and a more highly finished model, is preserved in the Thorvaldsen Museum in Copenhagen. The full-size group was made five times in marble, including versions in the Thorvaldsen Museum, in the Hermitage, Leningrad, and one in the Draper's Hall, London. There are also what appear to be replicas at Waddesdon and Chatsworth. It has recently been discovered that the Manchester version was bought by William Haldimand, a financier, who commissioned it in 1825–26 for the neo-classical house he was building in Belgrave Square. Haldimand, however, never lived there, and the group was sold to Henry Thomas Hope of Deepdene (a pun, meaning 'Long Hope'), Surrey, son of the banker and great connoisseur Thomas Hope (1769–1831), who formed an important collection of marbles (see entry to Algardi, no. 40). The Hopes also owned

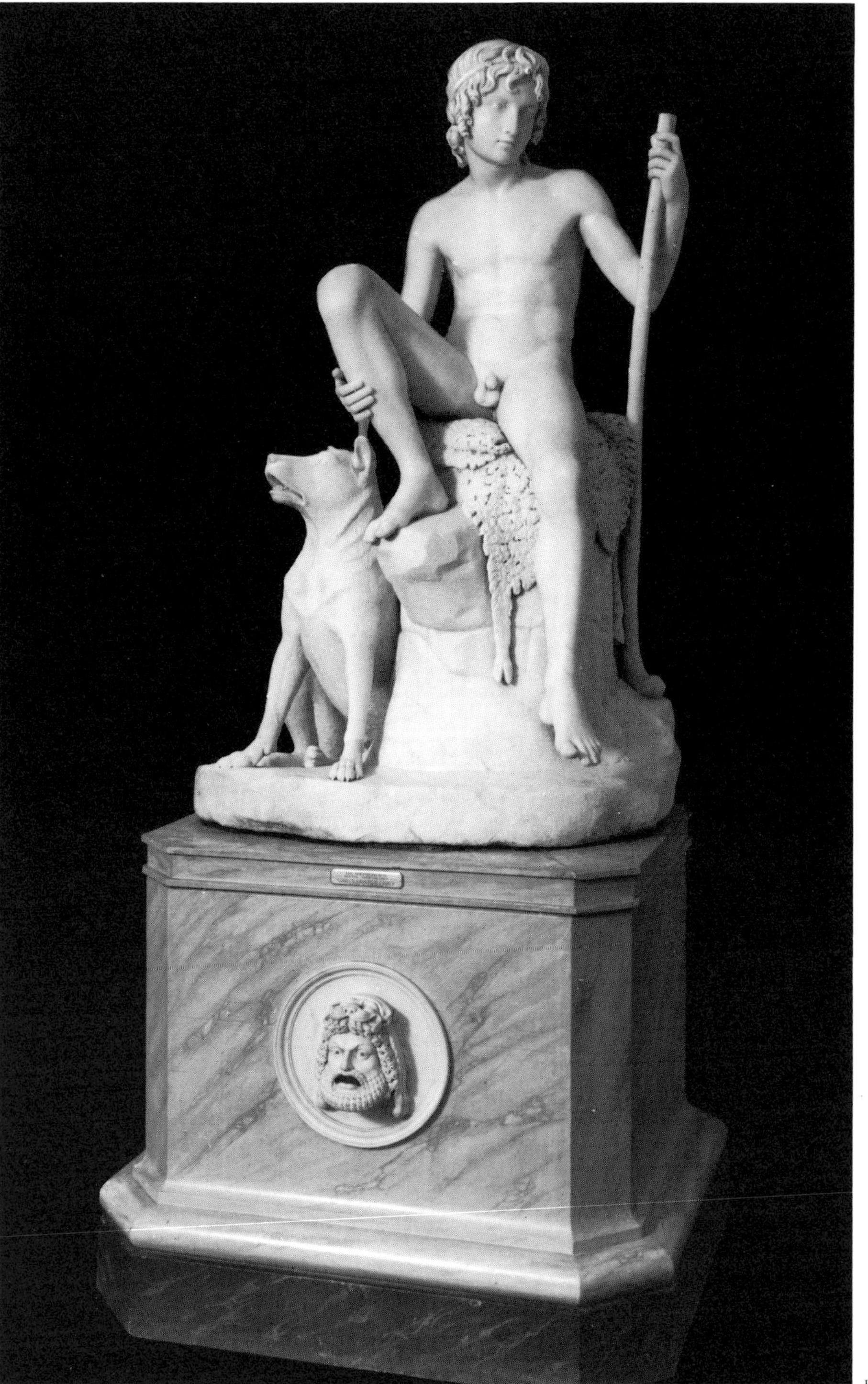

104

Merry Company by Jacob Ochtervelt (1634–1682), now in the Galleries' collection.

The marble mask of Hercules on the simulated marble timber pedestal was designed by Thomas Hope senior, as the design appears in his *Household Furniture and Interior Decoration* (London 1807), and was probably carved by John Flaxman RA (1755–1826).

105 *J. M. W. Turner*

(1775–1851)

THOMSON'S AEOLIAN HARP
exh. 1809

English; oil on canvas
166.7 × 306 cm (65⅝ × 120½ in)
Unsigned
Accepted by H.M. Treasury in 1979 in lieu of Capital Transfer Tax from the Trustees of the Walter Morrison Picture Settlement, and allocated to Manchester City Art Gallery (1979.7)

Aeolus was the king of storms and winds in classical mythology and the aeolian harp, placed on the pedestal in this picture, produced sound when the wind vibrated the strings. The pedestal decorating the tomb is inscribed with the word '*THOMSON*', referring to the poet, James Thomson who published *An Ode on Aeolus's Harp* in 1748. Thomson lived at Richmond, London, and Turner has depicted a view of the Thames from Richmond Hill. However, Turner's obscure choice of subject was more probably suggested by William Collins's *Ode occasion'd by the death of Mr. Thomson* written in 1749. Collins's poem, which is set on the Thames, near Richmond, mentions the harp of Aeolus and describes the poet's sylvan grave decorated by nymphs. Turner's painting was exhibited in 1809 with a poem composed by the artist on the subject of Thomson's tomb. Turner's lines invoke the four seasons – a reference to Thomson's famous poem *The Seasons* – and also mention Pope's Villa at Twickenham which was demolished in 1807.

Richmond Hill was a favourite sketching spot, and in 1810 Turner had a small villa, Sandy Combe Lodge, built to his own design on a plot of land not far from the site of Pope's demolished villa. Turner's view of the winding river and distant buildings is accurate but he has transformed the landscape into a Claudian vision of golden light and distant blue haze framed by the foreground vegetation. The composition is comparable to Claude's *Adoration of the Golden Calf* also formerly in the Walter Morrison collection (see no. 41).

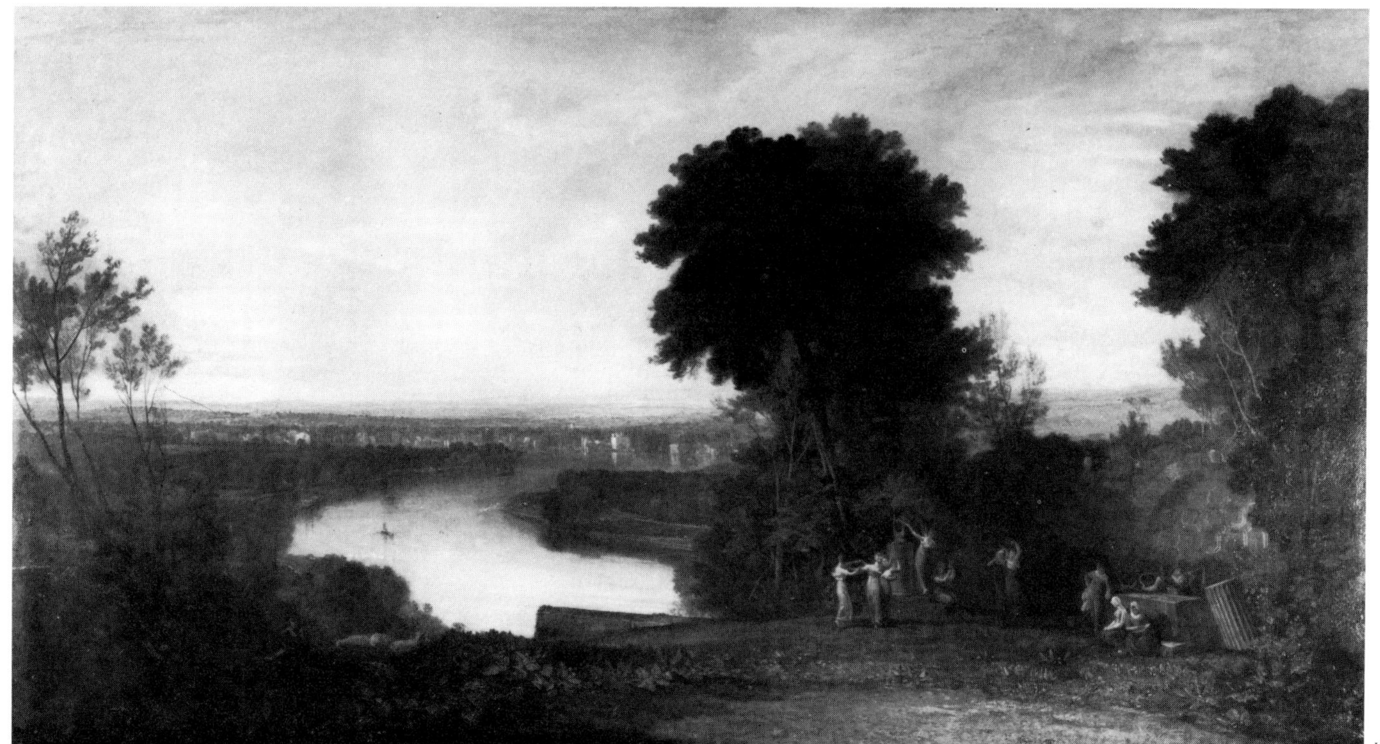

105

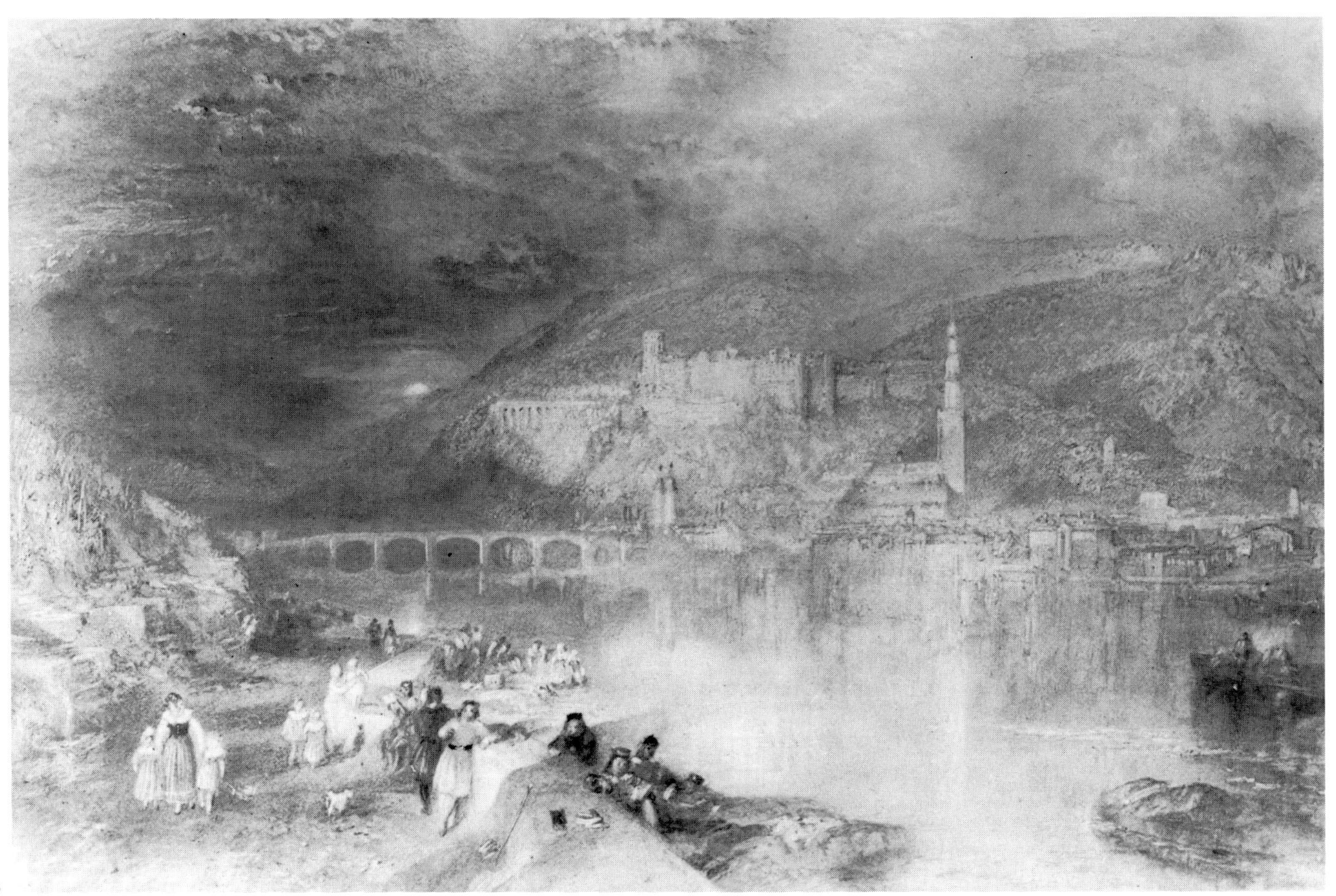

106

106 J. M. W. Turner
(1775–1851)

HEIDELBERG: SUNSET *c.* 1840–42
English; pencil, watercolour and bodycolour with scratching out
38 × 55.2 cm ($14\frac{15}{16} \times 21\frac{3}{4}$ in)
Unsigned
James T. Blair Bequest (1917.106)

Heidelberg, the picturesque university city in southwest Germany, is situated on the banks of the river Neckar. The castle (13th to 17th century) is perched on a hill ninety metres above the city. It was a favourite subject of Turner's in the 1840s, of which he made numerous drawings, watercolours and an oil. A preparatory study or 'colour beginning' in pencil and watercolour for this work is in the British Museum and is inscribed '10 Mar 41' suggesting that the finished watercolour was executed in this or the following year.

The atmospheric effects in *Heidelberg* were achieved by an intricate technique consisting of delicate touches of pure colour, predominantly blue and yellow, broken up by extensive areas of scratching out which create an intense, quivering light. Turner's technical powers evoke a grand, almost Claudian vision recalling his early landscapes. He may also have been influenced by Constable's use of scumbled white impasto in his late oils. Turner made frequent visits to the Continent in the early 1840s returning to the same familiar spots. *Heidelberg* is one of a magnificent series of brilliantly coloured and elaborately worked watercolours done in the penultimate phase of his career. It is one of thirty-five watercolours by Turner in the Gallery's collection.

107 John Crome
(1768–1821)

WOODLAND SCENE WITH SHEEP
English; oil on canvas
64 × 76.3 cm ($25\frac{3}{16} \times 30\frac{1}{16}$ in)
Unsigned
Purchased with the aid of a Government grant (through the Victoria and Albert Museum) (1979.47)

Crome, one of the greatest English landscape painters, was born in Norwich, the son of a journeyman weaver, and began his career apprenticed to a Norwich coach and sign painter. His gentle, introspective and atmospheric landscapes are based on Dutch 17th-century models with a considerable debt to Gainsborough and Wilson. Crome would have had ample opportunity to see works by these artists in the collections of his Norfolk patrons, and it is known he made copies of paintings by Hobbema, Gainsborough, and Wilson.

Woodland Scene has an obscure early history, but latterly belonged to the late Lord Mackintosh of Halifax, who owned a fine collection of Norwich School paintings. Crome's work is frequently difficult to date because many of his paintings were exhibited with vague titles and favourite views were often repeated. *Woodland Scene* was probably executed *c.* 1810–12 and can be compared with Crome's soft ground etchings of that date. The subject of *Woodland Scene* has not been identified, but Stoke Mills, near Norwich, and Chapel Fields, in Norwich, have both

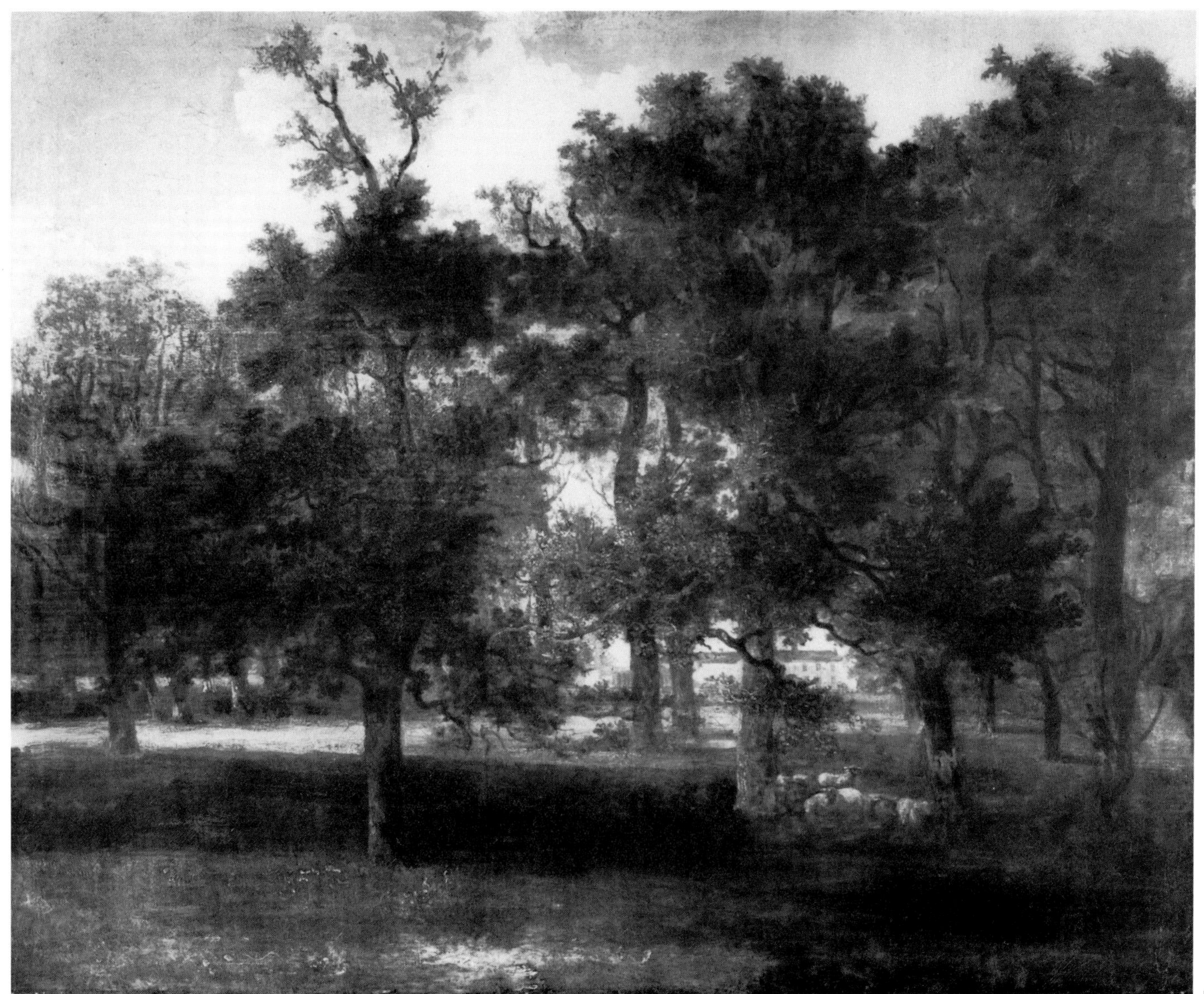

107

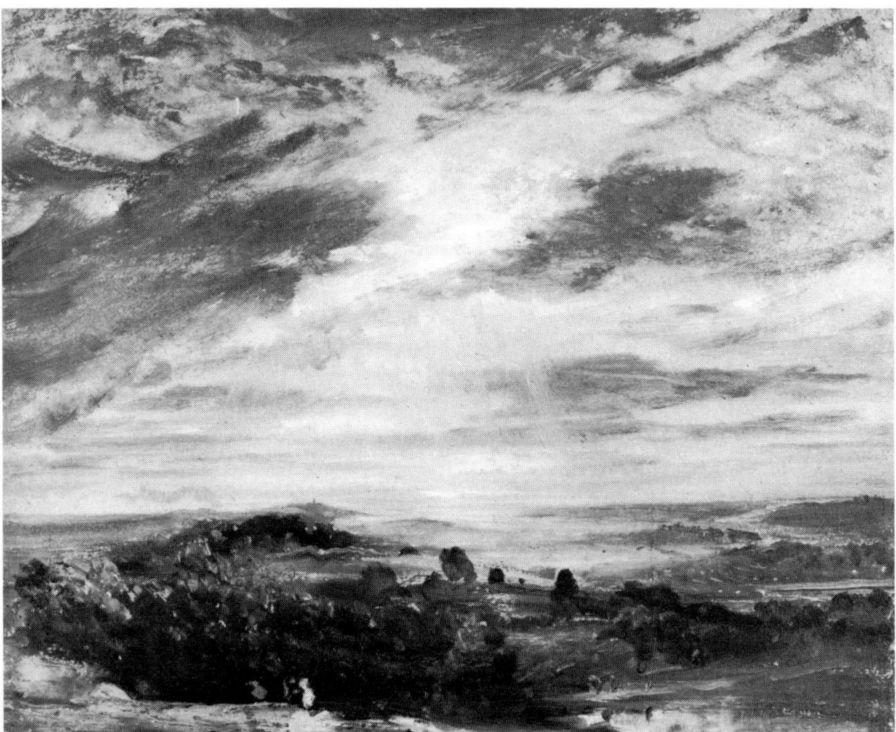

108

been suggested. The composition evokes the timeless tranquillity of the English rural scenery. It deliberately avoids dramatic incident or sharp highlighting and is a charming example of Crome's fresh and unpretentious observation of the Norfolk landscape.

108 John Constable

(1776–1837)

HAMPSTEAD HEATH LOOKING TOWARDS HARROW 1821

English; oil on paper
25 × 29.8 cm ($9\frac{7}{8} \times 11\frac{3}{4}$ in)
Unsigned
James T. Blair Bequest (1917.176)

A label pasted onto the stretcher is inscribed in the artist's hand: 'August 1821 / 5 o clock afternoon: very fine / bright & wind after rain slightly / in the morning.' By 1 September 1820, Constable and his family had settled at Hampstead. That year marked the beginning of a brilliant series of studies of sky and trees on which he continued to work in 1821. The rising ground at Hampstead was admirably suited to capturing the transient appearance of the sky. This sketch shows the spire of Harrow church on the horizon and Branch Hill Pond in the foreground. The explanatory inscriptions that Constable added to most of these rapidly executed oil sketches demonstrate his acute observation and understanding of weather as an ever changing phenomenon. In this example, he is interested not only in capturing the sunny, breezy afternoon light but in the rain of a few hours earlier which gives the sunshine its wet brightness.

The importance attached by Constable to sky painting is demonstrated in a now famous letter to his friend, the Rev. John Fisher, dated 23 October 1821. He wrote: 'I have done a good deal of skying, for I am determined to conquer all difficulties, and that among the rest . . . That landscape painter who does not make his skies a very material part of his composition, neglects to avail himself of one of his greatest aids . . . The sky is the source of light in Nature, and governs everything; even our common observations on the weather of the day are altogether suggested by it. The difficulty of skies in painting is very great, both as to composition and execution; because with all their brilliancy, they ought not to come forward, or, indeed, be hardly thought of any more than extreme distances are; but this does not apply to phenomena or accidental effects of sky, because they always attract particularly.'

109 Peter De Wint

(1784–1849)

HARVEST TIME

English; watercolour over pencil with highlights scratched out
34.4 × 54.9 cm ($13\frac{1}{2} \times 21\frac{5}{8}$ in) sight
Unsigned
James T. Blair Bequest (1917.132)

One of the finest of an important group of 13 watercolours and two oils by De Wint in the collection, this broadly-handled late work was probably finished in the studio after preliminary studies made directly from nature during one of the artist's annual sketching tours in the late summer and autumn months. De Wint's characteristic warm but sombre tones were produced with deep washes of ochre, burnt sienna, umber and indigo. As in this example, he preferred a thick, textured paper and rarely used bodycolour. The final watercolours were displayed in his own studio and from them a selection was made for the annual exhibition of the Old Water-Colour Society. Harvesting was a favourite subject. The extensive

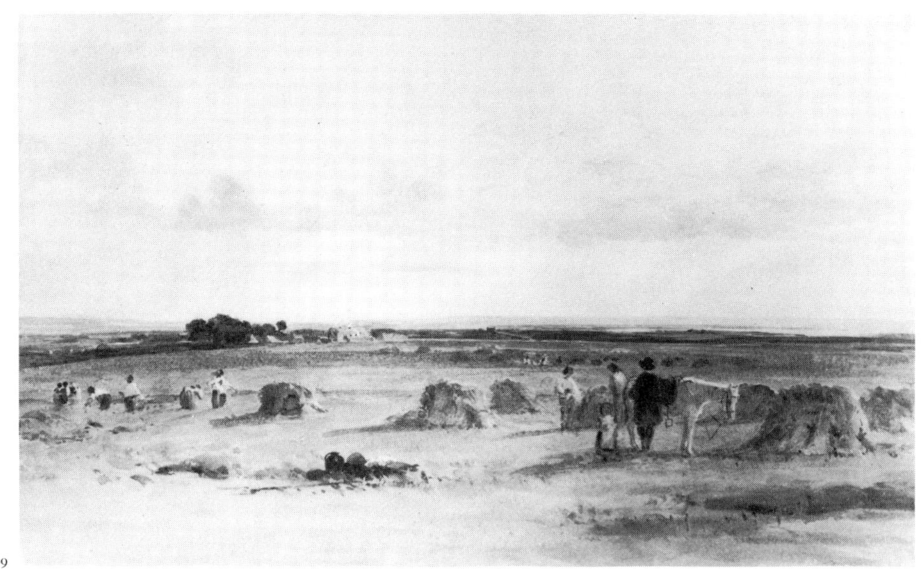

109

panoramic view and delicately painted skyscape vividly recall 17th-century Dutch landscape painting and De Wint would certainly have had the opportunity to study the work of, for example, Koninck and Ruisdael in the houses of his patrons.

110 R. P. Bonington

(1802–28)

THE DOGE'S PALACE FROM THE PIAZZETTA, VENICE *c.* 1826

English; pencil, watercolour, bodycolour and gum arabic
19.4 × 24.8 cm ($7\frac{5}{8} \times 9\frac{3}{4}$ in) sight
Signed (b.r.c.): *RPB 182* . . . .
James T. Blair Bequest (1917.90)

By the early 1820s, Bonington was making annual summer sketching tours and, inspired by Samuel Prout's extensive Italian tour in 1824, he made a two month pilgrimage to Italy in the spring of 1826. The beauty of Venice, in particular, held a strong attraction for many artists of the Romantic period. On 11 April, Bonington and his travelling companion, Charles Baron Rivet, had reached Milan where Rivet wrote to his family: 'Bonington thinks only of Venice; he makes sketches, and works a little everywhere, but without satisfaction and without interest in the country. He makes no effort to learn Italian, keeps to his tea, and requires the help of an interpreter in everything.'

Bonington and Rivet finally reached Venice on 20 April, remaining there until 19 May. The sparkling, vibrant quality of *The Doge's Palace* indicates that Bonington was truly inspired by the city. It appears not to have been done on the spot but is based on a detailed pencil drawing now in the Earl of Shelburne's collection. The watercolour may have been completed some months after Bonington had left Venice. The date may be 1826 or 7 (the margin, with the last digit, has been cut). Also, an almost identical undated watercolour version is in the Wallace Collection, London. From about 1824, Bonington used the fine point of a brush in rapid strokes of line or hatching to give structure. The confident technique of *The Doge's Palace* displays strong colour in combination with bodycolour and gum arabic, typical of his last works, giving brilliance and depth of tone.

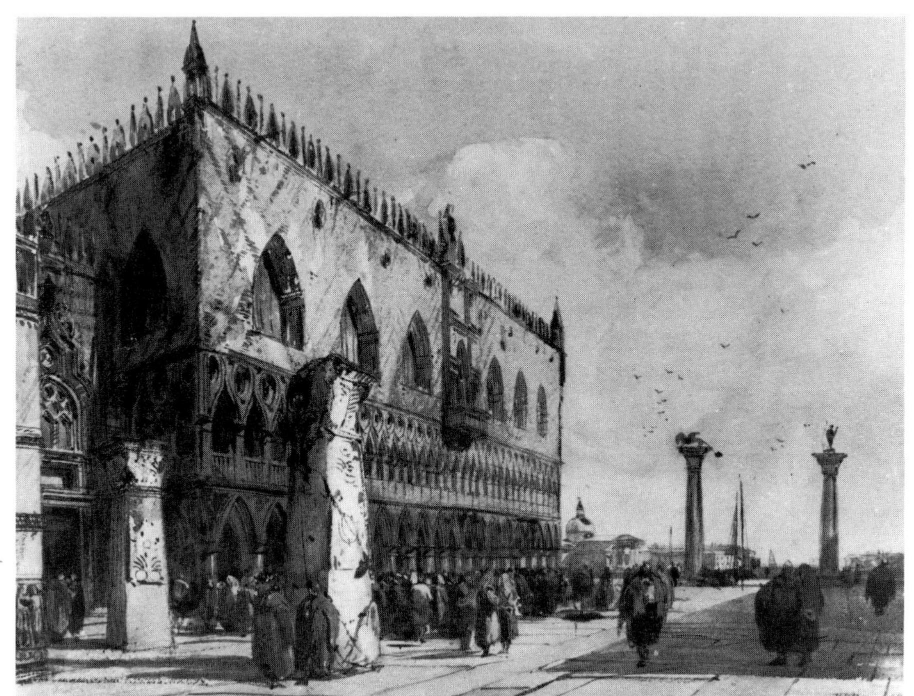

110

On 19 May, Rivet and Bonington left for Padua. Rivet wrote: 'Bonington has said nothing since we left the lagoons. He regrets Venice, though she treated him so badly with her rain and incessant storms, and he left the place with a presentiment that he would never see it again.' Bonington's already poor health deteriorated rapidly and he died two years later in London on 23 September 1828 shortly before his twenty-sixth birthday.

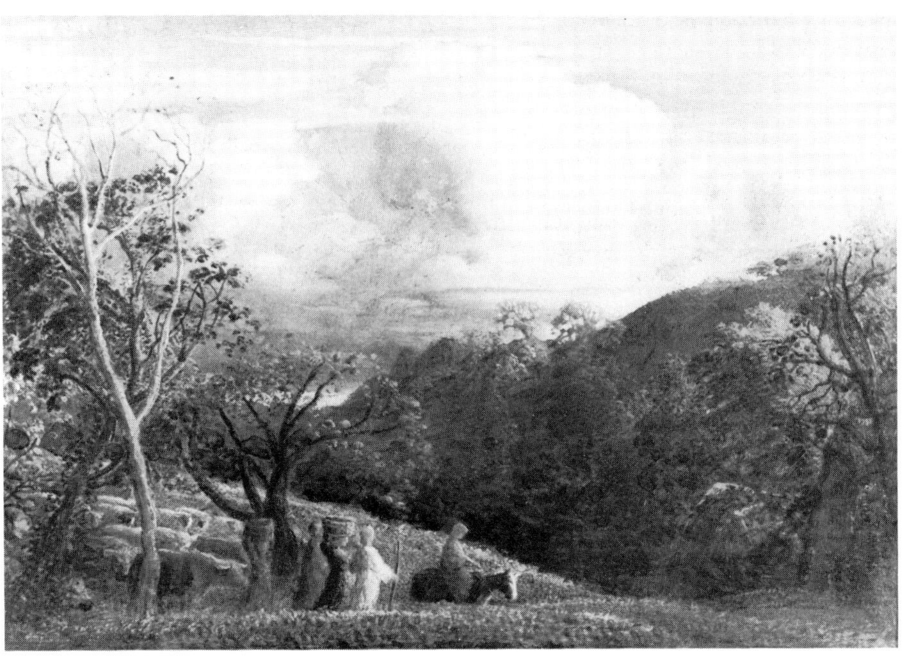

111

111 *Samuel Palmer*

(1805–81)

THE BRIGHT CLOUD 1833–34

English; oil and tempera on mahogany panel
23.3 × 32 cm ($9\frac{1}{8} \times 12\frac{5}{8}$ in)
Unsigned
Purchased with the aid of a Government grant (through the Victoria and Albert Museum) and the National Art-Collections Fund (1976.82).

The Bright Cloud is a work from Palmer's famous Shoreham period of *c.* 1826–35. Palmer was deeply inspired by the beauty of the landscape around Shoreham in Sussex. Many years later, in a letter to his wife of 1859, he referred to 'that first flush of summer splendour which entranced me at Shoreham.' During this period his small luminous landscape paintings and drawings took on a mystical intensity.

Milton and Bunyan were two of the most powerful literary sources of Palmer's inspiration and he must have known Milton's lines:

> .... yon western cloud, that draws
> O'er the blue firmament a radiant white,
> And slow descends, with something
> heavenly fraught.
>
> (Milton, *Paradise Lost*)

Palmer's exacting medium of oil mixed with tempera enabled him to recreate his haunting and mysterious vision of nature. In a letter to his friend and fellow-artist, John Linnell, dated 21 December 1828, Palmer evocatively described this vision which 'with mild reposing breadths of lawn and hill, shadowy glades and meadows, is sprinkled and showered with a thousand pretty eyes, and buds, and spires, and blossoms gemm'd with dew, and is clad in living green. Nor must be forgotten the motley clouding; the fine meshes, the aerial tissues, that dapple the skies of spring; nor the rolling volumes and piled mountains of light . . .'

A label on the back of the panel, in Palmer's hand, titles the work: *A Rustic Scene*. It is probably identifiable with *Rustic Scene* exhibited at the Royal Academy in 1833, or *A Rustic Scene* exhibited there in 1834. The present title first appeared in a sale of 1881. It relates to a group of earlier sepia watercolours of *c.* 1831–32 including *Bright Cloud and Ploughing*, also owned by the Galleries.

112 *David Cox*

(1783–1859)

RHYL SANDS *c.* 1855

English; oil on canvas
45.8 × 63.5 cm ($18\frac{1}{16} \times 25$ in)
Unsigned
James T. Blair Bequest (1917.170)

Manchester is fortunate to own eight oils and thirty-six watercolours from all periods of Cox's long and prolific career. It is worth noting that Cox did not begin painting in oils until 1840, at the age of fifty-seven, when he took lessons from William Müller (1812–45). North Wales was a favourite sketching ground and Rhyl Sands had inspired numerous watercolour sketches from as early as 1836. Cox was at Rhyl in August 1854, and a large oil of Rhyl Sands at Birmingham is dated 1854–55. It seems likely that the Manchester version dates from this visit.

Cox had already shown that he could capture in watercolour the breezy atmosphere of the open air. Nevertheless, the vivid sense of light and space in *Rhyl Sands* and the bold simplicity of composition are remarkable achievements for an increasingly elderly and infirm artist whose other experiments in oil were all too often laboured and dull. The translucent pale blue sky fills two-thirds of the composition contrasting with the pinkish tones of the sands.Groups of figures are deftly indicated with rapidly applied blobs and smudges of paint. *Rhyl Sands* stands out in the history of mid-19th-century British painting, and, like the work of Constable, anticipates the fresh coastal scenes of Boudin and the French Impressionists.

113 Sir Francis Chantrey

(1781–1841)

JOHN DALTON

English; marble
Height (including pedestal): 279.5 cm (110 in)
Signed (left side): CHANTREY / SCULPTOR / 1837.
Purchased by public subscription, 1837 (1882.48)

The scientist John Dalton (1786–1844), was born near Cockermouth and became a teacher of mathematics; he came to Manchester in 1793 to be Professor at the New College and was thereafter closely associated with the city. He was an active member of the Manchester Literary and Philosophical Society, and became its President in 1817. His work on meteorology and chemistry and, in particular, his discovery of atomic theory, made him world famous.

In 1833 the Royal Manchester Institution decided to commission a life-size statue of him, and raised £2,000 by public subscription. The statue was shown at the Royal Academy in 1837, and at the Royal Manchester Institution Autumn Exhibition in 1838. In August 1839 it was placed in the entrance hall of the Royal Manchester Institution. Its

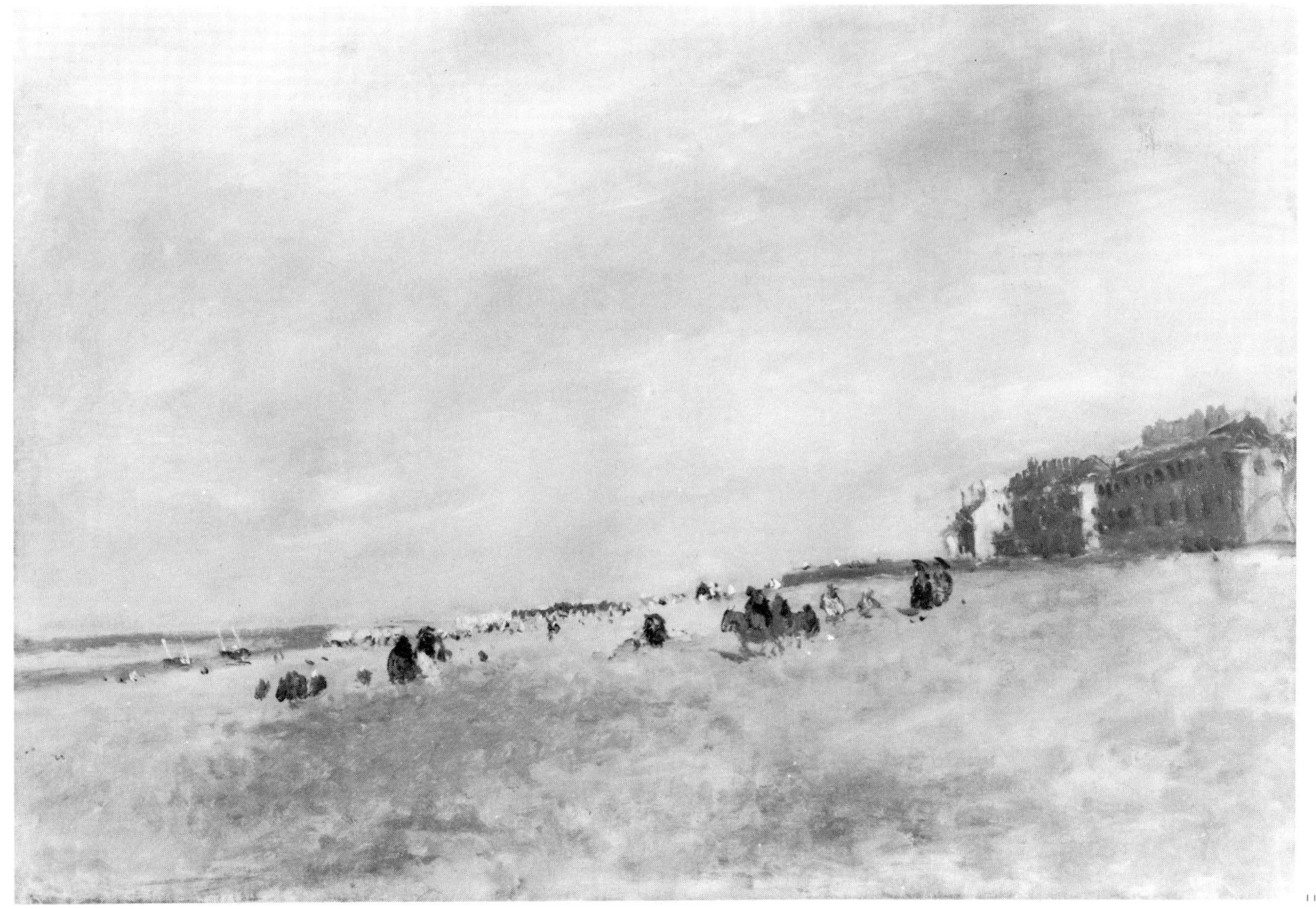

112

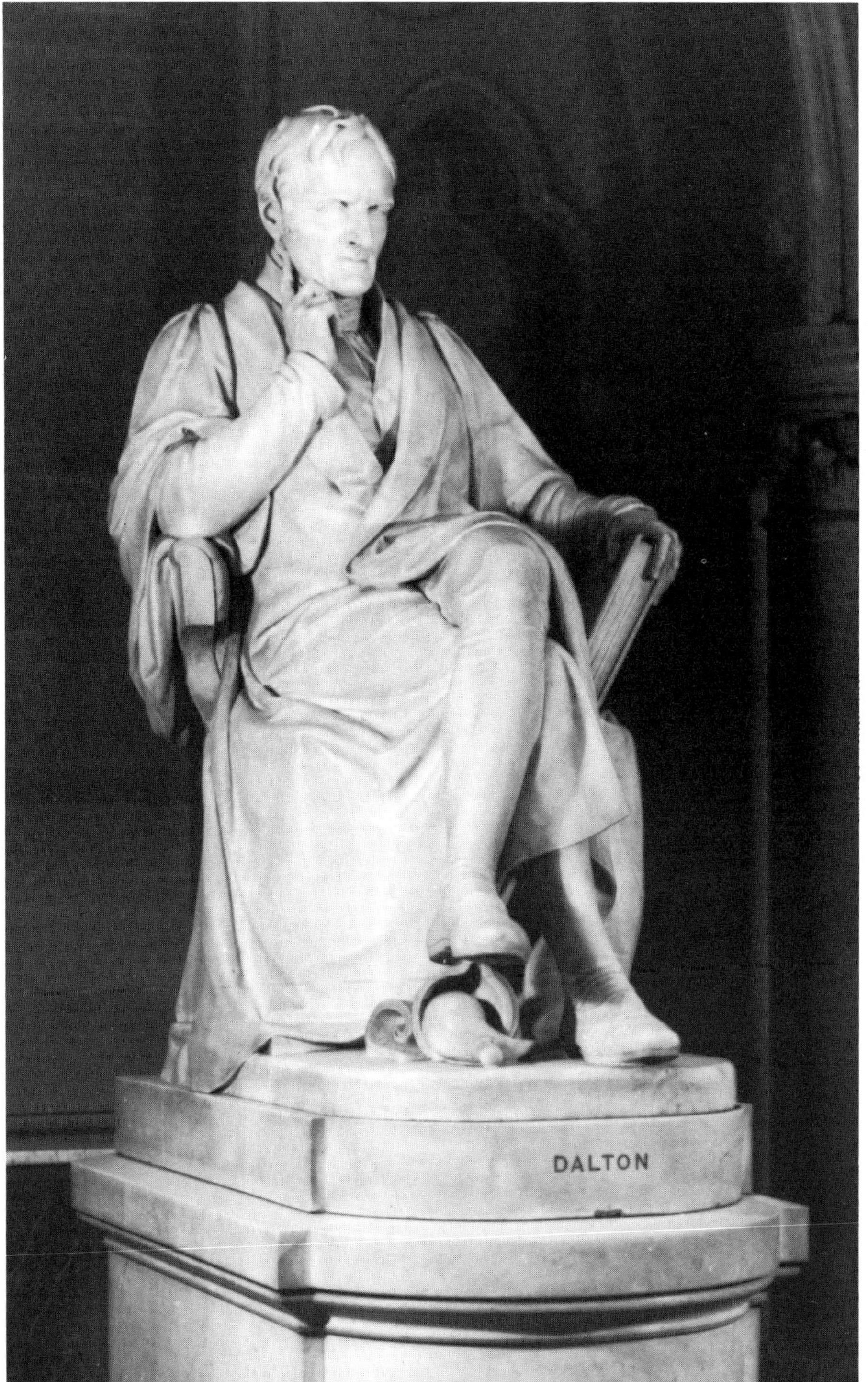

113

position there was criticised, and eventually, soon after the opening of Waterhouse's Town Hall in 1877, it was transferred to its present location, just inside the Town Hall entrance. Facing it is a statue of another Manchester scientist, *J. P. Joule* by Alfred Gilbert, dated 1893.

The sculptor chosen was Sir Francis Chantrey, the finest portrait sculptor of his day, renowned for his ability to portray intellect and dignity in his sitters, many of whom were men of science and learning. He has shown Dalton seated, following the type of his notable funerary statue of James Watt at Handsworth (1824). Chantrey preferred broad and simple effects and attitudes of natural repose: Dalton is deep in thought, resting his head in his right hand, and holding a book in his left, with scientific vessels and a scroll at his feet. Preparatory drawings are in the National Portrait Gallery, and a plaster model of the head is in the Ashmolean Museum, Oxford. Two busts by Chantrey are also in the Galleries' collection.

114 *William Etty*

(1836–37)

THE SIRENS AND ULYSSES
1836–37

English; oil on canvas
297 × 442.5 cm (117 × 174 in)
Unsigned
Transferred from the Royal Manchester Institution (1882.3)

The subject is taken from Homer's *Odyssey*. The wandering Ulysses had to sail past the sirens, whose beautiful song lured all who heard it to certain death. Circe the enchantress instructed Ulysses to fill the ears of his men with wax, and to have himself bound to the mast in order to resist. The prominence given by the artist to the voluptuously gesticulating nude sirens led to accusations of indencency, a criticism frequently levelled at Etty, who made the nude his principal study. He was also criticised for the gruesome realism of the remains of the sirens' victims, which were actually based on studies of decaying bodies made in a mortuary. But Etty claimed a moral purpose, described as 'the importance of resisting sensual delights, or an Homeric paraphrase on "The Wages of Sin is Death".'

Etty painted several such colossal exhibition pictures in the grand manner, displaying his command of depicting the human figure and his knowledge of the old masters. The theatrical gestures and chiaroscuro come from the Italian baroque, and the glowing colour from Venice, whilst the pose of Ulysses, with its exaggerated musculature, was based on the antique statue of Laocoon. The stormy sky and frenzied movement of the boatmen link Etty with contemporary French romantic painting.

The picture, based on a suggestion from Lord de Tabley, who lived at Knutsford and collected contemporary English painting, was begun in 1836, took five months to complete, and was shown in the Academy of 1837. It was bought unseen by Daniel Grant, a Manchester textile merchant, who gave it to his brother William. Not surprisingly, it did not stay long in the drawing room of a private house: after being shown at the Royal Manchester Institution in 1838, it was presented to the Institution the following year.

115 *Sir Edwin Landseer*

(1802–73)

PAGANINI PLAYING THE VIOLIN

English; pen, sepia ink and wash
22.2 × 17.8 cm ($8\frac{3}{4}$ × 7 in)
Unsigned
Gift of the nephews of Frederick Behrens (1945.181)

Landseer is best known for his animal paintings which were amongst the most

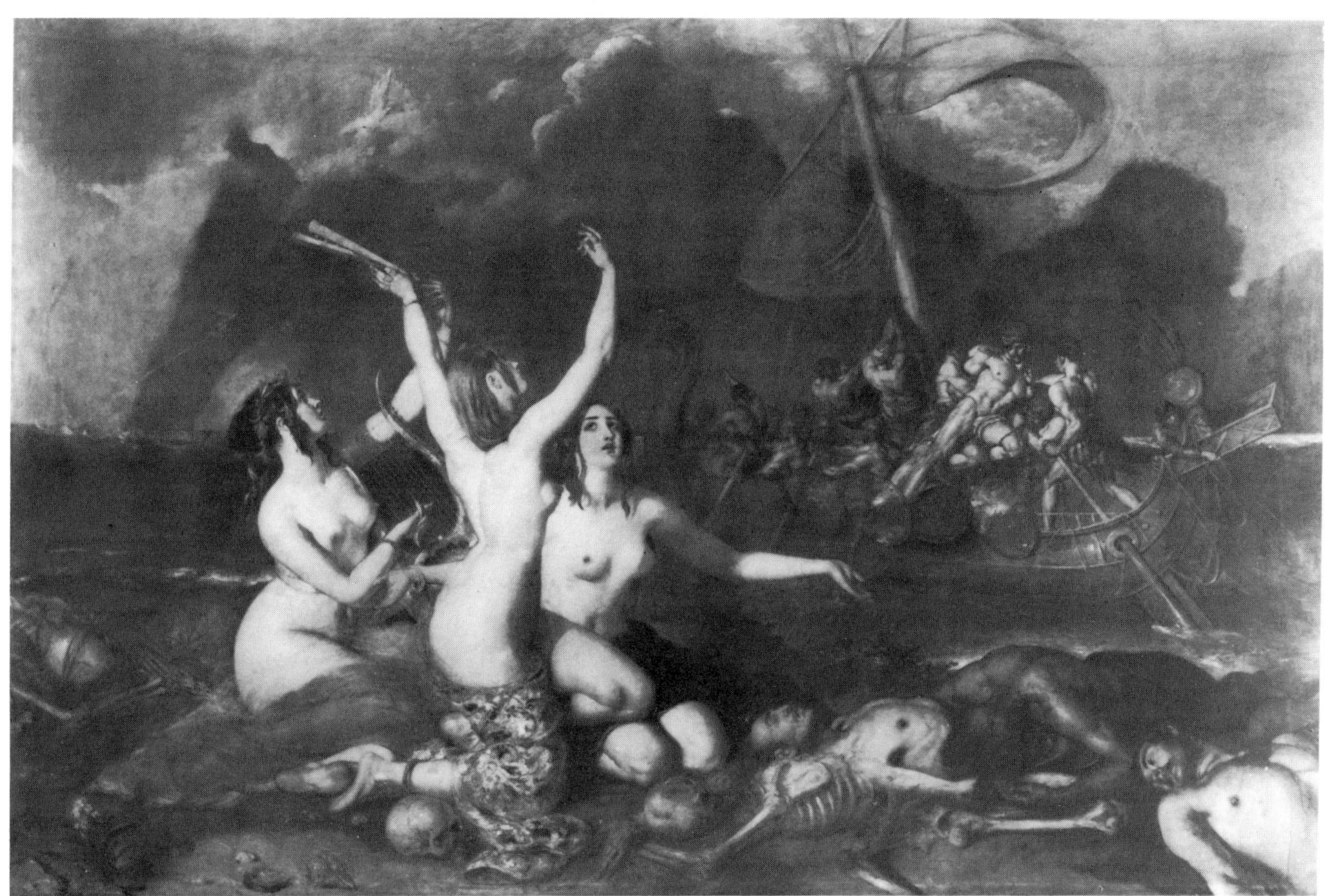

114

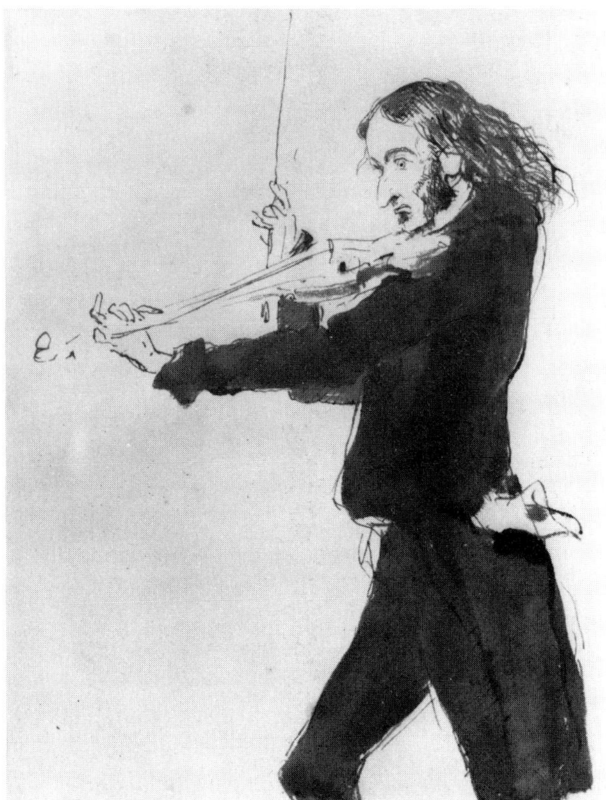
115

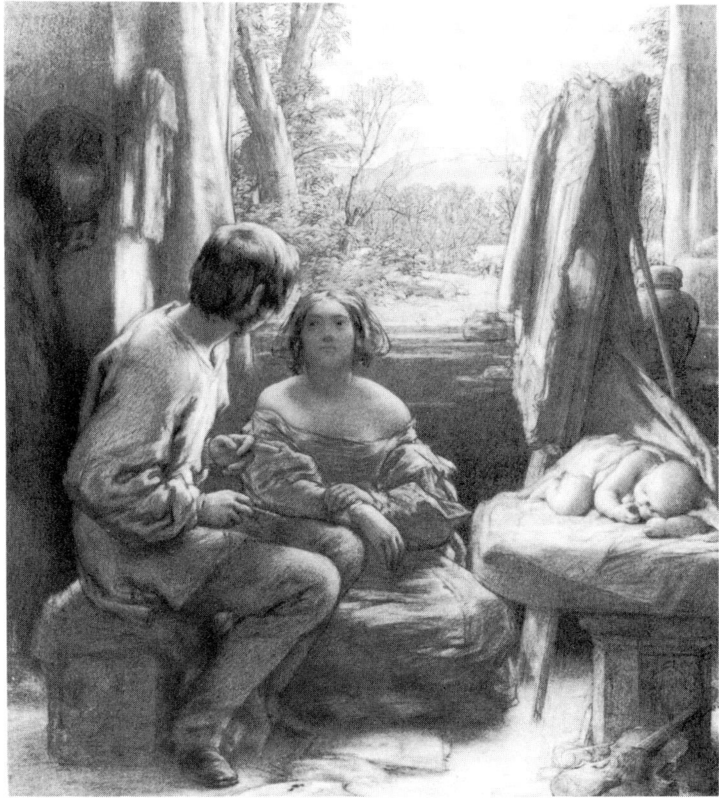
116

famous of all Victorian pictures. Quite different from these large, beautifully finished works, are his informal and witty sketches, tossed off quickly for the amusement of his friends and patrons. As a young man about town he moved in smart aristocratic and literary circles and his drawings and caricatures depict the fashionable personalities of London society at balls, suppers, theatres and country-house parties.

The great Italian virtuoso violinist Niccolò Paganini made his London debut to great acclaim at the King's Theatre on 3 June 1831. 'Scores of portraits of me made by different artists have appeared in all the print shops' he wrote. This drawing may have been made at one of his many later performances but must date from before 1840, the year he died. Several sketches of him by Landseer are recorded, at least one of which was engraved. The City Art Gallery has a second Landseer drawing, showing him bowing to applause. Another was formerly in the collection of the Countess of Blessington, authoress and hostess, who formed a notorious liaison with the Count d'Orsay, a dandy and amateur artist and a close friend of Landseer.

In this sketch, Landseer has caught *molto con brio* the tense concentration of the musical genius. Contemporaries recorded that he was a strange-looking man at all times, but his appearance when playing was as one 'half-demented'. The Galleries also own three Landseer oils.

116 William Mulready

(1786–1863)

THE ARTIST'S STUDIO *c.* 1839
English; chalk and pencil heightened with white
38.7 × 34.8 cm ($15\frac{1}{4} \times 13\frac{3}{4}$ in) sight
Unsigned
James Gresham Bequest (1917.260)

This beautiful red chalk drawing, with its view through a window, flooding the interior with daylight, demonstrates Mulready's brilliance as a draughtsman, though his contemporary reputation was based on his genre oil paintings.

The drawing is a highly finished study for an oil, now lost, which was exhibited at the Royal Academy in 1840, entitled *An Interior*, but also referred to by Mulready in his account books as *The Artist's Studio* or *Study*. This puzzling subject is unlikely to show Mulready's own studio, which was in Bayswater and probably did not have such a rural outlook, even in 1839. The artist's face in the picture is concealed (a frequent motif in Mulready's work), and the figure is probably too slight to be Mulready himself. He holds a brush and his palette is on the floor, but it is not clear whether he has been painting the landscape, or the baby, which is lying on a peculiar Gothic font-shaped pedestal, or whether the attentive girl he is addressing is his model, resting after posing. In any case, why is the picture he is painting on the easel framed? Nor do we know the meaning of the artist's gesture in pointing to the baby. Is the girl the baby's mother?

It is unusual for Mulready, at this date, to paint a picture without some kind of moral or narrative purpose. As Mulready gave the oil the title *An Interior* for its public showing, he perhaps wished to keep its meaning private.

117 *John Frederick Lewis*

(1805–76)

THE COFFEE BEARER 1857

English; oil on panel
30.4 × 19 cm (12 × 7½ in)
Signed (b.r.): *JFL / 1857* (mon)
Purchased (1977.2)

Though this little panel conveys the scented, luxurious atmosphere of the Middle East, it was painted in England. Lewis began as a pupil of Landseer, painting animals and Scottish subjects, but then turned to highly finished water-colours of Switzerland, Italy, and then Spain, earning for himself the name of 'Spanish Lewis'. But it is with the Middle East that he will always be associated. Probably inspired by seeing the *Odalisques* of the French painter Ingres, he visited Constantinople in 1840 and from 1841 to '51 settled in Cairo,

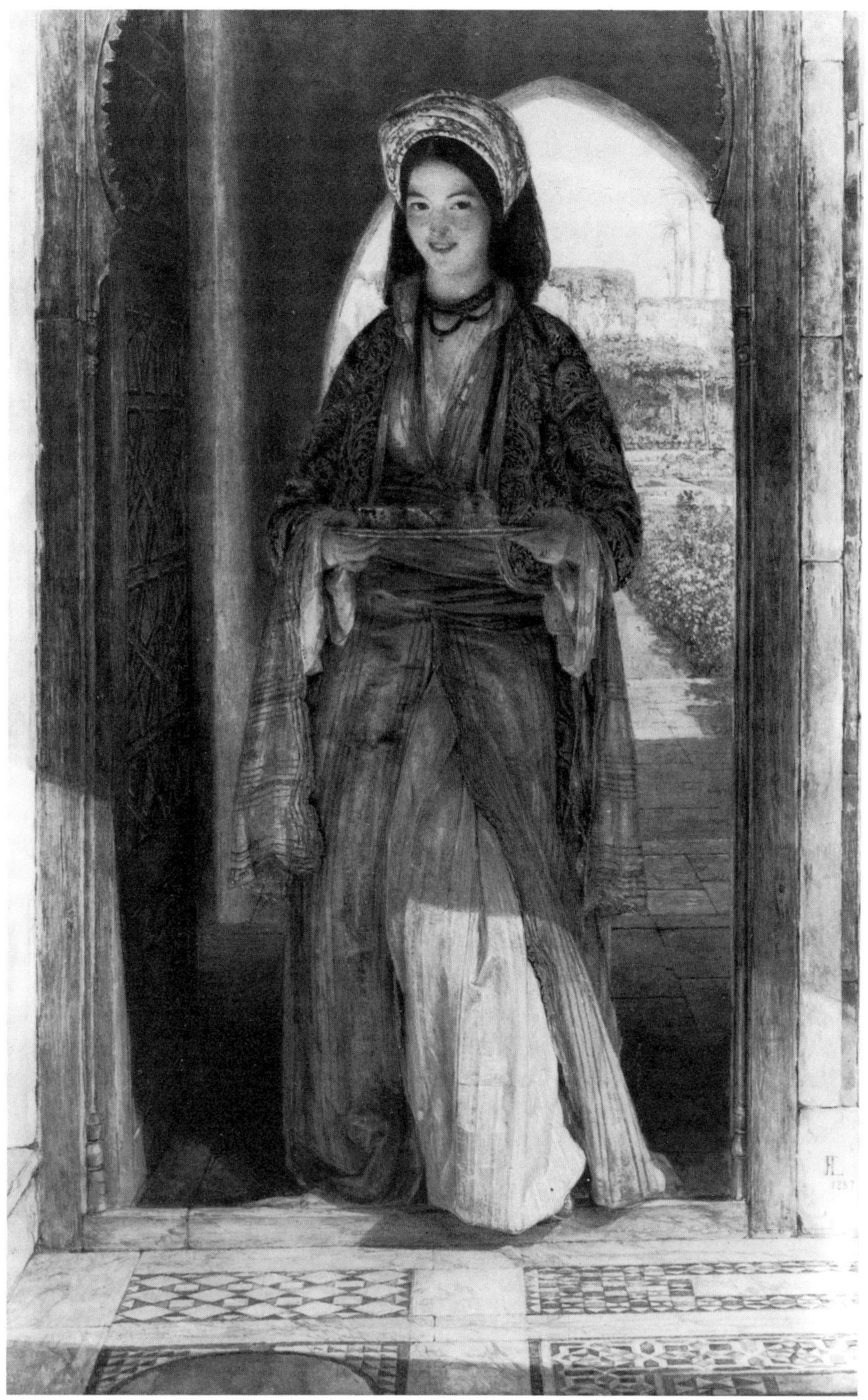

117

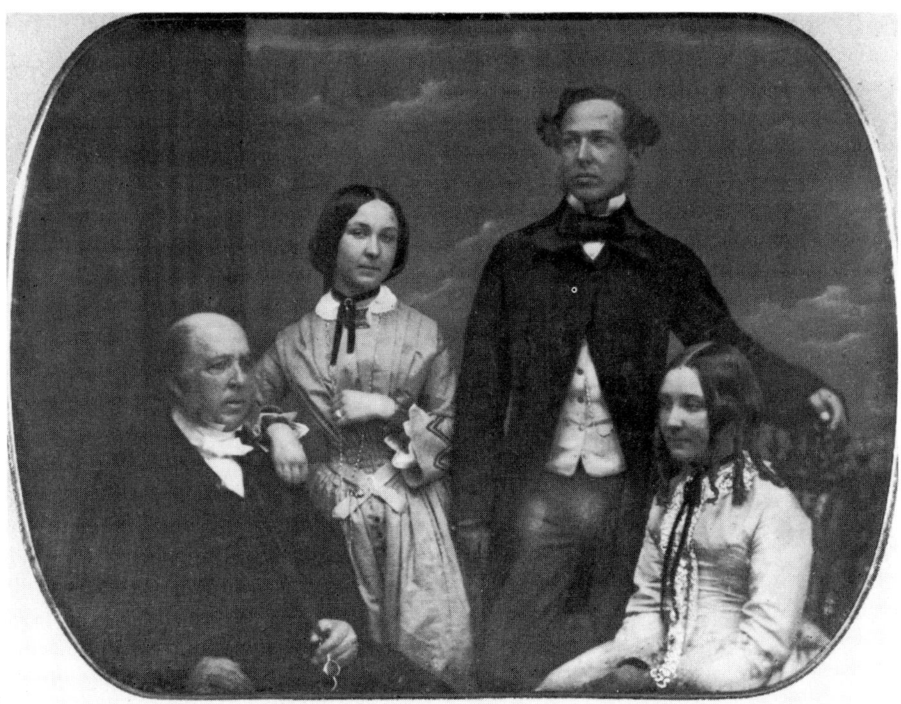

118

adopting oriental robes, travelling with bedouins in the desert and recording the crowded bazaars and the indolent life of the harem. He ceased to exhibit in England for nine years, and when, in 1850, he sent to London a harem scene, its jewelled brilliance as well as its exotic subject created a sensation.

After his return he painted only Middle Eastern scenes based on material he had gathered in Cairo. *The Coffee Bearer* dates from the period when he was changing from watercolour to oil, as it paid him better: but in oil he evolved a similar virtuoso technique to catch bright colour and detail. In this respect he had much in common with the Pre-Raphaelites, though he did not share their views on subject matter. But Holman Hunt, at least, followed in Lewis's footsteps to the Middle East.

The girl bearing a tray of coffee was repeated in a watercolour of 1858, where she is entering a harem to serve a girl lounging on silk cushions (Victoria and Albert Museum). There is also a watercolour of 1859, showing just the figure of the coffee bearer in the arch. In all three the artist beautifully captures the brilliant sunlight behind the girl and the reflected glow on her smiling face.

118 Daguerreotype

Tinted daguerreotype family group portrait.
English, by R. Low, Promenade, Cheltenham, 1850–55
Length: 12.5 cm ($4\frac{7}{8}$ in)
Cunnington Collection (1982.650)

The picture shows a typical middle class family of the early 1850s. The young woman on the left wears her hair pulled straight back with a fullness around the ears: an 1850s' development from the drooping loops of the previous decade. Her dress is a pink silk with a fine check. Its draped bodice was a popular style which lasted from the early 1840s through the 1850s. It is seen on many portraits and in surviving examples, but curiously, rarely in fashion plates. She is wearing a remarkable amount of jewellery. Round her neck she has a black velvet band fastened with a brooch, another large brooch, and a long-chain. She wears a ring and dark pink ruched ribbon bracelets. These were highly fashionable at the time, and there are several examples in the Platt Hall collection, which have the ribbon mounted on an elastic band. Her broiderie anglaise undersleeves and collar are similar to other examples at Platt Hall.

The other young woman wears her hair in the ringlets so popular in the early Victorian period. It is rather thin, and the effect was probably achieved by the use of grease or oil. Her bodice is extremely tight-fitting, as is shown by the many wrinkles, and her high bustline reveals the outline of her corset. The other woman's dress would actually have been equally constricting; the drapery was mounted on a tight lining. The old man's double-breasted coat with wide revers, and high white stock reflect the fashions of his youth. He holds a pince-nez in his hand, with its ribbon round his neck.

The young man is very up to date, with his coat fastening high up on his chest, and his huge bow tie – a style much lampooned by *Punch* at this time.

Mr R. Low took over the photographic studio in April 1850 from Richard Beard junior. Beard's father, an early pioneer and patentee of the daguerreotype process, had originally opened it in the early 1840s, as one of a chain of studios across the country. Low's business was a successful one, and he remained active in Cheltenham for some years. This photograph is one of approximately 8,000 19th-century prints in the collection at Platt Hall Gallery of English Costume.

119 *Noah's Ark*

Pine, painted in colours.
English, second quarter of 19th century
Length of ark: 68 cm ($26\frac{13}{16}$ in)
Mrs M. Greg Bequest (1922.486)

The Noah's Ark originated in Germany in the early 17th century; it was probably first made at Oberammergau. It became very popular in England in the 19th century and soon fitted into the useful category of 'Sunday toy'. All toys were forbidden in the nursery on Sunday, early in the century, but the Noah's Ark was eventually allowed, owing to its religious connections.

The Ark usually possessed figures of Noah and his wife, their three sons, Ham, Shem and Japheth, and their wives. There could be as many as 150 animals which fitted neatly into the body of the Ark; this example has ninety, a selection of which is illustrated. The animals and figures, usually made of wood, were mass-produced to a certain extent, being first cut in outline on the lathe and sliced into segments, then the carved work was finished by hand. Caleb Plummer, the toy-maker in Charles Dickens' *The Cricket on the Hearth* (1845), comments on the making of these items: 'There's rather a run on Noah's Arks at present. I could have wished to improve on the Family, but I don't see how it's to be done at the price. It would be a satisfaction to one's mind to make it clearer which was Shems and Hams, and which was Wives. Flies an't on that scale, neither, as compared with elephants, you know!'

120 *G. F. Watts*
(1817–1904)

THE GOOD SAMARITAN 1852
English; oil on canvas
254.7 × 189.2 cm ($110\frac{1}{4} \times 74\frac{1}{2}$ in)
Signed (b.r.): *G. F. Watts. 1852*
Transferred from the Royal Manchester Institution (1882.149)

The parable of the Good Samaritan comes from St. Luke, Chapter 10, and describes how a Jewish traveller was set upon and stripped naked by thieves. A

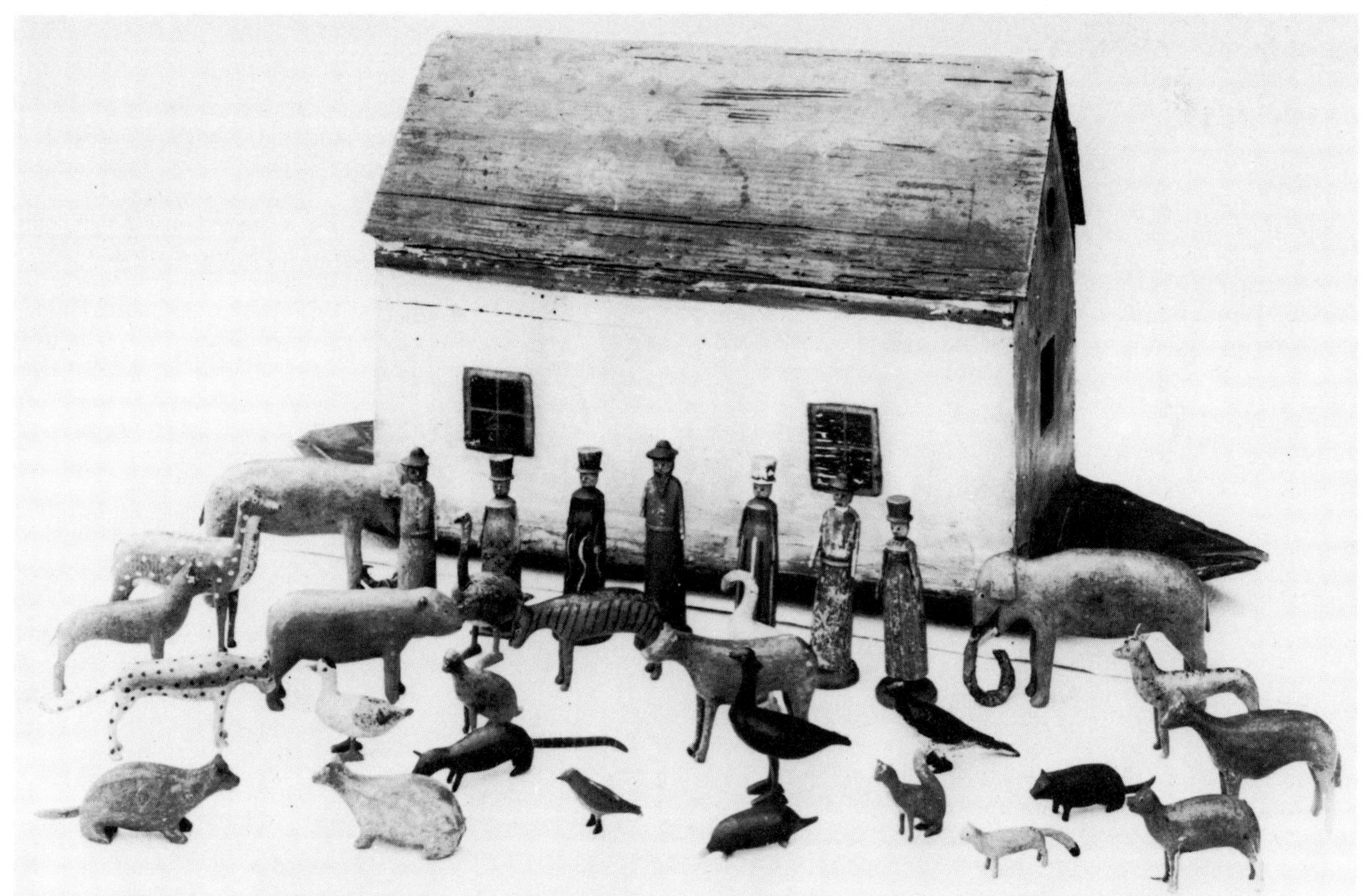

119

priest and a Levite, both Jews, 'passed by on the other side' but a Samaritan (a Gentile) stopped and helped him. Jesus concluded, 'Go thou and do likewise.' Watts's picture carries the same message, for it was presented to the citizens of Manchester as an expression of his admiration of Thomas Wright (1789–1875), a Manchester foundry worker who devoted his life to prison visiting and the rehabilitation of discharged convicts. Before the painting was transferred to the Gallery, it hung for many years in the old Town Hall, as an example to Mancunians.

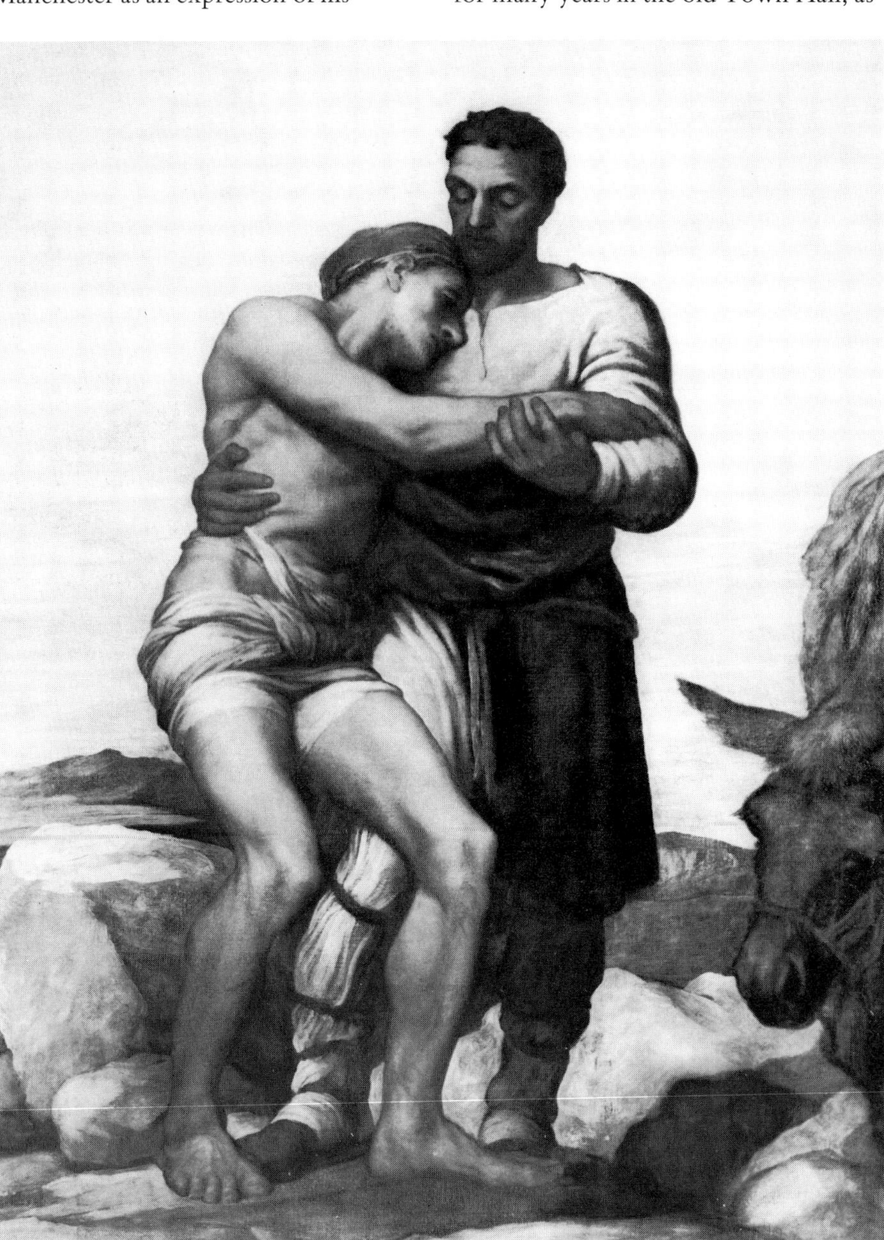

120

For Watts, art had a moral purpose, and he was a great campaigner to place pictures or frescoes in public buildings, for the improvement of the people. *The Good Samaritan* is dated 1852, and his other works of this period carry similar humanitarian lessons, though in more modern terms. They depict an Irish family starving in the famine, an exhausted seamstress in a garret, and a poor homeless woman huddled beneath an arch by the Thames. *The Good Samaritan*, however, is given a more generalised, timeless setting in a vast, bare desert. The sculptural breadth of the figures comes from his recent stay in Italy, from 1843 to 1847; the position of the figures is very close to Michelangelo's marble *Deposition*, then in the Duomo at Florence, while the palette resembles his *Last Judgment* in the Sistine Chapel.

An unfinished version is in the Watts Gallery, Compton, and the faces of both may be idealised portraits of Wright. Watts's later chalk drawing of Wright is in the National Portrait Gallery.

121 *W. Holman Hunt*

(1827–1910) *pl. 11*

THE HIRELING SHEPHERD 1851

English; oil on canvas
76.4 × 109.5 cm ($30\frac{1}{16} \times 43\frac{1}{8}$ in)
Signed (b.l.c.): *Holman Hunt. 1851. Ewell*
Purchased (1896.29)

Hunt began this famous picture in the summer of 1851, three years after the formation of the Pre-Raphaelite Brotherhood. The landscape was painted out of doors at Ewell, Surrey, in a novel technique, using a white porcelain palette to ensure the mixing of clear colours, and laying the colours on a wet white ground, renewed daily. This, together with Hunt's painstaking treatment of naturalistic detail, captures the brilliance of the sunlit landscape

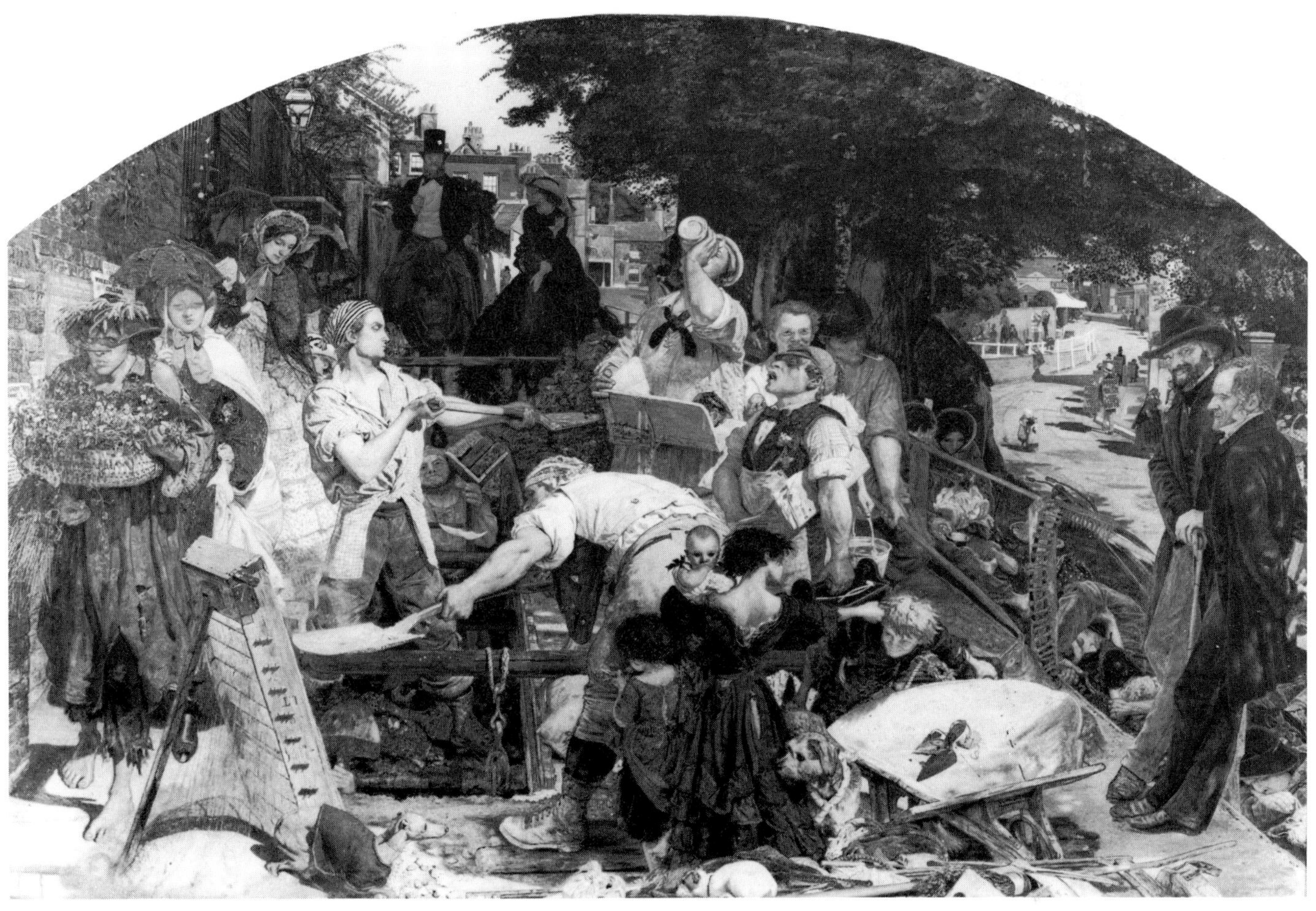

122

with an uncanny sharpness and brightness.

The subject is Hunt's own, but was based on St. John's Gospel (ch. 10, v. 12–13), where the Hireling Shepherd, neglectful of his flock, is contrasted with the Good Shepherd who 'giveth his life for the sheep'. Hunt also quoted a song from *King Lear* about another careless shepherd, who let his sheep wander in the corn. Later, in a letter in the Gallery's possession, Hunt explained that he meant his picture as a veiled criticism of the contemporary Church, which neglected its pastoral duty, the care of souls, for useless theological debate. The fatal results of spiritual neglect are shown by Hunt's symbolic use of the half-eaten apple of the temptress, and the death's head hawk moth caught by the shepherd.

But Hunt wrote that his first object was to paint 'not dresden china bergers, but a real shepherd, and a real shepherdess, and a landscape in full sunlight, with all the colour of luscious summer without the faintest fear of the precedents of any landscape painters who had rendered Nature before.' The shocked reaction of critics who saw it at the Royal Academy in 1852 shows that he succeeded.

Various sketches are recorded, and a small oil version, the original study, shows several variations from the finished picture. As well as Hunt's letter mentioned above, the Gallery's Hunt collection includes his spectacles, fountain pen, palette, paint brushes, admission ticket to the life school of the Royal Academy, and a quantity of drawings and oils.

122 *Ford Madox Brown*

(1821–93)

WORK 1852–65

English: oil on canvas, arched top
137 × 197.3 cm ($53\frac{15}{16} \times 77\frac{11}{16}$ in)
Signed (b.r.c.): F. MADOX BROWN 1852 – /65 (in one line)
Purchased (1885.1)

Inspired by the sight of navvies digging for drains in Heath Street, Hampstead, Brown made them the heroes of his masterpiece, an epic painting of modern life. It was begun in 1852 (the Galleries own a little oil sketch for the background, besides several figure studies), but it took thirteen years to complete, because of the many figures and the dazzling accumulation of tiny details. The bright colours and realistic outdoor sunlight are in accordance with Pre-Raphaelite ideas of truth to nature. But for all its surface realism, *Work* is an assemblage of types, each chosen to represent different facets of society.

Brown identified the characters in a long description. The honest toil of the navvies is contrasted with the other figures, the rich ladies who need not work, the outlandish herb-seller who has never learned to work; the ragged children and unemployed labourers in the ditch, who demonstrate the ill effects of the lack of work, and finally the two on-lookers on the right, who, seeming idle, are the 'brain-workers . . . the cause of well-ordained work and happiness in others.' They are portraits of Thomas Carlyle, the writer, and the Rev. F. D. Maurice, the pioneer of working class education. Brown admired Carlyle's *Past and Present*, which provided many of the ideas and some of the details in the picture, such as the election procession in the background. Brown taught at Maurice's Working Men's College, a poster for which is on the wall, on the left. Though Brown ignored the industrialisation of labour, his painting arose directly out of the social and intellectual ideas of its time: its purchase in 1885 by the City of Manchester, one of the industrial centres of the world, was entirely appropriate.

The Galleries house a large collection of paintings by Ford Madox Brown, who lived in Manchester in the 1880s whilst working on the murals in the Town Hall.

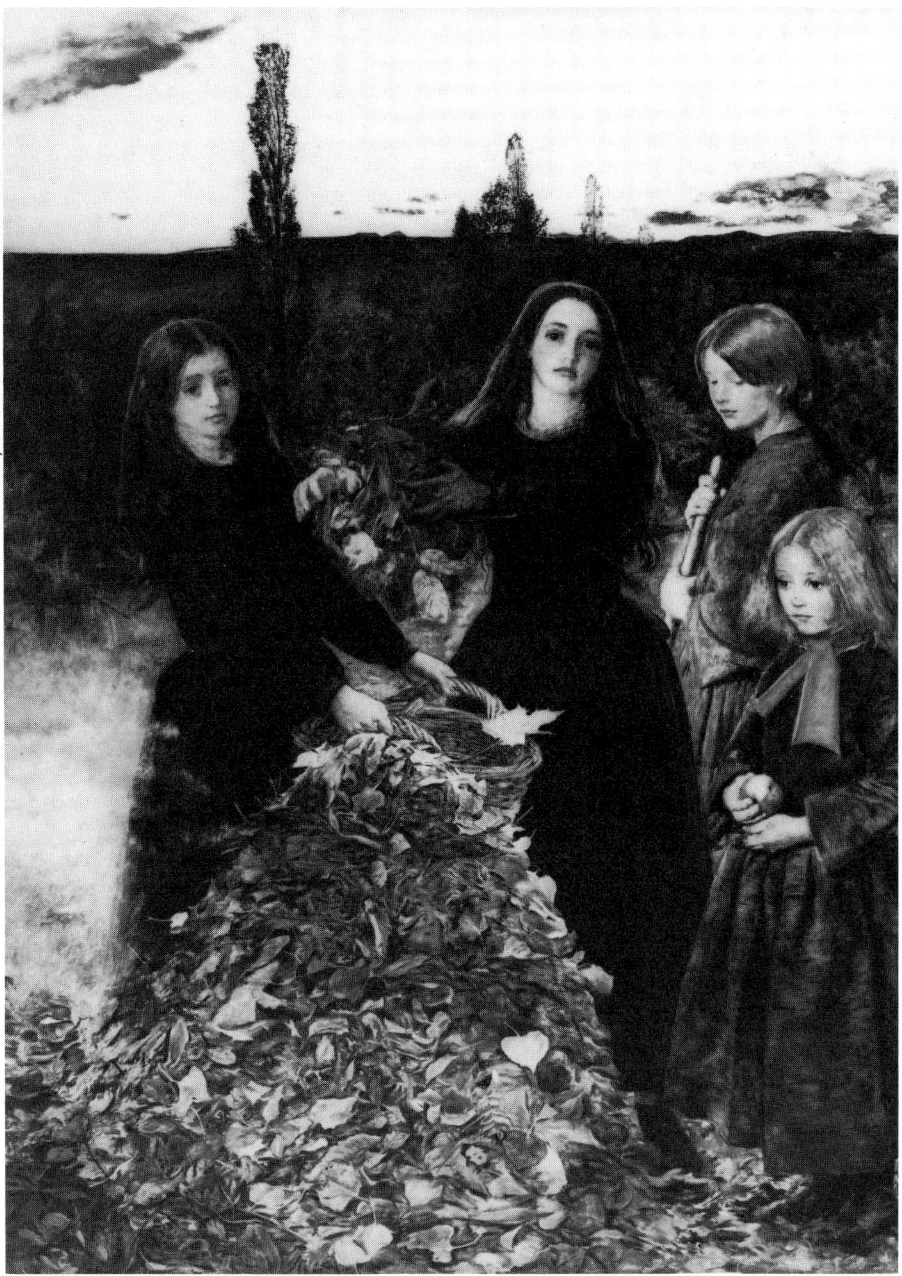

123

123 *John Everett Millais*
(1829–96)

AUTUMN LEAVES 1856

English; oil on canvas
104.3 × 74 cm ($41\frac{1}{16} \times 29\frac{1}{8}$ in)
Signed (b.r.c.): *18 JM 56* (mon)
Purchased (1892.4)

The haunting *Autumn Leaves* is an evocation of mood, not an attempt to put across a religious or moral message such as is found in *The Hireling Shepherd* or *Work*. Millais' wife wrote of it as 'a picture full of beauty, but without subject' and Ruskin called it 'the most poetical picture the artist has yet conceived'. The picture is invested with the wistful sadness associated with the season, the dying year and the passing of youthful beauty. 'Is there any sensation more delicious than that awakened by the odour of burning leaves', wrote Millais in 1851, according to Holman Hunt. 'To me nothing brings back sweeter memories of the days that are gone.'

The picture was painted in the autumn of 1855 in the garden of Annat Lodge, near Bowerswell, Perthshire, where Millais and his wife Effie had settled after their recent marriage. The models were Effie's sisters, Alice (left) and Sophie (centre), and two local girls. Millais has skilfully depicted the twilit glow of the sky, the smoke, the rich brown and gold of the leaves and the glowing colours of the girls. He has caught the atmosphere of autumn with precision and intensity, but the detail is less minutely handled than in his earlier works. Later he was to abandon the sharply observed Pre-Raphaelite style altogether.

Autumn Leaves was an extremely influential painting for the later phase of Pre-Raphaelitism, the forerunner of many sad-eyed beauties and purple horizons of the 1860s and 1870s.

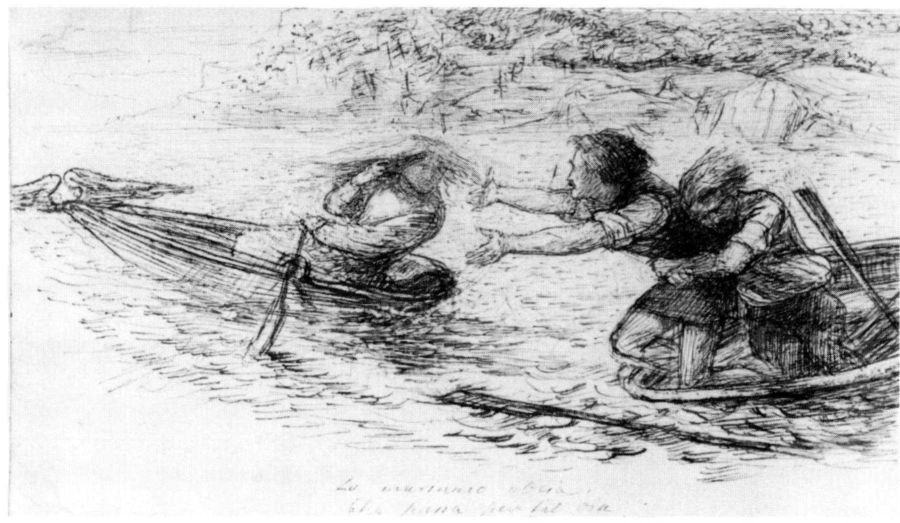

124

124 *D. G. Rossetti*
(1828–82)

BOATMEN AND SIREN *c.* 1853

English; ink
11 × 18.4 cm ($4\frac{5}{16} \times 7\frac{1}{4}$ in)
Unsigned
Inscr. (b.r.c.): *Lo marinaio oblia, / Che passa per tal via*
C. L. Rutherston Gift (1925.133)

A boatman is restraining his companion from being lured to death by the siren, whose hair streams out in the wind as her winged boat speeds by. The inscription 'Lo marinaio oblia, Che passa per tal via' comes from a *canzone* by the Italian Renaissance poet Jacopo da Lentino.

I am broken as a ship
Perishing of the song
Sweet, sweet and long, the song the sirens
know.
The mariner forgets,
Voyaging in those straits,
And dies assuredly.

The translation is by Rossetti himself who was an avid reader and writer of poetry. He was particularly fascinated with the relationship between poetry and painting: here he has made his drawing style echo the passion expressed by the poet.

A comparison with Etty's *The Sirens and Ulysses* (no. 114), inspired by a similar theme, shows the difference between the studied and grand manner of the Academician and the intensity and immediacy of the Pre-Raphaelite. Rossetti's work at this time (*c.* 1853) was all on a small scale. Between 1850 and 1860, he abandoned his few attempts at oil painting, preferring the more personal and intimate process of drawing or watercolour. The technique in this drawing, with its short, nervous strokes of the pen, is highly unorthodox. His subject matter was also unusual, closely bound up with his relationships with women. Such personal works were not publicly exhibited, but executed for a small circle of friends or private patrons; this drawing was given to his artist friend George Pryce Boyce in 1864.

125 *W. Holman Hunt*
(1827–1910)

DANTE GABRIEL ROSSETTI 1853

English; coloured chalks, oval
28.6 × 25.9 cm ($11\frac{1}{4} \times 10\frac{3}{16}$ in)
Signed (b.r.c.): *W. Holman Hunt / to his PR Brother / T Woolner / April 12*
Purchased (1922.25)

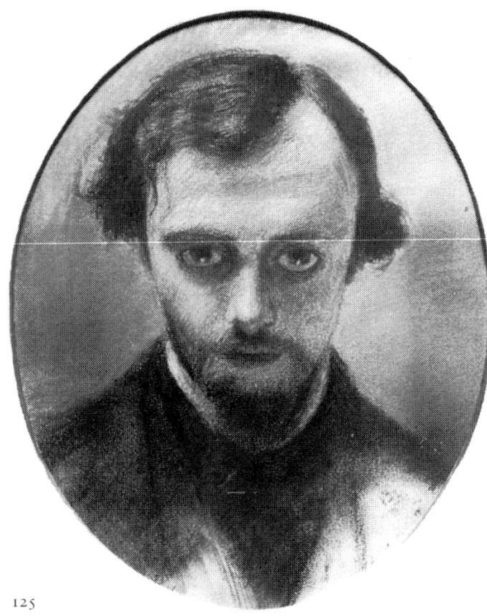

125

On 12 April 1853, members of the Pre-Raphaelite Brotherhood met for breakfast in Millais' studio and spent the rest of the day drawing portraits of each other to send as a memento to one of their number, the sculptor Thomas Woolner: in despair of making a living by his art, he had, in July 1852, emigrated to Australia to try his luck in the gold rush. This striking portrait of Rossetti, seen against a bright green background, was one of the seven portraits sent out to Australia. Hunt also made a less brilliantly coloured drawing of Millais (National Portrait Gallery).

'Are not Hunt's sketches wonderful? They are made with "Swiss Chalks" not Creta Levis', wrote Rossetti on 16 April in the letter accompanying the drawings to Australia. 'The "Swiss" are softer than the Creta, but I think much more beautiful in colour. Hunt will send you out some of both.'

Rossetti was aged twenty-five at this time, and Hunt's pastel vividly captures his good looks: his large luminous eyes, strongly highlighted, gaze out hypnotically as he tilts his head forward, doubtless concentrating on his own drawing of Hunt, now in Birmingham City Museums and Art Gallery.

Woolner's emigration had suggested to Ford Madox Brown the idea of *The Last of England* (Birmingham), but after failing to make his fortune, Woolner returned to England in 1854. After Rossetti's death in 1882, he gave the drawing to William Michael Rossetti, the sitter's brother, and Hunt, seeing how rubbed it had become, made the oil copy now in Birmingham.

126 D. G. Rossetti

(1828–82)

ASTARTE SYRIACA 1877

English; oil on canvas
185 × 109 cm ($72\frac{13}{16} \times 42\frac{15}{16}$ in)
Signed (b.l.c.): *D. G. Rossetti. 1877.*
Purchased (1891.5)

This is a late work by Rossetti, dating from the years when his love for Jane Morris had developed into an obsession, and every woman was seen by him in her image, with strikingly dark eyes, full lips, long neck and flowing hair. Here she is transformed into a cruel, impassive and overpowering *femme fatale*, in the person of a mythical combination of Venus, classical goddess of love, with Astarte, the forbidding queen-goddess of ancient Middle Eastern cults.

Rossetti wrote a sonnet for the painting. Part of it is written on the frame, and the Galleries also own a complete text in the artist's handwriting.

Mystery: lo! betwixt the sun and moon
Astarte of the Syrians: Venus Queen
Ere Aphrodite was. In silver sheen
Her twofold girdle clasps the infinite boon
Of bliss whereof the heaven and earth
commune . . .

Rossetti was never a mere illustrator of poetry, and the sonorous cadences of his sonnet have their visual equivalent in the heavy rhythms of the painting and its lurid green colour scheme. The goddess is placed in the centre, a formal hieratic image, flanked by near mirror images of

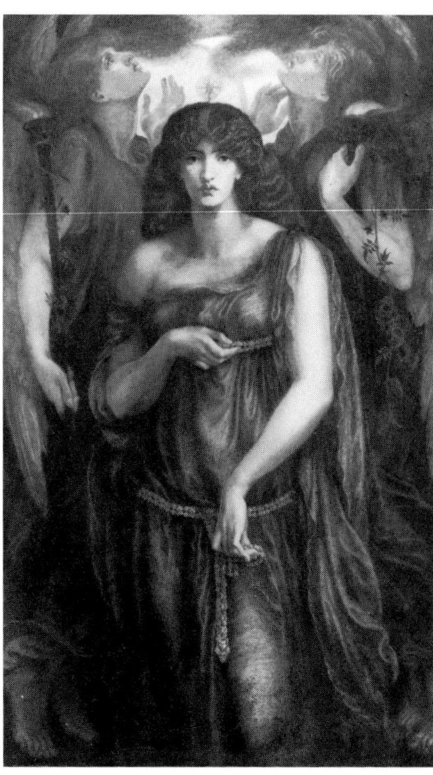

126

the torch bearers. A counterpoint of restless movement is set up by the flowing draperies, the curves of the tendrils and hair, and the coarsely exaggerated positions of the fingers toying with the silver girdle.

The picture was begun in 1875, and studies exist in Birmingham Museums and Art Gallery, the Victoria and Albert Museum, the Whitworth Art Gallery, Manchester, and elsewhere.

127 Alfred Stevens

(1817–75)

SEATED YOUTH

English; gilt-bronze
Height 40 cm ($15\frac{3}{4}$ in)
Purchased with the aid of a Government grant (through the Victoria and Albert Museum) (1980.265)

This broadly modelled figure on a

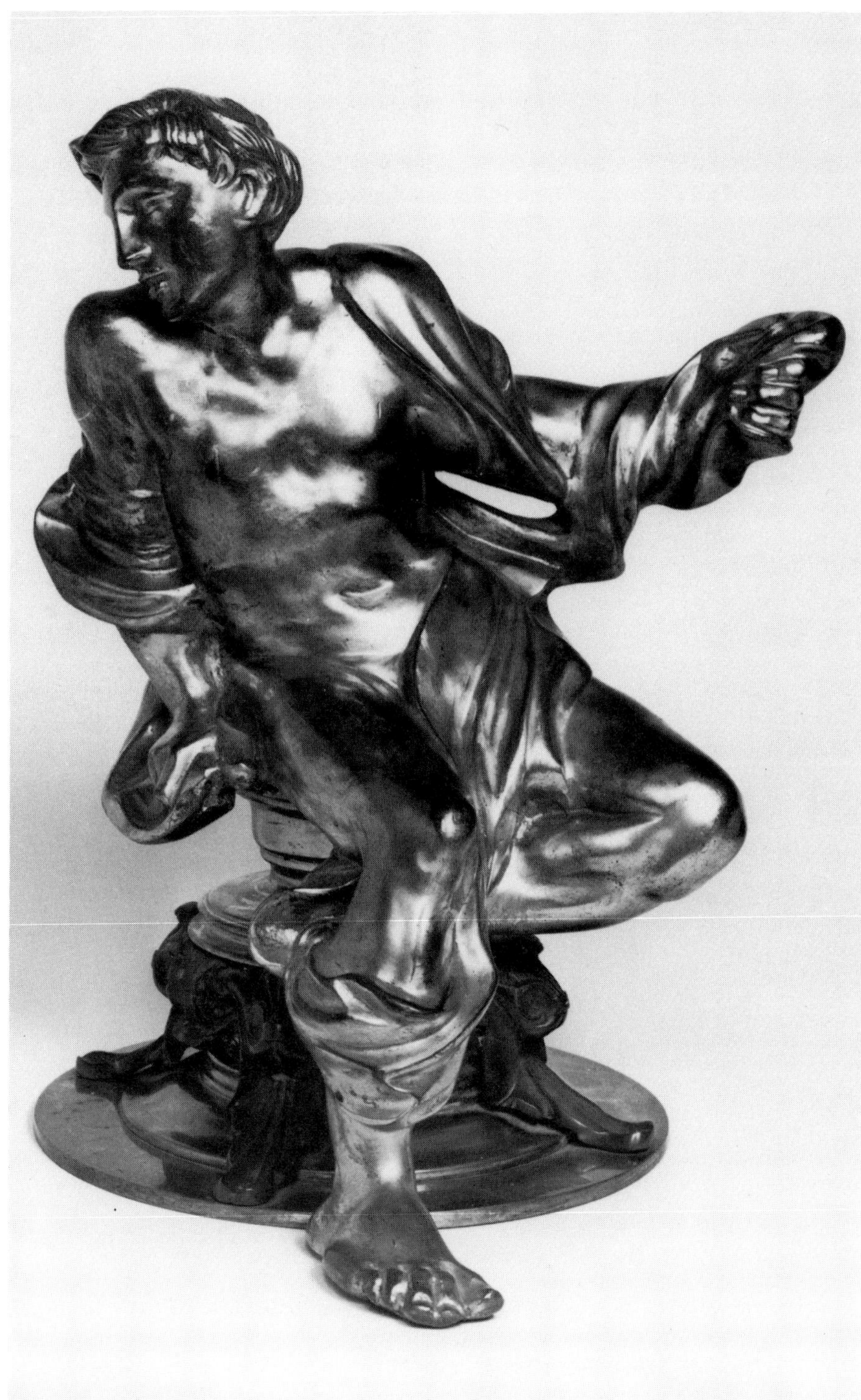
127

scrolled base was intended for use as a fire-dog for a grate, designed in 1852–53 by Stevens for Hoole & Co., a Sheffield firm of ironfounders. A drawing in the National Gallery of Victoria, Melbourne, shows the grate, flanked by upright panels decorated with inventive Renaissance grotesques, and in front is a pair of these andirons or 'figure-dogs'. A plaster model for the bronze is in the Victoria and Albert Museum.

Stevens worked as chief designer for Hoole's from 1850 to 1857, producing a series of fire-grates, stoves and fenders of superb, often complex, High Renaissance design, yet entirely suited to their purpose: there is no difference in quality between his work as a sculptor or painter and his designs for industry. The pose of this figure is derived from one of Michaelangelo's *ignudi* (nude youths) on the ceiling of the Sistine Chapel, Rome. Stevens spent the years from 1833 to 1842 in Italy, immersing himself in the painting, sculpture, architecture and decorative arts of the Renaissance, also studying its technical aspects such as modelling and casting. He was studio assistant to Thorvaldsen (see no. 104) from 1841 to 1842.

Stevens's versatility and distinction is further represented in the Gallery by a majolica vase he designed for Minton & Co., plaster figures for his Wellington Monument in St. Paul's, more plasters for an unexecuted scheme for the dome of St. Paul's, and a cast of the huge chimneypiece for Dorchester House, London, one of his great interior schemes.

128 *Table*

Ebony and boxwood, carved and set with a black marble top inlaid with agate, porphyry, serpentine, lapis lazuli and other semi-precious stones.
Italian (Florence); probably workshop of Ferri and Bartolozzi, *c.* 1885
Length: 173 cm (68 in)
Gift (1983.234)

This table originally stood in the library

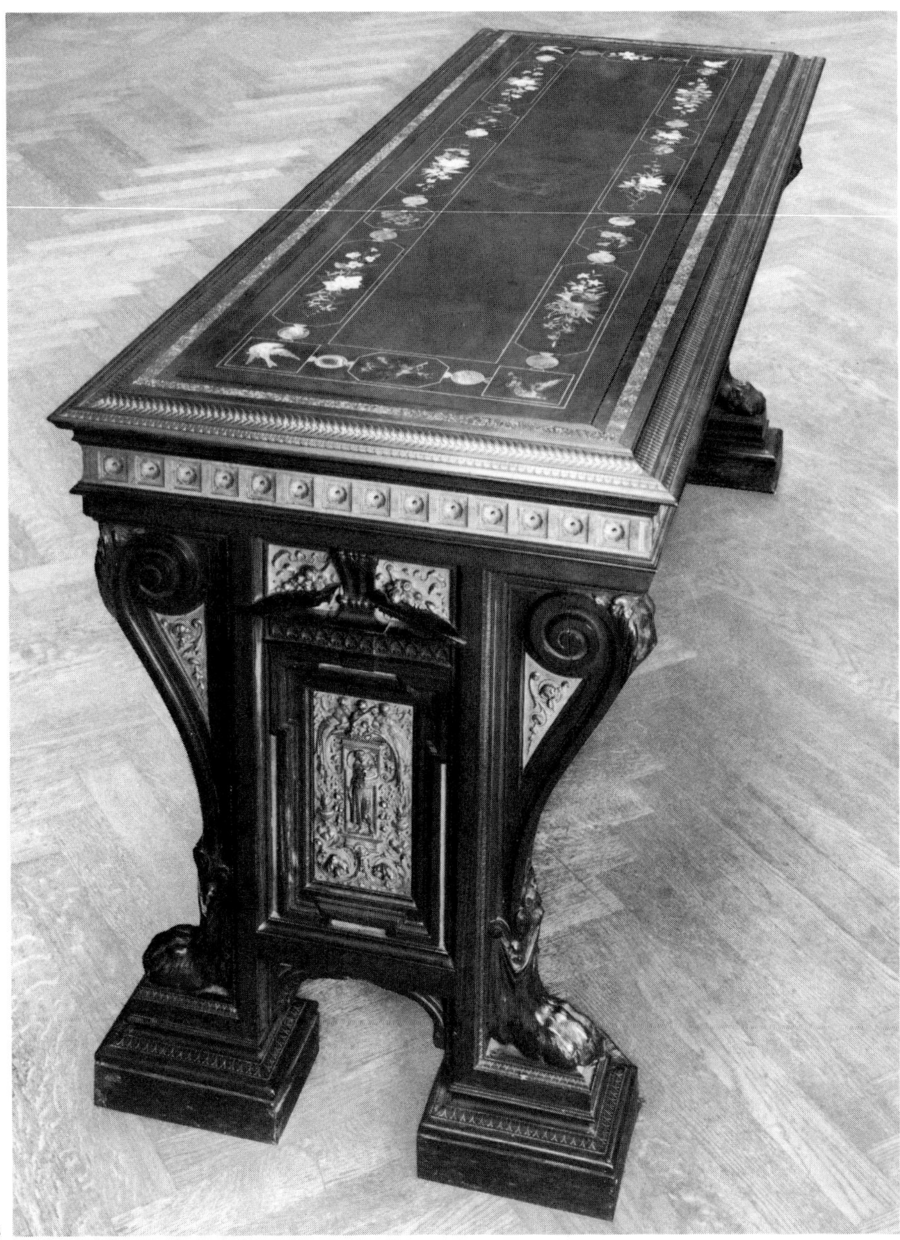

128

at Wythenshawe Hall, Manchester, formerly the home of the Tatton family. It is carved in shallow relief with panels showing the Muses Euterpe and Polyhymnia in the style of the mid-19th-century Renaissance revival. Prince Albert was an advocate of this style, and the English sculptor Alfred Stevens (1818–75) its most formidable exponent in the 1850s. However, this table appears to have been manufactured in the later 19th century. A Florentine ebony 'pietra dura' cabinet in the Renaissance style was commissioned by Henry Martin Gibbs (1850–98) of Barrow Court, Flax Burton, Somerset, in the 1890s. Signed 'Ferri & Bartolozzi', it was bought with a complete set of designs of the 'pietra dura' panels it contains, identifying the hardstones used. This is also the case with the Manchester table, which probably issued from the same workshop. The Wythenshawe Hall library was hung with an embossed wallpaper, *The Golden Age* by Jeffrey and Co., designed by Walter Crane (1845–1915) and exhibited at the Manchester Royal Jubilee Exhibition of 1887. The table was probably acquired at about the same time.

James Lamb of John Dalton Street, one of Manchester's leading cabinet makers and house furnishers, opened his first warehouse in 1843. His vast stock was discussed in *The Cabinet Maker and Art Furnisher* of February 1883, notably 'récherché' articles in various woods, ranging from 'the well known and very comfortable Lancashire rocking chair to the most costly specimens of Italian art furniture'.

129 *Plate and Flagon*

BREAD PLATE

Buff earthenware, inlaid with red-brown and blue slip in a design incorporating wheat ears and leaf scrolls.
Inscribed around rim: *waste not, want not*
English (Stoke-on-Trent); Minton, *c.* 1850
Diameter: 34 cm ($13\frac{3}{8}$ in)
Purchased (1972.42)

FLAGON

Silver gilt.
Inscribed around body: *Pascha Nostrum Immolatus Est Christus, IHS* on hexafoil foot, and a coat of arms *charged quarterly, the first or, a Trefoil slipped vert; second and third sable, three ducal coronets per pale or; fourth azure, a lion rampant surrounded by six roses or.*
Maker's mark: EB + JB for Edward Barnard & Sons Ltd.
English (London), 1866
Height: 26.7 cm ($10\frac{1}{2}$ in)
Purchased (1982.119)

The bread plate was designed by A. W. N. Pugin (1812–52), one of the leading architects of the Gothic Revival style. Pugin believed Gothic was 'the only correct expression of the faith, wants, styles and climate of our community' and adapted his Gothic style in architecture to flat patterns for wallpaper, tiles and plates, which were some of his most successful designs. Pugin was a friend of Herbert Minton, and began designing encaustic and printed tiles for the Minton factory in 1842 and tableware in 1849. The bread plate was designed at the end of the 'Hungry Forties' when the motto would have had particular significance; the problem of the hungry poor was the leading social topic of the time. The plate was reproduced in *The Journal of Design*, II, 1850, p. 97.

Pugin, as a Roman Catholic, was working in opposition to those who produced Gothic designs for the Anglican church. William Butterfield (1814–1900), the architect who designed this flagon, initiated a scheme to improve church plate design. He was adopted by the Cambridge Camden (later Ecclesiological) Society as supervisor of Gothic plate. In 1847 he published *Instrumenta Ecclesiastica*, which illustrated many of his designs, including this flagon. (A copy is in the Gallery archives.) Most are derived from pre-Reformation English silver; this flagon is based on a late 15th-century cruet.

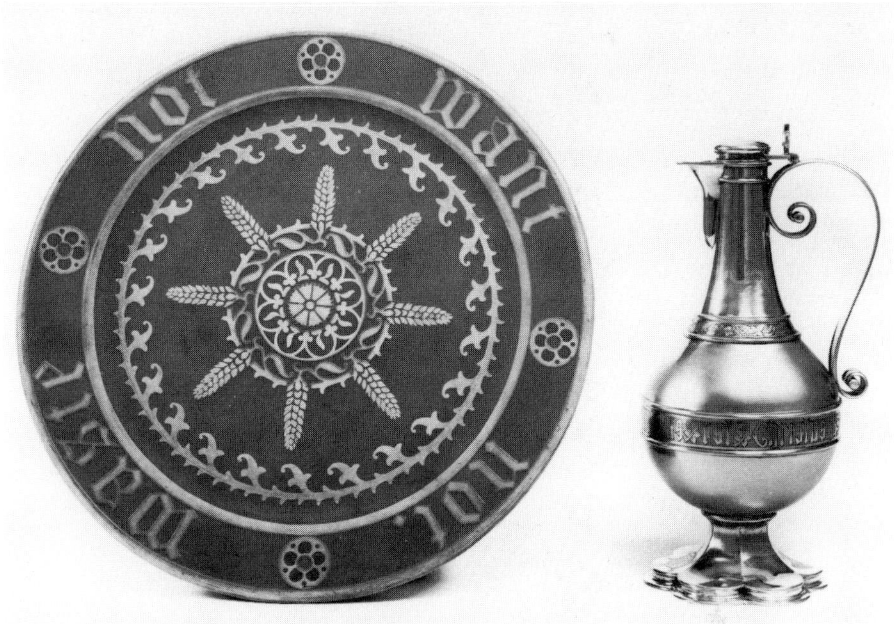

129

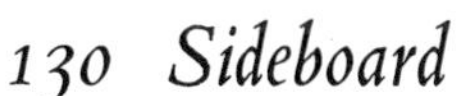

130 *Sideboard*

Oak, with ebony and walnut, and brass fittings.
Mark: LAMB/MANCHESTER/8911/178 impressed
English (Manchester)
James Lamb 1865–70.
Length: 228.7 cm (90 in)
Purchased (1978.48)

This sideboard is typical of the 'Medieval' Victorian furniture. Charles Bevan (fl.1865–73) made 'Medieval' designs which appeared in *The Building News* of 1865 and 1866. In 1865 Marsh and Jones of Leeds supplied Titus Salt of Baildon Lodge with furniture designed by Bevan in the same style. He also designed a bookcase made by Lamb of Manchester and shown in the Paris Exhibition of 1867.

At about this time Bevan's rival was Bruce Talbert (1828–81) an architect who also designed 'Medieval' furniture, and who published *Gothic Forms Applied to Furniture, Metalwork and Decoration for Domestic Purposes* in 1867. Lamb's tradecard of 1866, advertising 'Gothic

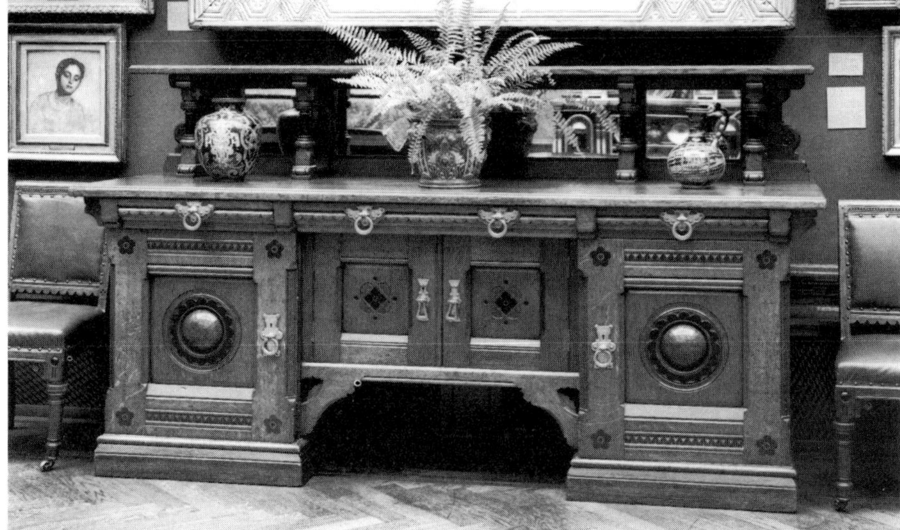

130

Domestic Furniture' bears a BT monogram. Talbert subsequently submitted a design for the Manchester Town Hall competition, won by Alfred Waterhouse.

Bevan's overtly architectural style, of which this piece is characteristic, features a restrained use of ebonised inlay and petal motifs, dwarf columns, curved bosses, cusp borders, and brass fittings.

James Lamb (1817–1903), the son of a builder, started a cabinet-making and upholstery business in 1843, opening a large warehouse on John Dalton Street in 1850, designed by Edward Salomons. His Castlefield works, bought in 1858, held an enormous stock of timber and the latest power cutting machines. Lamb exhibited at the Great Exhibition of 1851, the London and Paris Exhibitions of 1862 and 1867 (Bronze Medallist) and the Paris Exhibition of 1878 (Gold Medallist). On his retirement, his firm amalgamated with Goodall and Heighway and was dissolved in 1954.

131 Escritoire *pl. 13*

Painted pine and mahogany, with brass fittings and ceramic tiles.
Made by William Burges and Gualbert Saunders.
English 1865–67
Height: 248 cm ($97\frac{1}{2}$ in)
Purchased with the aid of a Government grant (through the Victoria and Albert Museum) (1979.132)

Burges (1827–81) was the most imaginative, brilliant and eccentric Victorian architect and designer. He rapidly established an international reputation by winning two competitions, for Lille Cathedral and the Crimea Memorial Church, whilst still in his twenties. His best buildings are truly 'High' Victorian in style, and include St. Finbar's Cathedral, Cork; Cardiff Castle; Castle Coch; and the Tower House, Melbury Road, London. All his work shows a deep appreciation of medieval buildings which are, in his words, 'glowing with imperishable colour'.

In 1865 W. Gualbert Saunders joined Burges at his Buckingham Street office in London and became the head of Saunders and Company, Burges's firm of craftsmen and cabinet makers. Burges had already received, in 1858, a commission for furniture from H. G. Yatman of Haslemere. The Yatman cabinet, in pine and mahogany, painted by E. J. Poynter (1836–1919) is now in the Victoria and Albert Museum. The Manchester desk, inscribed *Gualbert Saunders made ME AD 1865*, is, however, similar to Burges's own desk, and to an architectural cabinet once at Buckingham Street, which are both lost but known from photographs. The desk, sold in 1933, has similar iconography painted by C. Rossiter, also showing the five 'estates' of peasant, merchant, knight, priest and king, and the history of communication through Stone carving, Handwriting, Printing, Poetry, Telegraphy and the Press, painted on white tiles signed 'GS'.

The Buckingham Street architectural cabinet of about 1858 had more similar proportions to the Manchester desk, with painted sides, fish-scale 'roof' and carved crockets. Painted doors, gables and finials (what Christopher Dresser called Burges's 'doll's-house tricks') were all drawn from medieval prototypes. These were the painted armoire at Bayeux, published in colour by the French architect Viollet-le-Duc in 1858, and the Noyon armoire, published by Burges himself in 1853. Burges's furniture after 1858 combined architecture and painting admirably. It was admired by the Pre-Raphaelites. Morris, Rossetti and Burne-Jones also produced painted furniture in the 1850s epitomising their dream of recreating the artistic spirit of the Middle Ages in Victorian England.

132 Tile Panel *pl. 12*

Coarse earthenware, with hand-transferred underglaze 'Persian Colours'. Eight inch tiles with border tiles.
Mark: DE MORGAN/MERTON ABBEY, impressed oval
English (Surrey); William De Morgan and Company, Merton Abbey (1882–8)
Length of panel: 51.5 cm (20 in)
Horsfall Museum Gift (1918.292)

William de Morgan began decorating tiles from 1872 onwards, and making his own more durable tiles about 1876. Tiles, as well as vases and dishes, were either decorated with lustre, developed in Chelsea in 1873–74, or in 'Persian colours' of blue, turquoise, purple, green, black, iron-red and lemon yellow, on a white background. The same designs were used on tiles and vases, and the original watercolour sketch for a similar ship panel in Manchester's collections survives and is dated '13 March 82'. A vase with the design of two ships is in the Victoria and Albert Museum (1860.1905).

De Morgan, originally a painter and stained-glass designer, devised an ingenious method of transferring tile designs by hand, and filling the outlines with pigments. His 'Persian' designs are Syrian or Isnik inspired, but instantly recognisable as his own. The best known is *BBB*, a flower design named after the Company's first important tile customer Barnard, Bishop and Barnard.

De Morgan was introduced to Burne Jones and William Morris in 1863 and Morris & Co. became his customers during the 1860s. A tile in the 'new pineapple' series in Manchester's collections bears a Morris and Co. label with *60/-* over written in red *30/-*.

De Morgan also received commissions for Whistler's Peacock room (44 Princes Gate, London), Alexander III's yacht *Lavadia*, Leighton's Arab Hall in Kensington, the decoration of the P & O line ships, and work at the Bedford Park Estate, designed by Shaw and Godwin.

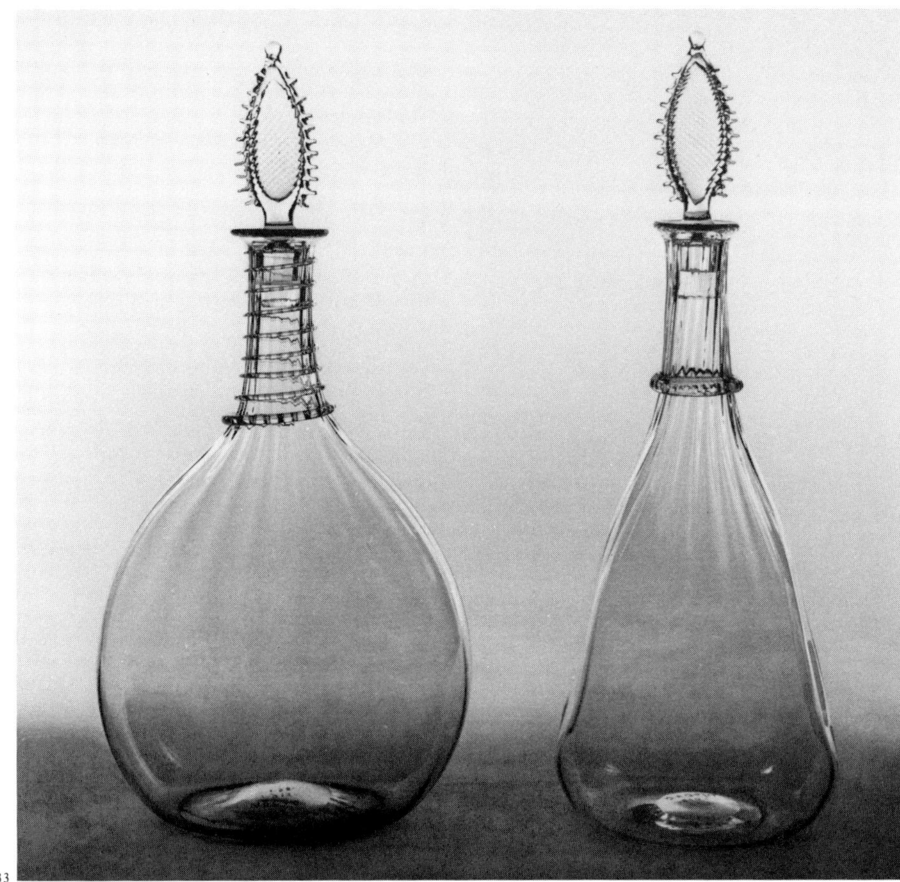

133

They used soda glass in preference to lead crystal to achieve a thinly blown, delicate form, to which they could add restrained pincered or trailed decoration in the Venetian style. The 'poppy-head' stopper on these decanters is the only obvious Venetian motif, used to create an imaginative, graceful design. This type of claret decanter was introduced in 1880; the four indentations in the body of one of the examples were intended to provide a secure grip.

133 *Glass Decanters*

DECANTER

Glass, colourless trail on the neck, 'poppy-head' stopper.
English (London); James Powell & Sons, Whitefriars Glassworks, 1880–85
Height (including stopper): 32.2 cm ($12\frac{5}{8}$ in)
Horsfall Collection (1918.198)

DECANTER

Glass, concave sides, 'poppy-head' stopper
English (London); James Powell & Sons, Whitefriars Glassworks, 1880–85
Height (including stopper): 32.8 cm ($12\frac{7}{8}$ in)
Horsfall Collection (1918.199)

By the mid-19th century there were strong reactions to the heavily cut glass of the earlier Victorian period. John Ruskin in *The Stones of Venice* (Volume II, 1853) claimed: 'All cut glass is barbaric', and Richard Redgrave had expressed similar views in his report of the 1851 exhibition. The firm of James Powell & Sons was the first to be influenced by this, and began to produce simple, uncut ranges of glass. They made a set of table glass designed by Philip Webb (1831–1915) for William Morris (1834–96) in 1859, and continued to execute other architects' designs.

Towards the end of the century Powell's began to imitate glassware of earlier periods, particularly Venetian glass of the 16th and 17th centuries.

134 *Ary Scheffer*

(1795–1858)

THE HOLY WOMEN AT THE SEPULCHRE 1845

French; oil on panel
108.8 × 86 cm ($42\frac{7}{8} \times 33\frac{7}{8}$ in)
Signed (b.l.c.): *Ary Scheffer 1845*
Lord Ashton of Hyde gift (1924.17)

This is a late work by Ary Scheffer, a Dutch artist who worked in France, where he became one of the most famous painters of the romantic movement, exhibiting regularly at the Paris Salon. He was a pupil of Guerin and Prud'hon, and employed the pure line and smooth, flat modelling of the French neo-classical school, derived from Ingres. Scheffer's style was also marked by a heightened sentimentality, frigid colour and the suppression of detail. His most famous subjects were from Dante and the romantic poets Schiller, Byron and, above all, Goethe.

Later in life he turned to religious subjects, and in this picture a mood of subdued pathos is set by the hypnotically undulating pattern of lines, the bowed heads and the Magdalen's large uplifted eyes. She holds a white shroud, which sets off Christ's pallid face, surrounded by a faint radiance. The Virgin's mantle is icy blue.

It was painted in 1845 and was shown at the Paris Salon of 1846, where it was seen by Baudelaire. In 1856–57, it was included in the first exhibition of

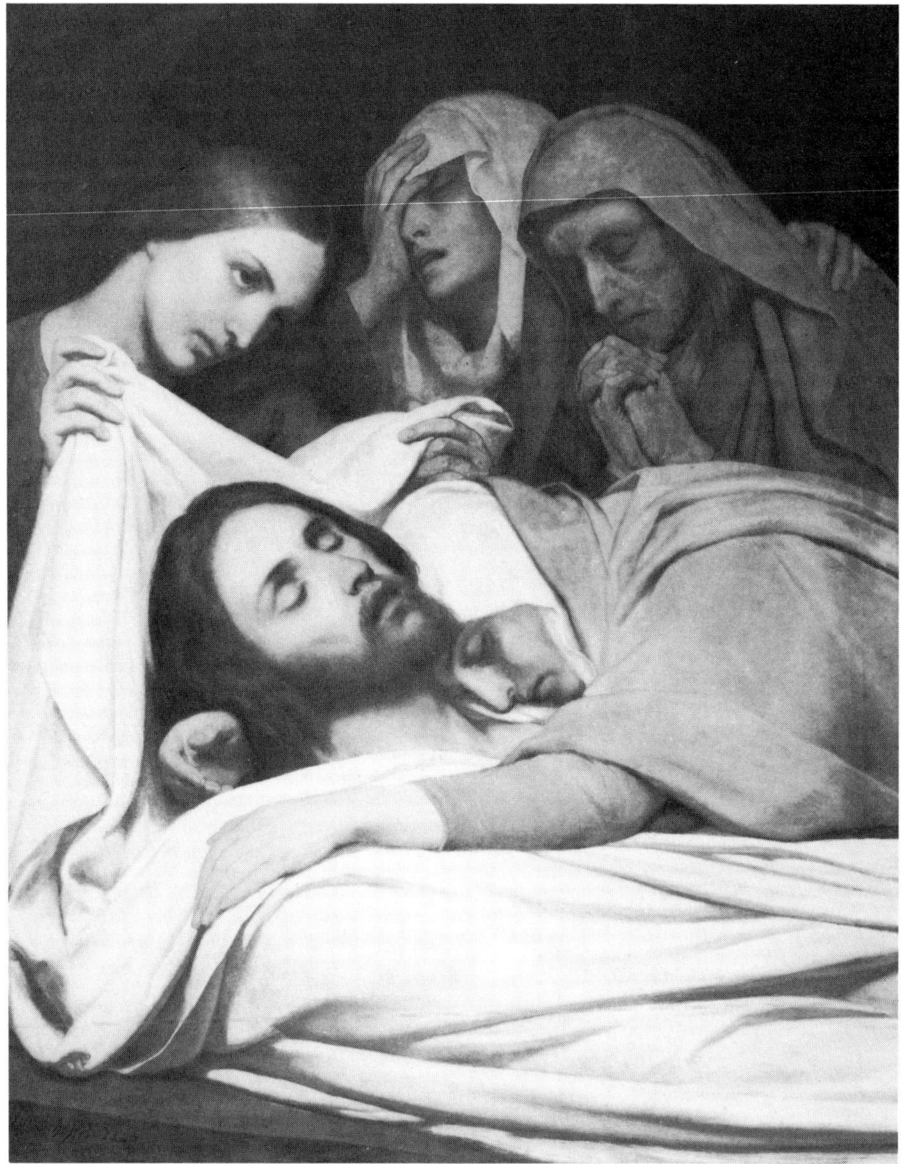

134

Modern French Art held at the Royal Manchester Institution, where it was purchased by Samuel Ashton, a cotton manufacturer. Scheffer had a large following amongst the English, particularly in the North West. In 1857 he visited Manchester to see the Art Treasures exhibition, and stayed for three weeks at the home of another of his patrons, Salis Schwabe, a Manchester merchant.

Like many of his pictures, *The Holy Women* became well known through engravings, in this case by Keller. Scheffer also painted a smaller version, dated 1854, which is now in the National Gallery of Victoria, Melbourne.

135 *Adolphe Yvon*

(1817–93)

MARSHAL NEY SUPPORTING THE REAR GUARD DURING THE RETREAT FROM MOSCOW

French; oil on canvas
179.8 × 301 cm ($70\frac{3}{4} \times 118\frac{1}{2}$ in)
Signed (b.r.c.): *Ad: Yvon. 1856*
Royal Manchester Institution, 1857, from which transferred (1882.7)

In September 1813 Napoleon entered Moscow, but the Russians had abandoned and set fire to the city, and the exhausted French invaders were thus deprived of shelter and supplies. Napoleon and his shattered army were forced to retreat across the barren countryside, and over 400,000 men are supposed to have perished in the terrible Russian winter.

Napoleonic subjects were extremely popular in mid-19th-century France. Napoleon III created at Versailles a vast Museum, with a large Napoleonic section devoted to the cult of his namesake. New paintings were commissioned from contemporary artists to show all Napoleon's military campaigns. There are two versions of this painting, this one and one at Versailles. The latter was exhibited at the Paris Salon of 1852, with a quotation from De Segur's book on Napoleon, describing the heroism of Marshal Ney: 'the last to leave that fatal Russia, showing to the world that adversity is powerless against so noble a courage, and that for a hero, everything turns to glory, even the greatest disasters.' Like this text, the painting is conceived in terms of unashamed propaganda for *la Gloire*, and is filled with gruesome details.

Yvon was a pupil of Delaroche, whose famous *Napoleon Crossing the Alps* (1848) is in the Walker Art Gallery, Liverpool. After a journey to Russia in 1843, Yvon began to specialise in battle scenes, historical and contemporary: he

135

was the only artist sent out officially to the Crimea.

The painting was purchased by the Royal Manchester Institution from the exhibition of Modern French Art held there in 1856–57.

136 *Henri Fantin-Latour*

(1836–1904)

SELF-PORTRAIT 1867

French; oil on canvas
64 × 55.2 cm ($25\frac{3}{16} \times 21\frac{3}{4}$ in)
Signed (t.r.c.): *Fantin*
Purchased (1919.8)

This self-portrait is one of nineteen works by Fantin-Latour in the collection, the others being five still-lifes in oil, and five oils and eight prints of mythological subjects. Fantin was a friend of the Impressionists, but his work is more conventional than theirs; it is dark, solidly modelled, with a finely worked surface and includes no landscapes.

Fantin-Latour painted many sensitive self-portraits, most of them dating from early in his career. These show the young artist posing informally, often in the act of painting himself, with an intent, searching expression. They are loosely handled, with strong chiaroscuro, in the manner of Rembrandt's self-portraits. Here the strong light and shade is retained, but the artist has assumed a more self-assured, public pose, probably corresponding to the growing success of his career. The self-portrait was exhibited in 1867 at the Paris Salon, with a portrait of his friend, the painter Edouard Manet (now in Chicago), which set the seal on his reputation.

Of self-portraits, Fantin-Latour wrote: 'The model is always ready and offers all sorts of advantages; he is exact, submissive, and one knows him before painting.' He was socially timid, and uneasy with sitters he did not know, which resulted in a sense of strain in many of his commissioned portraits. Indeed, he gave these up altogether after 1868.

This self-portrait was formerly in the collection of Constantine Ionides, born in Manchester, of a Greek merchant family. He settled in London in 1864, where he formed a collection, mostly now in the Victoria and Albert Museum, which included Old Masters, and English and French 19th-century pictures including three Fantin-Latour flower pieces.

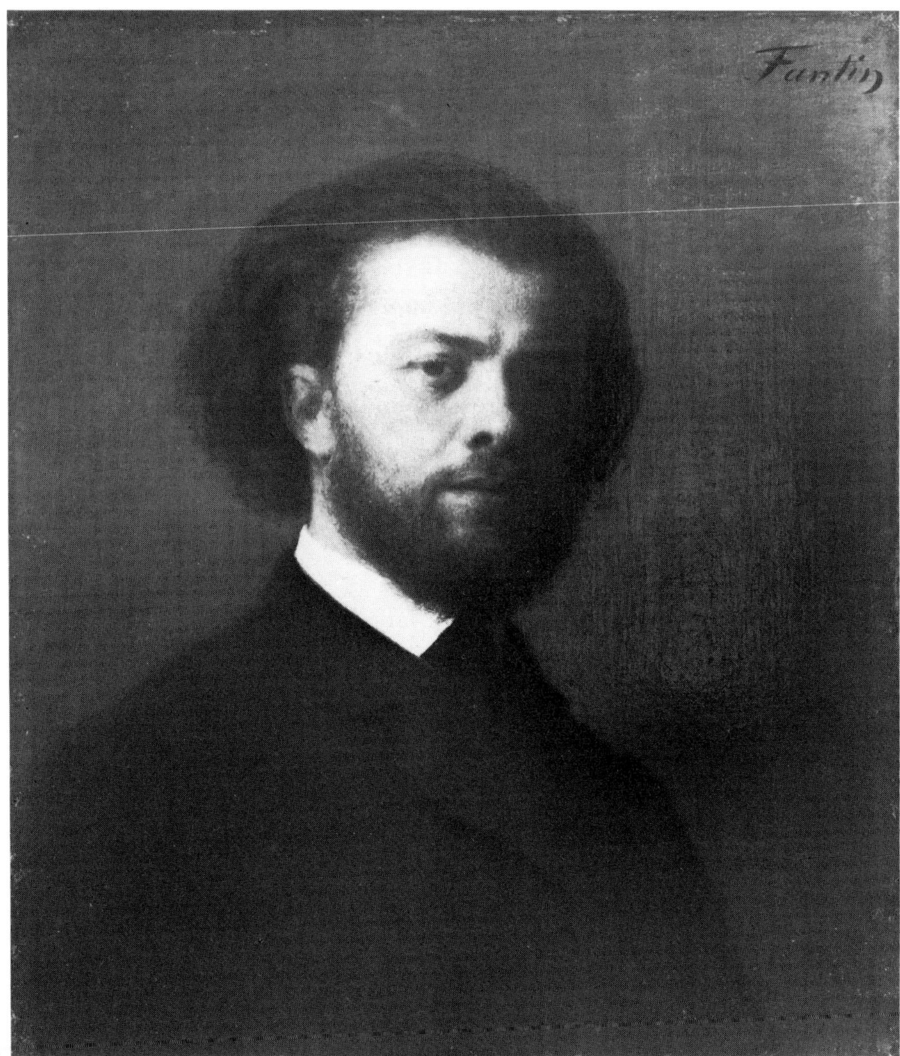

136

137 Camille Pissarro
(1831–1903)

A VILLAGE STREET, LOUVECIENNES 1871

French; oil on canvas
46 × 55.5 cm ($18\frac{1}{8} \times 21\frac{7}{8}$ in)
Signed (b.l.c.): *C Pissarro 1871*
Purchased from a descendant of Samuel Barlow with the aid of a Government grant (through the Victoria and Albert Museum) (1969.67)

Pissarro first went to live at Louveciennes, a village south west of Paris, in 1869, moving back to Pontoise in 1872. During this period, he painted a long sequence of views of streets and small houses at Louveciennes mostly with steep perspectives and small figures. This view has been identified as of the Rue de Voisins. A similar work taken from a more distant viewpoint was painted by Alfred Sisley around 1870 (*Early Snow at Louveciennes*, Boston Museum of Fine Arts). Judging by the cool tonality of Pissarro's painting and the clumps of leafless trees, the work was executed in the autumn of 1871. The freely applied dabs of colour and loose brushwork show the influence of Monet. The observation of light at a particular time of day was important to Pissarro and his fellow Impressionists: here, the sun is low in the sky casting long shadows and picking out the figures in aureoles of light. Areas of light and shadow are expressed by light and dark tones of the same colour.

Soon afterwards, the picture became one of the earliest Impressionist paintings to be purchased by a British collector. It was bought through an art-dealer, probably Durand-Ruel, by Samuel Barlow (1825–93) of Stakehill, Middleton, Manchester, the owner of a bleach works. It seems likely that it entered his collection in the 1870s at a time when the public regarded Impressionist paintings as mere daubs. It was a remarkable acquisition for any collector of the time, and Barlow himself may have had second thoughts as he attempted, but failed, to sell it at Christie's in 1883. It was bought in for twenty-one guineas. Today it is one of the most delightful examples of Impressionist painting in the Galleries collection.

138 Paul Gauguin
(1848–1903)

LE PORT DE DIEPPE ?1885

French; oil on canvas
60.2 × 72.3 cm ($23\frac{11}{16} \times 28\frac{7}{16}$ in)
Signed (b.r.c.): P Gauguin
Presented by Mrs P. Duxbury (1944.46)

Le Port de Dieppe is an early work by Gauguin, painted in the Impressionist style. It pre-dates the poetic, symbolist paintings of Breton peasants made between 1886 and 1890, and the later, highly individual, brilliantly coloured vision of Tahiti. Gauguin was purely a

Sunday painter until 1883 when he resigned his job as a stockbroker to become a full-time artist. He had been encouraged to do this by meeting Pissarro and exhibiting with the Impressionists, whose work he began to collect from 1875. The low tones of *Le Port de Dieppe* show a fairly conservative approach to Impressionism, which is perhaps closer to Corot and Boudin than to Monet or Renoir; but the isolated patches of vibrant colour, such as the pink of the roof tops, presage something of the exceptional colourist Gauguin was to become.

On stylistic grounds, the painting can be dated between 1883 and 1885. It was mostly probably painted in September 1885, when Gauguin was staying for a few days in Dieppe before a three-week visit to London. No other visit to Dieppe is recorded, but he may have gone there earlier while living in Rouen. Another view of Dieppe, *La Plage à Dieppe* (Ny Carlsberg Museum, Copenhagen), dated 1885, was almost certainly made during this visit.

The scene is painted at half-tide from the east end of Quai Henri IV on a level with its junction with the Rue de la Rade. To the left can be seen the spire of Nôtre Dame des Grèves built in 1841–49.

The Gallery also owns two woodcuts by Gauguin: *Te Po, the God of Night* and *Auti Te, Pape*.

139 *Auguste Rodin*

(1840–1917)

THE AGE OF BRONZE

French; bronze
Height: 183 cm (72 in)
Signed (top of base on r.): *Rodin*
Marked, back of base: ALEXIS RUDIER / FONDEUR. PARIS
Purchased from the artist (1911.109)

The Age of Bronze was the first full-scale figure Rodin exhibited. His model was a Belgian soldier, Auguste Neyt, and the

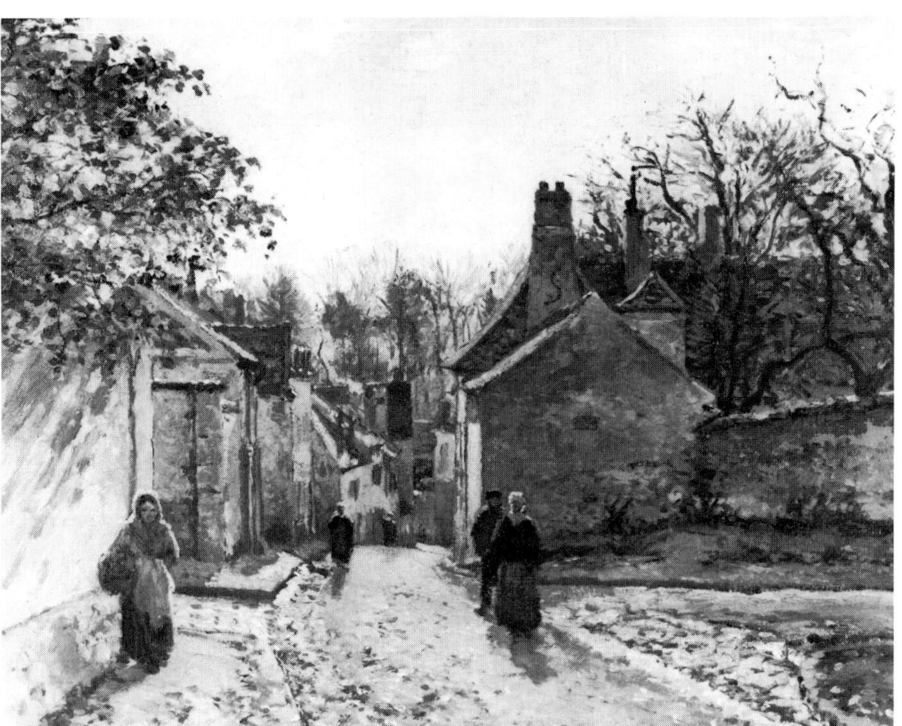

137

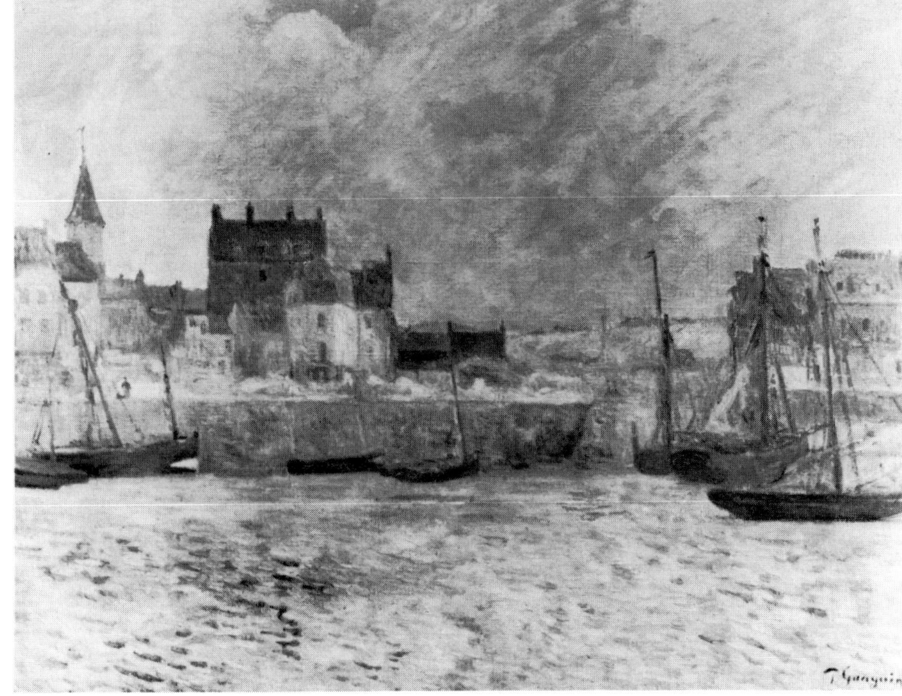

138

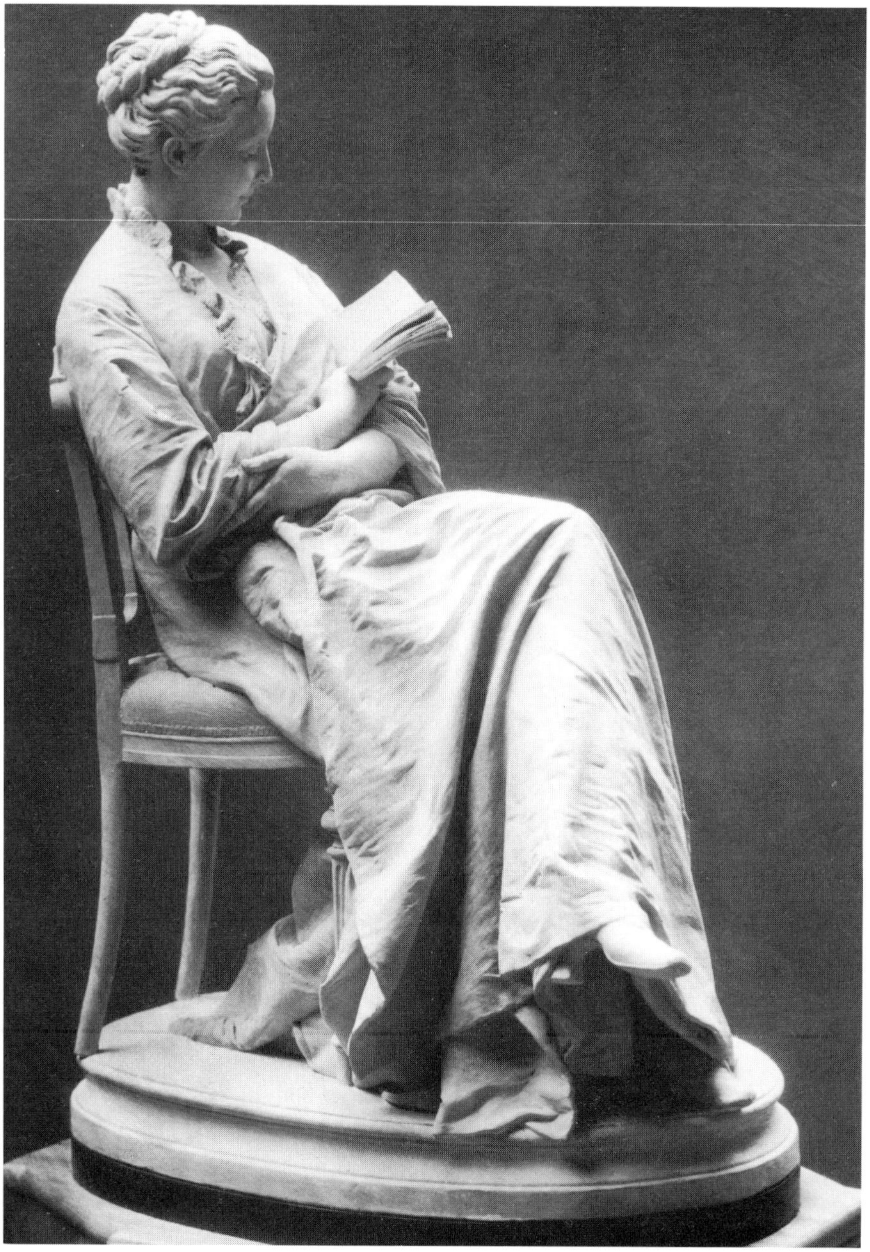

140

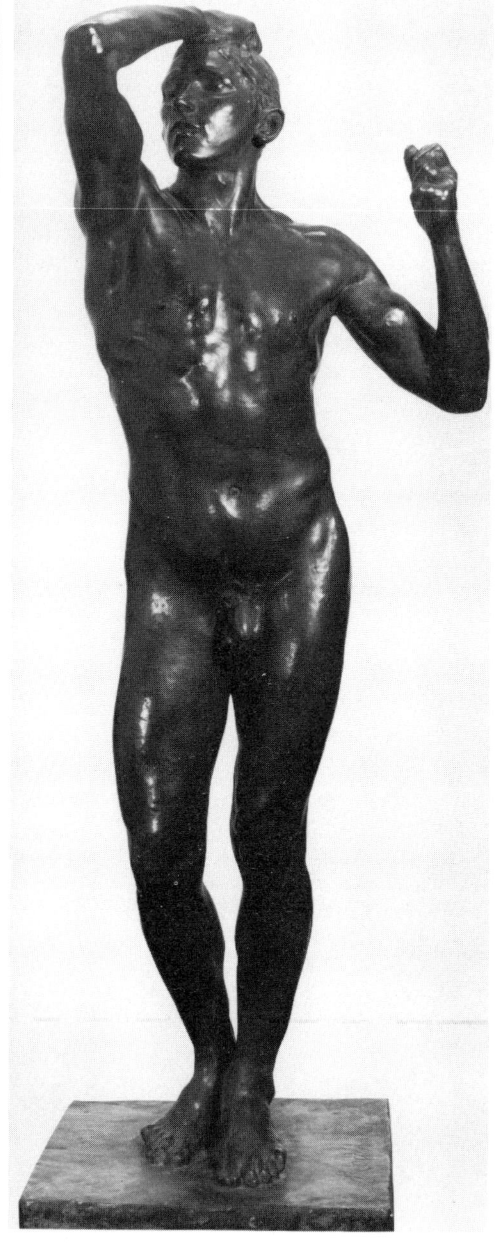

139

sculptor worked for eighteen months, observing the form from all angles, using a step-ladder to see from above. He also studied clay sketches of Neyt by candlelight. When exhibited, the figure looked so natural that Rodin was accused of casting it directly from the figure: but he subtly modified correct anatomy to give the impression of life and movement in a static material. Neyt was given a staff, probably to help him keep his pose. According to an ink drawing of 1876, this was changed to a spear, which may have suggested the first title, *The Vanquished*. The spear was removed before January 1877 when the plaster model was shown at the Brussels Salon. Later in the year it was exhibited at the Paris Salon, for which Rodin gave it the title *The Age of Bronze*.

The exact meaning of the title is not clear, and the pose is ambiguous. There is a general air of uncertainty about the gesture; the figure seems to be on the point of stretching. Possibly Rodin wanted to show early man, physically perfect, becoming aware of his powers. The upper part resembles Michaelangelo's *Bound Captive* (Louvre).

This is a late cast, commissioned specially for the Galleries in 1911, after a visit to Rodin's studio by the Chairman of the Art Galleries Committee. It is one of four works by Rodin in the collection.

140 *Jules Dalou*

(1838–1902)

THE READER 1877

French; terracotta
Height 79 cm (31 in)
Signed and dated: *Dalou 1877*
Presented by Helen Ionides (1921.24)

The French sculptor Dalou came as a political refugee to London in July 1871. After the Franco-Prussian War and the fall of the Second Empire he was actively involved in the Commune. When it fell, he escaped with his family to London, and in his absence was sentenced to hard labour for life. He did not return until 1880, after a general amnesty.

In London, the French emigré painter Alphonse Legros, by then professor at the Slade, introduced him to prospective patrons, such as the amateur artist and friend of the Pre-Raphaelites, George Howard, later 9th Earl of Carlisle. One of Howard's early commissions was a portrait of his wife seated on a chair. This inaugurated a series of similar genre figures, nursing, sewing or reading. *The Reader*, modelled in terracotta in 1877, was inspired by Madame Dalou, though it is not a portrait. It was purchased by another of Legros' friends, C. A. Ionides (see entry on Fantin-Latour, no. 136).

From his first teacher, J. B. Carpeaux, Dalou inherited a fluent touch and the ability to catch fleeting expressions. *The Reader* beautifully portrays the papery texture of the silk dress, the lace collar and the graceful hint of a smile. In the Victoria and Albert Museum is a 9-inch-high terracotta sketch which preserves the speed of the first idea, refined in the Manchester piece to a gentle naturalism, without over-finishing.

From 1877 Dalou taught modelling at what is now the Royal College of Art and played a decisive role in the emergence in Britain of the 'new sculpture', a reaction to the monumentality and bland smoothness of mid-Victorian sculpture.

141 *A. von Wagner*

(1838–1919)

THE CHARIOT RACE

German; oil on canvas
138.3 × 347 cm ($54\frac{7}{16}$ × $136\frac{9}{16}$ in)
Signed (b.r.c.): *A Wagner* (AW in mon.)
Mrs H. Higgins Bequest (1898.12)

In the late 19th century Munich was the centre of a school of painters specialising in the production of vast operatically-conceived reconstructions of historical events. The founder of the school was Karl Piloty, who was much influenced by French and Belgian historical painters such as Delaroche and Gallait, and one of Piloty's pupils was Alexander von Wagner. Born in Hungary, but trained in Vienna and Munich, he became

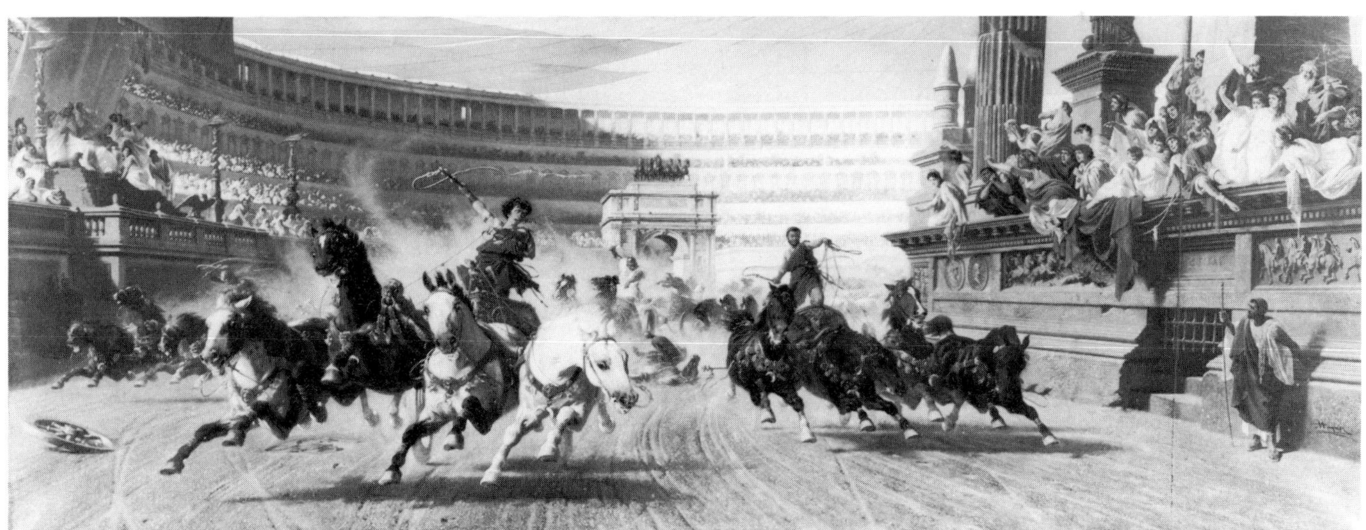

141

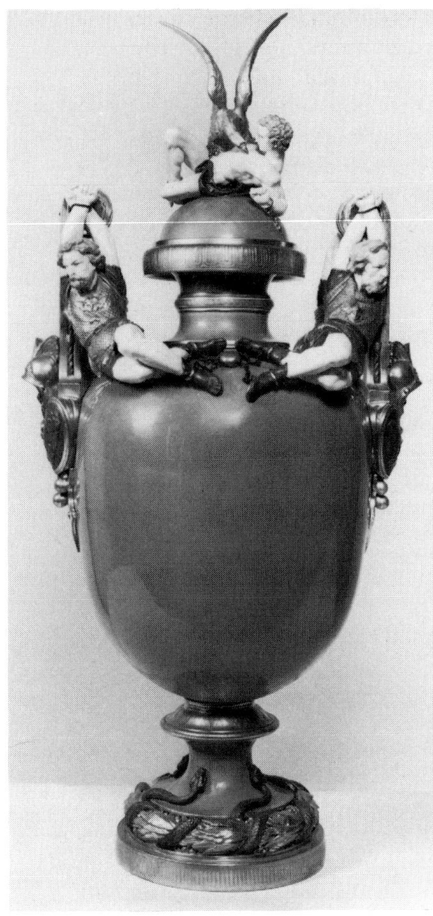

142

Professor of Art at the Munich Academy. Like his master, he covered acres of canvas and wall with crowded figure subjects depicting battles, triumphal processions and deaths of famous personages. He was also proficient at genre and landscape, but scenes of Greek and Roman history were important in his work: one of his greatest paintings, in both senses, was *The Entrance of Constantine the Great into Rome*, commissioned by the Panorama Society of Munich, but also shown in England and America. It was 5 ft high and 42 ft long.

The Chariot Race shows a greater concern for vulgar spectacle than for beauty of drawing, touch or colour: yet it vividly captures the wild excitement of the charioteers, rushing headlong at the spectator, in a composition which foreshadows the effects of the wide screen. Such popular Victorian pictures fulfilled the same need as the epic films of the 20th century. There may well be a connection between the two, for directors such as Cecil B. de Mille were brought up when paintings like this were at the height of their fame. When making *Ben Hur*, he and his designers may well have had in mind a picture like *The Chariot Race*.

142 *Prometheus vase*

Bone china, with applied, slip cast figures of Prometheus and captive Gauls, gilt, silvered and bronzed. 'Bleu céleste' turquoise glaze.
Mark: *1328, MINTONS/N* (impressed); *3* (incised)
English (Stoke-on-Trent); Mintons, 1875–78
Height: 110.5 cm ($43\frac{1}{2}$ in)
Purchased (1884.45)

The Prometheus or 'Captive' vase is attributed to Victor Simeon, referred to in the Minton archives as 'an able French modeller', active about 1858. Victor Étienne Simyan was a successful French Salon sculptor who came to London in the 1860s to produce *de poteries d'art*. The Prometheus vase was exhibited in 1867 at Paris, and has a cover with a figure of Prometheus tortured by an eagle eternally feeding on his liver. The subject, taken from classical mythology, relates closely to a painting by Rubens, *Prometheus bound on Mount Caucasus*, of about 1617, now in the Philadelphia Art Museum.

At least two other Prometheus vases are painted with further Rubens subjects. One, now in the Victoria and Albert Museum, is decorated after *The Rape of the Sabine Women* of 1635, now in the National Gallery, and another which was recently sold at auction is painted in majolica colours after Rubens' *Hippopotamus and Crocodile Hunt*, now in the Alte Pinakothek, Munich, and *The Lion Hunt*, 1615–20, for which there is a sketch in the National Gallery, Peel Collection.

The Manchester vase is, however, undecorated, and would seem to be the piece recorded in the Minton Estimate Book for the Paris 1878 Exhibition, costing 90 guineas.

> China turquoise ground, R gilt Bands at top, around neck and foot. Figures twisted Armour in Bronze and silver. Snakes in silver in GR.

The vase is one of a fine group of Minton wares acquired in 1884, from an exhibition at Queen's Park Art Gallery, Manchester. It was purchased for £94 10s.

143 *James Tissot*
(1836–1902)

THE CONCERT

English School; oil on canvas
73.7 × 112.2 cm (29 × $44\frac{3}{16}$ in)
Signed (b.r.c.): *J. J. Tissot*
Purchased (1933.56)

This was originally shown at the Royal Academy in 1875 under the much more atmospheric title *Hush!* Tissot has captured the momentary pause when the audience is settling down before the concert begins. Fans flicker, satins rustle, figures are caught in movement and cut off by the edge of the picture as in a snap-shot. Tissot was born in France, and was a friend of the Impressionists and of Degas, all of whom were interested in instantaneous and casual effects and much influenced by the recent invention of photography. He came to England as a political refugee after the Commune of 1870, and settled in London where he achieved great success with his sparkling depictions of English fashionable occasions. These were unfairly derided by Ruskin as 'mere colour photographs of vulgar society'.

Many attempts have been made to

identify the figures. The painting is said to have been inspired by a musical soirée at the Coopes', at which Madame Neruda (the second Lady Hallé) played, but the violinist has also been identified as Mlle Diaz de Soria and Mlle Castellan. Others present are alleged to be the painters Lord Leighton, Heilbuth and de Nittis, and the composer Arthur Sullivan. However, the figures are not meant to be portraits, just types, and some professional models are included. The costumes, with their frothy layers of tulle, silk flowers and beribboned head-dresses, give an extremely accurate picture of fashionable dress. Each ensemble must have been very expensive, the product of hundreds of hours of labour, yet none were designed to last through more than one or two such evenings.

144 *Lord Leighton*

(1830–96) *pl. 10*

CAPTIVE ANDROMACHE

English; oil on canvas, 197 × 407 cm (77 × 160 in)
Unsigned
Purchased from the artist with the aid of Friends of the Gallery (1889.2).

One of Lord Leighton's largest and grandest compositions, exhibited at the Royal Academy in 1888, it typifies his desire to recreate for the Victorian age the ideal art of ancient Greece. The subject was suggested by the episode in Homer's *Iliad* where Hector, armed for battle, takes leave of his wife Andromache and, resisting her passionate appeals to stay, reminds her of what might happen if the war were lost and the Trojans enslaved. The painting depicts the fulfilment of Hector's prophecy and shows the noble Andromache as an exile in a strange land. Dressed in black, she stands in the centre of the painting, isolated from the Greek slave women and awaiting her turn to draw water at the well. She gazes sadly at the charming group of the baby playing with its parents, and perhaps recalls her own family in happier days. Three travellers and a Fate-like old crone remark upon her presence.

Leighton has depicted the scene in the

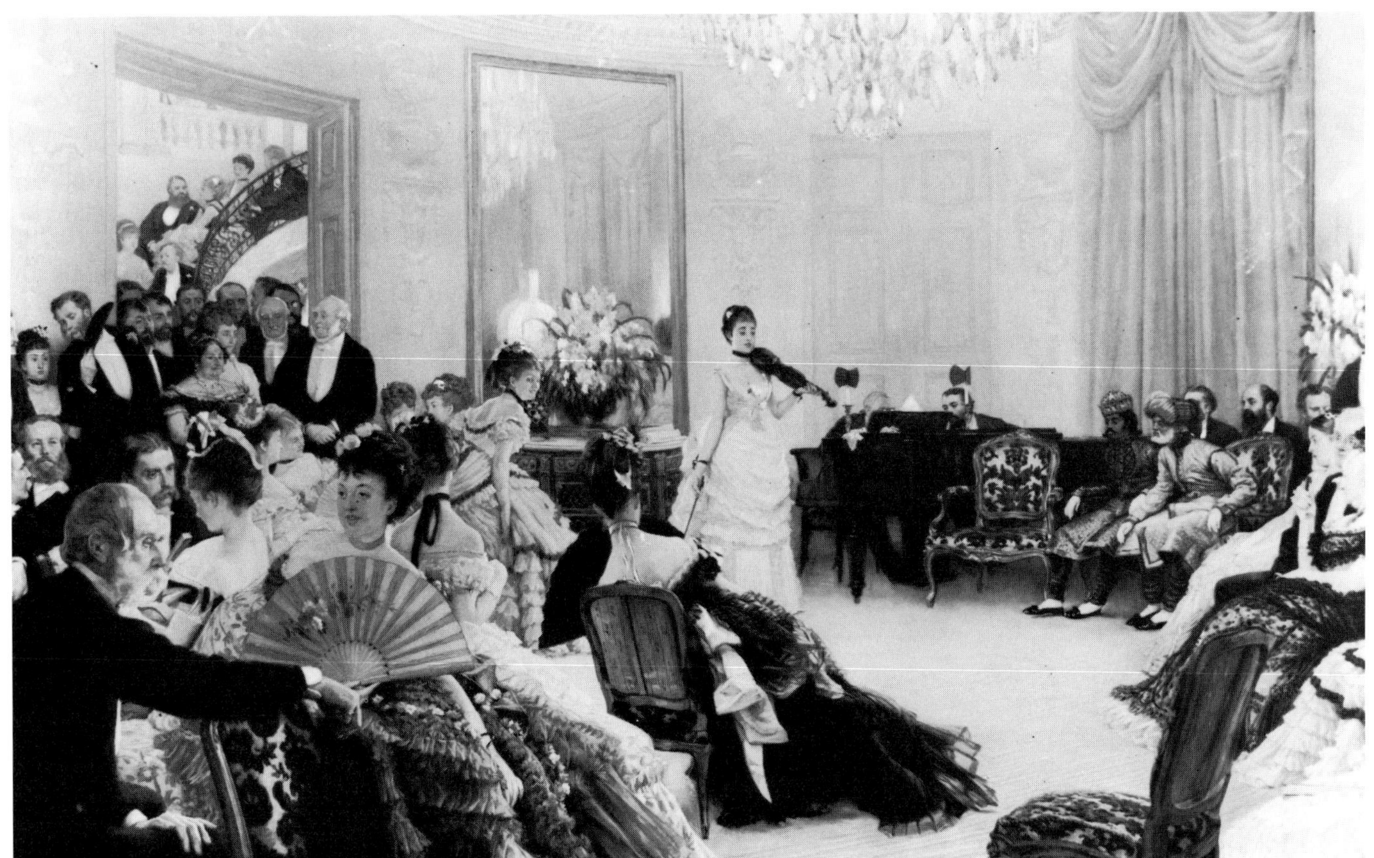

143

145 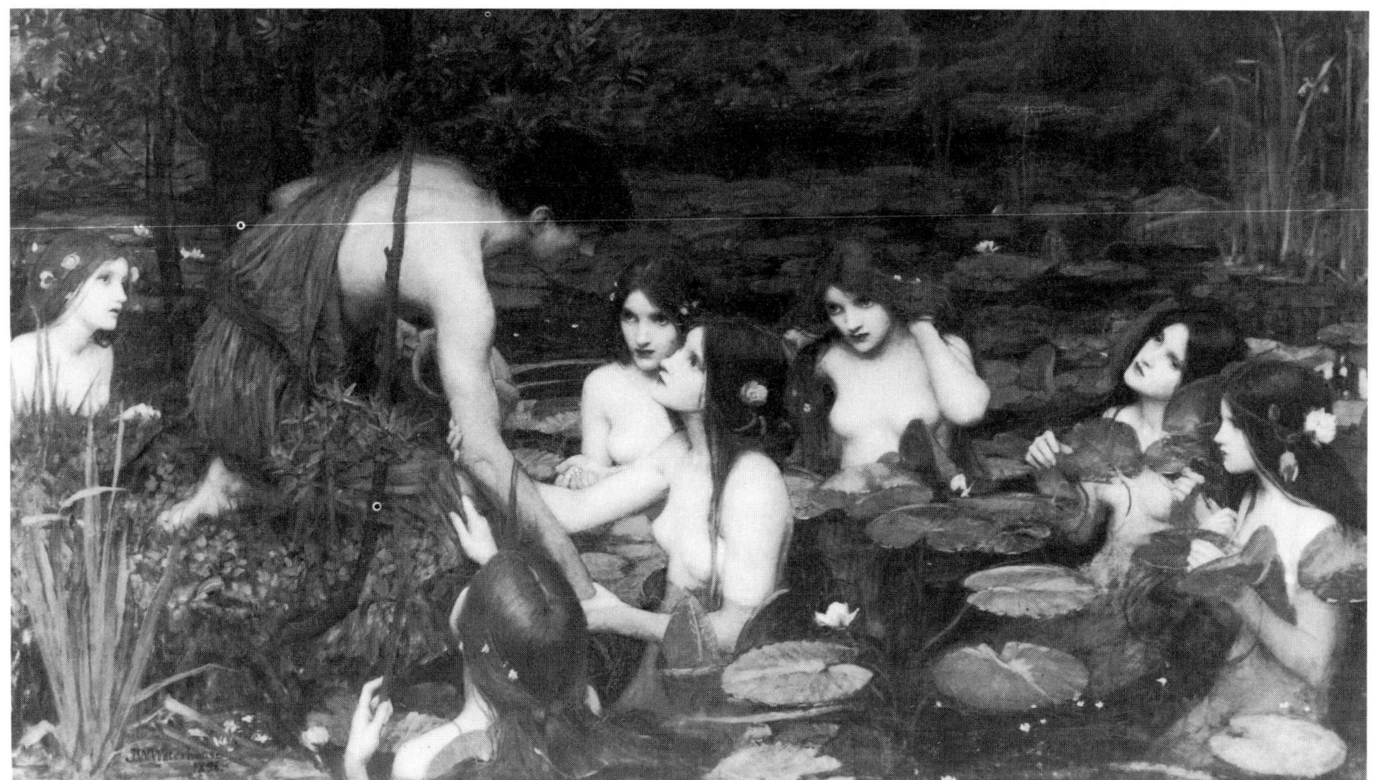

form of a Greek frieze, the figures elegantly posed in an almost musical progression, their vases copied from Greek originals and their ripplingly decorative draperies modelled on those from the Parthenon sculptures. The brilliant landscape background is based on oil sketches made on trips to Greece and Asia Minor, whilst the sumptuous use of colour shows Leighton's links with the aesthetic movement of his own day. The Gallery also owns Leighton's famous *The Last Watch of Hero*, oil sketches of *The Temple of Philae* and the *Isle of Chios*, and a fine group of exquisitely soft chalk studies for both *Captive Andromache* and *The Last Watch of Hero*.

145 J. W. Waterhouse
(1849–1917)

HYLAS AND THE NYMPHS
English; oil on canvas
98.2 × 163.3 cm ($38\frac{5}{8} \times 64\frac{1}{4}$ in)
Signed (b.l.c.): J. W. Waterhouse/1896
Purchased from the artist (1896.15)

Hylas, as recounted in Homer's *Odyssey*, was the handsome young companion of Hercules on the Argonauts expedition led by Jason. When their ship reached the coast of the Troad, Hylas was sent ashore in search of water. He discovered a spring inhabited by nymphs, whose nourishment of ambrosia kept them always young and beautiful. They lured Hylas into the water and he was never seen again.

Waterhouse began painting scenes of ancient Greek life in the manner of Alma-Tadema, but then fell under the influence of the second phase of Pre-Raphaelitism, with its rich colouring, decorative effects and dreamy *femmes fatales*. The water nymphs in this painting, though their faces are too much alike, recall the female figure-types of Rossetti and Burne-Jones.

Waterhouse achieved immense success towards the end of the century with a series of poetic subject pictures, rather repetitive and lacking the imaginative force of their earlier Pre-Raphaelite models. Nevertheless, this is a strong and memorable image. Typically for the period, Waterhouse has taken a cruel pagan myth about the brutality of nature and made it soft and pretty. The picture's mild eroticism also contributed to its popular appeal. After its purchase by the Gallery in 1896, it achieved fame through frequent appearances at British and international exhibitions, including Paris in 1900, Glasgow in 1901, St. Louis in 1904, Wembley in 1925.

146 Sir L. Alma-Tadema

(1836–1912)

SILVER FAVOURITES (exh. 1903)

English; oil on panel
69.1 × 42.2 cm ($27\frac{3}{16} \times 16\frac{5}{8}$ in)
Signed (b.r.): *L. Alma Tadema Op. CCCLXXIII*
James Blair Bequest (1917.235)

Three Roman ladies are idling in the brilliant sunshine by a marble pool, feeding fish from a tambourine filled with bread. Sir Lawrence Alma-Tadema, the painter of this serene vision of classical life, was born in Holland, hence the minute finish and the pleasure in fine detail and trivial domestic incident, which he inherited from 17th-century genre painters such as Dou and Metsu. After studying art in Antwerp, he worked for Professor Louis de Taye, a famous archaeologist, and later studied Roman and Pompeiian ruins. Thus his re-creation of antiquity was based on profound knowledge, and as an aid to his art he formed a huge archive of photographs and measured drawings of classical sites and objets d'art (now at Birmingham University). Finding a ready market amongst the English for his classical scenes, he settled in London in 1870 and became one of the most successful of Royal Academicians.

This is a late work, dating from 1903, and it bears the artist's own opus number 373 (out of a total of 408), a numbering system devised as proof of authenticity. The picture demonstrates Alma-Tadema's sensuous love of flowers and diaphanous draperies, his ability to reproduce the effect of sunlight on marble, and the sparkle on the water, and his fondness for bold and immediate effects of composition, with the marble seat curving close to the spectator, contrasting with the distant brilliant blue sea. The title refers to the fish, and the classical frame, designed by the artist and bearing his monogram, is inscribed with lines from Wordsworth's *Gold and Silver Fishes in a Vase*.

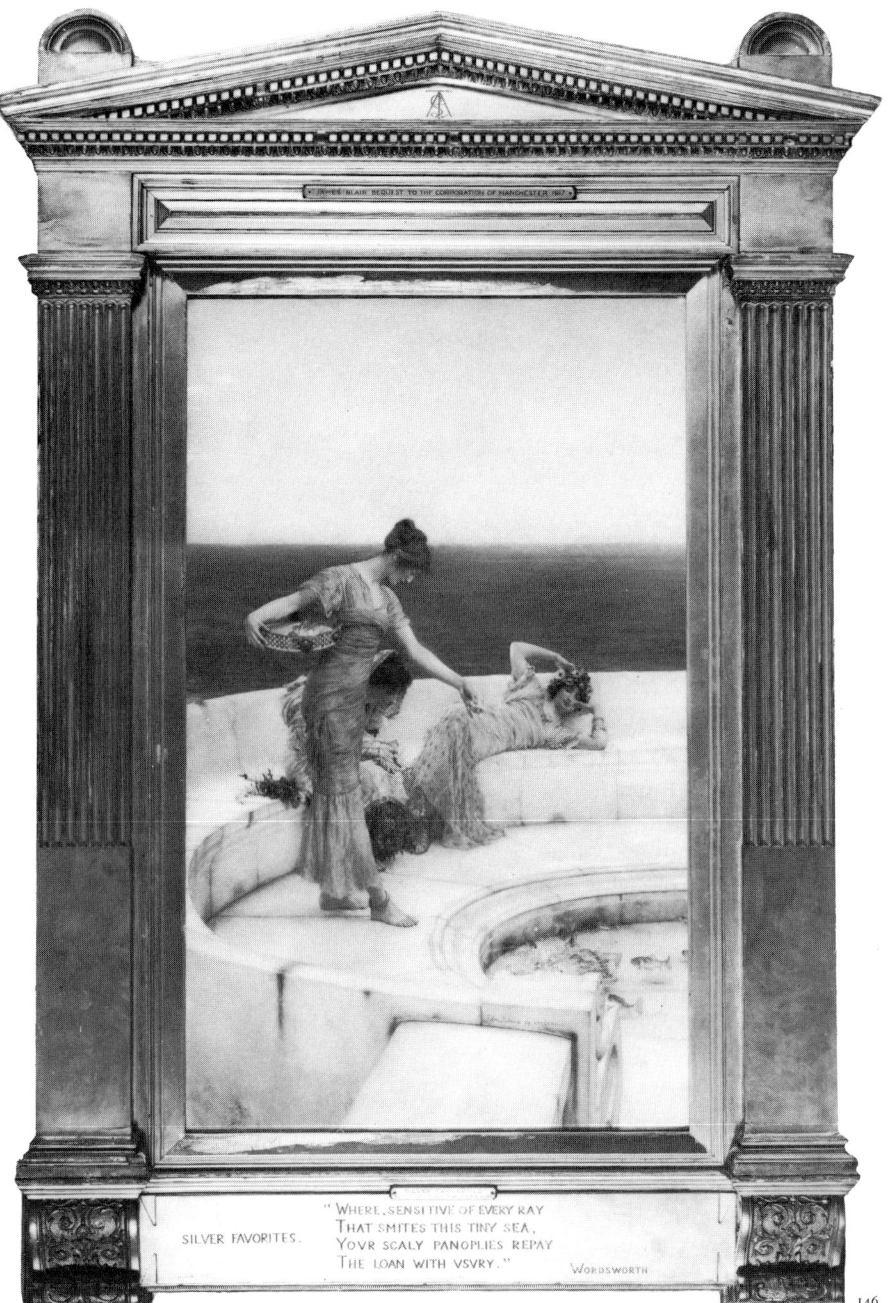

146

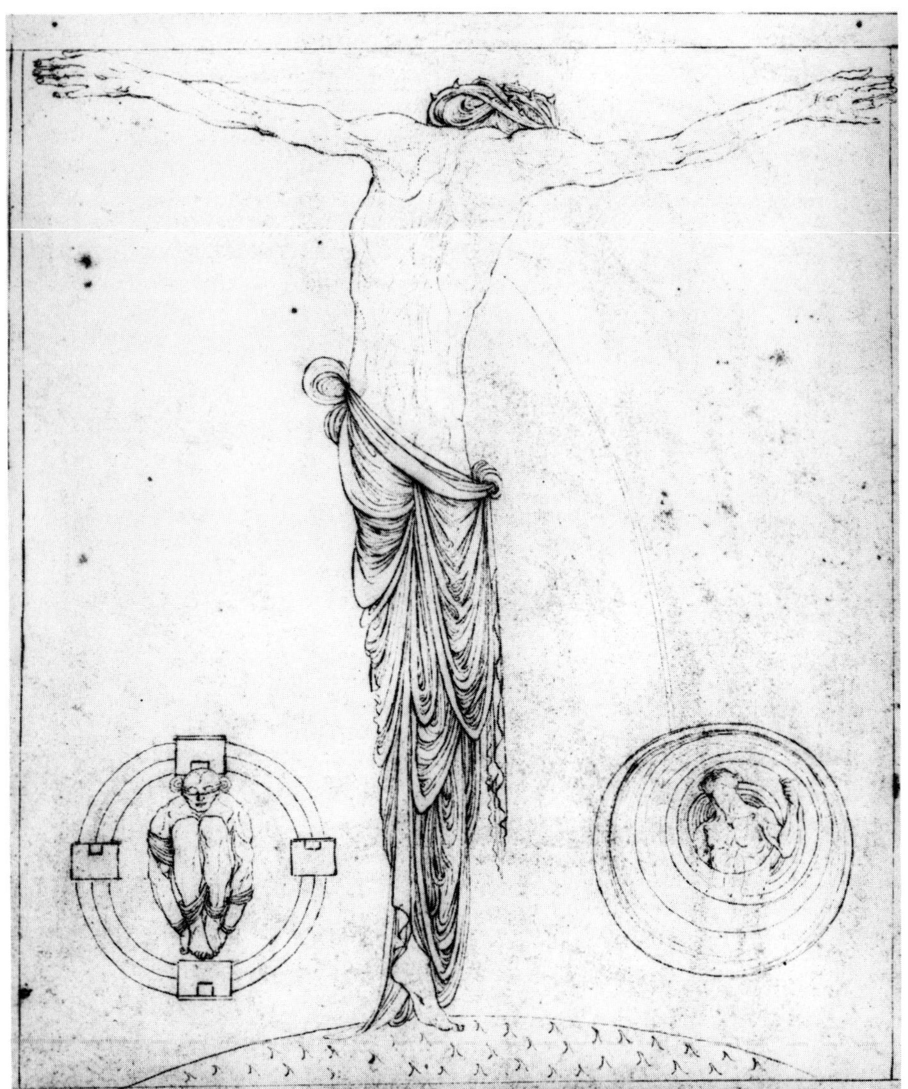

147

147 *Charles Ricketts*

(1866–1931)

CHRIST CRUCIFIED

English; pen and ink
17.5 × 14.6 cm ($6\frac{7}{8} \times 5\frac{3}{4}$ in)
Unsigned
Charles Rutherston Gift (1925.419)

This is one of three drawings in the collection executed for one of the most exquisite illustrated books of the 1890s, *The Sphinx*, by Oscar Wilde, designed and illustrated by Ricketts and published in 1894 by Elkin Mathews and John Lane at the sign of the Bodley Head. Only 250 copies were printed, most of which were destroyed in a fire in 1899, so it is also one of the rarest of Ricketts' early books.

The drawing illustrates Wilde's lines describing Christ: 'Whose pallid burden, sick with pain, watches the world with wearied eyes, And weeps for every soul that dies, and weeps for every soul in vain.' Ricketts' illustrations exhibit the nervous line and elongated curves of *art nouveau*, but the hieratic quality of this page is derived from Romanesque illuminated manuscripts. The book was beautifully printed and bound in vellum with a Beardsley-like design blocked in gold on the cover. All aspects of the book's production were supervised by Ricketts, but in 1896 he founded his own private press, the Vale Press, named after the house in Chelsea which he shared with his friend Charles Shannon. They were both painters and printmakers, and Ricketts was also a sculptor and theatrical designer. Devoted to the cult of the beautiful, they formed a rarefied collection, which included Old Master prints and drawings, paintings, Greek and Egyptian antiquities, Japanese woodcuts and Persian miniatures.

148 *Egg Coddler*

Sheet silver plate with ebony handle.
Mark: impressed *1* on the stand and lid.
English (Birmingham and London), designed by Christopher Dresser for J. W. Hukin and J. T. Heath, *c.* 1880, probably design no. 2875
Height: 19.7 cm ($8\frac{3}{4}$ in)
Purchased (1978.73)

Christopher Dresser (1834–1904) was a pioneering Victorian freelance designer who practised the doctrines of Functionalism or 'fitness for purpose'. By devising designs and manufacturing methods appropriate to sheet metal, cast iron or glass, he established forever the role of the industrial designer. In a way, he applied natural selection to the world of design (Darwin's controversial theory had been announced in 1859, the year before Dresser received his doctorate in Philosophy from Jena University). Unlike Morris, he seemed to welcome the machine age, and understood how to design for it.

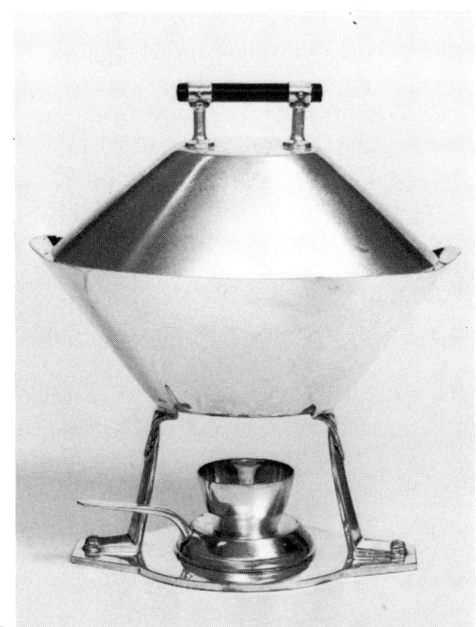

148

Dresser designed for Hukin and Heath from 1878 until 1887, as he did for James Dixon and Elkington's, designs being produced long after the date they were registered. Sheet metal enabled Dresser to simplify shapes and work in solid, curved, perfect forms of cone, cube and sphere, so light and cheap to make. Dresser's metalwork items therefore anticipate the European styles of the mid-1920s, emanating from the Bauhaus.

In *Principles of Decorative Design* (1873), Dresser, an opponent of naturalism, illustrated conventional floral designs. Elements from a famous illustration to the book (Fig. 12, 'Design Exemplifying Power') are used to decorate the outer surface of the coddler's legs. This particular piece was also made in sheet silver, a material less appropriate for Dresser, who believed that the best vehicles for art are the least costly materials. A silver plate teapot and a Minton pilgrim bottle ornamented with cranes flying against a full moon, both designed by Dresser, are also in the Galleries' collections.

149 *Jar and Cover*

Salt-glazed stoneware, slip cast and carved, and decorated in red, blue, green and brown slips.
Marks: *22/5/1905 / R. W. Martin / Bros. / London / & Southall*, and also on the cover, dated *20.5.05*
English 1905
Height: 24 cm (9¾ in)
Joan Sutcliffe Gift (1981.4)

The Martin Brothers were England's first artist-potters, designing and making their own pottery at Southall from 1878–1920; the wares were sold from their shop in Brownlow Street, London. Wallace Martin (1843–1924), an aspiring sculptor, lived, worked and went to Art College in Lambeth, a centre for architectural and ornamental stone carving, where there were also a number of potteries, including Doulton's. At Southall, the *chef d'œuvre* of the Martins were Wallace's bird jars and other ceramic *grotesqueries*, which were made from about 1880 onwards.

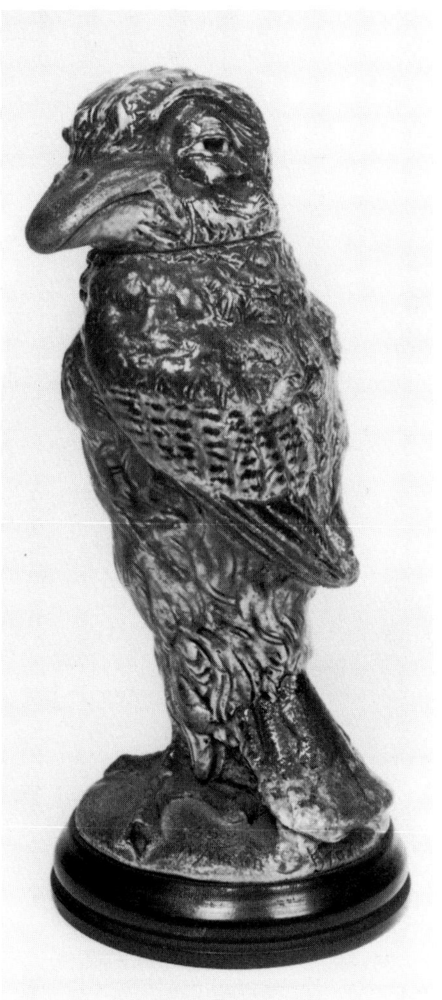

149

As a sculptor schooled in the Gothic Revival of the 1860s, Wallace developed the traditional form of an English slipware owl jug and cover into something immensely creative and imaginative. His wonderfully sly birds have a fundamental naturalism about them, as do his leering face jugs and nightmarish spoon warmers. The birds are especially vital, thinking creatures with cruel eyes and ruffled plumage. Half parrot, owl or cuckoo, they adopt human attitudes and physiognomies. Drawings from the Martin studio of *c.* 1895 include a sheet of human face studies, characterised as weird birds. Some of the earlier (1873–77) Martin studio clock cases made at Pomona House in Fulham were decorated with imaginary animals and figures which anticipate the bird jars and other work of the 1880s.

Walter Martin (1857–1912), Wallace's brother responsible for throwing pots and firing the kiln at Southall, developed a range of coloured clay slips in the 1880s. These are unrivalled in the history of salt-glaze, contributing significantly to the realism of Wallace's bird jars. Both he and the younger brother Edwin (1860–1915) were incapable of reproducing Walter's colours after he died in 1912.

This jar, with others, was bought in 1905 by the parents of Miss Joan Sutcliffe of Manchester from the Martin Brothers during a trip to London. They also purchased a smaller fantastical bird, incised *Joan*.

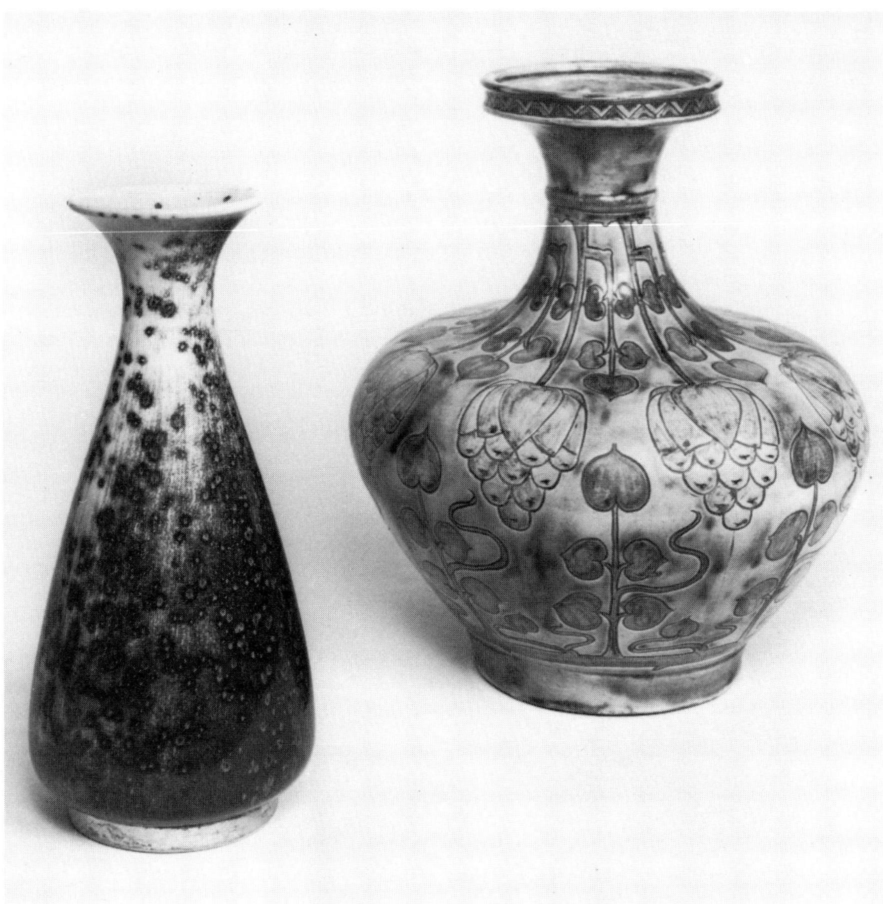

150

150 *Two Vases*

RUSKIN VASE

'High-fired' stoneware with strawberry red flambé glaze, speckled with black and green. The footring has a silver mount.
Mark: RUSKIN POTTERY WEST SMETHWICK in an oval. Shape '*?261*' impressed. Silver hallmark for 1906–7, maker's mark '*S?B*'.
English (Birmingham), The Ruskin Pottery (W. Howson Taylor), 1906
Height: 24.1 cm ($9\frac{1}{2}$ in)
Purchased (1910.5)

The vase was acquired, with other art pottery, from the exhibition *Modern Decorative Pottery* held at Queen's Park Art Gallery, Manchester, from 31 August 1909 to 11 April 1910. The exhibitors were Ashworth Brothers, Macintyre's, Bernard Moore, Pilkington's and Howson Taylor, and their work was shown with two cases of Minton's pottery (see no. 142) in the High Victorian style, regarded as 'typical of the ideals of 30 years ago' by the Manchester press. Howson Taylor (1876–1935) came from a family of potters, and his father was head of Birmingham School of Art. Like other French and English 'master-potters', he sought to reproduce the arcane, miraculous glaze effects of Chinese 18th-century porcelain, particularly the so-called 'Flambé' and 'Transmutation' glazes. By 1907 Taylor had spent £15,000 on pottery experiments and glaze trials. Shortly before his death he was offered £20,000 for his notebooks, which he preferred to destroy. Thus Taylor secured forever the promise made with each Ruskin 'high-fired' vase or bowl produced in the mysterious 'Red Kiln' at Smethwick: 'This piece can never be repeated'.

DELLA ROBBIA VASE

Lead-glazed red earthenware covered in white clay slip with a sgraffito design of flowers and leaves in the Art Nouveau style, with yellow, green and deep purple underglaze colours.
Mark: incised galleon, *D R Birkenhead*, *C* within a circle, *ELL, 161, 1898*. Painted in green: *LW* and *1904*.
English (Birkenhead, The Della Robbia Pottery), 1904
Height: 27 cm ($10\frac{5}{8}$ in)
Purchased (1981.43)

Named after the Italian maiolica workshops founded by Luca della Robbia (1399–1482), the Birkenhead works of Harold Rathbone had showrooms in 7 Berry Street in Liverpool, selling 'Vases, panels, fountains, friezes & etc.' Rathbone, a pupil of Ford Madox Brown, shared the optimism of William Morris (1834–96) and his circle for a revival of craftsmanship in Victorian England, and a renewed application of artistic qualities to everyday things. Lizzie Wilkins was a colourist who signed this vase, and one of Rathbone's 'set of refined and artistic girls'. Charles Collis carved the sgraffito design, and a similar vase appeared on page 3 of the 1896 Della Robbia catalogue (no. 19). Rathbone had anticipated a market in prosperous Liverpool for ceramic architectural decoration, employing as partners the sculptors Conrad Dressler (1856–1940) and G. C. Manzoni (1855–1910). A typical example, signed by Dressler and in the manner of the Italian Della Robbia School, is in the Gallery's collection.

151 *Pair of Vases*

'Lancastrian Lustre' earthenware, painted with figures in silver lustre on a burgundy flambé glaze, inscribed: *PHOEBUS, JUNO/IRIS, HEH, ABD.*
Marks: *P/L* and bees, ENGLAND (impressed); four scythes motif, APRIL. 25TH 1906. FROM W & EB (painted)
English (Manchester), The Pilkington Tile and Pottery Company, designed and painted by G. M. Forsyth (1879–1952)
Height: 20.9 cm ($8\frac{1}{4}$ in)
Purchased (1981.329/2)

Pilkington's manufactured tiles under the directorship of William Burton (1892–1915). At the Paris 1900 Exhibition the Company displayed some 'artistic vases' to show the glazes developed by Burton and his brother Joseph, which were unsuitable for tiles. In 1903 Burton commenced trials for another kind of pottery decorated with painted lustre, producing it commercially after 1906. With Lancastrian Lustre Burton indulged his fascination for glaze chemistry, first acquired at Josiah Wedgwood's, where in the 1870s an Italian workman had carried out lustre experiments.

To revive vase painting in the ancient technique of Persian lustre, Burton called together an élite group of artists, led by the up-and-coming G. M. Forsyth (1879–1952). His plans for Pilkington's to make fine pottery were encouraged by the company's brilliant tile designer Lewis F. Day (1845–1910), who had made lustre designs for tile firms J. C. Edwards' and Maw's.

The 'Burton' vases are the earliest datable examples of Lancastrian Lustre, decorated by Forsyth, and from the inscription on the bases they seem to have been commissioned by Burton and his wife, 'E.B.' The names *PHOEBUS* and *JUNO*, and the initialled covers *HEH* and *ABD* suggest the vases were intended for a married couple. Juno would have been especially significant in this context, her festival being celebrated by married women in Roman times on 1 March.

Stylistically the vases belong to a group of lustrewares of 1906–7, all decorated with classical subjects in yellowish opaque lustre on a dark, usually red flambé glaze. The classical designs, usually attributed to Forsyth and including *Poseidon, Dionysus* and other *Phoebus* vases, derive from ancient Greek and south Italian vase painting.

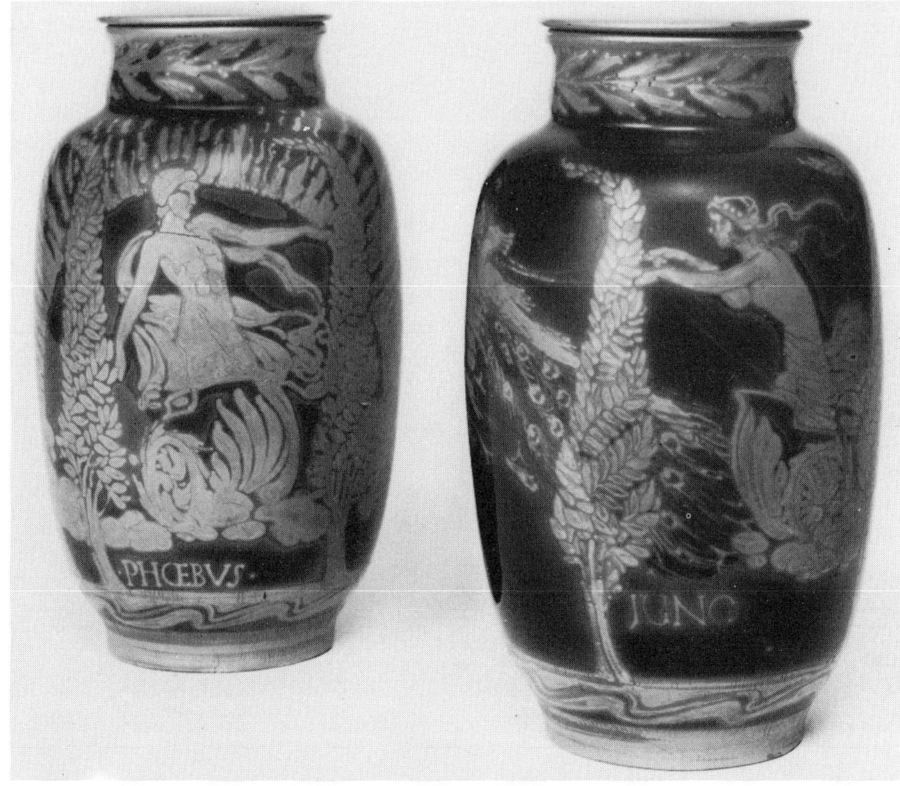

151

152 *Peacock Vase*

Iridescent glass inlaid with 'peacock eyes'.
Mark on base: *L C Tiffany. Inc. Favrile 857N*
American (New York), *c.* 1900
Height: 20.3 cm (8 in)
Purchased (1979.72)

Louis Comfort Tiffany (1848–1933), the son of the foremost New York jeweller Charles Tiffany, was the leading designer of glass in the Art Nouveau style. He studied painting in New York and Paris, and on his return to America began designing windows for churches and large houses. In 1885 he established a glass factory and began his experiments into iridescence.

Interest in iridescent glass had been stimulated by the excavation of ancient glass, which had acquired an iridescent surface through being buried. It was first produced in Europe around 1860 and at Thomas Webb's, Stourbridge, in 1878. Arthur Nash, the glass technologist, came from Webb's in 1893 to run the glassworks and carry out experiments. Tiffany filed for a patent in 1894 for 'favrile' glass (from the old English word 'fabrile', meaning hand made). The patent stated the iridescence was achieved 'by forming a film of a metal or its oxide, or a compound of a metal,

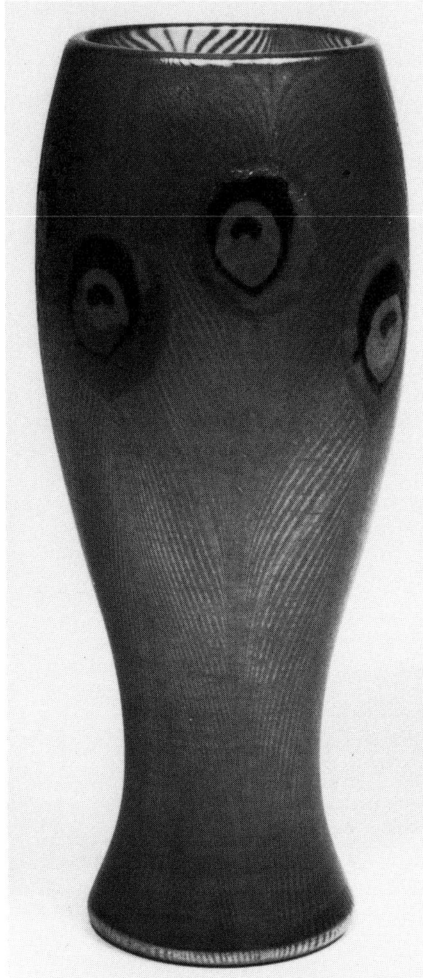

152

on or in the glass either by exposing it to vapours or gases or by direct application.' Earliest examples were sent to Paris for the opening of S. Bing's shop, *La Maison de L'Art Nouveau*.

The peacock feather, one of the symbols of Art Nouveau, forms the basis of this design. The formula was probably developed by the gaffer, George Joseph Cook (resigned from Tiffany Furnaces in 1908). A sketch of a similar Peacock vase, dated 1899, pattern number 0.7250, features in a notebook kept by Cook. The vase was created by blowing the shape and fusing rods of coloured glass to the surface to form the peacock 'eyes'.

153 *Bowl and Stand*

Green Siberian nephrite bowl and triangular stand, with three cast silver-gilt dolphin mounts and paw feet.
Marks: on the silver, CF, FABERGÉ (in cyrillic), HW, *91*, Kokoshnik mark. English import marks: Leo mark, *·925*, *P*.
Russian (St. Petersburg), Henrik Wigström for Carl Fabergé, 1903–10
Height: 22.6 cm ($8\frac{7}{8}$ in)
Yates Bequest (1934.256)

Wigström (1862–1930), a Finnish craftsman, became head of the main St. Petersburg workshop in 1903, specialising in pieces in the French Louis XVI and Empire styles. As a maker of fantasy ornaments and jewelry in gold, silver, enamel, gemstones and hardstones, Fabergé, of French Huguenot descent, was patronised by the Imperial Family from about 1884, and subsequently by the Kings and Queens of Europe. The Yates bowl and stand is unusually large, and is similar to a piece made for Rama VI of Siam, which arrived in Bangkok in 1914: a bowl in nephrite supported by three figures derived from Hindu mythology on a triangular stand, said to be over

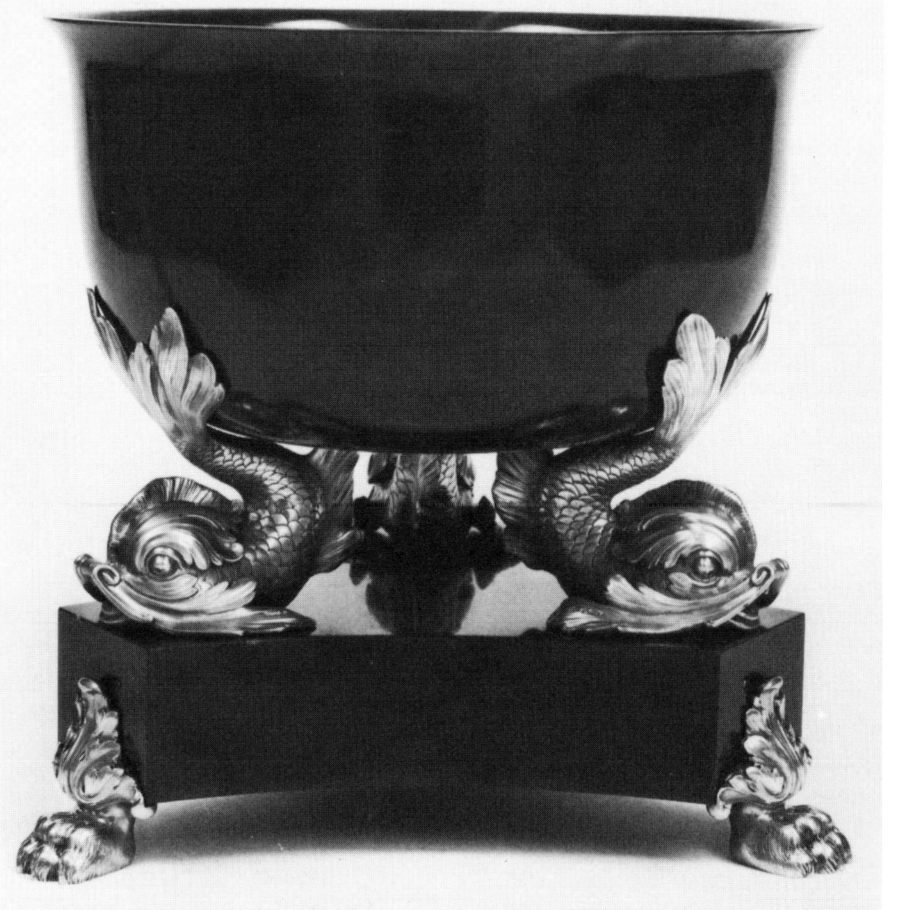

153

15 inches in diameter.

As an imported piece, the Yates bowl must have come from Fabergé's London shop at 48 Dover Street, opened in 1906 and patronised by King Edward and Queen Alexandra, sister to the Imperial Dowager Empress, Maria Fedorovna. Yates considered himself to be a rival of Queen Mary, the wife of George V, as a collector of 19th-century hardstones. She was reputedly the underbidder for his massive 'mutton-fat' jade vase, also in the Yates Bequest (no. 19).

154 *L'oiseau de Feu*

Surtout de table, moulded glass plaque engraved with a firebird, set on an illuminated bronze box.
Mark: *R. LALIQUE*
French; *c.* 1925
Height including base: 43 cm ($16\frac{5}{8}$ in)
Purchased with the aid of a Government grant (through the Victoria and Albert Museum) (1981.361)

René Lalique (1860–1945) made his name as the most original designer of jewellery in Paris in the 1890s. An accomplished goldsmith, he often incorporated glass into his jewellery in place of precious stones. He became interested in glassmaking after 1900 and his first commercial success came in 1907 when he was commissioned by François Coty to design perfume bottles. In 1921 he opened his large glassworks, Lalique & Cie, at Wingen-sur-Moder (Bas Rhine). He was determined to make fine quality glass using modern industrial methods. His work attained wide recognition after the Paris *Exposition Internationale des Arts Decoratifs et Industriels Modernes* in 1925. He exhibited a wide range of articles from his factory and also designed the gates and fountains of the fairgrounds and many of the doors, screens and lighting fixtures in the pavilions.

The subject for this *surtout*, a mythical creature with the head and torso of a woman, was inspired by Igor Stravinsky's *The Firebird*, first performed by Diaghilev's *Ballets Russes* in Paris in 1910, with costumes by Leon Bakst; the ballet formed part of their repertoire until 1922.

Lalique designed a series of *surtouts* from 1925 to 1935; they were probably intended for the sideboard or the centre of the dining table. The bronze bases were cast in his own foundry.

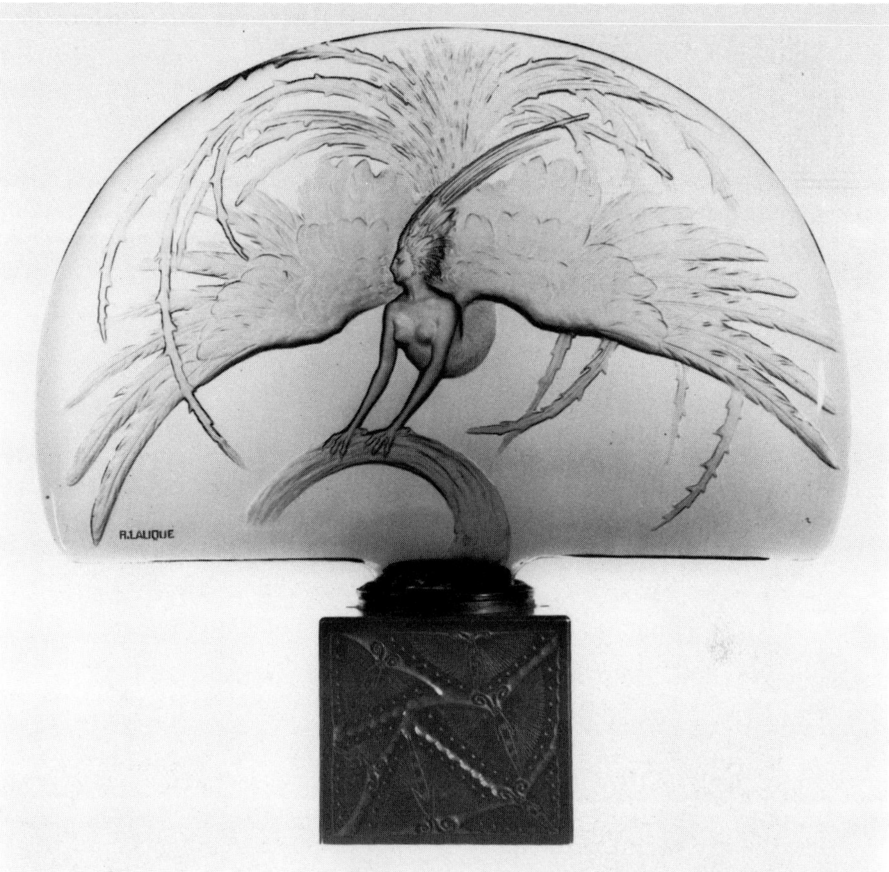

154

155 *Sir William Orpen*

(1878–1931)

HOMAGE TO MANET 1909
English; oil on canvas
162.9 × 130 cm ($64\frac{1}{8} \times 51\frac{3}{16}$ in)
Signed (b.l.c.): ORPEN 1909
Purchased from the artist (1910.9)

Orpen's prototype for this subject was Fantin-Latour's *Hommage à Delacroix* (Louvre) which was painted after Delacroix's death in 1863 and included, amongst others, portraits of Whistler and Baudelaire. The scene is a room in Sir Hugh Lane's London house in South Bolton Gardens, which was later acquired by Orpen and used as his studio. Sir Hugh Lane was one of the first London art dealers to admire and buy Impressionist paintings. Manet's *Portrait of Eva Gonzales*, hanging in the background centre of this picture, had special significance for Orpen, because he had introduced it and Impressionism to Lane in Paris in 1904. Lane bought the Manet, which is now in the National Gallery.

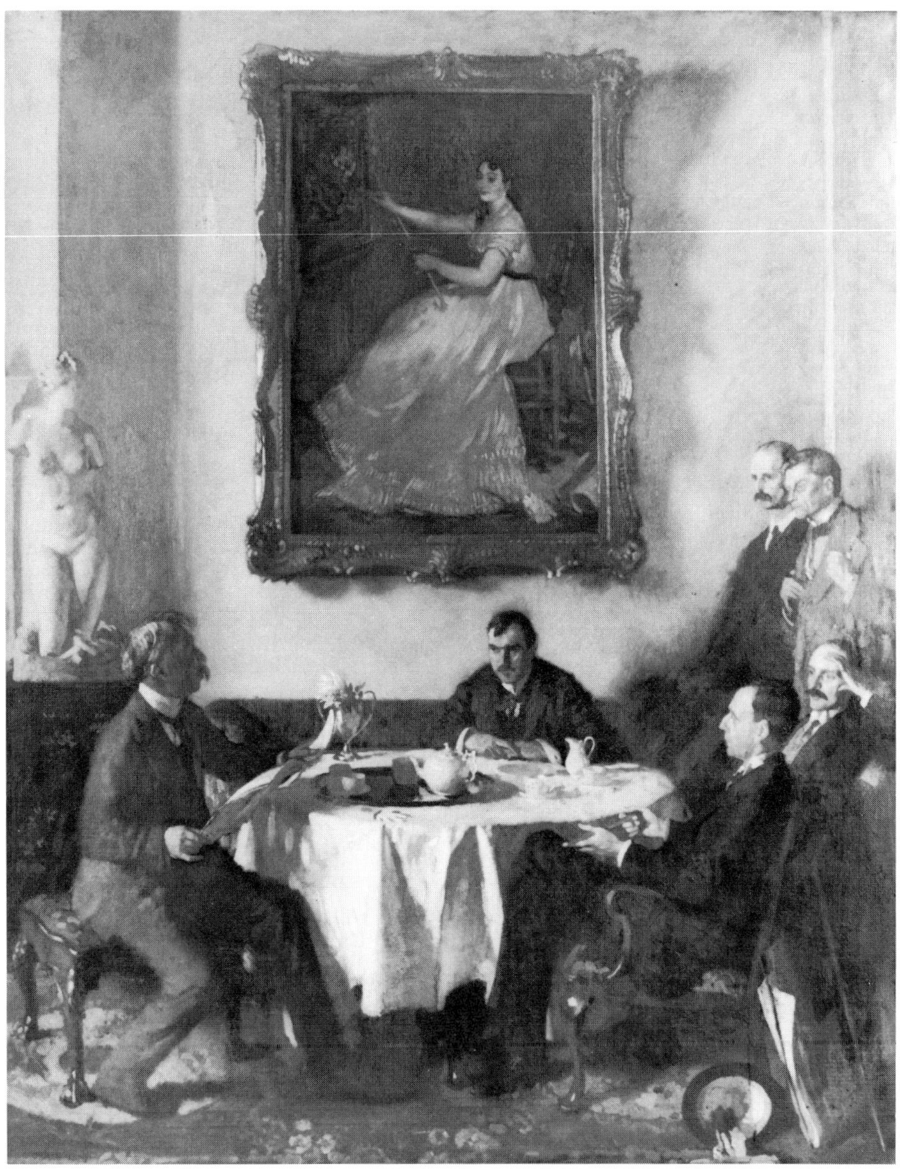

155

Orpen began work on the picture in 1906 and spent longer on it than any other canvas. Numerous preparatory studies survive, including three in the Gallery's collection, which reveal a slow and difficult progress towards the final composition. Orpen also made several changes in the final version, including covering the table with a white cloth and introducing a sixth figure.

The figures in Orpen's picture are, from left to right, George Moore, Wilson Steer, D. S. MacColl, W. R. Sickert, Sir Hugh Lane and Henry Tonks. George Moore, at that time, was the chief supporter, in England, of French painting. Steer and Sickert were the principal exponents of English Impressionism, and, with Tonks and D. S. MacColl, were the most influential figures in modern English painting, art criticism and teaching. The painting, therefore, is a record of the growing relationship between French Impressionism and English artists.

It is interesting to note that it was bought by Manchester directly from the artist in 1910, for it was only two years earlier that Messrs. Durand-Ruel of Paris had held an exhibition of Impressionist paintings at Manchester. The Art Gallery Committee were also clearly becoming interested in this 'new' French phenomenon.

156 *Adolphe Valette*

(1876–1942)

ALBERT SQUARE, MANCHESTER 1910

French; oil on jute
152 × 114 cm ($59\frac{7}{8} \times 44\frac{7}{8}$ in)
Signed (b.r.c.): *A. VALETTE.* 1910.
Purchased (1928.37)

This large, atmospheric painting of Albert Square is one of nine, impressionistic views of Manchester produced by the French artist, Adolphe Valette when he lived in the City, and acquired by the Art Gallery when he left in 1928. Four other paintings by Valette, including a self-portrait, are also in the Galleries' collection.

Valette, born in St. Etienne near Lyon, visited England in 1904 on a travelling scholarship. He probably came to Manchester to undertake commercial work, but was soon invited to teach at the School of Art, where his knowledge of contemporary French art had much impact on the students, amongst whom was L. S. Lowry. Between 1908 and 1913, Valette produced a remarkable group of small, low-toned impressionist sketches of Manchester from which he painted a number of large canvases showing its canals, streets and bridges veiled in fog

156 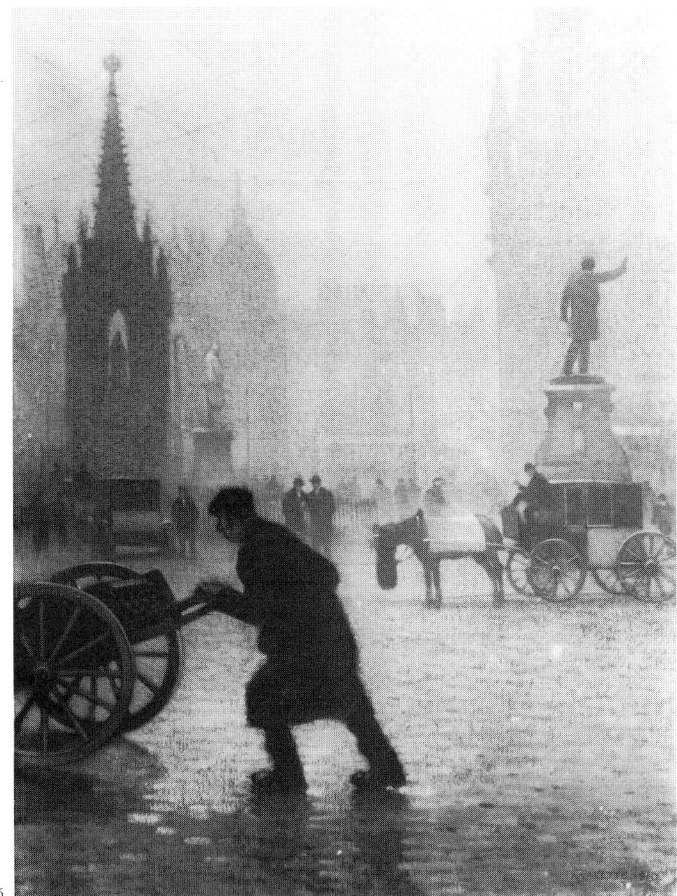

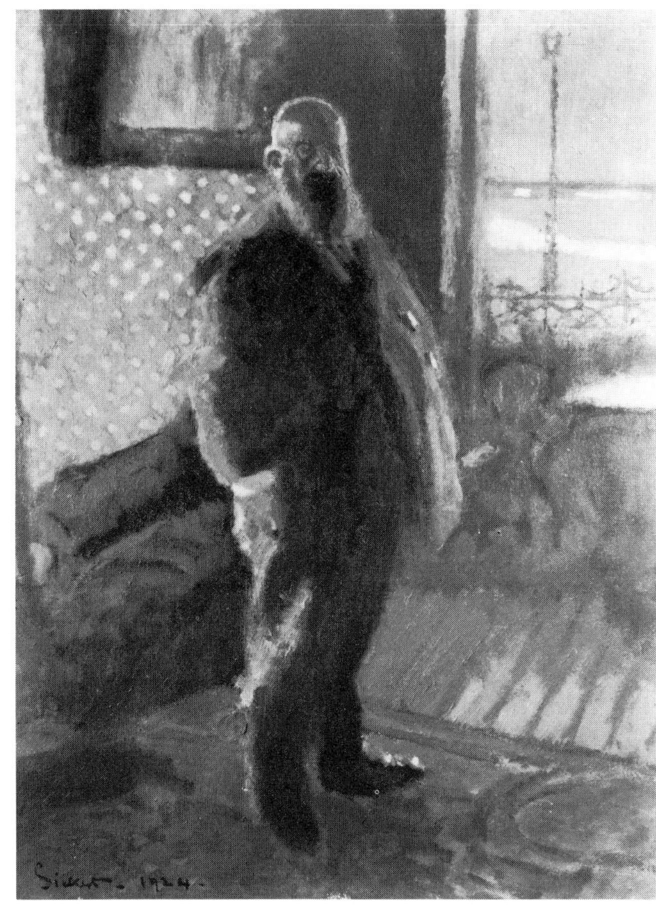 157

or mist. *Albert Square* was one of the earliest of these. The view is from the south-west side of the square, showing, from left to right, the Albert Memorial, the statues of Heywood and Gladstone, and part of Alfred Waterhouse's great Town Hall of 1877. The frame, with a simplified leaf moulding, was made by Robert Carruthers, a local framemaker often employed by the artist.

Valette has painted the scene on one of Manchester's then typical, wintry days, the lights from the commercial buildings twinkling through the fog. The Victorian city can be seen gradually moving into the 20th century: the old cabs running side-by-side with the newly invented motor cars, and tram-lines overhead cutting across its Victorian Gothic spires and pinnacles. The almost caricature-like figure of the cellarman pushing his barrow, who dominates the foreground, is silhouetted against the pale, pearly background, anticipating the work of L. S. Lowry, who has acknowledged his debt to his teacher.

157 *W.R. Sickert*

(1860–1942)

VICTOR LECOUR 1922–24

English; oil on canvas
81.3 × 60.5 cm (32 × $23\frac{13}{16}$ in)
Signed (b.l.c.): *Sickert. 1924.*
G. Beatson Blair Bequest 1941 (1947.165)

Referring to Sickert's art, Virginia Woolf commented: 'The life of the lower middle classes interests him most – of innkeepers, shopkeepers, music hall actors and actresses.' Sickert's interest and curiosity in the sitter for this portrait is vividly felt. Victor Lecour was proprietor of a restaurant, the 'Clos Normand' at Martin Eglise, a few miles outside Dieppe. Sickert's enthusiasm for his subject is also conveyed in a letter dated January 1922 to his sister-in-law in which he describes Lecour as 'a superb, great creature like a bear.' The powerful physical presence of the figure, resolutely immobile, is complemented by the boldly patterned wallpaper and heavy bulbous furniture. The way the setting is used to suggest the character of the sitter recalls Degas although, in fact, the room was rented in Dieppe by Sickert and had nothing to do with Lecour. In contrast to the cluttered interior with its tilted perspective, the view through the window over the promenade to the sea is treated as a pattern of flat colours: the broadly-applied, brilliant turquoise, indian reds and sharp yellows recall *fauve* painting and Lecour's dark suit is startlingly lit with yellow and blue highlights.

Like Degas, Sickert painted in the studio from memory and from preparatory drawings – a squared-up study is in the collection. *Victor Lecour* was begun in Dieppe in 1922 but completed in London in 1924. It is one of thirteen oils and forty-four drawings by Sickert in the City Art Galleries.

158 Augustus John
(1878–1961)

DORELIA IN A HAT

English; red chalk
33.5 × 24.5 cm ($13\frac{3}{16}$ × $9\frac{5}{8}$ in)
Signed (b.r.c.): *John*

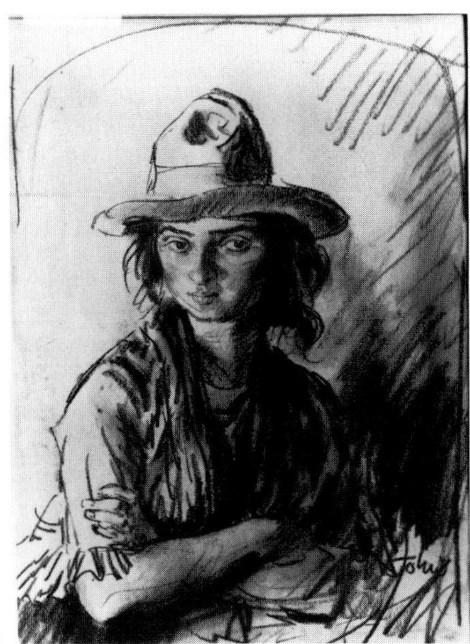

158

Presented by Charles L. Rutherston
(1925.370)

A portrait of the artist's second wife, Dorelia McNeill (1881–1969) whom he first met in early 1903. John became instantly infatuated with the mysterious and enigmatic beauty of Dorelia and continued to draw and paint her obsessively over a period of sixty years. John liked to dress her in fanciful costume to suit the vision of his ideal woman and she is often depicted wearing long gathered skirts with high waistlines and tight bodices. In this

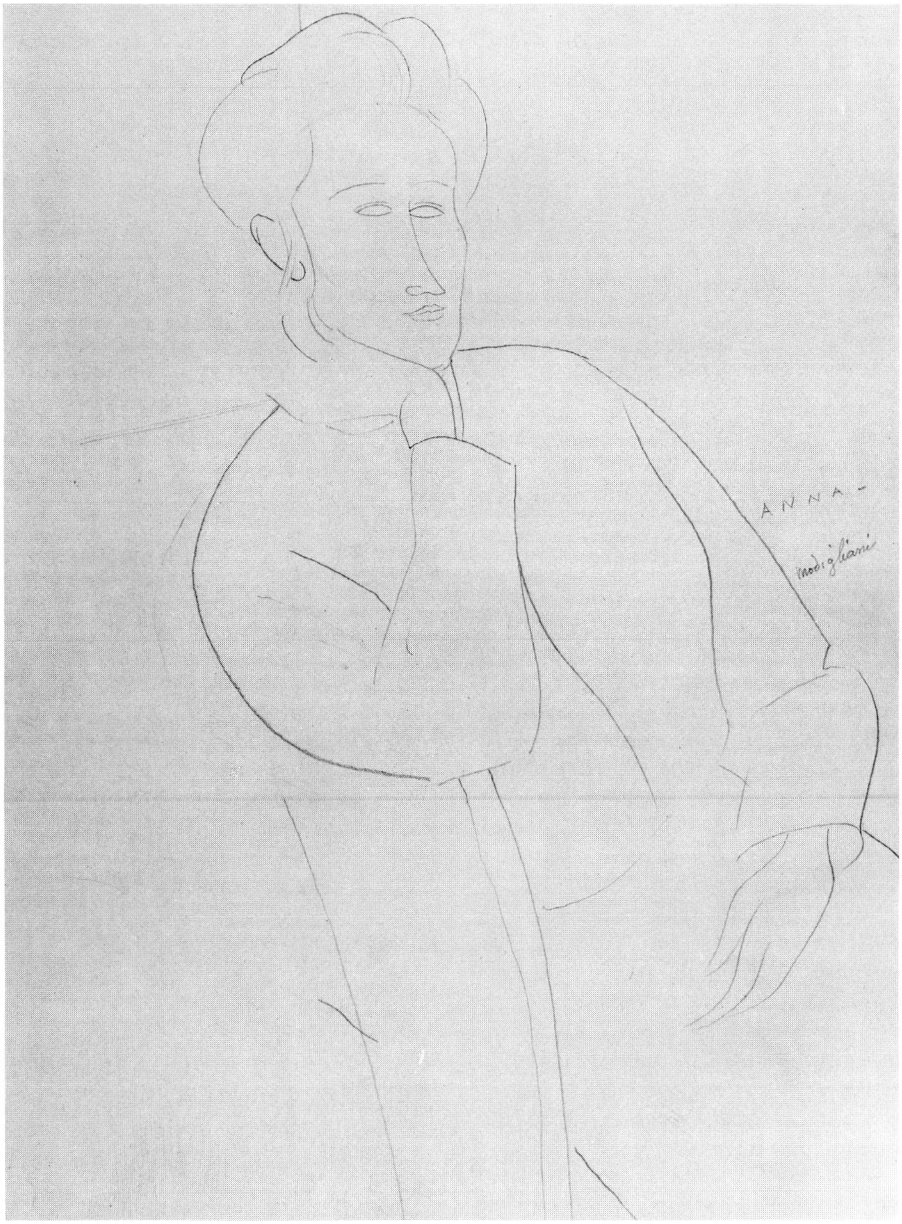

159

freely-drawn chalk portrait the sitter's tousled hair and battered hat suggest the gypsy origins that John invented for her. Dorelia preferred to conceal her respectable, middle-class background and, under John's tuition, had learnt the Romany language.

A similar drawing of Dorelia in a hat is at the Fitzwilliam Museum, Cambridge. The Manchester drawing is not dated but was bought from the Carfax Gallery in 1907 by Charles Rutherston. It is one of the Galleries' fine collection of eight oils and twenty-four drawings by John and four oils by his sister, Gwen John.

159 *Amedeo Modigliani*

(1884–1920)

ANNA

Italian; pencil
49.5 × 32.5 cm (19½ × 12¾ in)
Verso: slight sketch of a woman's head
Signed (b.r.): *ANNA – / MODIGLIANI*
Presented by Charles Rutherston (1925.502)

Modigliani is perhaps one of the greatest Italian artists of the 20th century. Handsome, amorous, addicted to drugs and alcohol, his life was cut tragically short by tuberculosis. Born into a distinguished Italian/French-Jewish family, he began painting in 1898 in the Macchiaioli tradition. In 1906, he went to Paris and was influenced by Gauguin, Toulouse-Lautrec, Cézanne and the Fauves. In 1909 he met Brancusi, whose elegant simplifications of form dramatically affected him, and from 1910 to '14 he made stone carvings which show a significant debt to African sculpture. After an illness, he began to paint again, this time in a linear, rhythmical style with echoes of Botticelli and the Trecento; oval heads, elongated necks, and almond-shaped eyes without pupils became the hallmarks of his style.

This drawing belongs to this latter period. The sitter is Anna (Hanka in Polish) Siespowska (sometimes written Cirowska). She came from an aristocratic family, and was in Paris studying to be a teacher. In 1914 she met, and probably later married, the Polish poet, Leopold Zborowski, who in 1916 became Modigliani's dealer and intimate friend. Whether out of kindness or self-interest, Hanka took care of the artist, especially during his illnesses. Although they did not particularly like each other, Modigliani painted and drew Hanka many times; and she once claimed to have a 'Modigliani look'. Modigliani habitually drew from life to capture the spontaneous and fleeting aspects of his sitters, each one given individuality by some subtle gesture or look. This graceful sketch was bought in May 1921 by the collector Charles Rutherston from Zborowski himself.

160 *Wyndham Lewis*

(1882–1957)

PORTRAIT OF THE ARTIST AS THE PAINTER RAPHAEL 1921

English; oil on canvas
76 × 68.5 cm (30 × 27 in)
Signed (b.r.): Wyndham Lewis
Presented by Charles L. Rutherston (1925.579)

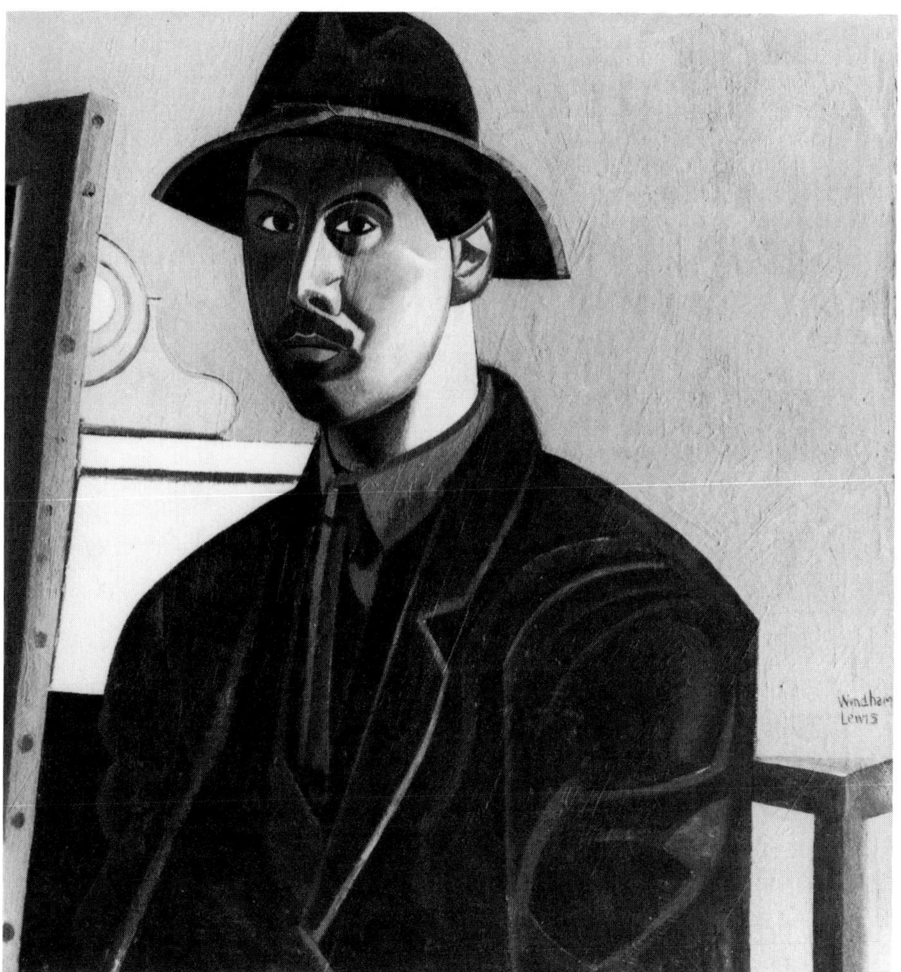

160

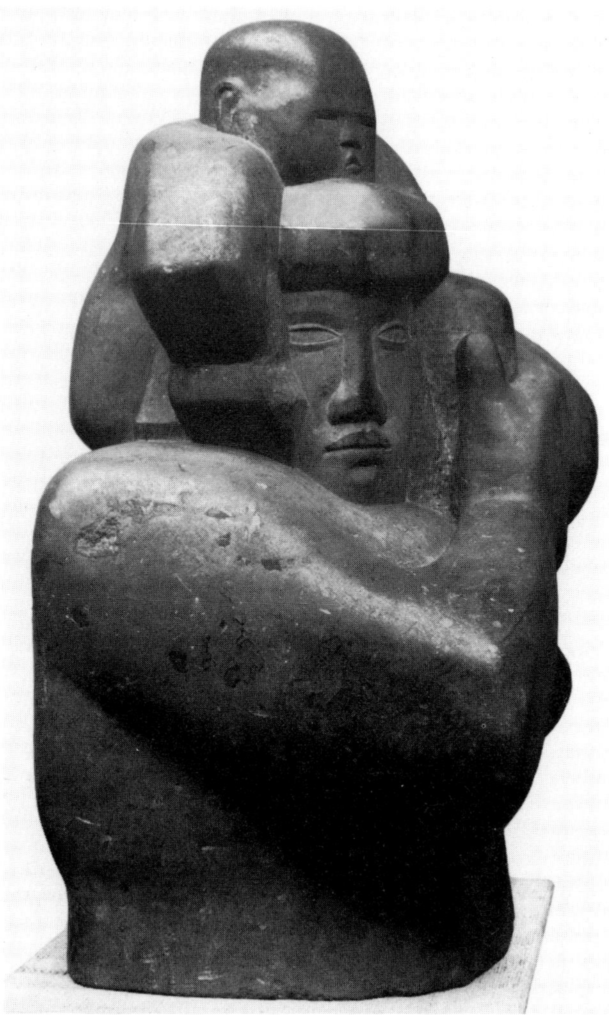
161

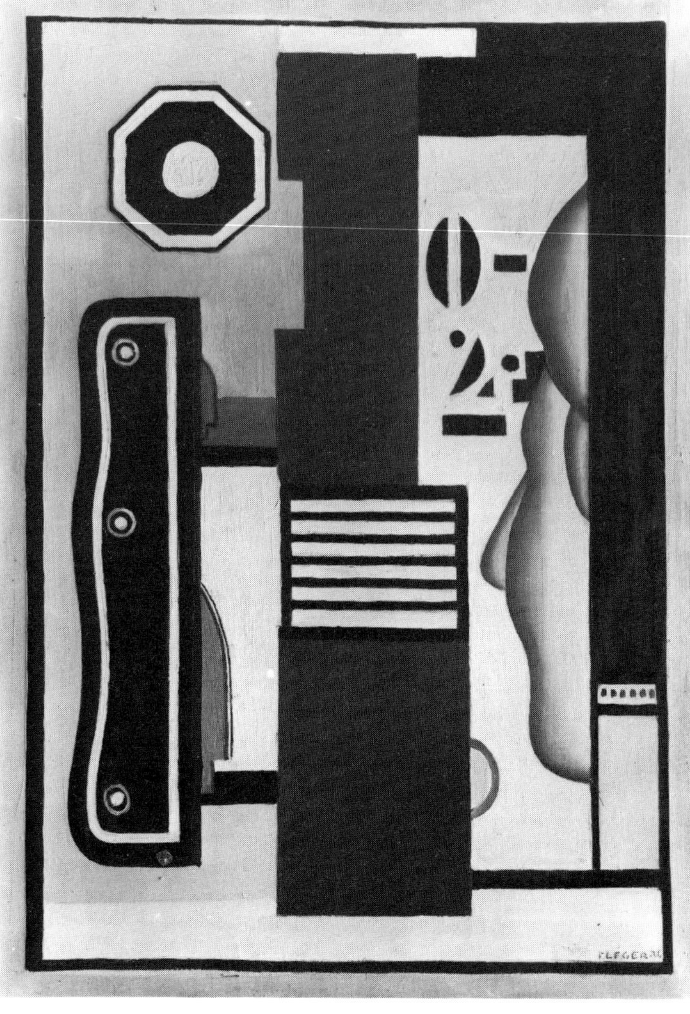
162

Wyndham Lewis, a leader of the Vorticists, was responsible for bringing British art to the forefront of the modern movement in the months leading up to the outbreak of the First World War. Manchester has two of his works from the Vorticist period, *Girl Asleep* of 1911 and *The Dancers* of 1912. Of a total of 25 works by him in the collection, all but one were given to the Gallery by Charles Rutherston, a friend and early patron of Lewis. This splendid group includes the self-portrait, which was added by the artist to his one-man exhibition at the Leicester Galleries in 1921 with a typed placard which read: 'Portrait of the Artist as the Painter Raphael'.

Although Lewis's views on classicism and romanticism in art are often paradoxical, he considered himself to be a classical artist. The intriguing title of this self-portrait, therefore, shows the artist identifying himself with a great classical painter of the Renaissance period. To achieve a classic, rigid stability and timelessness in his art, Lewis concentrated on the external appearance of things. Tarr, the hero of Lewis's first novel, speaks for the author when he states that the two most important conditions of art are deadness and absence of soul: 'Anything living, quick and changing is bad art always. . . . Deadness is the first condition of art: the second is absence of soul, in the human and sentimental sense.' Significantly, Lewis remarked to Michael Ayrton that there are no highlights on the eyeballs of the self-portrait because it would give the wrong kind of life to the head. No doubt glinting eyes, hinting at an inner presence, would disturb the harmony of this sculptural, hieratic image.

161 Henry Moore

(b. 1898)

MOTHER AND CHILD 1925

English; Hornton stone
Height: 56 cm (22 in)
Unsigned
Purchased (1939.144)

Mother and Child took Henry Moore from autumn 1924 to autumn 1925 to complete. It is carved out of Hornton stone, a soft, fine-textured limestone, found mostly on the borders of Oxford and Warwickshire, with a colour-range from blue to brown. Derived partly from Cubism, the block-like forms have many right angles, which Moore believed gave his sculptures a sense of vigour. The group also reflects his interest in Pre-Columbian, Mexican and African primitive sculpture which he had begun to examine at the British Museum while studying at the Royal College of Art.

The two themes which recur most frequently in Moore's work are the *Reclining Woman* and the *Mother and Child*. The latter became conspicuous from the early 1920s and Moore has acknowledged his early obsession with the theme; he discovered, when drawing, that he 'could turn every little scribble, blot or smudge into a "Mother and Child".' The Manchester *Mother and Child*, one of the sculptor's finest early works, has particular significance because, once finished, it made him question his own and his contemporaries' preference for carving over modelling. In retrospect, Moore felt that, in these early pieces, forms were buried inside each other and heads given no necks, because he was concerned not to weaken the stone out of an exaggerated respect for his medium. This powerful work was bought from Moore's first exhibition at the Warren Gallery, London, in 1928 by the painter Henry Lamb, from whom it was subsequently acquired. Manchester also possesses three other sculptures by the artist and four drawings.

162 Fernand Léger

1881–1955

PAINTING 1926

French; oil on canvas
65.1 × 46 cm (25⅝ × 18⅛ in)
Signed (b.r.c.): F. LÉGER. 26
Purchased (1949.102)

This picture was almost certainly the first in a series of oils, painted in 1926, which culminated in a larger version, *Composition avec Profil*, owned by the architect Le Corbusier until his death. A smaller gouache study for the final version also exists (Private Collection). The image, with its muted colouring and severe, architectural structure, would have fitted perfectly with a Le Corbusier interior, and belongs to Léger's most 'Purist' and monumental period.

In this work, Léger blended various artistic currents of his era. The stencilled figures refer to Cubism, with which he was associated from 1910, developing his own cylindrical version of the style. The flat, architectural elements reveal his association with Mondrian and the De Stijl group, and perhaps his early career as an architectural draughtsman. The painting is closest in spirit, however, to the 'Purist' works of Ozenfant and Le Corbusier, in which machine-made objects are flattened into a harmonious geometric arrangement; the door-handle and finger-plate in *Painting 1926* have been simplified to become abstract forms.

Highly individual, Léger was strongly inspired by modern life and the products of the machine age. Fascinated by the cinema and the close-up, he had made use of the fragmented image in his avant-garde film of the previous year, *Le Ballet Mechanique*, in which a profile also appears. Ambiguously, the profile in *Painting 1926* can be seen as a lifeless bust with echoes of De Chirico, or as a shaded face watching a screen.

The picture also demonstrates Léger's 'Theory of Contrasts', developed and refined by him from 1912 onwards, in which lines, colours and rhythms are contrasted to produce powerful, dynamic effects. In this work, black is played off against white; the acid yellow against the warm brown; rounded contours against angles; and the flat areas, which are quickly perceived, are relieved by the profile, successfully altering the rhythm of the work.

163 Vase *pl. 16*

Earthenware, glazed, decorated with a geometric design in black, white and red.
Painted mark: KERAMIS MADE IN BELGIUM, D 1293, initials, probably for Charles Catteau
Belgian (Hainault); Boch Frères, 1920–25
Height: 26.5 cm (10½ in)
Purchased (1979.5)

Boch Frères, one of the leading manufacturers of ceramics in Belgium, was founded in 1841 and opened works at La Louvière and Tournai in Hainault, and at Septfontaines in Luxembourg. A large range of art pottery was produced, trading under the names Keramis and Grès Keramis. Much of this was decorated by Charles Catteau (b. 1880), who had studied at the École Nationale de Sèvres, before working for Boch Frères in 1900–1925. He specialised in vases like this example, decorated with geometric patterns in slips or glazes.

This vase, with its angular qualities, shows the strong influence of De Stijl, the Dutch style exemplified by the paintings of Piet Mondrian (1872–1944) and the furniture of Gerrit Rietveld (1888–1964). De Stijl (Dutch for 'The Style') was the name of a magazine founded by Theo van Doesburg

(1883–1931), the artist and writer. This gave its name to the characteristic style of those who contributed to the magazine or were associated with it: a belief in abstraction, the use of pure colour, and the absence of decoration. De Stijl had a widespread influence on the development of architecture, painting, decorative arts and graphic design in the 1920s and '30s.

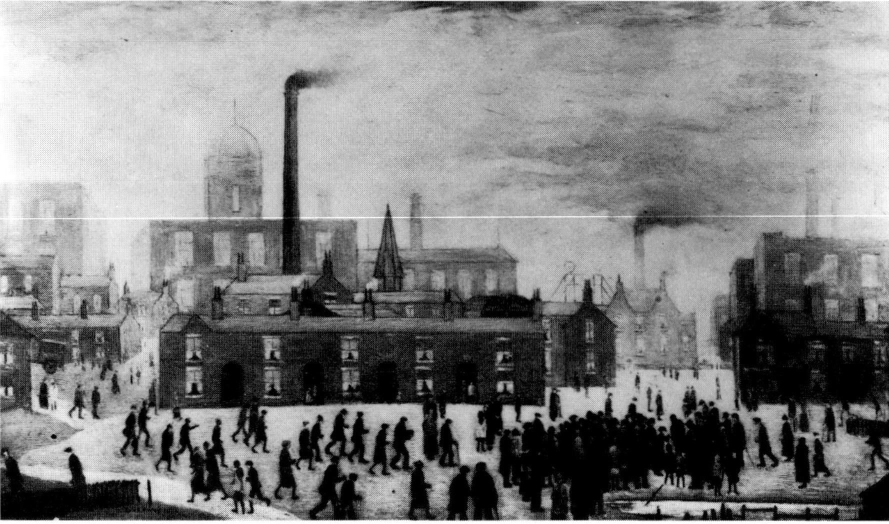

165

164 *Sir Jacob Epstein*

(1880–1959)

BUST OF CHARLES PRESTWICH SCOTT 1926

English; bronze
Height: 58 cm ($22\frac{3}{4}$ in)
Unsigned
Presented in 1926 by a body of subscribers in commemoration of Scott's eightieth birthday and his fifty-five years' editorship of the Manchester Guardian (1926.74)

Born of Russian and Polish parents in New York, Epstein, the monumental carver and portrait sculptor, knighted for his achievements in 1954, began making bronze portraits not long after settling in England in 1905. Although his carved work received more acclaim, he considered his modelled portraits to be of equal importance. The bust of C. P. Scott is one of thirteen sculptures by Epstein owned by Manchester City Art Galleries: most of them are bronze portraits of famous men, such as Joseph Conrad and Ralph Vaughan-Williams, and one is the monumental bronze *Youth Advances*, executed for the Festival of Britain in 1951. The Gallery also owns a watercolour by Epstein of *Epping Forest* painted in 1933.

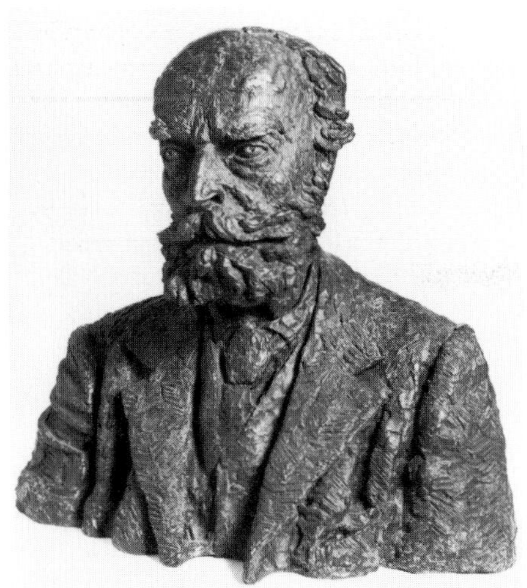

164

C. P. Scott (1846–1932), JP, born in Bath, was, from 1872 to 1929, the Editor of the Manchester Guardian, which he transformed into one of the world's greatest newspapers. He was a Liberal MP for Lancashire (Leigh Division, 1895–1906), a Governor of the Manchester Grammar School and of Manchester University, and was recognised for his fruitful involvement in the social and political affairs of the City.

To celebrate his eightieth birthday in October 1926, local worthies, who included Lord Derby, the Bishop of Manchester and the Vice-Chancellor of the University, decided that the bronze bust of Scott, which Epstein had been working on in May, should be acquired by public subscription and presented to the City. The bust was exhibited in June and July at the Leicester Galleries, London, where it was bought. Subscribers, who were not allowed to contribute more than one guinea, included some of the most eminent men in politics, religion and the arts. Three ex-Prime Ministers – Asquith, Lloyd George and Macdonald – two archbishops, leading politicians from all parties and important artists and writers, including George Bernard Shaw, J. M. Barrie, H. G. Wells, John Galsworthy, William Rothenstein and Max Beerbohm, contributed; also the Manchester artist Francis Dodd, whose portrait of Scott, painted in 1916, was acquired in 1978. The life-size bronze bust of Scott is typical of Epstein's work of this period; the original clay model is boldly and freely manipulated to achieve maximum surface liveliness and facial expression.

165 *L. S. Lowry*

(1887–1976)

AN ACCIDENT 1926

English; oil on panel
36.3 × 61 cm ($14\frac{1}{4} \times 24$ in)
Signed (b.l.): L · S · LOWRY 1926
Purchased from the Six Manchester Art Clubs Exhibition (1930.153)

The City Art Gallery has eight paintings and eleven drawings by this much-loved, and best-known of all Northern artists. L. S. Lowry was born in Old Trafford, Manchester. He was employed as a rent collector and clerk until he retired at sixty-five, but all his spare time was devoted to depicting scenes of life in industrial Lancashire as he saw it. While he often made on-the-spot sketches on his walks through Manchester and Salford, the paintings were done at home and were usually imaginative inventions based on his own experience.

From the earliest years, while he was still unknown, Manchester City Art Gallery showed much interest in his work. *An Accident* was the first oil painting by him to enter a public collection; the first drawing was *Stony Brow*, a view of Ancoats which the Gallery had acquired earlier the same year. In a letter to the Curator (20 September 1930), Lowry wrote of *An Accident*: 'It was done on wood on a white ground – laid in solidly at one shot, then the roughness scraped off and the whole gradually worked up in detail to the end. No oil or varnish – I do not use either. Have not varnished a picture for some time . . . As to the subject, it was a case of a woman found drowned (suicide) some years ago in Pendlebury – a large crowd seemed to come from absolutely nowhere in no time. The incident rather got hold of me.' The woman was apparently drowned in a canal, not evident in the picture, which is a composite view, and not a specific location. Lowry knew Pendlebury well, having moved there with his parents in 1909. It is typical of Lowry's compositions that the viewpoint is a distant one, indicating his fascination with the movements and reactions of the crowd rather than the woman's tragic physical condition, from which, with his sensitive temperament, the artist would certainly have recoiled.

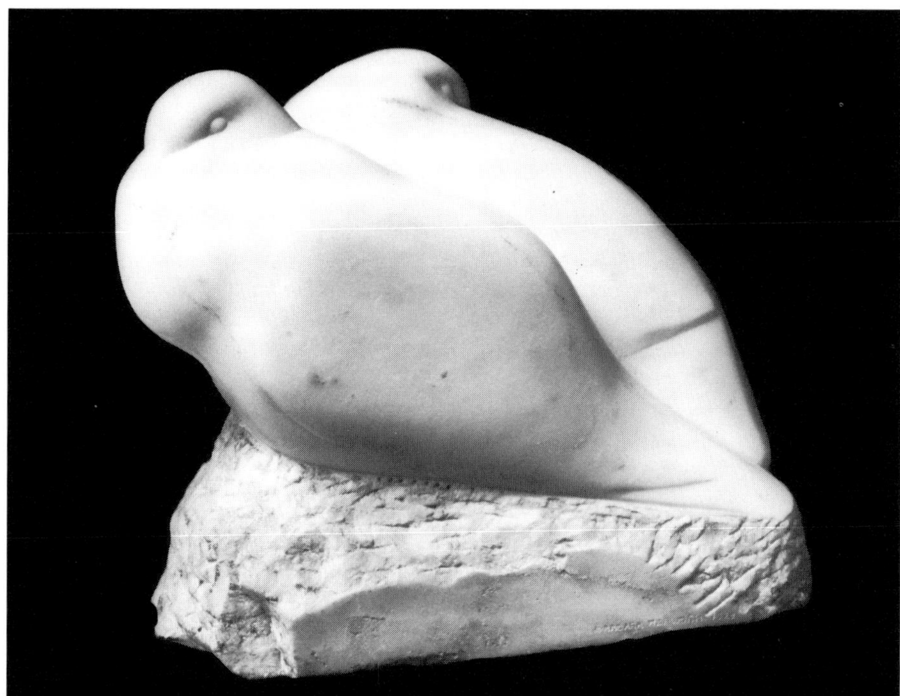
166

166 Barbara Hepworth

(1903–75)

DOVES 1927

English; Parian marble
Height: 29 cm ($11\frac{1}{2}$ in)
Signed (verso, on base): *BARBARA HEPWORH* [sic] 1927
Purchased (1942.91)

One of Hepworth's earliest sculptures, *Doves* demonstrates the particular interest in direct carving which the sculptress shared at this time with Henry Moore, a former fellow student at Leeds College of Art and at the Royal College of Art. Both artists admired the work of Brancusi, Epstein, and Gaudier-Brzeska and regarded direct carving as a way of breaking free from the influence of Rodin and from 19th-century academicism.

While on a scholarship in Italy in 1925, Hepworth met and married the animal and figure sculptor, John Skeaping. Receptive to the carvings of Modigliani and Gaudier-Brzeska, Skeaping was very friendly with Epstein. Hepworth would certainly have known Epstein's *Doves* of 1915, but his angular forms are here replaced with rounded and flowing contours and a less aggressive, more sentimental, treatment of the subject (the Skeapings loved birds and kept an aviary while in Rome). In Italy, Hepworth became very receptive to light and how forms reflect it. This is particularly evident in her choice and treatment of the marble in *Doves* which, like all her early carvings, is compact with little undercutting of the forms to preserve the block's solidity. An earlier sculpture of a dove of 1925 (now lost) was even more simply carved, in the manner of Brancusi.

Doves was apparently bought from Hepworth's first exhibition, held jointly with Skeaping at their studio in St. Johns Wood in December 1927, by George Eumorfopoulos, a wealthy

167 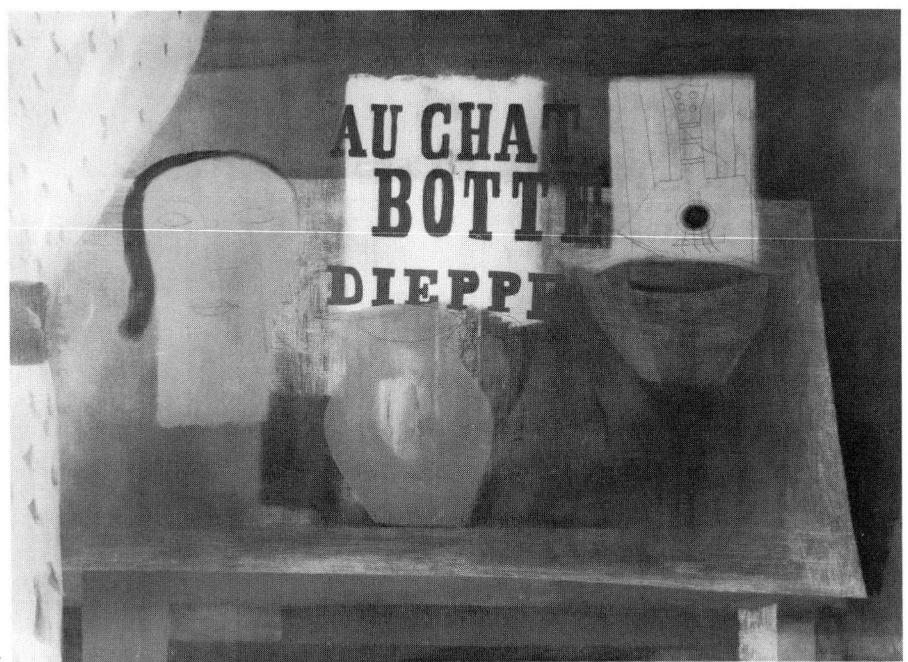

connoisseur of Chinese porcelain. Eumorfopoulos had been introduced by Richard Bedford, then Keeper of Sculpture at the Victoria and Albert Museum; he became a life-long friend of Hepworth's and bought several of her works of this period. However, he was not credited with ownership of this particular piece at the second exhibition, held in June 1928 at the Beaux-Arts Gallery in London, where the sculpture was exhibited as *Doves Group* and was reproduced on the front of the catalogue. He certainly possessed it by 1930, and, after his death in the Second World War, the Beaux-Arts Gallery sold it to Manchester.

167 Ben Nicholson

(1894–1982)

AU CHAT BOTTÉ 1932
English; oil and pencil on canvas
92.3 × 122 cm ($36\frac{3}{8}$ × 48 in)
Signed (verso): *Ben Nicholson 1932*
Purchased (1948.316)

By 1932, Ben Nicholson had become increasingly involved with Cubism. In the spring of that year, he met Picasso and Braque in Paris. Later, he visited Dieppe with Barbara Hepworth. *Au Chat Botté* (Puss in Boots) was painted during this visit and, in an article published in 1941, the artist gives a lucid account of the inspiration behind the work.

He wrote: 'About space-construction: I can explain one aspect of this by an early painting I made of a shop-window in Dieppe, though, at the time, this was not made with any conscious idea of space but merely using the shop-window as a theme on which to base an imaginative idea. The name of the shop was "Au Chat Botté", and this set going a train of thought connected with the fairy tales of my childhood and, being in French, and my French being a little mysterious, the words themselves had also an abstract quality – but what was important was that this name was printed in very lovely red lettering on the glass window – giving one plane – and in this window were reflections of what was behind me as I looked in – giving a second plane – while through the window objects on a table were performing a kind of ballet and forming the "eye" or life-point of the painting – giving a third plane. These three planes and all their subsidiary planes were interchangeable so that you could not tell which was real and which unreal, what was reflected and what unreflected, and this created, as I see now, some kind of space or an imaginative world in which one could live.'

The different elements of the picture are deliberately confused. The head, the jug and the bowl are rounded shapes, but the flat surface of the canvas is emphasised by the linear outlines and the thinly applied paint. The two pale rectangles are flat shapes, but the blackness of the hole in the guitar suggests depth. This draws attention to the work of art as an object rather than as a picture of something else. Like Nicholson's later, more abstract work, the carefully grouped objects and restrained colour give a sense of balance and calm.

168 Leach Vase

Stoneware, with a matt white glaze decorated with two sprays of flowers.
Mark: BL, SI, impressed in seals
English (St. Ives); Bernard Leach, 1931
Height: 30.7 cm ($12\frac{1}{8}$ in)
Gift (1938.369)

In 1920 Bernard Leach (1887–1979) established a pottery at St. Ives, Cornwall, with Shoji Hamada (1894–1978), and built the first oriental climbing kiln in Europe. Leach, who studied drawing at the Slade School and etching under Frank Brangwyn, worked in the Far East from 1909 to 1920, learning pottery under Ogata Kenzan. St. Ives pottery was a mixture of oriental influences and traditional English decorative techniques.

Leach's own work is usually decorated in an inimitable, calligraphic style, also seen in his wash or pen drawings and etchings. The shapes of his pots follow closely those of the Korean Yi and Chinese Song dynasties, and often re-occur, since he believed in 'repeat work' as a method of acquiring skill and eventually perfection in pottery.

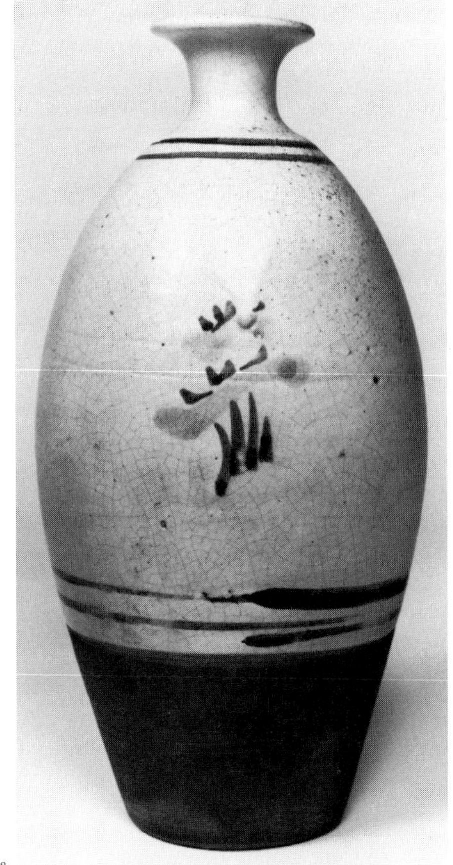

168

In 1940 Leach published *A Potter's Book*, which had an enormous impact on the ceramic industry, on those who reacted strongly against his ideas, and ironically on his own work, which was raised to the status of *Art*. Leach, however, always retained the principle that potters were artists who made useful as well as decorative wares.

In 1931 Leach was making a series of these tall vases, which he called 'fish bottles'. His excellent book on his friend Hamada contains a description of the glaze he used, made from bracken ash. 'It was velvety white, it took pigment on its surface with gentleness, it did not look mechanised, it was hard and soft at the same time. We attempted the same effect in successive years but never got it again.'

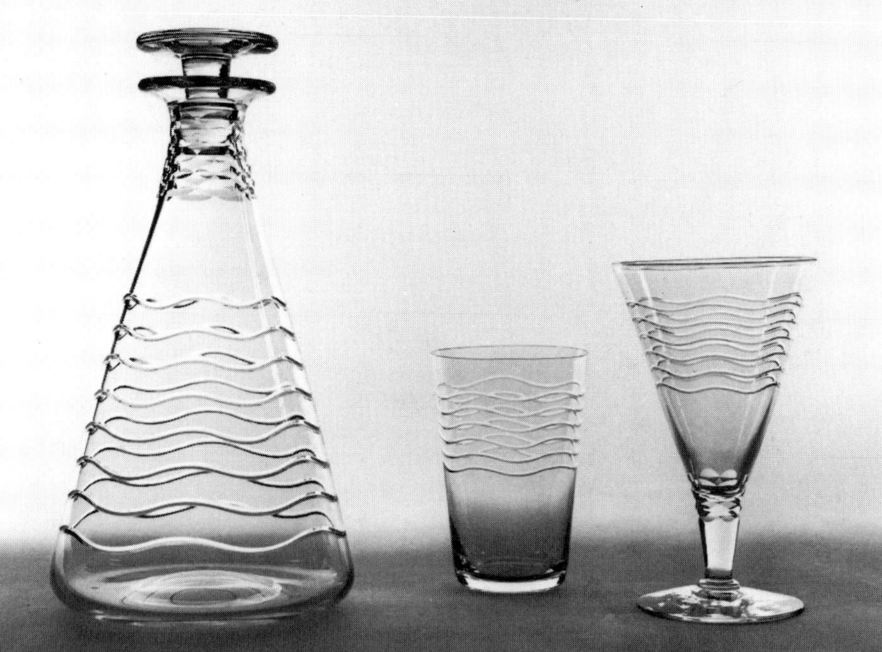

169

169 Modern Wine Service

Lead glass decanter, tumbler and cocktail glass, blown, with polished intaglio cutting.
English (Stourbridge), Thomas Webb and Corbett Ltd., Coalbournhill Glassworks.
Design 14089, 1933
Height of decanter: 25 cm ($9\frac{7}{8}$ in)
Thomas Webb and Corbett Ltd. (1933.97/6)

Manchester's almost unknown collection of so-called 'Industrial Art' was acquired in the '30s under the enlightened directorship of Lawrence Haward (1914–44), often through the large contemporary exhibitions he arranged at the City Art Gallery. One of them, *British Industrial Art*, held in 1933, comprised some 600 exhibits 'made for circulation in the provinces', selected from a larger exhibition at Dorland Hall, Lower Regent Street, London. Exhibit 280, 'Goblet, Sherry, Tumbler, Finger bowl, Plate, Decanter' by Webb and Corbett was design 14089, and appeared in their 1937 catalogue.

'Modern' glass in the '30s showed a reaction, in both form and decoration,

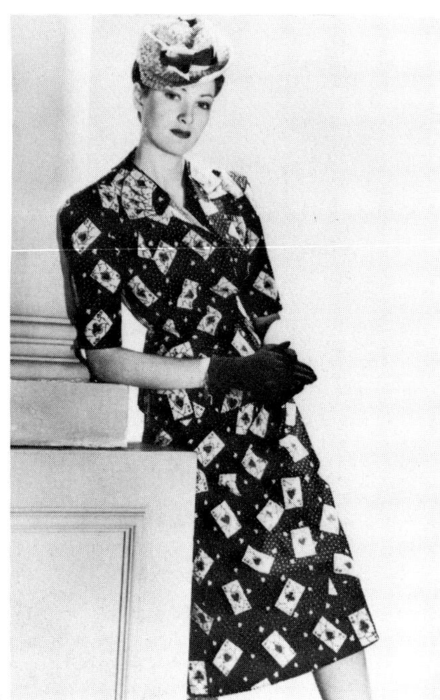
170

against the traditional cut and engraved styles established in the 19th century for table glass. The new style may have been encouraged by Scandinavian glass design of the '20s, notably at Sandvik/ Orrefors in Sweden. In fact, Thomas Webb had employed a Swedish works manager, Sven Fogelburg.

Other firms in the Stourbridge area, the centre of 19th-century glass making in England, began to take on 'modern' designers like the ubiquitous Keith Murray (b. 1892). Stuart and Sons invited contemporary artists to provide designs, including Graham Sutherland, Paul Nash, Laura Knight and Eric Ravilious.

The free and simple cutting on Webb's 14089, called 'polished intaglio', is very close to that found on designs by Murray for Stevens and Williams of Stourbridge. At this time Webb's director in charge of decorating was Mr William Kny (fl. 1922–42), a son of F. E. Kny, one of Webb's most famous glass engravers of the 1870s.

170 *Jacqmar Summer Suit*

Printed cotton.
Designed by Bianca Mosca (fl. 1930–45) for Jacqmar. Original press photograph
English, 1942
Waist: 55.9 cm (22 in)
Gift of the Cotton Board (1957.482)

Navy cotton with cream spots, sprigged with playing card 'pips'. The four aces of the pack are in red and blue on a cream ground, the surface of the cards being 'crazed' with red and navy lines. Deliberately off-register colour printing gives the fabric a lively surface, resembling Manchester export indigo prints.

In June 1940, *Queen* featured other Jacqmar fabrics on the theme of games: 'Snooker' and 'Harlem' (poker-dice).

The jacket is narrow waisted, with short basque weighted at the back, and fastens with two pairs of small, self-covered buttons. Shoulder pads give the fashionable square shape to the elbow-length sleeves. The narrow skirt is gored, and reaches just below the knee. Since this is a model suit, it has a great deal of hand-finishing, and is made for a very slim woman.

Pockets and collar are cut and arranged to make perfect card hands of four aces – a witty designer touch, typical of the jaunty optimism of Jacqmar wartime fashions.

This suit is part of a large collection of couture clothes of the 1940s to early 1960s, given to the Gallery of English Costume by the Colour Design and Style Centre of the Cotton Board.

During the Second World War, the Board of Trade successfully boosted British textile and fashion exports, with sales drives in South America and the USA. Artists were commissioned by the Cotton Board to produce fabric prints, which were then featured in *Vogue* in June 1941: designs by Graham Sutherland and Paul Nash were reproduced with the cartoonist

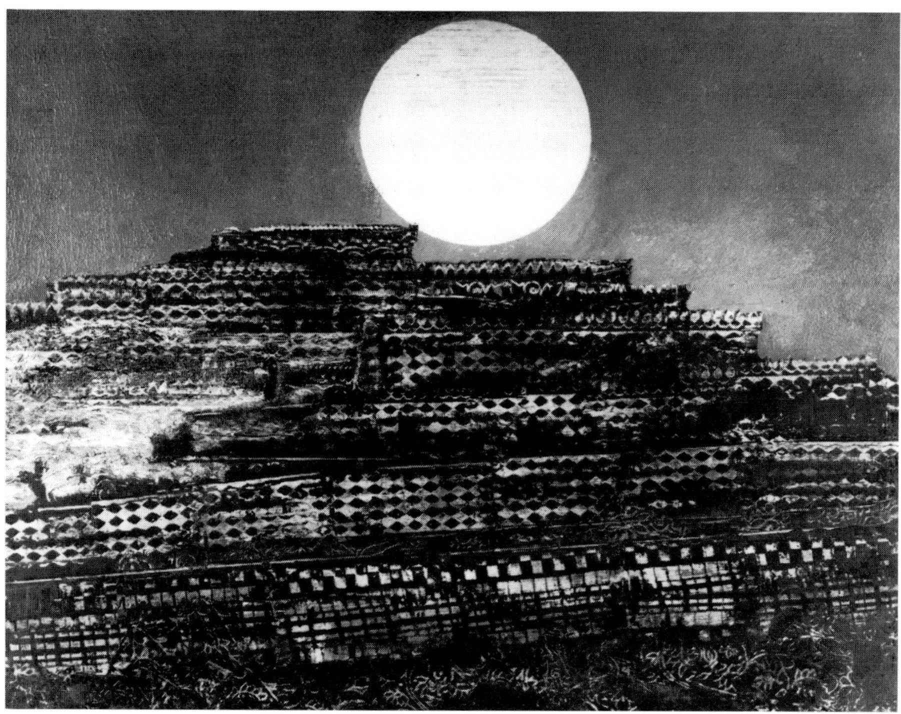
171

Fougasse's famous slogan 'prints' for Jacqmar. In the same year, the Incorporated Society of London Fashion Designers was formed, first for export collections, and then, in 1942, to design prototype austerity clothes. Bianca Mosca, who had worked for many years with Schiaparelli in Paris, came to London and joined Jacqmar at the start of the war, and was one of the first members of 'Inc. Soc.' With Molyneux, Charles Creed, Digby Morton, Hardy Amies, Victor Stiebel and Worth, she was one of those invited to produce Utility costume (top-coat, suit, afternoon dress and cotton overall dress). The most appropriate designs were mass-produced anonymously, putting elegantly restrained designer clothes within the means of a large number of women.

Bianca Mosca also made blouses, dresses and aprons from the much-loved Jacqmar patriotic scarves.

The Gallery's collection includes work by all the 'Inc. Soc.' designers, as well as a wide variety of Utility garments, from corsets and child's vests to dresses.

171 Max Ernst

(1897–1976)

LA VILLE PETRIFIÉE 1933

German; oil on paper stuck on board
50.5 × 60.9 cm ($19\frac{7}{8} \times 23\frac{15}{16}$ in)
Signed (b.r.c.): *max ernst*
Purchased (1955.112)

Ernst painted *La Ville Petrifiée* (*The Petrified City*) while in Gascony visiting the English Surrealist Roland Penrose. It later belonged to another Surrealist, Paul Eluard. Surrealism, defined in 1922 as 'psychic automatism closely allied to the dream state', was influenced by the theories of Freud and Jung. Attempting to free thought from reason, logic and moral preoccupations, the Surrealist painters abandoned the conventional pictorial representation of the natural world. They sought instead to express their unconscious visions by automatic techniques where chance played a significant part.

While studying philosophy and psychology, Ernst became interested in art through looking at the work of the insane. From 1919 he developed a semi-automatic technique called *frottage*, which involved placing paper over a surface such as wood and making a rubbing with pencils or paint-soaked rags. By this method, new images, unrelated to the original materials, emerged. In *La Ville Petrifiée* a similar technique, called *grattage* was employed, in which paper was covered with several layers of ground paint, then pressed over a textured surface and the paint scraped away to reveal different layers. The result, suggestive of an abandoned citadel, was then finished with a brush. It was the first in a series, which culminated in *La Ville Entière* (*The Entire City*; Künsthaus, Munich). In both pictures, block-like forms are piled up as in an ancient ziggurat. The effect is of a ruined civilization; fossilized, with weeds beginning to encroach on its outskirts. Whether the pale disc which hovers above *La Ville Petrifiée* is the moon, a symbol of the dark, enigmatic side of life, or the sun, drained of its life-giving force, is hard to determine. It was painted in 1933, the year the Nazis came to power, Hitler became Chancellor of the Reich, and Ernst's work was condemned by the new régime.

172 Alberto Giacometti

(1901–66)

THE ARTIST'S MOTHER 1949

Swiss; oil on canvas
74.3 × 38.8 cm ($29\frac{1}{4} \times 15\frac{5}{16}$ in)
Signed (b.r.c.): Alberto Giacometti 1949
Presented by the Contemporary Art Society (1952.277)

Giacometti was famous for his stick-like sculptures of standing and walking

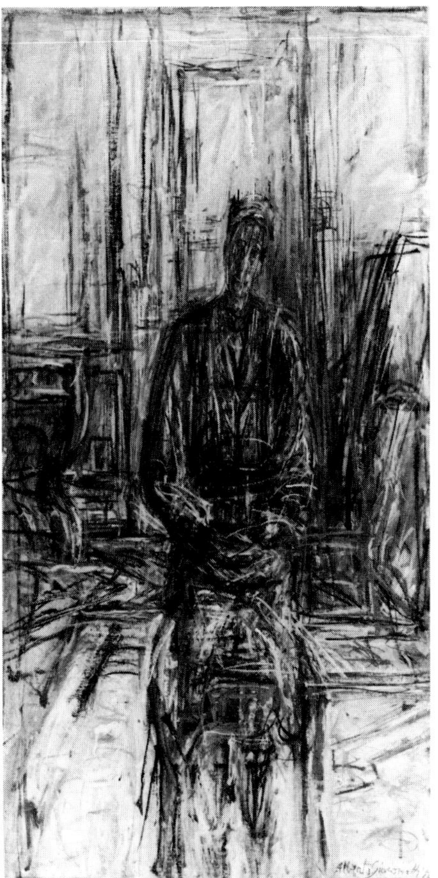

172

figures. He consciously limited his models to certain types and to specific people he knew well, notably his wife, Annette, whom he married in 1949, the year this picture was painted, and his brother, Diego, who was his assistant in Paris from 1925 onwards.

Although Giacometti painted and drew from an early age, it was not until the late 1940s that painting became a regular activity equal to that of his sculpture. His early paintings, like this one of his mother, tend to be small in size. One of several portraits he executed of her, *The Artist's Mother* is stylistically close to a larger one of the following year, *My Mother in the Parlour*, now in the Museum of Modern Art, New York. Two other full-lengths and several studies of her head also exist, as well as two early sculptures: one of 1927 reflected his interest in African and Cycladic sculpture, and the influence of the Cubist sculptors Archipenko (his teacher), and Henri Laurens (a close friend). The odd proportions of the figure in this painting are typical of Giacometti, who, when drawing from life, found it difficult to make his figures large enough for the setting. He developed this elongated form in the 1940s, when he began to pare down his figures, investing them with stiff movements and skeletal proportions. Sketched in with loose, nervous brushwork, the painted surface is similar to the rough, fluid textures of his sculptures; the dense, cloudy background creates a claustrophobic space in which the sitter seems trapped. This expressive figure, both pathetic and disturbing, probably owes something to Surrealism, with which the artist was involved in 1929–34, and is reminiscent of some of Francis Bacon's work. With an almost featureless face, yet with a kind of compressed energy, she seems, simultaneously, both alive and dead.

173 Lucian Freud

(b. 1922)

GIRL WITH BERET 1951

English; oil on canvas
35.5 × 25.6 cm (14 × 10$\frac{1}{16}$ in)
Unsigned
Purchased (1952.278)

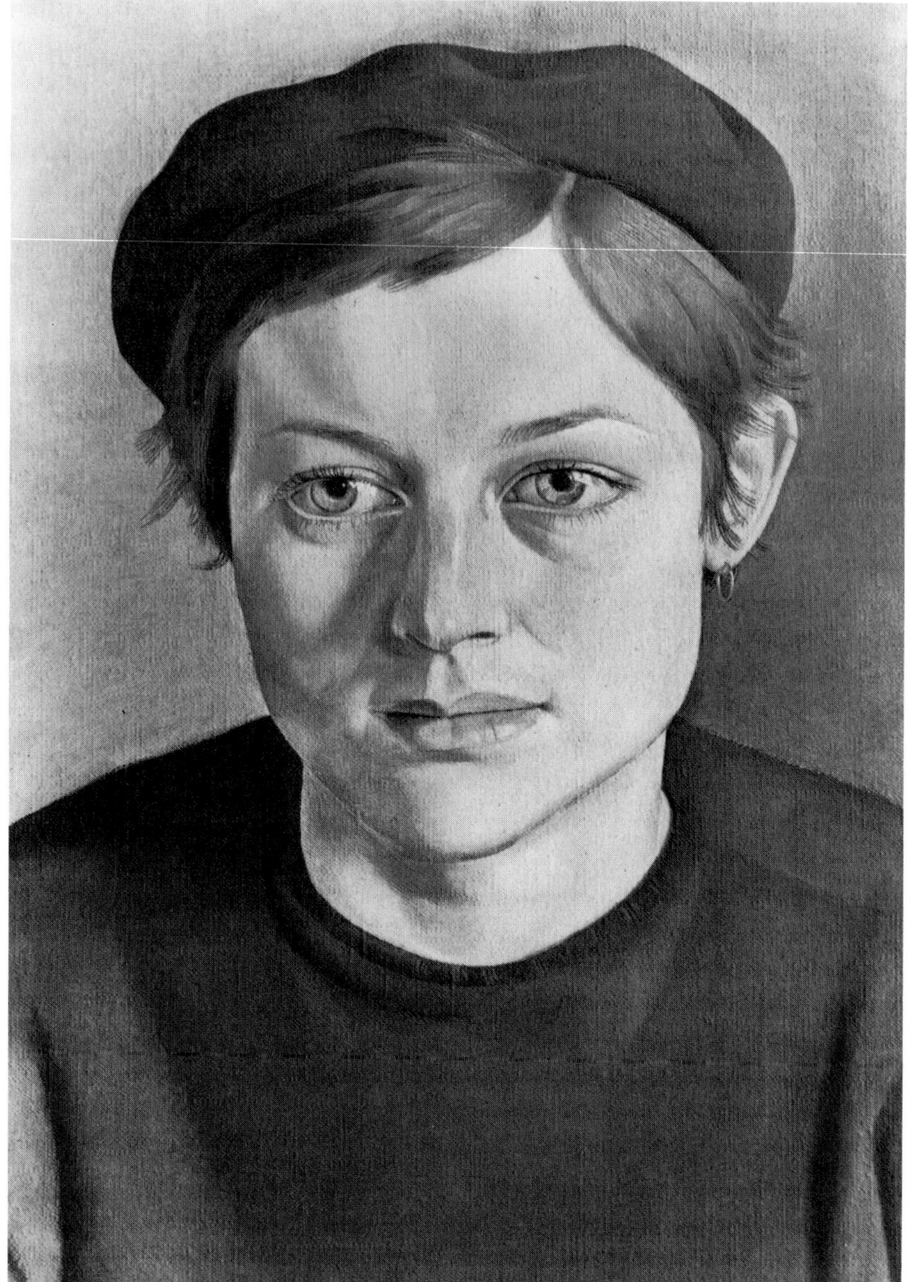

173

The grandson of Sigmund and brother of Clement, Lucian Freud was born in Berlin where he lived until he moved with his family to England in 1932. Here, he studied art at the Central School and at Cedric Morris's school in Suffolk. Influenced by Picasso and De Chirico, and befriended by Graham Sutherland, his earliest work shows Surrealist tendencies. Despite being adopted by the London art world, however, Freud felt he lacked talent and dedicated himself to drawing, attempting by the scrupulous observation of people and objects to improve his technique. This discipline he extended to his oil paintings. From 1945 the early works such as *Girl with a Beret* tend to be small with a 'close-up' effect; from the late 1950s, he enlarged his scale and employed looser brush-work, demonstrating his admiration for artists like Soutine and Bacon.

Freud's work tends to be autobiographical. He works directly from people he knows and who interest him rather than from the imagination using them to 'invent' the pictures. Very few of his sitters are named and this is deliberate; nevertheless their presence and personality is usually strongly felt. *Girl With Beret* is a memorable little portrait of an unknown girl, intimate but with a striking tension. The meticulous execution, shallow picture space, and cool palette is characteristic of Freud's work between 1947 and 1957; the pale skin, glassy eyes, and slightly distorted jawline transform the girl's face into an unusually compelling image.

174 *Francis Bacon*

(b. 1909)

PORTRAIT OF HENRIETTA MORAES ON A BLUE COUCH 1965

English; oil on canvas
198 × 147 cm ($77\frac{15}{16} \times 57\frac{7}{8}$ in)
Unsigned
Purchased with the aid of the Wilfred Wood Bequest Fund, and a Government grant (through the Victoria and Albert Museum)
(1979.603)

Francis Bacon is one of this century's most controversial and provocative artists, whose grotesque, expressionist figure-paintings still have the ability to shock. Born in Dublin of English parents, Bacon settled in England in the late 1920s and had some success as an interior decorator. Self-taught, he began to paint about 1928, but rarely exhibited until after the Second World War. He subsequently destroyed most of his early pieces and others which did not satisfy him. In the '50s, he suddenly became famous for his paintings of screaming popes, seemingly caged in a plate-glass void. Today, he enjoys an international reputation.

Henrietta Moraes is the former wife of the Indian poet and essayist, Dom Moraes. In the 1960s, she and her husband, along with Francis Bacon, frequented 'The Colony Room', a bohemian club in Dean Street, Soho, which was a popular haunt of writers and artists. After separating from her husband, Henrietta Moraes lived in a studio near the Chelsea Yacht and Boat Company, and became famous for her Sunday afternoon parties attended by the demi-monde.

Bacon's first painting of Henrietta

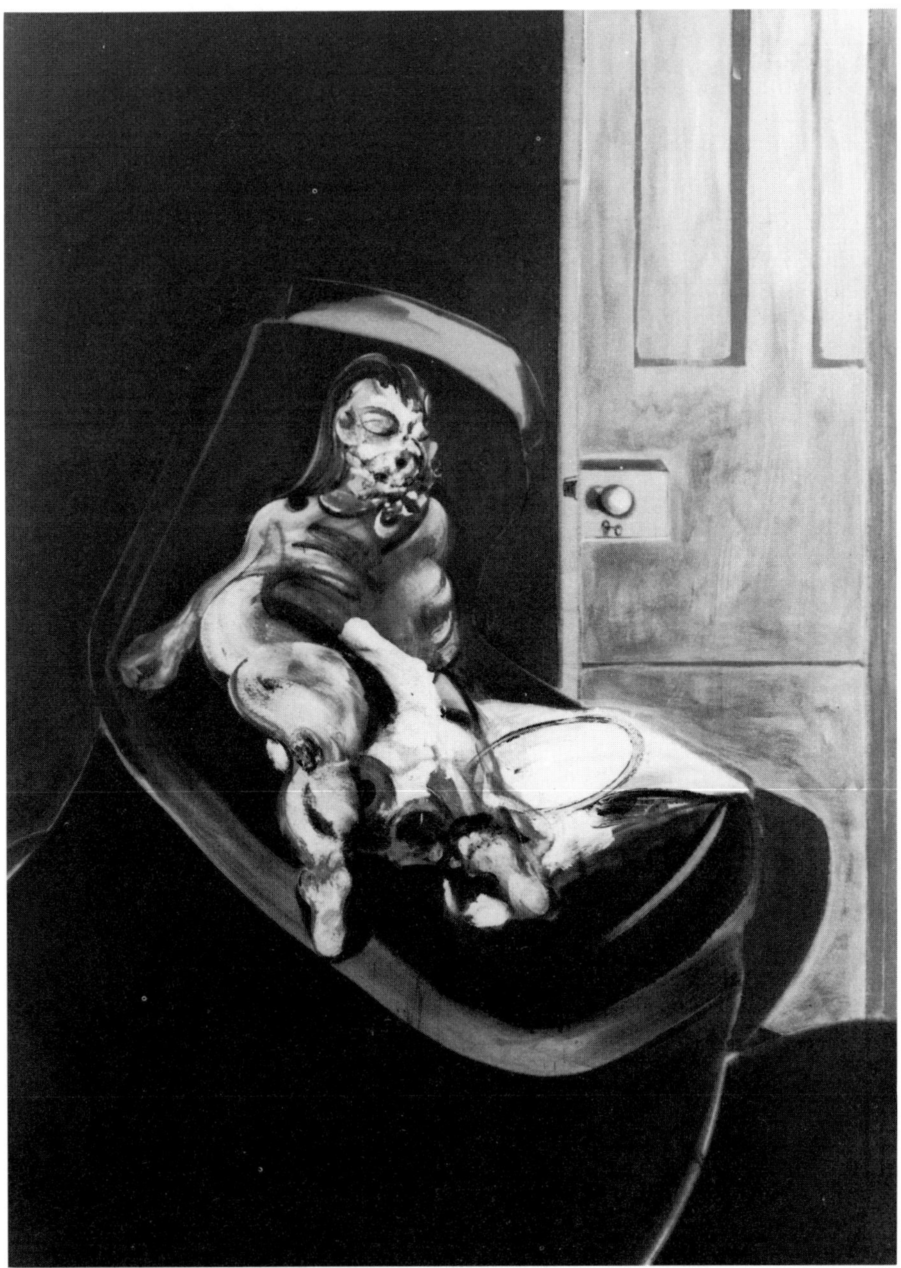

174

Moraes was executed in 1963, and he produced several studies and paintings of her from that date until 1969. Three full lengths were completed, of which this is the second. In general, Bacon worked from memory or photographs rather than life, and the paintings of Henrietta are based on nude photographs taken in 1963 by Bacon's friend, the Vogue photographer John Deakin. These photographs belong to a series which Bacon commissioned Deakin to take of his Soho friends to provide material for paintings. Among others were Lucian Freud, Frank Auerbach, Frank Norman, and John Deakin himself.

In this, as in most of his paintings, Bacon has created an image of tension and violence. The brutal, expressive brushwork and meaty flesh colours stand out sharply against the smooth mass of the blue couch which envelops the figure. The thinly painted door, opening into a mysterious vacuum, enhances the mood of foreboding.

This portrait is little known in this country as it was purchased by Manchester from a private collection in America.

175 *David Hockney*

(b. 1937) *pl. 15*

CELIA 1973

English; coloured crayons
33 × 28 cm (13 × 11 in)
Signed (b.r.c. in crayon): *DH Paris / 73*
Purchased (1981.51)

David Hockney, who was born and grew up in Bradford, came to prominence in the '60s as one of the leading British 'Pop' artists. His paintings of California, such as *A Bigger Splash*, are now regarded as classics of popular imagery. His work has been influential in re-establishing the figurative tradition in contemporary art.

The subject of this exquisite portrait is Celia Birtwell, a close friend and favourite model of the artist, whom he first met in 1968. Born in Salford, Celia Birtwell studied textile design at Manchester College of Art and became a fabric designer. She later married the fashion designer Ossie Clark. Hockney immortalised the couple in his well-known painting *Mr. and Mrs. Clark and Percy* (1970), now in the Tate Gallery. During the last decade the artist has lived alternatively in Paris and California. His first drawing of Celia was made in Paris in 1969, but this study dates from 1973, when he first went to live there. The drawing belongs to a series made between 1971 and 1975. Most show Celia clothed and pay special attention to her costume, but in this rare nude study Hockney has concentrated on the delicate texture of her skin and the expression of her eyes. With its sensitive use of line and sweet colouring, this portrait epitomises Hockney's facility with coloured crayons.

The Galleries also possess *Cushions* (1973) in the same medium, and seven prints by the artist.

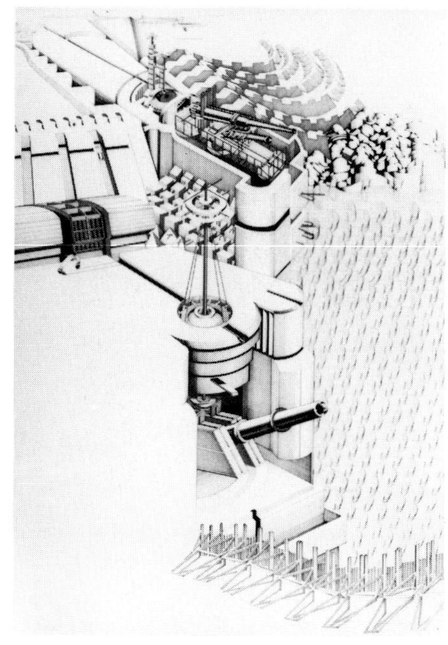

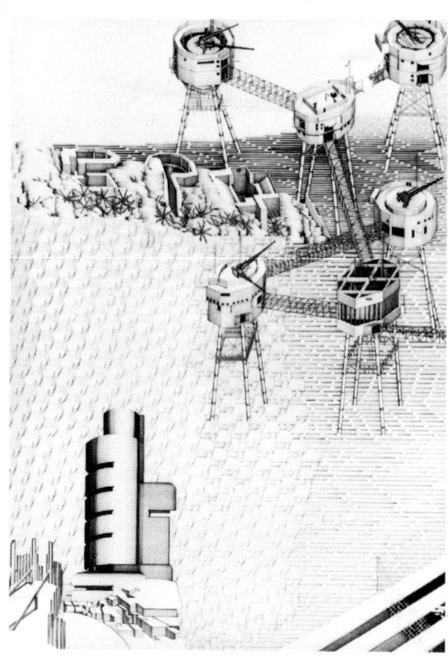

176 *Deanna Petherbridge*

(b. 1939)

THE CONCRETE ARMADA 1978

English School; pen and ink
143 × 500 cm ($56\frac{1}{2}$ × 197 in)
Signed (b.r.c. of fifth panel) in monogram
Purchased (1982.713)

The Concrete Armada is an enormous drawing on the universal theme of war. In it, mechanistic symbols of destruction confront each other in a formalised, futuristic landscape, devoid of people but seething with human aggression. Drawn over eight months, it is the second in an intended series of three imaginary 'battlepieces' linked loosely by theme and style. The first, *The Iron Siege of Pavia* (1975), took two years to complete. Employing medieval and Renaissance imagery, it represents a land battle with army formations assembling to besiege a central citadel. *The Concrete Armada* is a sea or coastal battle and, according to the artist, 'uses imagery of the First and Second World Wars, block

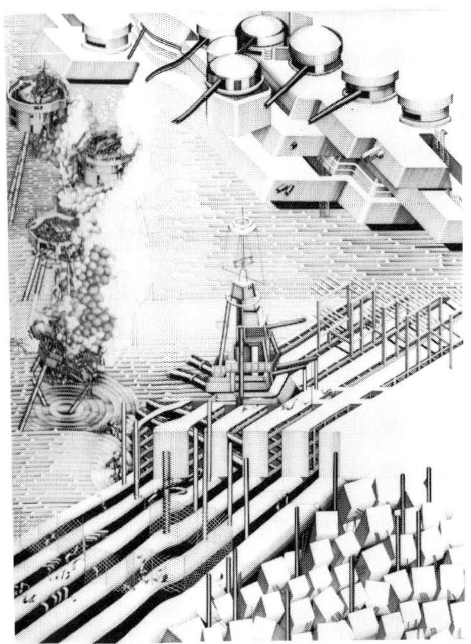

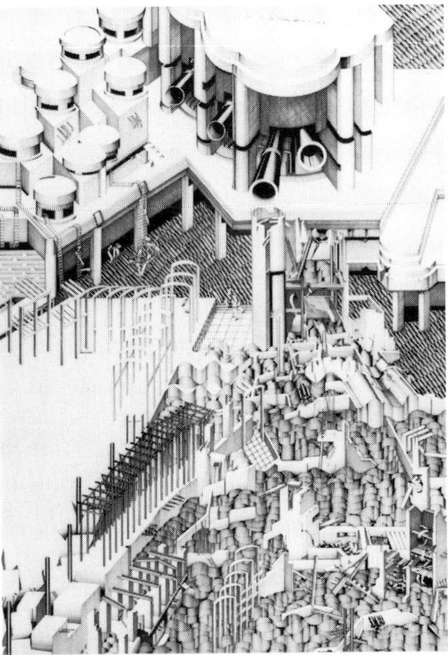

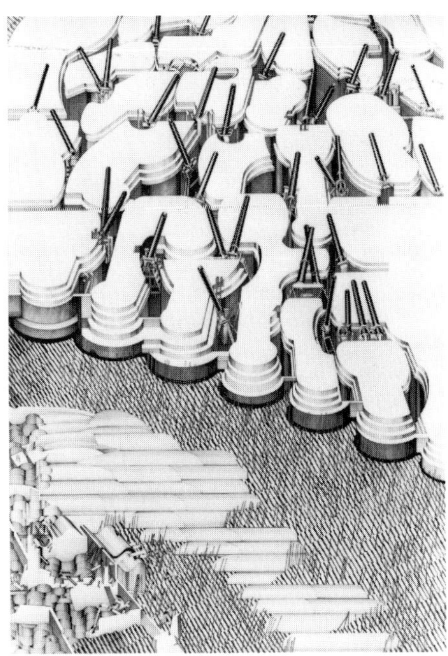

176

houses, army and navy sea-forts, all the awful paraphernalia of Hitler's Atlantic Wall . . .' The final battlepiece, not yet completed, is intended to employ images suggestive of aerospace and the advanced technology of present and future warfare, in which the distance between weapon and target grows increasingly remote. The artist originally intended that the three works should form a 'total environment in the spirit of Uccello's *Rout of San Romano* or the Pisanello Arthurian battle cycle.' *The Concrete Armada* was bought when Deanna Petherbridge was the City Art Gallery's first 'Artist-in-Residence'.

Educated in South Africa, the artist came to England in 1960; later she lived in Greece, where she turned from broad expressionist painting and soft sculptures to drawing in black and white. She bases much of her work on oriental architectural forms, repeating basic modular units to create rhythm, and using contradictory perspectives to confuse and entice the eye. Frozen into an architectonic harmony, the battlepieces are allegorical, archetypal conflicts, both spiritual and physical. The format used is that of the Japanese folding screen, divided into five panels, the 'narrative' of which can be read in an unfolding continuum. The effect is distant and panoramic, like battles of the drawing board, where troops, supplies, and armoury are redeployed about large-scale maps by the dispassionate architects of war.